P9-ARR-089

Contemporary Group Work

Second Edition

Contemporary
Group
Work

CHARLES D. GARVIN

The University of Michigan

CARNEGIE LIBRARY
LIVINGSTONE COLLEGE
SALISBURY, N. C. 28144

Prentice-Hall, Inc.   Englewood Cliffs, New Jersey 07632

122117

Library of Congress Cataloging-in-Publication Data

Garvin, Charles D.
   Contemporary group work.

   Bibliography: p.
   Includes index.
   1. Social group work—United States. I. Title.
HV45.G37 1987   361.4   86-9334
ISBN 0-13-170218-1

Editorial/production supervision: Linda Benson
Cover design: Lundgren Graphics Ltd.
Manufacturing buyer: John Hall

©1987 by Prentice-Hall, Inc.
A Division of Simon & Schuster
Englewood Cliffs, New Jersey 07632

All rights reserved. No part of this book may be
reproduced, in any form or by any means,
without permission in writing from the publisher.

Printed in the United States of America

10 9 8 7 6 5 4 3 2 1

ISBN   0-13-170218-1   01

Prentice-Hall International (UK) Limited, *London*
Prentice-Hall of Australia Pty. Limited, *Sydney*
Prentice-Hall Canada Inc., *Toronto*
Prentice-Hall Hispanoamericana, S.A., *Mexico*
Prentice-Hall of India Private Limited, *New Delhi*
Prentice-Hall of Japan, Inc., *Tokyo*
Prentice-Hall of Southeast Asia Pte. Ltd., *Singapore*
Editora Prentice-Hall do Brasil, Ltda., *Rio de Janeiro*
Whitehall Books Limited, *Wellington, New Zealand*

DEDICATED TO

*The members of my men's support group
who have taught me much about the meaning
of membership: Richard, Tom, Michael A., Cam,
Peter, Gary, Jim, Michael J., Brian, Mark.*

Contents

2

GROUP WORK ACTIVITIES
AND SETTINGS   24

Part Two
The Phases of Work

3

THE PREGROUP PHASE   54

4

BEGINNING A GROUP 80

5

ACHIEVING GROUP PURPOSES THROUGH CHANGES IN GROUP CONDITIONS 106

6

ACHIEVING INDIVIDUAL CHANGE THROUGH GROUPS   149

7

GROUP WORK AND ENVIRONMENTAL CHANGE   175

8

THE EVALUATION OF GROUP
WORK PRACTICE   190

9

THE GROUP AND
ENDINGS   211

Part Three
Variations in Practice

13

WORKING WITH GROUPS FOR ALTERNATIVE ROLE ATTAINMENT   269

14

WORKING WITH OPPRESSED PEOPLE IN GROUPS   285

15

WORKING WITH COMMITTEES AND OTHER TASK GROUPS   301

Preface

This book is intended as an introductory text on group work in social welfare settings. As such its purpose is to help the reader to understand how to select members for groups, facilitate the development of groups through beginning, middle, and ending phases, and evaluate with the members the impact of the group experience. Groups are used for many different reasons in such settings and no one book can convey the range of approaches required for all of these. We, therefore, focus much of our attention on groups established to enhance the functioning of individual members. However, a broad, rather than a narrow, conception of enhancing functioning is intended, so as to preclude this book's application to work with a variety of groups. Interest groups, committees, educational groups, and representative groups can all have this as a major thrust. In our last chapter we focus on task groups, such as committees. We have, consequently, included content that is applicable to all of these situations.

The selection of content for this book has also been guided by several of the author's convictions. First, the actions of the group worker should be to help the group and its members attain mutually agreed on goals. The first major task of the worker and the members is to determine such goals and then to guide subsequent events by these goals or to revise them accordingly. This premise leads to the second proposition that movement toward goals should be monitored and that the worker and the group should acquire the means to do this. Third, the worker's actions should be based on an understanding of research and theory from the social sciences, and throughout this book we have included content on monitoring changes and on relevant social science material. Fourth, we believe that social workers with groups should use any effective means that are consistent with social work values and purposes. We, therefore, have incorporated many ideas from other disciplines and professions.

An important approach taken in this book is that learning requires an experiential element that includes carefully structured observations. To assist with this, many chapters conclude with a structured exercise or an observational guide. Throughout the book, we present many practice illustrations; the chapters in Part Three are devoted to applications of group methods in groups formed for different purposes; in addition, each contains detailed practice examples.

While extensive discussions of concepts are presented later, it should be noted that the author utilizes many systemic notions. Thus the idea of the worker as a mediator among members, between members, and the group-as-a-whole, and between the group and external institutions is a view that is maintained throughout the book. Also relevant is a group dynamics approach that views group changes in terms of interactions of forces within as well as outside of the group. Finally, we hold a sociobehavioral view that individual behavior is a consequence of social forces and interactions. Cognitive factors are not overlooked, however, as the author is committed to an approach in which group members determine their own destinies by being guided to awareness of group forces as they affect individual behavior.

The organizing principles of the book are twofold: first, a group developmental approach is taken that views worker and member tasks as occurring differently at each stage of group development. Second, a "functional" approach is taken that sees group development as affected by group purposes and agency functions. For this reason, a typology of such purposes is presented early in the book and forms the major basis for the final chapters.

The book is divided into three parts: Part One is devoted to background material that will help the reader to understand the historical as well as current forces from which contemporary approaches to group work emerged. Part Two presents the group phenomena that occur at different phases of the development of the group and the tasks of workers and members in these phases. These include actions prior to the first group meeting, during the "formation" period, the subsequent sessions when members and workers act to attain member goals, and the termination of the group. The chapters on the worker's actions are divided into those devoted to changing group, individual, and environmental situations. In a separate chapter ways of evaluating these efforts are presented.

Part Three presents the ways group services differ when purposes differ. The chapters in this part utilize the frameworks developed earlier in the book as a way of presenting variations in group development as related to group purpose.

ACKNOWLEDGMENTS

Throughout my years as a practicing group worker, supervisor of this practice, and trainer of social work students, the ideas of a number of people have been of great benefit to me. First, I wish to acknowledge the debt I owe to my first supervisors of group work practice, Edna Hansen and Rose Cohn; second, to such writers as Robert Vinter and William Schwartz, who on many occasions encouraged and supported my development and who undoubtedly found places where they saw that I benefitted as well as strayed from their contrasting inputs. The work of revising this book was greatly helped by the constructive suggestions from Beulah Rothman.

Next, I owe much to my colleagues at the University of Michigan and particularly to such fellow group work teachers as Harvey Bertcher, Sallie Churchill, Charles Wolfson, and Frank Maple. Of great importance to this work is its typology of group purpose, developed jointly with Paul Glasser.

Finally, all of the ideas here have been expressed, critiqued, and often changed in interaction with social work students. They and their experiences have been a major stimulus for everything I have written.

Contemporary
Group
Work

1

Contemporary Group Work: An Overview

Group work, as a social work method, has evolved and changed in the half century since its origin. These changes are the result of altered circumstances, increased knowledge, and an expansion in the number and variety of practice settings. A consensus has developed during this period as to what constitutes social work with groups although different practice models have been created and coexist within this broad consensus.

In the first two chapters of this book we shall provide information on the history of group practice so that the reader might gain a better understanding of the ideas that unify, as well as divide, practitioners of this social-work method. This chapter will present our approach to group work and how it relates to other workers, from both inside and outside the field of social work.

In a recent article, Middleman and Goldberg describe the essential elements of social work with groups.[1] They state that the first element is that the worker "must focus on helping members to become a system of mutual aid." The main source of help for each member in the group is seen as coming from other members, individually and collectively. A major task of the social worker, consequently, is to assist members to understand this and to work to create a group where mutual aid can and does occur. The specific techniques used by the worker to contribute to this task will be described throughout the book.

---

[1]Ruth Middleman and Gale Goldberg, "Social Group Work," in *Encyclopedia of Social Work* (New York: National Association of Social Workers, forthcoming).

The second element of social work with groups is that the worker understands and makes use of group processes and helps the members to do the same. We shall have much more to say about group process later in the book. At this point, the reader should understand that we are speaking of the unfolding of events in the group as members solve problems together, express feelings to and toward each other, evolve a pattern of relationships, and influence each other. Group processes can be very powerful forces for the members and may or may not be beneficial in helping members attain their goals. The tasks of the worker are to support processes that are beneficial, to diminish those that are not, and to help members of the group to do the same.

The third element cited by Middleman and Goldberg is that the worker strives to enhance the ability of the members to function more and more autonomously as individuals and as a group. They view the worker to be easing him or herself "out of a job." To function autonomously may be feasible in some situations as when groups continue wholly on a "self-help" basis; in other situations this may not be possible, at least in the short run during the "life" of the group.

Middleman and Goldberg cite a fourth element which they describe as helping the members to "re-experience their groupness at the point of termination." We view this as part of the third element in that all of life's experiences have beginnings, middles, and endings and members are helped to understand and to cope with this when they become conscious of the unfolding of these phases of the group. We believe, therefore, that members should be helped, as much as possible, to understand their group experience as a means of dealing with the many other group experiences they have faced and will face in their lives.

THE ORGANIZATIONAL AND ENVIRONMENTAL APPROACH

Our practice model was developed from the model generated by Vinter and his colleagues at the University of Michigan.[2] This extension of the ideas of Vinter and others was originally described by Glasser and Garvin, who sought to develop principles to guide effective practice in the broad variety of social welfare agencies that now sponsor group services.[3] Their model, termed "an organizational and environmental approach," incorporates a diversity of practice procedures by declaring that the purpose or purposes for which the group is established determines the way the members will respond to their group experience and the way the worker will work with the group.

---

[2]Martin Sundel, Paul H. Glasser, Rosemary Sarri, and Robert Vinter, eds., *Individual Change Through Small Groups,* 2nd ed. (New York: Free Press, 1985).

[3]Paul J. Glasser and Charles D. Garvin, "An Organizational Model," in *Theories of Social Work with Groups,* eds., Robert W. Roberts and Helen Northen (New York: Columbia University Press, 1976), pp. 75–115.

Clarification of Purpose

The organizational and environmental approach to group purpose recognizes that the ultimate fulfillment of the purpose will be as a result of interactions involving the agency, the worker, the members, as well as others in the environment. In certain situations, for instance, where the agency recruits members for the group, the agency's view of group purpose will affect even the selection of the worker and the members.

To help the worker understand group purposes and to use this understanding in making decisions, we have developed a typology of group purposes. While this will be discussed fully in the next chapter, we describe it briefly here. Our categorization takes into consideration whether the group is meant to enhance the social development of members who have joined the group voluntarily and whose development is viewed as proceeding normally *(socialization groups)* or whether the group is to remedy the social development of members whose previous socialization is viewed, in a sociological sense, as deviant and where group participation is often a consequence of some form of social pressure *(resocialization groups)*. Each of these purposes is subdivided further and this shall also be described in the following chapter.

The categorization of group purpose allows us to offer one resolution of an important concern of group work practice, as well as all of social work: to present appropriate ways of modifying both individual and environmental circumstances in order to attain individual goals. For each of the types of purposes we identify, singly or in combination, there are relevant targets of change related to the individual member, the group, and the larger social environment. Elsewhere, when we criticized the unfortunate tendency to dichotomize the choice of *either* individual or environmental targets, we made the following statements:

> The use of groups is seen either as a means to achieve social goals in a community context or as a method to encourage individual growth and change in an educational or rehabilitative context. It may be argued that this is consistant neither with modern social science theory nor with common sense. A broad view sees the social environment as a source of individual behavior patterns, as influential in maintaining such patterns, and as a useful tool in altering them. On the other hand, the individual—often together with others—can play a significant role in making more constructive use of his environment or change it in ways that will provide greater satisfaction of his or her needs.[4]

Whether the purpose of the group is to facilitate the socialization or resocialization of the member, we view all member goals as related to optimal *social functioning*. This concept refers to the way individuals seek to cope with their

---

[4]Paul H. Glasser and Charles D. Garvin, "Social Group Work: The Organizational and Environmental Approach," in *Encyclopedia of Social Work* (New York: National Association of Social Workers, 1977), II, 1338.

social situations by modifying themselves, their environment, or both so as to achieve the best fit among individual needs and capacities and environmental opportunities.

We have found role concepts to be useful in an analysis of social functioning because they describe individual behaviors as responses to social circumstances. Thus the ways wives and husbands function in their marital roles, their children in their child roles, the parents in their work roles, and all family members in their roles in the community (for example, student, church member, or member of friendship groups) are examples of social functioning.

Problems in social functioning occur when people's roles do not fit their needs and capacities, when they are not satisfied with their enactment of their roles, when the way one person performs his or her role is in conflict with the actions of others, or when others are critical of one's actions in relationship to roles. Problems can also occur when the environment fails to provide resources for role performance or hinders such performance in other ways.

Social work clients may seek to modify their role performances through acting differently, feeling differently, or thinking about their situations in new ways. They may also seek to change their environment so that it affects their role-related activities differently.

Social workers can seek to enhance social functioning on many levels by working solely with the individual concerned or with that individual in concert with family members, friends, and so forth. People may help each other with problems in social functioning in group situations and that is what this book is about. Individual social functioning can also be enhanced by changes brought about on a community level or by changes in national social policies. Such changes in the environment may be sought by the individual, often with the help of social workers, or may be sought by social workers on behalf of individuals, whether known to them personally or as members of such classes of people as the handicapped or of ethnic minorities.

Group workers have made contributions to alleviating many social functioning problems. For example, groups can provide people with recreational and educational resources, or group members can join with each other to obtain these. Groups can also help people who are "at risk," such as adolescents facing developmental stresses, parents who fear that their stresses may provoke them to mistreat their children, or unemployed people who seek ways to regain employment.

Focus on Goals

Another facet of our approach is its emphasis on individual goal specification and attainment—the goal being enhanced social functioning. A *goal* relates to a group member's condition, situation, or both that the member and the worker agree should be changed through group experience. A goal should be expressed in terms that are so sufficiently concrete that the member will be able to recognize when it has been reached. In order to achieve member goals, the goals regarding group and environmental conditions must also be clearly specified. Later we shall present in detail procedures and examples regarding such goal specifications.

A Mutual Aid System

Even though we see group work as facilitating individual goal attainment, we, like all group workers, view the group as a mutual aid system. Many approaches to groups describe the worker as interacting with individuals in the context of the group. While we see this as a necessary activity of group workers from time to time, we join with other group work theorists in placing the major emphasis on how the worker facilitates the members in helping one another to achieve their individual and collective aspirations.

Evaluation of Practice

The goal attainment of the members in this approach to practice should be assessed at regular intervals for several reasons: first, the effectiveness of the group process and the worker's facilitation of this process should be determined so that the individual members, the group, and the worker can, when necessary, change group conditions; second, the member, when goals have been achieved, should either leave the group or select new goals; third, the agency and the worker should gather evidence as to the effectiveness of group services. Throughout this book, therefore, we shall present ways of measuring changes in individual, group, and environmental conditions.

Worker Tasks

The actions to be taken by the worker to help members achieve their goals and to create a group to accomplish this are specified in this practice model. Since the worker is sometimes required to seek changes in the environment outside the group, this is also detailed. Although other models do not necessarily present worker behaviors in this way, our reason for doing so is that group workers should be able to generate and test propositions about the effects of different kinds of worker actions; effective ways of helping the member can then be identified and taught to others.

Values

There are three values basic to our practice model. First, our approach to group work shares with others in social work a commitment to respect the worth of all people; the importance placed on self-determination is derived from this as is the importance placed on the right of individuals to obtain support from society to achieve their maximum potential. In this sense, we define our approach as human-istic while recognizing that other group workers might define this term differently.

Self-determination requires that we uphold voluntary participation in groups and insist on a "contract" between the worker and members and the worker and the group-as-a-whole specifying goals and member and worker tasks. The worker should negotiate these tasks with members and renegotiate them whenever changes take place. A related principle is that workers may intervene in the group in ways that do not benefit all members but must not intervene in ways that can harm any member even if others are benefited.

The second social work value inherent in group work is the value placed on human life. This means not only the biological preservation of the individuals but the nurturance of growth toward maximum utilization of capacities. Thus an alcoholic accelerates the approach of biological death and psychological impairment, and the latter, in at least a metaphorical sense, is death. Similarly, the adolescent who embarks on a criminal career also has chosen a psychological death in terms of killing his or her talents even if the crimes do not lead to a threat to biological existence.

The third value issue addressed by our model arises around priorities for the development and staffing of services. Social work has always had a commitment to serve those who, as a result of being the most exploited, the most needy, or the most vulnerable, are, or may become, impaired in their social functioning. Group workers, throughout their history, have worked with the poor, those oppressed by virtue of their ethnic group, the immigrants, and those in the cities who have grievances related to urban conditions. In a later period of group work history, workers served other oppressed groups such as mental patients, children in conflict with their schools, and prisoners. The oppression of women has also been a concern of group workers.

Some writers argue that it is not the obligation or prerogative of the profession or its educational institutions to influence practitioner's choice of settings. We do not agree with this position. For example, health care institutions are often enjoined to provide medical care to people deprived of such service and lawyers are increasingly expected to advocate for persons treated unjustly by the criminal justice system. As much, if not more than these professions, social work has a mandate to serve socially oppressed persons.

The greatest problem for the practitioner seeking to function ethically is that following some of the values mentioned can conflict with others. In later chapters we shall discuss responses to this issue.

DIFFERING APPROACHES TO PRACTICE

In the following discussion, our model will be related to other contemporary approaches to group work in an effort to place it in both historical and contemporary contexts. One of the earliest comparisons of these approaches was that of William Schwartz, who identified three models.

There was a kind of "medical" model in which "the steps of the helping process are described by assuming a sequence of movements through which the worker investigates, diagnoses, and treats the problem under consideration." There was a "scientific" model "in which the steps in the helping process resemble closely the problem solving sequence by which the scientific worker moves from the unknown to the known." And there was a "model of the organic system in which the total helping situation is viewed as a network of reciprocal activity, and in which it is impossible to describe accurately any part of the system without describing its active relationship to the other moving parts."[5]

A year later, Vinter described three orientations to group work that he believed succeeded each other historically. The first emphasized "democratic decentralization," the second "socialization," and the third, "rehabilitation."[6]

A paper that stood as a definition of group work models for at least a decade and is still influential today was prepared by Papell and Rothman for the 1966 meeting of the Council on Social Work Education.[7] In their presentation the "social goals," "remedial," and "reciprocal" models were identified.

The social goals approach, perhaps the oldest, is clearly the outcome of the democratic decentralization orientation referred to by Vinter. This model, because of its relationship to a view of social work as a "cause" and because of its relevance to contemporary struggles for human rights, continues to influence all of social work practice as well as its group work component.

The remedial model emerged during the movement of group work into rehabilitation settings. It focused on treatment goals for individuals, with the group viewed as a means and context to attain such goals. This model is the one out of which our approach emerged.

The reciprocal model sought to identify and enhance the processes whereby individuals, groups, and larger social systems engaged each other to undertake activities of mutual benefit. The worker, therefore, was described as a "mediator," involved, for example, in the ways a group member sought to use the group, the demands the group placed on the members to ensure its own survival, the pressures the group placed on the agency, and the agency requirements transmitted to the group and its members.

The assumption that group work practice included three models was influential for a number of years; the editors of two consecutive editions of the *Encyclopedia of Social Work* in 1971 and 1977 commissioned three articles to present the state of group work theory: one by William Schwartz, the exponent of the reciprocal model, one by Garvin and Glasser, who wrote in the tradition of Vinter's remedial model, and the third, "The Developmental Approach" by Emanuel Tropp which, although not identified by its author as the "social goals" model, was

[5]William Schwartz, "Social Group Work: The Interactionist Approach," in *Encyclopedia of Social Work* (New York: National Association of Social Workers, 1971), II, 1255.

[6]Robert D. Vinter, "Social Group Work," in *Encyclopedia of Social Work* (New York: National Association of Social Workers, 1965), pp. 715-24.

[7]Catherine P. Papell and Beulah Rothman, "Social Group Work Models: Possession and Heritage," *Journal of Education for Social Work* 2, no. 2 (Fall 1966), 66-77.

described as "starting with a strong emphasis on the common group goal and the democratic process of group involvement."[8]

As one would expect, movement toward an integration of models and a reaffirmation of the core ideas of what constitutes social work with groups is now occurring. A recent edition of the *Encyclopedia of Social Work* has returned to presenting one article on group work that emphasizes its central ideas.[9]

The most recent effort to codify models of group work was the publication of *Theories of Social Work with Groups.* This volume was planned as a companion to *Theories of Social Casework*[10] with the expectation that the "single systems theoretical models" (that is, casework, group work, family treatment) "will serve as the major building blocks of multi-system integrated practice theories."[11]

It was quite clear to Roberts and Northen, who edited the group work volume, that the papers included did not represent distinct approaches to group work although some authors' values or other foundations of their theories contrasted sharply. In a final review chapter, Roberts and Northen compared the articles on such dimensions as behavioral science foundations, target populations, criteria for group member selection, and worker activity. They found that authors who had a similar position on one of these dimensions often had different postures on another. Clearly, while the authors may claim, with some justification, to have internally consistent models, all seek to achieve this by assembling a basic set of practice elements in different ways.

We would like to encourage the reader to choose appropriate strategies for group composition or group formation from among various alternatives. It is premature to assemble all group work ideas into a master plan in which the group circumstances and the array of group work approaches can be totally accommodated, although some have tried.[12] In this book, therefore, while we do favor one model, we shall often identify alternative approaches. Whatever else may be argued, all groups have beginnings, middles, and endings, even though different ideas exist as to how to approach these events.

[8]Emmanuel Tropp, "Social Group Work: The Developmental Approach," in *Encyclopedia of Social Work* (New York: National Association of Social Workers, 1977), II, 1322.

[9]Middleman and Goldberg, "Social Group Work."

[10]Robert W. Roberts and Robert Nee, eds., *Theories of Social Casework* (New York: Columbia University Press, 1970).

[11]Robert W. Roberts and Helen Northen, eds., *Theories of Social Work with Groups* (New York: Columbia Univeristy Press, 1976), p. xi. The volume includes the work of the same authors from the *Encyclopedia of Social Work* (Tropp, Schwartz, Garvin, and Glasser) and, in addition, proponents of still other group work practice theories. Some wrote group work texts (Northen, Hartford); one is a proponent of the "functional" (Rankian) approach; several were individuals associated with casework models with group work applications (McBroom on socialization groups, Parad and colleagues on crisis intervention in groups, and Garvin, Reid, and Epstein on task-centered groups). A chapter by Gertrude Wilson on group work history and by Mary Louise Somers on approaches to problem solving in groups completed the volume.

[12]See, for example, Norma Lang, "A Broad Range Model of Practice with the Social Work Group," *Social Service Review* 46 (1972), pp. 76–89.

INFLUENCES BEYOND SOCIAL WORK

Criteria for Use

Group activities for personal growth are proliferating and include many elements not included in the social work models we have just described. Group workers in social work, as well as their counterparts in psychiatry, psychology, nursing, and education do not live in a vacuum. Professionals read each other's works and borrow ideas across institutional boundaries. When new ideas such as gestalt therapy or transactional analysis are promoted, practitioners from all disciplines hear of them through books and workshops and seek to utilize what they have learned. Clearly, then, no set of techniques fully distinguishes any profession's work with groups, and goals and methods overlap.

The social worker with groups will, therefore, utilize techniques from many sources if they are (1) compatible with social work values; (2) helpful to those who are customarily served by social workers; (3) appropriate to the institutions that employ social workers; and (4) encompassable in the educational program prescribed for social work. Those techniques that are easily integrated into the practitioner's model will be the most utilized.

Needs of Social Work Clients. Any discussion of the use of non–social work approaches must begin with a reiteration of the idea that social work focuses on individual-environmental transactions. Thus, social work approaches should be concerned with enhancing not only the behavior of individuals but enhancing the way environments meet their needs as well. In a sense this is inevitable in group work since the group has been widely viewed as a social microcosm that can reflect many of the forces the individual copes with in other situations. The group is one aspect of the member's environment. It is possible, of course, to use groups so that the social component is minimized. Group workers sometimes use the phrase "case work in the group" to describe groups that primarily focus on worker-member communications rather than communications among the members. Approaches from outside of social work that operate in a similar way are inappropriate to group work in social work because of its concern for social functioning.

Requirements of Social Work Agencies. An even more difficult issue is to determine approaches that are appropriate to the institutions that employ social workers. The following organizational variables have implications for this:

1. Social work agencies often have limited budgets. Approaches that require training that is well beyond that usually received by social workers, expensive equipment, several workers working simultaneously, or consultants who normally demand very high fees may be unfeasible.
2. Social work organizations should operate with an emphasis on voluntary participation, on personal freedom, and on noninfliction of pain. Some approaches are of limited applicability in such agencies because of their use of compulsion or of aversive measures. Even the strong confrontation style sometimes used in

correctional and drug programs may be unacceptable to many social work agencies.

3. Social workers may have less power over their organizational environments than members of other professions. Approaches that require control over broad aspects of that environment may also not be feasible for group workers.

4. A few approaches require more training than can be encompassed in a social work curriculum for the worker to acquire even minimally acceptable competence. Some social workers, after receiving their degree, may secure such training. The purpose of this text, however, is to portray ways of working that can be taught to social workers in the normal course of a professional program. Thus, for example, the full scope of gestalt therapy, transactional analysis, or analytic group psychotherapy cannot be offered in a social work program. Nevertheless, there are techniques and concepts, drawn from these treatment systems, that can be so incorporated.

The following discussion describes some of the major approaches to work with groups developed outside of social work. In presenting each approach, we shall note those aspects that can be integrated into social work practice and taught in a social work curriculum. We shall focus on eleven approaches, grouped into four clusters, that we believe incorporate most of the major contemporary trends in work with groups for personal growth and change. Some of this material shall be elaborated on in later chapters when we discuss practice issues. We omit ideas (for example, rational emotive therapy and reality therapy) which, while they may have group applications, are not conceived of primarily as ways of working with groups.[13]

Approaches Utilizing or Originating from Psychoanalysis

Gestalt Therapy. The framework of gestalt therapy owes its origin and much of its development to Fritz Perls.[14] Its theoretical foundation draws from gestalt psychology, particularly the idea that perception is organized around attention to some aspect of a total situation (figure) with the balance (the ground) forming a context. A particularly important concept for the gestalt therapist, then, is *awareness* inasmuch as one's needs and feelings may often be blocked and remain as *ground* and, thus, out of awareness. These concepts are also closely related to the notion that the individual may deny aspects of his or her own desires, potentialities, or experiences that might be drawn upon to enhance one's life.

Techniques developed by Perls and his colleagues to increase awareness and subsequent integration of rejected aspects of one's self include drawing a person's attention to body positions and movements and role playing components of his or her own body, dreams, fantasies, or attitudes. The individual may then actually hold a "dialogue" among these aspects, while "occupying" what is referred to as

---

[13]For a thorough discussion of many of the approaches commented on here see, John B.P. Shaffer and David Galinsky, *Models of Group Therapy and Sensitivity Training* (Englewood Cliffs, N.J.: Prentice-Hall, Inc., 1974).

[14]Fritz Perls, R.F. Hefferline, and Paul Goodman, *Gestalt Therapy* (New York: Julian Press, 1951).

the "hot seat." The worker in a gestalt group may also use "exercises" to help members increase self-awareness.

Perls involved group members to a very limited degree with each other as the person in the "hot seat" worked primarily with the therapist. Many contemporary gestalt therapists, however, use awareness exercises in which group members interact with each other; they may also encourage the group to discuss with the individual issues raised while in the "hot seat."

Whether or not group workers fully understand gestalt therapy, they can use gestalt exercises to promote awareness. For example, exercises can be used at the beginning and ending of the group so that feelings about these phases can be elicited. Group workers can also use these techniques to help members to "own" beliefs and feelings such as anger or rejection, which they project onto others. Ambivalence, also, is a very frequent problem that inhibits decision making, and gestalt approaches such as double chairing are useful in exploring issues around alternative choices facing members.

Group workers have used nonverbal activities in groups. These are drawn upon to enhance relationships, encourage expressiveness, and build skills. The gestalt concepts regarding awareness may help group workers to add another dimension to their understanding and use of program experiences.

Transactional Analysis. Eric Berne, the founder of transactional analysis, like Fritz Perls, was originally trained and experienced in psychoanalytic therapy.[15] His system is based on an analysis of how transactions among people are affected by their "ego states," which are defined by Berne "as a set of coherent behavior patterns; or pragmatically, as a system of feelings which motivates a related set of behavior patterns." Most readers are probably familiar with the ego states that Berne has labeled as the *child, parent,* and *adult.* Through Berne's writings and those of many of his followers, the indicators of these ego states and many subtypes of each ego state have been identified. These concepts are used in the transactional analysis therapy situation to analyze transactions of the individual with others.

Such transactions are also found in more complex interactions, and Berne developed ways of conceptualizing these. One technique examines sequences that substitute for "intimacy," which Berne called *games.* Long-lasting interactional patterns in life are labeled *scripts,* and means have evolved for identifying these. The intent of this conceptual framework is to help people to examine transations so that both immediate interactions as well as life-long patterns may be consciously modified.

In the group therapy situation, members are trained in the analysis of ego states, games, and scripts. Subsequently, with the help of the therapist and each other, they apply this analysis to behavior in the group as well as to the environment outside of the group.[16]

[15]For Berne's own explication of his system, see Eric Berne, *Transactional Analysis in Psychotherapy* (New York: Grove Press, 1961).
[16]Ibid., pp. 165–87.

Within the social work group, it is often essential to examine the trans-actions between the worker and the members or among members. There are many approaches to this ranging from those that call attention to what is taking place to those that utilize a generalized set of concepts as in transactional analysis. Without any research on how effective one approach is compared to another, the worker will have to draw upon what seems most appropriate to the population represented.

Psychoanalytic Group Therapy. With the exception of some early experi-ments with tubercular patients and World War I veterans, group psychotherapy was developed within a psychoanalytic framework. The early group psychotherapists adopted many approaches to group therapy that were drawn from individual psychoanalysis, including free association and the analysis of transference. One group of writers, namely Foulkes, Ezriel, Whitaker, and Lieberman sought to understand how affects and drives were related to group forces.[17] The following are some of the propositions from these analytically oriented theories:

1. Members of groups will identify common ideational and emotional reactions among themselves and direct their discussion to these. These often relate to individual drives and psychological states.
2. Reactions to therapists include both realistic elements as well as distortions determined by members' past experiences (i.e., transference).
3. Conflicts occur between a desire to fulfill individual needs and a fear of the consequences of striving to meet these needs, and these are often shared by members. The concensus reached as to the resolution of such conflicts may be compatible with the goals of therapy or may be a hindrance on both group and individual levels.

The role of the therapist is to stimulate examination of these issues and to make the kinds of interpretations that will bring about conflict resolution through reality oriented therapist–member interactions. Common psycholo-gical themes can be dealt with and resolved in ways that can help members with their individual difficulties.

The application of these concepts is dependent on the therapist's under-standing of psychoanalytic theory and how it illuminates group phenomena. Group workers have not had such training in depth but are usually taught basic information on human development, often from a psychoanalytic (usually ego psychological) perspective.

Many group work clients are not motivated to engage in the long-term verbally and psychologically oriented activities that group analytic approaches require. Nevertheless, an understanding that members may distort the reality of the worker and each other and that such distortions may hinder group and

---

[17]H. Ezriel, "Psychoanalytic Group Therapy," in *Group Therapy,* eds. L.R. Wolberg and E.K. Schwartz (New York: Intercontinental Medical Book Corporation, 1973); S.H. Foulkes, *Therapeutic Group Analysis* (New York: International Universities Press, 1965); and Dorothy Stock Whitaker and Morton A. Lieberman, *Psychotherapy Through the Group Process* (New York: Lieber-Atherton, Inc., 1965).

individual problem solving is important to effective work with groups. The ability of the worker to identify group themes and to analyze the meaning of these in terms of affects and drives is also useful in order to "make sense" out of the many pieces of information provided by group members. Workers should have a point of view with regard to member's personality manifestations and the meaning of their behavior, and psychoanalytic and ego psychological theory certainly provides one such system.

The Tavistock Approach. When we refer here to the *Tavistock approach,* we have in mind primarily the work of Wilfred Bion.[18] Bion was psychoanalytically trained and subsequently became impressed with group phenomena. One of Bion's major ideas was that groups often avoid "work" by operating according to "basic assumptions." A major reason for responding to a basic assumption is a reaction to the authority of the leader. Basic assumptions include dependence on the leader, fight-flight responses, and pairing among members. Typically, in a Tavistock group, the leader, who is analogous to the psychoanalyst with individuals, remains relatively inactive so that the basic assumptions, as they emerge, do so presumably out of the members' needs rather than worker reality.

This model may be useful for people seeking to understand these emotional processes in groups. The short-term, more focused nature of social work groups militates against this as a central framework. Nevertheless, in order to work toward their goals, all groups must be helped to free themselves from emotional reactions that are hindering, especially those toward leadership. The leader who has participated in a Tavistock-type experience will be particularly sensitive to this issue and will be able to impart this understanding to group members.

Approaches Utilizing or Originating from Social Psychological Theories

Guided Group Interaction. The guided group interaction approach has been utilized primarily with delinquent adolescents in institutional settings.[19] One of the earliest studies of the guided group interactions concept, published in 1958, reported on its use in a New Jersey institution, Highfields.[20] There is also another related approach that has been called *positive peer culture.*[21]

Guided group interaction was designed by sociologists who believed that delinquent behavior was determined in the main by peer group rather than psychological processes. Efforts to encourage change must, therefore, be

[18]W.R. Bion, *Experiences in Groups* (New York: Basic Books, 1959).

[19]LaMar T. Empey and Maynard L. Erickson, *The Provo Experiment: Evaluating Community Control of Delinquency* (Lexington, Mass.: Heath, 1972).

[20]Lloyd W. McCorkle, Albert Elias, and F. Lovell Bixby, *The Highfields Story* (New York: Holt, Rinehart & Winston, 1958).

[21]Harry Vorrath and Larry Brendtro, *Posititive Peer Culture,* 2nd ed. (Chicago: Aldine Publishing Co., 1985).

directed at these social processes. Interventions in the guided group approach require frequent, usually daily, interactions among group members who are also aware of each other's extra-group behavior, usually within an institutional program.

The group is given considerable salience for the youth in that major decisions regarding current privileges and future plans are evaluated there. These decisions are based on whether members have identified and worked on *problems*. A terminology for such problems is either developed by the group or, as in positive peer culture, taught to it. This "language" describes problems in direct, often colloquial, ways.

A major norm that is developed in the group is one of *candor* (as opposed to *conning*). Staff members motivate the members to develop such norms by creating initial ambiguity regarding the group, by confronting the group, and by fostering the dependency of members on the group. As one text on guided group interaction states, a program based on sociological theory will have to concentrate on "changing reference group and normative orientations; utilizing ambivalent feelings resulting from the conflict of conventional and delinquent standards; and, providing opportunities for recognition and achievement in conventional pursuits."[22]

In some ways, these ideas can be drawn upon by group workers; in others, they are problematic. Those that are most usable relate to how the group shapes norms and how workers can mold this process, since group workers *do* work with people branded by society as deviant and placed in institutions involuntarily. On the other hand, the manipulative style and the type of confrontation that is encouraged pose value dilemmas to social workers.

Self-Help Groups. A study of self-help groups estimated a membership of several million in the United States with the number of different organizations as large as two hundred and sixteen.[23] The actual number of such groups is much larger if all the local affiliates of such organizations as Alcoholics Anonymous, Weight Watchers, and Parents Anonymous are considered. The range of concerns addressed by such groups is vast and includes addictions (Synanon, Alcoholics Anonymous), aggressive behavior (Parents Anonymous), mental illness (Recovery, Inc.), disability (Emphysema Anonymous), loss of children (Compassionate Friends), loss of spouse (Parents without Partners), gamblers (Gamblers Anonymous), weight control (Weight Watchers), and sexual orientation (Gay Liberation Front).

This type of group activity is classified as a sociological approach for several reasons. The emphasis of the groups is on interpersonal support rather than psychological uncovering; a major component of what such groups have to offer is successful role models; these groups often have social action goals, such as securing better services or overcoming the stigma directed at group members.

---

[22]Empey and Erickson, *The Provo Experiment,* p. 7.

[23]Morton A. Lieberman, "Group Methods," in *Helping People Change,* eds. Frederick H. Kanfer and Arnold P. Goldstein (Elmsford, N.Y.: Pergamon Press, 1975), p. 440.

The use of these groups is also an outgrowth of social forces as members are likely to have been rejected by mental health professionals and are often viewed as deviant.

Several similarities are found among the groups, although vast differences in programs exist. These include procedures to provide support for members between sessions, an opportunity to tell one's full "story" in an accepting atmosphere, an occasion to enhance one's self-esteem by helping others, and the availability of successful role models. The groups are also, with a few exceptions, such as Parent's Anonymous, without professional leadership and, in fact, are often suspicious of it. While supportive, many of the groups at times, are quite direct and confronting in their style; it is presumed that those who take this stance have earned the right by having shared similar problems and by having overcome them.

The importance of the approaches to group work used in self-help groups is severalfold. These groups remind us of the great value of peer helping and this challenges professional self-importance. Even in professsionally led groups, the techniques of peer support, as well as confrontation, can be cultivated to a greater degree than usual. There is value in nonprofessionally led groups, because of the sense of competence that they nurture. The task of the group worker is to support and offer consultation to such group without taking them over.

Psychodrama. The psychodrama approach has been associated largely with the work of one man—J. L. Moreno.[24] Many of the techniques now in use, particularly gestalt and encounter sessions, were anticipated or even simulated by Moreno's work. We classify this approach as social psychological because of Moreno's stress on the "public" aspects of one's activities rather than the psychological components.

The methods of psychodrama include casting the individual into a problematic role and other individuals present into related roles and then enacting actual and potential scenes. Out of this, insights are elicited, emotional catharsis is secured, and other group members benefit through discussion as well as vicariously.

Moreno also developed another concept, sociodrama, where the focus is on social factors such as intercultural conflict. In fact, Moreno was interested in applying his techniques to the resolution of issues raised by the civil rights movement.

Dramatic devices have always had a place in group work; nevertheless, the type of emotional expression and confrontation brought about in psychodrama is not usually elicited by social work practitioners. However, the emergence of gestalt and encounter techniques has probably made us less apprehensive about such events, although lack of proof of their effectiveness may sometimes create skepticism.[25] Because of this effectiveness issue, group workers, will benefit by an

---

[24]J.L. Moreno, *Psychodrama* (Beacon, N.Y.: Beacon House, Inc., 1964).

[25]For research on the effects of these groups, see M.A. Lieberman, I. Yalom, and M. Miles, *Encounter Groups: First Facts* (New York: Basic Books, 1973).

examination of the carefully specified and illustrated techniques developed by Moreno and his successors.

Approaches Developed from Educational–Psychological Frameworks

Behavior Modification in Groups. One of the greatest impacts on the human service field today comes from the contemporary behaviorists. Drawing from the laboratory work of many people, particularly experimental psychologists, a vast array of behavioral procedures has emerged for treatment of the same problematic conditions at which other approaches are directed. It is not surprising, therefore, that behavioral therapists, like other practitioners, saw the potential of group contexts for behavioral treatment.

Behavioral therapy in groups shares several features with individual behavioral therapy, including a commitment to precise goal specification and initial (baseline) and subsequent measurement of the behaviors to be modified. These changes in behavior are obtained using interventions planned as applications of the principles of conditioning,[26] such as those having to do with behavior that is a result of antecedent or consequent events (operant conditioning) or as a conditioned response (respondent conditioning). Such behavior may consist of thoughts or actions or both. The precise procedures to be used are selected after an analysis to determine the controlling conditions for the relevant behaviors.

Group settings offer a number of additional possibilities for the application of the principles of behavior therapy. Members can help each other to assess behaviors and can reinforce one another for change. In addition, since many of the behaviors to be modified occur in interpersonal contexts, members can engage in assessment and change activities related to behaviors occurring in the group.

The group worker can draw on many behavioral techniques in social work groups, and new behavioral approaches are being developed to facilitate this. Specific procedures, such as assertiveness training, social skill training, and communicational training, draw on behavioral concepts and are frequently and appropriately utilized in a variety of social work groups.[27]

Laboratory Training (T-Groups). While behavior modification grew out of an effort to apply psychological principles that had first been studied in laboratories to therapeutic situations, laboratory training evolved serendipitously from observations of "natural" group situations. Specifically, the laboratory training approach developed out of experiences of members of the staff of the Research Center on Group Dynamics at a workshop held in 1946 to help community leaders

---

[26]For a discussion of such principles, see J. Fisher and H. Gochros, *Planned Behavior Change: Behavior Modification in Social Work* (New York: The Free Press, 1975).

[27]For extensive discussions of the application of behavior therapy in social work groups, see Sheldon Rose, *Group Therapy: A Behavioral Approach* (Englewood Cliffs, N.J.: Prentice-Hall, Inc., 1977), Sheldon Rose, *Treating Children in Groups* (San Francisco: Jossey-Bass, 1972), and Sheldon Rose, ed., *A Case Book in Group Therapy* (Englewood Cliffs, N.J.: Prentice-Hall, Inc., 1980).

implement the Fair Employment Practices Act. Evening sessions were held at which interactions that occurred during the day were analyzed. To the participants attending, it became apparent that a powerful force for change was unleashed as members examined their behavior in the group and the reactions of others to it. Initially, the intent of the participants was to mold an effective social action device but soon the major emphasis was placed on individual learning.[28]

Laboratory training typically takes place at a two-week residential experience where the individuals are isolated from their usual activities. In the beginning of the period, few instructions are given and the members struggle with this ambiguity. After such efforts, members are helped to examine the interpersonal behaviors elicited by this situation. The learning thus induced was utilized to develop applications to real-life situations outside the laboratory. Some of the key ideas of the trainers who facilitated this experience are that participants in groups can learn "how to learn" from experience; that this learning is facilitated by a "here and now focus"; and that feedback from members on their reactions to each other's behavior is an essential condition for interpersonal learning.

The ideas generated by laboratory training, selectively employed, can enrich all work with groups. Giving and receiving feedback is an important tool when used appropriately, but it can produce a great deal of anxiety if introduced into the wrong group or at the wrong time. Members can also be seduced into avoiding the very real purposes of groups by too extensive a focus on internal processes. Nevertheless, some attention to process is valuable in all groups and essential in therapeutic groups. Group workers involved in training and program development may recommend to a staff and professional groups that they examine their group process, when problems in group functioning occur.

Approaches Developed from Social Movements

Social Change Movements. In discussing some approaches, the designation *social movement* is relevant. By this phrase, we mean an organized set of people dedicated to a social ideal that is often viewed as "radical" by status groups in the society. The term "radical" is justified by the principles embodied in the movement as well as the fact that efforts are usually directed at combatting specified ills of the society and even to create a society devoid of such problems. In this respect, it is important to reflect on the fact that during the early period of its history, group work had many of the characteristics of a social movement and this was also true of the entire profession of social work.

Other movements also have developed approaches that have relevance to social group work. Black, Chicano, and similar ethnic groups have formed organizations that emphasize themes of group pride and conduct activities consistent with these themes. Social workers often work with groups composed of members of ethnic minorities and these people's problems relate strongly to lack of social support for their identities. A similar phenomenon is found among women's

---

[28]This discussion of laboratory training draws heavily on Shaffer and Galinsky, *Models of Group Therapy,* pp. 189–210.

movement groups in their approaches to consciousness raising, group support, and confrontation of sexism as ways of meeting members' needs. This also has relevance for groups conducted by social workers. Even political groups committed to specific ideologies provide important normative climates and supports for their members that have parallels in social work situations. The programs of these groups utilize techniques similar to those employed by "grass roots" community organizations. Group workers should become familiar with these techniques.

The Encounter Movement. So-called encounter groups probably form a continuum with those identified as sensitivity groups. Many encounter groups quite clearly present at least the rudiments of a social movement and have been so characterized by many writers.

The movement aspect of encounter groups, according to Shaffer and Galinsky, is "designed to put the normally alienated individual into closer contact—or encounter with himself, with others, and with the world of nature and pure sensation."[29] The socially critical stance of writers on encounter groups stems from their charge that our society and its institutions alienate individuals from themselves and their bodies. Values, such as spontaneity, honesty in interactions, and the validity of one's own feelings, are offered as a basis for the encounter experience. As with many other aspects of the "counterculture," authority is downgraded, particularly that based on the training and certification of the group leader. Instead, there is an emphasis on what can be gained from the creation of a sense of community.

Workers in encounter groups usually come from sensitivity group, psychoanalytic, and psychotherapeutic backgrounds and are often influenced by writers, such as Wilhelm Reich, who stress the relationships between physiological and emotional states. They inevitably recruit group members who hold social values different from those who enter traditional psychotherapies.

The techniques used in encounter groups include encouragement of direct emotional expression, physical exercises, physical interaction among participants (for example, hugging, arm wrestling, communication by touch), as well as the use of exercises drawn from approaches such as gestalt. The leader is active in introducing these procedures and is often a participant, thus lessening social distance between the leader and group members.

Some of the techniques used in encounter groups will not be accepted by social work clients who come from working class, as opposed to academic and professional, backgrounds and who seek help with specific circumstances and behaviors. On the other hand, the lowering of social barriers may be accepted by many clients of social work groups, particularly children and young people. Also, clients who are inhibited in emotional expression can be helped by various nonverbal exercises and clients with bodily tensions can profit from learning ways to relax these. Finally, many clients do seek ways to develop closer ties with others by freeing themselves from various restraints and seeking new life styles.

[29]Shaffer and Galinsky, *Models of Group Therapy,* p. 211.

SIMILARITIES AND DIFFERENCES AMONG
APPROACHES

A number of similarities such as the following can be found among virtually all group work writers.

1. Purposes. All approaches to group work incorporate the professional purposes of preventing breakdown of social functioning, providing resources to meet human needs, and rehabilitating individuals whose functioning has been impaired. Some writers focus on one or another of these purposes but none deny the legitimacy of social work's responsibility for all of these purposes and the contribution that group work can make to each.

2. Knowledge and Theory. All approaches to group work draw from a common source of knowledge from the behavioral sciences. Some lean more heavily upon one kind of knowledge than others but all utilize small group theory as it describes group development, group leadership, group problem solving, and other group conditions. All also utilize an understanding of individual development and ways of coping, primarily related to participation in small groups. Role concepts abound in the group work literature and are used to describe positions occupied by group members such as leader, expert, or scapegoat. Role concepts are also used to discuss the processes of socialization as affected by group participation.

Group work writers will differ, however, in the degree to which they draw on concepts from behavioral theory, systems theory, or ego psychology. In these, the differences among group workers parallel those among all human service professionals.

3. Problem Solving. Although differing somewhat on how the problems confronting groups and their members are to be analyzed, group workers are usually problem focused. As Somers states, "Problem solving characterized the formulations of social group work practice across the spectrum of fifty years."[30] Somers explains this focus, not only in terms of the intellectual history of group work but also because "The social and intellectual history of the United States is replete with examples of the pragmatic philosophy and experimental approach that form the matrix in which problem solving is embedded, and that provide the source of its essence and continuing energy."[31]

4. Intervention. Different group work writers describe many similar worker interventions. These actions, which shall be discussed thoroughly in subsequent chapters, include enhancing program activities, eliciting the expression of affect, and supporting honest presentation of one's experiences and beliefs.

---

[30]Mary Lousie Somers, "Problem Solving in Small Groups," in *Theories of Social Work with Groups,* eds. Roberts and Northen, p. 331.
[31]Ibid., p. 333.

Workers help members to try out roles in the group in order to rehearse for their performance outside the group and to give suggestions and feedback to one another regarding their behavior *both* within and outside of the group.

A number of ideas have been developed and used more extensively by the adherents of one approach as opposed to another. We shall now summarize some of these.

William Schwartz

William Schwartz, the initiator of what he has called the *interactionist approach,* draws more strongly than others from systems concepts to portray members, groups, agencies, and other complex environments in interaction with each other and in a constant process of mutual adaptation. The social worker facilitates this process by functioning as a *mediator.*[32]

The interactionist model focuses on the process whereby individuals engage with others to meet mutual needs. An emphasis of this approach is on the quality of the process rather than on the long-term consequences (goals). Schwartz's analysis of process enriches all of group work practice, particularly his portrayal of phases[33] and the tasks of group workers in relationship to such phases.[34]

Robert Vinter

Robert Vinter developed some of the major aspects of what he referred to as a *social treatment* or a *problem oriented* model although others have referred to it as either the *remedial* or *preventive and rehabilitative approach.*[35] This work is based on the idea that the individual group member is the focus of change and the group is the means and context of such change. Vinter and his colleague's ideas contrast with those of Schwartz in that they place a strong emphasis on establishing individual goals, often long term in nature, that are precise and operational.

This model calls for an empirical base for practice: practice principles should be scientifically tested for effectiveness and can and should be employed in the service of goal attainment. Philosophically, therefore, this framework is closer to a positivist rather than an existential stance. The writings of Vinter and related theorists have been of value in the development of group work because of their efforts to specify group worker activities and their effects: these include worker acts (1) at different phases of group development,[36] (2) in relationship to different

---

[32]William Schwartz, "Between Client and System: The Mediating Function," in *Theories of Social Work with Groups,* eds. Roberts and Northen, p. 178.

[33]Ibid., pp. 186–94.

[34]William Schwartz, "The Social Worker in the Group," in *New Perspectives on Service to Groups* (New York: Columbia University Press, 1961).

[35]For writing on this approach, see Sundel, Glasser, Sarri, and Vinter, eds., *Individual Change Through Small Groups.*

[36]Rosemary C. Sarri and Maeda Galinsky, "A Conceptual Framework for Group Development," in *Individual Change Through Small Groups,* eds. Sundel, Glasser, Sarri, and Vinter, pp. 70–86.

group processes,[37] (3) for various program approaches,[38] and (4) toward the social environment.[39]

Emanuel Tropp

Emanuel Tropp considers his approach as in the "mainstream" of the development of group work in social work; he regards many other group work writers as "special offshoots."[40] Tropp sees the mainstream as stressing the principle that "group self-direction toward a common goal is the most effective group vehicle for the social growth of its members";[41] the individual is helped to achieve growth through participation in establishing and accomplishing the group's goal or purpose. Because Tropp sees the group as the vehicle of such growth, he describes the worker (or "leader") as helping to establish group goals and to attain them.

In sharp contrast to Vinter's conceptualization, Tropp does not seek to articulate his model with social science and other research findings. He believes that these endeavors have not created, and are not likely to create, a basis for social work practice. Rather, he finds the empirical evidence for group work in the experiences of its practitioners.

Finally, Tropp does not describe group work as "treatment" and its beneficiaries as "abnormal or pathological." As he states, "All are seen as people who face stressful developmental stages, life situations, challenges, and crises with which they must cope in some way."[42] Thus, Tropp has made major contributions to an understanding of how workers function when their intent is to provide the group context for individual growth experiences.

Alan Klein

Alan Klein, an author whose books on group work span almost three decades (the most recent published in 1972),[43] like Tropp, emphasizes the potential of group experience to help individuals acquire interpersonal skills. Klein, however, refers to his model as a "matching" one in which individual needs are related to environmental opportunities. Klein, as well as Tropp, places strong emphasis on the role of the group in nurturing and encouraging the freedom and autonomy of the group member. In this respect, Klein and Tropp draw on the extensive heritage in group work of analyses of the democratic process.

[37]Charles D. Garvin, "Group Process: Usage and Uses in Social Work Practice," in *Individual Change Through Small Groups,* eds. Sundel, Glasser, Sarri, and Vinter, pp. 203–25.

[38]Robert D. Vinter, "Program Activities: An Analysis of their Effects on Participant Behavior," in *Individual Change Through Small Groups,* eds. Sundel, Glasser, Sarri, and Vinter, pp. 226–36.

[39]Charles Garvin and others, "Group Work Intervention in the Social Environment," in *Individual Change Through Small Groups,* eds. Sundel, Glasser, Sarri, and Vinter, pp. 277–93.

[40]Emanuel Tropp, "Developmental Theory," in *Theories of Social Work with Groups,* eds. Roberts and Northen, pp. 198–99.

[41]Ibid.

[42]Ibid., p. 213.

[43]Alan F. Klein, *Effective Group Work* (New York: Association Press, 1972).

Margaret Hartford

Margaret Hartford has developed concepts that place group work in the context of generic practice,[44] in that the worker "uses the methodological approaches most appropriate for the given situation." She sees common as well as unique elements to all social work with groups and for this reason has developed a typology of the full range of such services. Her classifications include, for example, work focused on individual participants, problem solving or task achievement, the group context, the institution outside the group or the wider society.[45] In this respect, Hartford differs from other writers who might see only one function for workers wherever they are located (for example, as mediators) or who limit their model to selected functions (for example, prevention and rehabilitation). Hartford describes "stances" for group workers depending on the type of group and the specific circumstances of the group (for example, stage of development). These stances include directing, facilitating, permissive, and flexible postures.

Boston University School of Social Work

The work of Saul Bernstein and other persons associated with the Boston University School of Social Work has also been very influential for current practice.[46] Their impact is due to their identification of key practice issues. Their approaches and solutions are drawn from extensive experience as well as from theory—examples of which are their discussions of worker activities in different stages of group development, in group conflict situations, and in decisions on group purpose.

Helen Northen

Helen Northen has incorporated systems theory into group work in order to provide a theoretical foundation for a *psychosocial* model.[47] She employs concepts regarding individual assessment and goal setting that are also used in the preventive and rehabilitative model. Her model also emphasizes the concept of group development and the ways worker tasks vary in relationship to the group's developmental stages. She presents a comprehensive review of the way changes in group conditions and member behaviors relate to the process of goal setting, interpersonal relationship development, confrontation, and feedback.

[44]Margaret Hartford, "Group Methods and Generic Practice," in *Theories of Social Work with Groups,* eds. Roberts and Northen, pp. 45–74. Also see her effort to portray knowledge about groups for all social workers, in *Groups in Social Work* (New York: Columbia University Press, 1972).

[45]Margaret Hartford, "Group Methods and Generic Practice," pp. 54–55.

[46]Saul Bernstein, ed., *Exploration in Group Work* (Boston: Boston University School of Social Work, 1965).

[47]A recent statement of her model is Helen Northen, "Psychosocial Practice in Small Groups," in *Theories of Social Work with Groups,* eds. Roberts and Northen, pp. 116–52. An earlier and more extensive presentation of her ideas is found in Helen Northen, *Social Work with Groups* (New York: Columbia University Press, 1969).

Behavioral Group Work

Roberts and Northen in explaining how they chose the models they included in their book on contemporary group work theory justify excluding behavior modification as a model.[48] It is seen, rather, as a set of procedures initially developed by psychologists and incorporated into many models. This is true; yet the reader's attention should be drawn to the writings of Sheldon Rose and Martin Sundel, and Harry Lawrence,[49] all social workers who have identified themselves with group work as well as with behavior modification. The behavior modification approach, like the preventive and rehabilitative model, focuses on individual behavior change to achieve mutually agreed on goals. Procedures for achieving such changes are usually introduced by the worker and are derived theoretically from conditioning concepts. Change is carefully monitored and data is used as feedback for modifying the procedures. Rose's work differs from that of many behaviorists, however, in that it incorporates small group theory and describes how group conditions (for example, cohesiveness, leadership, deviance) may be modified so as to enhance individual goal attainment.[50] These writers, as well as many others who use behavior modification in social work with groups, had been closely associated at one time or another in their careers with Vinter, Glasser, and Garvin at the University of Michigan.

SUMMARY

In chapter 1, we made a presentation of the model of group work to be utilized in this text, which included an explanation of how this model seeks to be relevant to the many settings in which group work is practiced through the use of a typology of group purposes. Each of these purposes requires adaptations of the model including variations in procedures directed at individual members, the group, and the extra-group environment. Other features of the model that were discussed include: the view of the group as a mutual aid system; the requirement that goals and means of achieving them be specified behaviorally; and, that outcomes be evaluated. The professional values embedded in the model were enumerated.

---

[48]Roberts and Northen, eds. *Theories of Social Work with Groups,* p. 373.
[49]Sheldon Rose, *Group Therapy;* Harry Lawrence and Martin Sundel, "Behavior Modification in Adult Groups," *Social Work* 17 (1972), pp. 34–43.
[50]Sheldon Rose, *Group Therapy.*

2

Group Work Activities and Settings

THE SIGNIFICANCE OF THE AGENCY

Most group work, as well as social work, is practiced under the auspices of social agencies. These agencies have been established either by government or private citizens to meet a variety of social needs such as those related to physical and mental health, to specified populations (children, the aged), to resource deficits (financial assistance), or to the enhancement of the quality of life (education and the use of leisure time).

Chapter 2 will discuss the agency settings in which group work is practiced and how these settings affect the group and will be followed by a summary of the history of group work to help the reader understand its scope and diversity.

Some social workers, including group workers, engage in private practice in which the worker directly recruits clients who then pay a fee. Private practice, therefore, tends to serve the more affluent. Because of the emphasis of our model on service to the oppressed, we do not discuss private practice, although many group work principles do apply to it.

The agencies that offer group services include those in the public sector, such as departments of welfare or community mental health, state institutions for the mentally ill, and schools. Those maintained by private boards (often with government assistance), are many family agencies, child guidance clinics, and community centers. These agencies do not merely promote a group in a neutral way and then disengage from it; they influence the group at all stages of its development from conception to termination. A worker cannot effectively work with a group, therefore, without understanding, utilizing, and sometimes seeking to change agency conditions. Major issues related to this are how to involve the group and how to cope with the fact that the worker is an employee of the agency as well as a professional.

As a consequence, in this book we identify with what Hasenfeld calls "an organization practice model" and not a "clinical practice model."[1] The latter "focuses primarily (and often exclusively) on client-change agent relations and the purposeful use of these relations for change, with minimal attention given to the organization within which such relations exist or to the impact the organization has on the entire change process."[2] This chapter will be devoted to helping the reader to understand organizational effects on group work: Chapter 7 will present related change strategies.

The current range of group work activities and their relationship to the sponsoring agencies will be more meaningful if the history of group work is understood. This history is an exciting one in which group workers struggled to develop their ideas and to overcome opposition to them. An understanding of history should also help the reader to see why the models described in the previous chapter were created as well as the controversies surrounding them.

GROUP WORK HISTORY

In discussing the history of group work, we must describe events that occurred before the phrase *group work* was even used. This is because important developments took place that would later be labeled "group work" and the individuals involved in these would later come to call themselves "group workers." This history, then, can be divided into four periods: the emergence of group work (1861 to 1927); the clarification of the method (1928 to 1946); the diffusion of practice (1947 to 1963); the move to the generic (1964 to 1979); and the revitalization of group work (1979 and after).

The Emergence of Group Work: 1861 to 1927

Developments in American society during this period that gave the greatest impetus to group services were the emergence of the United States and other countries as industrial societies, the shift of large populations from rural to urban living to support such industrialization, and the immigrations from Europe, Mexico, and Asia. This led to the entrapment of people in communities that were overcrowded, unhealthy, and deteriorating. Many of the residents of these

---

[1]Yeheskel Hasenfeld, "Organizational Factors in Service to Groups," in *Individual Change Through Small Groups,* eds. Martin Sundel, Paul H. Glasser, Rosemary Sarri, and Robert Vinter (New York: Free Press, 1985), p. 294.
[2]Ibid.

communities were also hindered from improving their occupational status and they experienced themselves as powerless to change these conditions. These factors stimulated the creation of organizations to ameliorate these circumstances through progressive social reform activities.

One of the first agencies to respond to these problems through group services was the Young Men's Christian Association, organized in the United States in 1851 "to improve the spiritual condition of young men in the drapery and trades"; this developed into the broader objective of improving the "mental, social and physical condition of all young men of good moral character."[3]

The Young Women's Christian Association was founded in the United States fifteen years later. In the years after that, many additional organizations with similar orientations emerged such as the Girl's Friendly Society of the United States (1877) and the Boy's Clubs of America (1906). According to one writer, these organizations "looked to the face-to-face group to restore opportunities for the good life taken from people by the speed and ruthlessness of post-Civil War industrialization."[4]

A more vigorous reform thrust, however, was provided by the introduction of the settlement house into the United States, inspired by similar institutions developed in England. Stanton Coit, after a visit to Toynbee Hall in London, established the Neighborhood Guild on the lower east side of New York in 1886. The settlement idea spread rapidly and in 1891 there were six settlements in the United States; by 1900 the number was more than four hundred.

The idea behind the settlements was that people interested in the problems of the poor could understand them better by participating in their community life. Settlements sought to create a variety of programs to ameliorate the specific problems of their communities. Thus settlements sponsored such diverse activities as kindergartens and preschool sessions, adult education, leisure time and cultural arts groups, social action committees, and neighborhood councils—all group-oriented activities. Settlements, in contrast to many other social services that emphasized adjustment to the social order, had a social change focus. Their workers sought changes in social conditions as a way of attaining their objectives.

Closely related to the development of the Ys and the settlements was the emergence of the Jewish Community Centers, and Young Men's and Women's Hebrew Associations. These organizations had philosophies that were similar to those of the Ys. A difference, however, was that they were often sponsored by the more affluent western European Jews who, having come to this country before the Jews from Eastern Europe, used these associations as a means to "Americanize" the latter group.[5]

---

[3]Gertrude Wilson, "From Practice to Theory: A Personalized History," in *Theories of Social Work With Groups,* eds. Robert Roberts and Helen Northen (New York: Columbia Universtiy Press, 1976), p. 6.

[4]William Schwartz, "Social Group Work: The Interactionist Approach," in *Encyclopedia of Social Work* (New York: National Association of Social Workers, 1971), II, 1253.

[5]For a discussion of this, see Irving Howe, *World of Our Fathers* (New York: Simon & Schuster, 1976), p. 230.

During this period, there was a lack of professional identification among workers in these various agencies who were referred to by their settings such as Y or Scout leaders or settlement workers. While people from a number of professions, such as education, psychology, sociology, and social work, discussed with each other how to utilize groups, there was no agreement among them regarding a professional auspice.

Within social work itself, beyond those people who worked with groups, there was little appreciation of the value of group experience. However, Mary Richmond, one of the pioneers in the development of casework practice, began, in her later works, to emphasize a broad conception of social work practice and in 1920 wrote of the importance of "small group psychology."[6]

One writer who influenced these early workers was Mary P. Follett, a political scientist. In her book, *The New State,* Follett states that she thought solutions to social problems would emerge from the creation of groups in neighborhoods and around social interests.[7] Another thinker who was important to these workers was John Dewey, who developed the idea of progressive education. According to one view of the period, the social group work method "was an application of the principles of progressive education to small informal groups in leisure time settings."[8]

Group work, at first, was closely associated with community development concepts, and, in fact, the origins of community organization method and its citizens participation focus cannot be distinguished from the beginnings of group work. Another writer who influenced these developments was Eduard C. Lindeman, who was interested in the fostering of community groups, also, and their role in a functioning democracy.[9]

Although these ideas and programs were developed in an atmosphere of excitement among reformers, educators, and social workers involved in them, it was not until the end of this period that a course in group work was introduced into a school of social work. The first course was taught by Mildred Chadsey at Western Reserve University in 1923. This began a long and productive period of that school's commitment to the development of group work. Virtually all of the pioneers among group-oriented social workers either taught at Western Reserve or were closely associated with its faculty.

We chose the year 1927 to mark the end of this period of group work history because by then it was clear that a new approach had emerged. Evidence for this was that Western Reserve University, in that year, significantly increased its group services curriculum. A large number of agencies were committing their

[6]Mary Richmond, "Some Next Steps in Social Treatment," *Proceedings of the National Conference of Social Work* (Chicago: University of Chicago Press, 1920), p. 256.

[7]Mary Parker Follett, *The New State* (New York: Longman, 1926).

[8]John Dewey, *How We Think* (Lexington, Mass.: Heath, 1933).

[9]Harry Lawrence, "The Origins of Social Group Work" (unpublished manuscript, p. 13), quoted in Scott Briar, "Social Casework and Social Group Work: Historical Foundations," *Encyclopedia of Social Work,* p. 1241.

resources to group activities, and people such as Kaiser, Newstetter, and Williamson were drawing upon these experiences to conceptualize a theory of practice.

Clarification of the Method: 1928 to 1946

The further development of group work from 1928 until the end of World War II was affected by two major cataclysms that occurred at the beginning and ending of this period: the depression and the war. The depression posed a new challenge to social reformers who believed that their earlier efforts had contributed to progress toward a humanitarian society. Social workers now were forced to question the validity of adjusting people to the existing social order. This gave impetus to group workers who saw groups as a vehicle for promoting social change. It is not surprising, therefore, that these years were productive ones for group work.

First, this increased awareness of the importance of group services was associated with an enhanced professional identity. Gertrude Wilson relates an interesting anecdote associated with this process. In 1927 Wilbur Newstetter of Western Reserve University and Walter Pettit of the New York School for Social Work (now Columbia University School of Social Work) were traveling together on a long train ride to the National Conference of Social Work. Newstetter could only describe the group work project at Western Reserve that had just begun as he did not know what to call it. "Pettit said that it sounded to him as if the project would demonstrate the delivery of social services through groups and that at his school they call the delivery of social services to individuals *casework*; why not call this Western Reserve project *group work*."[10] Wilson explains that the phrase "group work" had been used before this time, in a programmatic sense, in religious education, and adult education contexts. Newstetter was innovative in using "group work" to designate a social work method.

During the 1930s and 1940s group work continued to be practiced primarily in the Ys, settlements, Jewish Centers, and scouts. It was a productive and peaceful phase of development in these agencies as they strove to meet the needs of people affected by depression and then war. Controversy, when it existed, was found between some professionals and educators as they struggled with the creation of a practice theory and a professional identity for group workers.

The creation of a *social work* identity for group workers posed a challenge. People interested in group work, such as Coyle, Kaiser, Wilson, and Newstetter, were closely related to social work; but it took several years for their efforts to take organizational form. The years 1935 an 1936 were important ones in this respect. In 1935, the National Conference of Social Work agreed to institute a section on group work and a number of important papers were delivered at the

---

[10]Wilson, "From Practice to Theory," p. 18.

1935 meeting.[11] Group workers were also active on another organizational front. The National Association for the Study of Group Work was formed in 1936, and provided an organizational form for group workers to further their practice interests.

As group work pioneers advanced their ideas through social work channels, major conflicts appeared. One speaker at the 1935 National Conference saw group work as a "social mechanism perfectly competent people utilize to achieve their own ends."[12] He saw social workers' use of groups as an adaptation of something broader and more basic than simply a social work method. At the same time, caseworkers took issue, not with group work philosophy, but with the seriousness of group work as an enterprise. Wilson explains that group workers were described stereotypically as people who "play with children" or "run dances."[13]

Nevertheless, by 1937, ten schools of social work offered courses in group work. Others rejected this type of education because of its ties to recreation. Within the next two years, nevertheless, the number of schools offering group work education grew to seventeen. Six more schools taught about group work but did not provide an appropriate field experience.[14]

Coincident with these organizational activities was the development of group work practice theory. The audience for this was expanded when the National Association for the Study of Group Work established a publication in 1939—*The Group—in Education, Recreation, Social Work*. A number of texts were also written in the 1930s that continue to have an influence to the present day.[15]

We consider this period of clarification of the method to have ended in 1946 because by then group workers had consolidated their existence as practitioners of an established method. They had formed the American Association of Group Workers, produced a consensus document on professional standards, and expanded their activities into new settings. This latter development was an important component of the next period as the influence of group work continued to grow.

---

[11] These include Coyle's classic presentation of a philosophy for group work entitled "Group Work and Social Change," Grace L. Coyle, *Group Experience and Democratic Values* (New York: Women's Press, 1947); and Newstetter's clarification of semantic and conceptual issues: W.I. Newstetter, "What is Social Group Work?" in *Proceedings of the National Conference of Social Work* (Chicago: University of Chicago Press, 1935), pp. 291-99. Coyle in her presentation stressed the dual function of group work to transmit cultural values to individuals while at the same time helping people to transform these values through democratic processes. Newstetter identified group work as a "field," a "process," and a "set of techniques."

[12] Schwartz, *Encyclopedia of Social Work*, p. 1254.

[13] Wilson, "From Practice to Theory," p. 25.

[14] Ibid., p. 18.

[15] For example, Grace Coyle, *Studies in Group Behavior* (New York: Harper & Row Pub., 1937); Clara A. Kaiser, *The Group Records of Four Clubs* (Cleveland: Western Reserve University, 1930); S.R. Slavson, *Creative Group Education* (New York: Association Press, 1937); and Margaretta Williamson, *The Social Worker in Group Work* (New York: Harper & Row, Pub., 1929).

The Diffusion of Practice: 1947 to 1963

As a result of the depression and the war, the idea of large-scale government involvement in programs and services led to the expansion of social work practice. On the other hand, the state of foreign affairs, particularly the cold war with the Soviet Union, was associated with fears of an "internal communist menace." The accusation that reformers were "subversive," impeded the social reform spirit of the previous period. Since many group workers were associated with the spirit of social reform this period had an effect on their endeavors.

These decades of the forties and fifties, therefore, were not ones in which group workers sought to attain social change, but were ones in which they endeavored to clarify and expand group work practice theory and the movement of that practice into new settings. The connection of group work with social action was muted. An example is provided by the comparison of two discussions of social action printed during this era. The first, written by Grace Coyle in 1948, describes a situation in which a group of young people planned a lobbying strategy for Fair Employment Practice legislation.[16] Five years later, Alan Klein, in his discussion of social action, gave an example of a member of a group who was expelled by the police from a park. Through subsequent visits to the police station, the group was helped to develop a closer relationship with the police.[17] This latter type of accommodation to society was typical of the fifties and contrasted with Coyle's illustration.

At the beginning of this period, ambiguity existed as to whether group work was a social work or an educational specialization. A crucial consensus was reached at the meeting of the National Conference on Social Work in 1946 in support of Grace Coyle's conclusion that "group work as a method falls within the larger scope of social work *as a method.*"[18] Coyle came to this conclusion through her analysis of the common concerns of caseworkers, group workers, and community organizers. This consensus led to the formation of the American Association of Group Workers (AAGW) as a professional membership organization, with membership based on the possession of professional training.

In this organizational environment theoretical developments received great encouragement; many influential books were published and *The Group,* now under AAGW sponsorship, continued to play an important role.[19] With this type of progress, it was inevitable that group workers would bring their skills to the performance of new tasks in new settings.

[16]Grace Coyle, *Group Work with American Youth* (New York: Harper & Row, Pub., 1948).
[17]Alan Klein, *Society, Democracy and the Group* (New York: Morrow, 1953).
[18]Harleigh B. Trecker, ed., *Group Work: Foundations and Frontiers* (New York: Whiteside, Inc., 1955), p. 340.
[19]For example, Gertrude Wilson and Gladys Ryland, *Social Group Work Practice* (Boston: Houghton-Mifflin, 1949); Harleigh B. Trecker, *Social Group Work* (New York: Women's Press, 1948); Grace Coyle, *Group Experience and Democratic Values;* Gisela Konopka, *Therapeutic Group Work with Children* (Minneapolis: University of Minnesota Press, 1949); and a few years later Helen Phillips, *Essentials of Social Group Work Skill* (New York: Association Press, 1957).

While the predominant employment of group workers continued to be in settlements, Ys, and youth organizations, demonstrations of the group technique were conducted in psychiatric services, hospitals, family agencies, correctional institutions, and schools. This was enhanced by the use of groups for the treatment of World War II veterans having psychiatric problems,[20] with reported beneficial effects. Support for many of these experiments with group work was provided by government funds as well as by the National Association of Social Workers.[21]

The entry of group workers into rehabilitation settings, nevertheless, led to considerable debate during the 1950s. Writers such as Robert Vinter argued that the preponderance of group workers in community agencies was a "retreat from the profession's historic mission of service to those most in need."[22] On the other hand, some group workers saw this shift as withdrawal from social action responsibilities.[23] Others also feared that the preventive function of group work would be lost.

A factor that created dilemmas for group workers was the idea that the social work method could be viewed in a generic sense. The "generic" idea was paralleled and enhanced by the 1962 decision of the National Association of Social Workers to eliminate "sections" devoted to separate methods such as group work. The next phase of group work history found many writers, as well as group workers, seeking to conceptualize social work as a single method.

The Move to the Generic Method: 1964 to 1979

The events in the society that affected the development of group work in the sixties and seventies were the War on Poverty and the Civil Rights Movement. Both of these led to pressures on social workers to see problems from new, often more sociological, perspectives and to seek ways to solve such problems that were not restricted by the traditional dogmas.

Thus the government was committed to supplying money to be used for experiments with new solutions to delinquency, poverty, and mental illness. In conceiving of such experiments, professionals were influenced by the Civil Rights struggles to consider comprehensive interventions. In addition, data from the evaluation of previously utilized interventions led to serious concern about their effectiveness. Thus one idea that emerged was that a combination of these methods would be more effective than the utilization of only one.

Developments in group work practice theory during the 1947 to 1963 period facilitated the development of a generic approach. Because group work was increasingly practiced in psychiatric, medical, child welfare, correctional, and other

---

[20]Wilson, "From Practice to Theory," pp. 32–33.

[21]*Use of Groups in the Psychiatric Setting* (New York: National Association of Social Workers, 1960).

[22]Robert D. Vinter, "Group Work: Perspectives and Prospects," in *Social Work with Groups* (New York: National Association of Social Workers, 1959), pp. 128-49.

[23]Wilson, "From Practice to Theory," p. 33.

"special" settings, the needs of group members were now similar to casework clients. Approaches to group work evolved in practice that utilized concepts familiar to caseworkers. For example, Robert Vinter, in his writings in the 1950s, prescribed the development of treatment goals for individuals served in groups and indicated these should be related to individual diagnoses. He saw the group as a means for achieving such treatment goals rather than as an end in itself. Writers such as Fritz Redl and Gisela Konopka also wrote about group work utilizing psychoanalytic concepts that were also employed by caseworkers.[24]

These trends in group work practice also led to the recognition that there were now schools of group work practice, namely the ones described in the preceding chapter. Some of these schools were compatible with the generic practice idea, but writers associated with other schools feared that the essence of group work would be lost in a generic approach.

The current controversies that surround group work stem from the historical events just described. Those who maintain that the group as an entity has a vital role in a democracy and should be nurtured by social workers are the heirs of the tradition of Follet and Lindeman, who wrote at a time when democracy was seen as threatened by rapid industrialization, war, and economic depression. Others who are more likely to emphasize the group as a means to individual change are in the tradition of Redl and Slavson, who were allied with psychology and psychiatry. The development of group work as therapy began during the individually oriented years of the 1920s[25] and continued in the 1950s when an ideology of individual rather than social responsibility for one's problems was strong.

The Revitalization of Group Work: 1979 and After

During the 1960s and 1970s when major efforts were underway to integrate direct practice methods in social work, little attention was paid to the development of group work theory and to the quality and quantity of practice with groups in agencies. Nevertheless, there was growing concern regarding this inattention among practitioners and teachers who remained committed to work with groups. Several important steps were taken by such individuals to reaffirm the importance of work with groups *within* the arena of direct practice and the necessity of continuing to develop the theoretical base for work with groups.

One such step was the creation of the journal *Social Work with Groups* under the creative and capable editorship of Catherine Papell of Adelphi University and Beulah Rothman, first of Adelphi and then of Barry University. This journal is not only devoted to articles for direct service practitioners but also to those involved with group issues in the agency and the community. It filled a gap

---

[24]Konopka, *Therapeutic Group Work;* Fritz Redl, "The Therapeutic Ingredients in the Group Work Program in a Residential Treatment Center for Children," in *Group Work in the Psychiatric Setting,* ed. Harleigh Trecker (N.Y.: Whiteside, Inc., and Morrow, 1956), pp. 43–46.

[25]See, for example, T. Burrow, "The Basis of Group Analysis," *British Journal of Medical Psychology* 8, Pt. 3 (November 1928), 198–206.

that was left when *The Group* ceased publication under the mistaken assumption that the more general journals in social work could provide sufficient coverage of group related developments.

Another important step occurred when a number of people concerned about group work assembled during the 1978 Annual Program Meeting of the Council on Social Work Education. They created the Committee for the Advancement of Social Work with Groups. The initial activity of the committee was to sponsor the first Annual Symposium on Social Work with Groups, which was held in Cleveland, Ohio, in October, 1979. This location was chosen in recognition of the seminal role played by Grace Coyle in the creation of contemporary group work practice and her association with Case Western Reserve University in Cleveland. The opening session of the symposium, in which Gisela Konopka, Mary Louise Somers, Margaret Hartford, James Garland, and William Schwartz were participants, was devoted to a panel discussion of the contributions of Grace Coyle. Over four hundred individuals were in attendance, which was double the expectation of the symposium organizers. Many excellent presentations on all aspects of practice were offered and the atmosphere of the meetings resembled a long postponed reunion with old friends.

The symposium has become an annual event with over a hundred presentations each year devoted to all aspects of work with groups. These offerings have been finding their way into all social work publications, as well as the proceedings of the conferences themselves and have enriched all of direct practice. The conferences are sponsored by local planning groups whose geographical spread attests to the international nature of this reemphasis on groups. Sponsorship has come from such local areas as those surrounding Arlington, Texas; Hartford, Connecticut; Toronto, Ontario; Detroit, Michigan; Chicago, Illinois; and Los Angeles, California. People attending these meetings have come from Asia, Europe, and South America.

These events have undoubtedly affected education as well as practice in social work. Schools have reexamined their group offerings and practitioners have sought post-graduate education in group work. A number of other activities have emerged such as a seminar on group work research at the University of Wisconsin-Madison in June, 1985 and the creation of local group work associations. Consideration is also being given to whether the current structure of the Committee for the Advancement of Social Work with Groups meets the many needs for expressing the growing interests in group work.

This is truly an exciting time for people interested in work with groups. We anticipate that the above activities, as well as many we do not have space to cite, will lead to a vigorous growth period for group practice.

In conclusion, when the social climate is one in which there is concern in the society for its democratic functioning, then the role of the worker as facilitator of group process is favored, as in the thirties when Grace Coyle's work was influential and in the sixties when Schwartz's ideas influenced group workers profoundly. In contrast, in the more conservative atmosphere of the fifties, group work was defined by one writer as "the systematic ways in which the worker affects social and group process to achieve specified objectives," and group process in social work groups was defined as "group process when consciously affected by the worker toward specified ends."[26]

In the later 1970s, when movements for social change were in abeyance, behavior modification approaches were of considerable interest and a leading theorist on social work with groups wrote that "treatment planning involves choosing from a number of highly specific procedures that have been demonstrated to be related to achieving behavioral change goals."[27] The intent here is not to express criticism of these sets of ideas but rather to place them in the social and historical contexts that were conducive to their development.

The 1980s, while representing a conservative political climate in the society, is a period in which social workers have sought to maintain social commitments despite the prevailing political atmosphere. The reaffirmation of group work with its historical investment in individual empowerment and social change is part of this current professional mission.

The expert versus facilitator dichotomy is also affected by the state of social science knowledge regarding human behavior and its control. As London points out so well: ". . . means are being found, in all the crafts and sciences of man, society, and life, that will soon make possible precise control over much of people's individual actions, thoughts, emotions, moods and wills."[28] Both practitioners and philosophers have speculated on the possibility that such a development can be halted because of the threat posed to liberty. London, however, is pessimistic in his statement: "It is plain to anyone who troubles to look that once the potential for a particular technological development is clear, the actual technology follows, sometimes sooner, sometimes later, but without fail."[29] London's inevitable conclusion is: "The future, already upon us, must be controlled."[30]

As far as group work is concerned, group workers considered themselves as facilitators of group process before the emergence of technologies of behavior control. Some workers, now, with the creation of behavioral techniques seek to implement group work procedures that have immediate and potent effects. In this respect, group workers join the ranks of teachers, psychologists, and producers of the mass media who can be divided into those who maintain a facilitative and educational stance as opposed to those who seek to attain predetermined goals by the most expeditious means possible.

Now that we have examined the evolution of group work theories and practice settings, we shall analyze in detail the way settings currently affect practice. This discussion, as we stated earlier, should help the practitioner to see ways of using agency conditions as well as, on occasion, seeking to change them.

[26]Marjorie Murphy, *The Social Group Work Method in Social Work Education* (New York: Council on Social Work Education, 1959), p. 312.
[27]Sheldon Rose, *Group Therapy: A Behavioral Approach* (Englewood Cliffs, N.J.: Prentice-Hall, Inc., 1977), p. 9.
[28]Perry London, *Behavior Control* (New York: Harper & Row, Pub., 1971), p. 4.
[29]Ibid., p. 7.
[30]Ibid., p. 21.

AGENCY CONDITIONS THAT AFFECT GROUP WORK

Why Agencies Establish Groups

In order to supply a foundation for the worker's evaluation of agency conditions that affect group services, we will first list and discuss such conditions. We will then describe the current range of group work activities in terms of a classification of types of agency purposes.

Example: The X Family Agency decided to offer a "drop-in group" to help mothers with young children discuss concerns around child rearing. Baby sitting services were also provided to them while they attended the group.

Example: The Planned Parenthood Clinic offered "rap sessions" for teens concerned about sexuality and sexual behaviors.

Agencies always have a reason for allocating staff time to group work services as the above examples imply. Sometimes these reasons are explicit and embodied in formal proposals or descriptions of services. Thus an agency may state that it supports groups to enhance the classroom behavior of school children or to assist previously hospitalized psychotic patients to cope with a return to the community. At other times, there is no specific statement about the group work program and one must refer to the overall program descriptions of the agency to infer agency purposes for groups. There also can be "hidden" purposes, such as the transfer of clients from individual treatment caseloads because their workers no longer wish to work with them. Purposes may also be stated in very general terms, such as "helping children adjust better to institutional conditions" or they may be very specific, such as "helping unwed mothers decide whether or not to place their children for adoption after delivery."

The agency purposes for the group will have a strong influence on group processes throughout the life of the group and will influence who is referred to the group, how the member is prepared (or not prepared) for the group, what kinds of group activities are reinforced, and how the agency is likely to respond to requests from the group and its worker.

An example of the way purpose is influential is that of a group of ten- and eleven-year-olds meeting in a community center. The agency composed the group from children who were referred from the local public school because of complaints about their classroom behavior. The agency had contacted the youths and their families, explained the *purposes* of the group, and inquired as to the youths' interest in participation.

When the youngsters got together, they asked if they could take trips. They were informed that this was not the *purpose* of the group as the workers had explained prior to the group's first meeting. A trip might be taken, however, to reward the group for working out the details of how the group's meetings will be used to accomplish its *purposes*. The agency had equipped a room with some school supplies so that the youngsters might, at some point, simulate their school room. The worker had asked for this resource because of the *purpose* of the group.

Group workers have the responsibility, before the beginning of a group, to help the agency to consider purposes that can be accomplished through groups. Some purposes should not be implemented, such as attempting to cause members to accept agency injustices. Other purposes may be unethical, such as manipulating members to accept goals that they might otherwise reject. The worker should also help the agency to evaluate how its purposes are being achieved through groups so that unfeasible ones might be modified. Workers should make clear to members what the group's purposes are and should help members to negotiate with the agency regarding these purposes either through the worker or directly.[31]

How Members Are Referred to or Recruited for the Groups

Example: In a psychiatric clinic, a worker asked other workers to refer socially isolated young adults to him as he planned to start a group to help such persons make friends.

Example: In a child and family service agency, a policy was announced that all unmarried, pregnant women seeking help with decisions about adoption will be offered membership in a group established for that purpose. Those who expressed concern about group participation or who had other reasons for not being included in a group will be offered individual service.

Example: In a residential treatment center, a group worker offered to hold weekly meetings with the youths living in Cottage D.

These examples illustrate several of the ways people may be secured for group work services. The agency usually establishes recruitment procedures that have substantial influence on the future of the group, including agency intake itself, and when this process eliminates or recruits clients of specified ages, ethnic groups, social statuses, or with certain problems, the range of group services is predetermined. Subsequent to agency intake, the way clients are recruited for groups varies; for example, people may be offered individual services first and then may be referred to groups by "caseworkers." This may be before or after individual services have begun. Alternatively, group work may be presented as an option when individuals enter the agency.

When the agency stresses individual services, Hasenfeld hypothesizes that group work services will be considered marginal and group work practice ". . . confronts the problem of formulating a common basis for clients to interact as a group."[32] Thus the worker and clients will spend a substantial amount

---

[31]For example, see Rose, *Group Therapy.*
[32]Hasenfeld, "Organizational Factors," p. 299.

of energy identifying and maintaining the rationale for the group's existence.

In some cases, the agency interacts primarily with all its clients on a group basis as, for example, in residential institutions, where the group workers will often be in competition with other people who also transact with groups, such as teachers, nurses, and custodial personnel. This can blur the particular functions that are to be served by the group work experience.

When enrollment for groups is decided at the point of agency intake, who decides and how this is decided are important. One of the major influences a worker has on group events is through the composition of the group (see page 58) and this depends on a sufficiently diverse pool of potential members. The composition procedures the worker utilizes can be implemented better when they are part of decision making for services rather than when they are "political" and must depend on the beliefs of staff to whom the clients have been assigned and who must relinquish them.

Another major dimension of the intake process of concern to group workers is whether agency services as well as group work services are voluntary or compulsory. Again, according to Hasenfeld, in the latter case "the group is likely to develop apathy, self-aggression, frustration, and inability to adapt to free situations, which could undermine any treatment objective."[33]

For example, group services are offered frequently in prisons and psychiatric treatment facilities where group members are pressured to attend. Much time is then spent by the worker discussing member reactions to determine if a basis for working together can be developed. (This process of identifying such a basis—the development of a contract—is discussed in Chapter 4; a more extensive discussion of issues in working with involuntary clients is presented in Chapter 12).

The way each member experiences entering the agency and then the group is important. As Yalom demonstrates, members will be more committed to the group and will interact more with each other if prepared individually for the group.[34] This procedure, however, takes time prior to the first meeting of the group, and the agency must facilitate this.

The ability of the worker to have an effect on these intake events is a function of his or her status in the agency, an issue which we turn to now.

What Are the Status and Role of the Group Worker in the Agency

Example: John's job assignment included work with individuals, families, and groups. He was seen as a professional equal by the other social workers in the Community Mental Health Center.

---

[33]Ibid.

[34]Irvin D. Yalom, *The Theory and Practice of Group Psychotherapy,* 2nd ed. (New York: Basic Books, 1975), p. 294.

Example: Alice was a group worker in a residential treatment center. When the caseworkers in the agency saw her, they always jokingly asked her where her whistle was to call the children to activities.

Example: Bill was one of a staff of workers in a large settlement house. All of the workers spent most of their time either working with groups or supervising people who did.

The way the agency defines the job of the group worker and the location of this person in the agency hierarchy will have impact on the group. If the major technology in the agency is one-to-one treatment, a separate cadre of workers usually offer group services and initial assignments of cases are made to caseworkers; the activities of the group worker are then likely to be seen as relatively unimportant. Members of groups often perceive the low status of their worker and react accordingly, even to the extent of rejecting group services.

The status of group workers can vary beyond the division of labor between work with individuals and work with groups. People with expertise and interest in work with groups may or may not be represented in the administration of the agency. On the other hand, group workers might be either supervised by people defined as caseworkers or else segregated into a separate unit. Even though this pattern may become less dominant as social work practice becomes more generic, it will be found in a number of agencies. The impact of such arrangements is less power for the worker to secure resources for the group, influence the pattern of referrals to the group, and have his or her ideas taken into consideration in agency determination of group purposes.

The resolution of this issue is affected by whether group workers define their method as unique amidst the methods of casework and community organization, or whether work with groups is seen as a skill developed by all workers. In the former case, it is important that group workers have as much power as other practitioners to influence policy, particularly policy on how services are offered. In the latter case, people who work with groups will, by definition, have as much power as any other worker. As indicated earlier, we prefer to conceive of group work as part of a generic range of skills to be developed by most workers.

Which Resources Do Agencies Allocate to the Group

Example: The Child Guidance Clinic rented the gymnasium of a nearby YMCA for the use of an adolescent group.

Example: The family agency furnished one of its rooms with comfortable sofas and arm chairs for use as a group therapy room.

Example: The probation service established a small budget for refreshments at group meetings.

Group activities are enchanced if the worker has space, equipment, consultation, and other resources available. With the possible exception of play therapy and other treatment modalities for use with children, there is more of a tradition regarding the use of material objects and space in group work than in other social work approaches. This is because of the use group workers have made of a variety of program media to provide new experiences for members. Group workers have often required suitable space to engage, for example, in games with children or to help adults feel that this is a different experience than a class or committee meeting. Group members in residential situations may want to visit places outside of the institution as part of their learning experiences and this leads to such costs as transportation and worker time beyond the "therapeutic hour." All of these contingencies require agencies to consider the costs involved in group sessions. Group workers, in helping agencies establish such services should be forthright in making this known to agency administration.

How Targets for Change Are Selected by Agencies

Example: A school system defined the targets of its school social work program as those classroom behaviors that would enhance learning. Family and peer relationship problems were not to be dealt with. Workers were expected to refer such situations to other agencies.

Example: The Child Guidance Clinic, because of the psychiatric orientation of its administrator, the focus of its consulting psychiatrist, and the material asked for on agency recording forms oriented its efforts to parent-child, parent-peer, and child-authority transactions. Little attention was paid to job, or community resource issues also of concern to clients.

As illustrated by these examples, agency conditions may predispose a worker to select some aspects of client-agency-environment transactions rather than others as targets for change. This is related to our proposition that the targets of social work intervention are created by the interactions of people and their situations. This is similar to the contention of many family therapists that "problems" in families are defined by the family in ways that are based on the family's systemic requirements.[35]

The workers have a number of options as to how to approach this issue of the agency's preferred targets. One way is to describe agency definitions of problems to clients, who may then choose to seek services elsewhere. On the other hand, some clients may wish, often with the help of the worker, to seek to change the agency's orientation so that attention is given to the clients' targets. When the agency's and client's preferred targets coincide, either fortuitously or as a result of negotiation, it is more likely that necessary resources for the group

[35] James Framo, "Symptoms from a Family Transactional Viewpoint," in *Progress in Group and Family Therapy*, eds. Clifford Sager and Helen Kaplan (New York: Brunner/Mazel, 1972), pp. 271–308.

and the worker will be forthcoming. The worker, then, will not be caught in a conflict between member and agency desires that can be immobilizing for all concerned.

What Effect Agencies Have on Groups' Social and Physical Environment

Example: In the Child Guidance Clinic, the agency assigned the social relations group, a group formed to help socially isolated teenagers, to one of the agency's club rooms. The group was given a set of drawers in which to keep records of how members were performing "social tasks" and a bulletin board to post clippings and quotations selected by members.

Example: A community center assigned several workers to "reach out" to teenage gangs in the area. When one of these groups decided to come to the agency for meetings and activities, the agency assigned one hour a week in the gym for the group's exclusive use.

Again, according to Hasenfeld, "the capacity of the group to develop well-defined boundaries and identity is partly determined by its ability to establish and shape its own 'territory' according to its needs."[36] The same writer also states that "development of the group requires a space that provides some insulation from the environment and protection from excessive external disturbances."[37] As we shall see in Chapter 4, a *sine qua non* for the effectiveness of the group to help its members is the attraction it holds for them, that is, its cohesiveness. An often neglected factor in enhancing this is the environment the agency offers the group. This includes the physical setting for the group meeting as well as the following:

1. The ways that other people in the agency, in addition to the group worker, interact with group members. These people include other clients, receptionists, other professional staff, secretaries, and maintenance workers.
2. The decor of the agency. Whether the agency looks orderly and maintained is often interpreted by members as showing the esteem with which clients are held; also relevant is the meaning to the members of visible objects in terms of their culture. For example, one agency placed pictures of its benefactors in its rooms and these were mostly caucasians. The largely black clientele did not feel the agency valued them until important people in black history were also honored by having their pictures prominently displayed.
3. The "social" aspects of the agency. Workers should attempt to see the agency through the eyes of the group members who will usually be willing to share their perceptions when asked. The "social" environment of the agency includes the degree to which the staff members function as a team, understand and support one another, and have high morale. The workers cannot ignore these variables any more than they can ignore internal actions in the group.

[36]Hasenfeld, "Organizational Factors," p. 305.
[37]Ibid.

How Agencies Interact with Groups' Indigenous Leaders

Example: In Agency A, the director sent a letter to the group asking it to nominate from among its members an advisory committee on group services.

Example: In Agency B, the worker notified the group that the type of services received by the group were to be discontinued by the agency. Several group members sought out the agency director to discuss this decision but were told by her receptionist that she would not be available for an appointment for several weeks.

People tend to emerge in groups who have greater influence over group processes than others, who function as spokespersons for the group, or who are authorized by other group members to represent the group in external affairs. Agency definitions of clients' status will affect these individuals. In some group work situations, however, members conceive of themselves as recipients of a service and do not expect to be involved in any processes with the agency after they have joined the group. This is most often true of those voluntarily seeking help with personal problems in psychiatric outpatient facilities.

In other cases, group members conceive of themselves as constituents rather than clients, in the traditional sense of the word, and *do* expect to be consulted by the agency and involved in its affairs. This is usually true in community centers. In yet another type of agency, clients may feel alienated and powerless in relationship to social institutions (for example, welfare agencies or prisons). The noninvolvement of these persons in the agencies offering them group experiences is more evidence of their powerlessness. In these cases, such involvement may be therapeutic in itself.

An asset of the group experience is the group members' awareness that they may share similar concerns. Out of this springs the possibility of joint action and this creates even more power for members. Some agencies may seek to reinforce this possibility while others may fear the consequences of group pressures and may act to inhibit them.

This issue of involvement of group members in extra-group processes is related, also, to how much control the agency has over clients. The agencies that have the most control are those in which the client is institutionalized, such as mental hospitals, residential treatment centers, and prisons. Substantial control is also exercised by agencies given legal legitimation for control, such as probation and psychiatric aftercare programs. The least control is, of course, exercised by agencies in which the client is there voluntarily (a community center) or where the client may be performing a service for the agency (adoptive parents of hard-to-place children).

Group members are often least involved in those agencies with the greatest degree of control over them. The control issue will have effects on the way members exercise options related to group program, create indigenous leadership, respond to worker decisions, and participate in selecting group goals and targets.

What Are Agencies' Attitudes to Service Ideologies and Technologies

Example: An institution for adolescents was committed to the use of positive peer culture (PPC). Staff received training in this approach and referral agencies were informed of this emphasis. As soon as youths were admitted, other group members explained the way the PPC group was conducted.

Example: The Child Guidance Clinic was directed by a psychoanalytically oriented psychiatrist. Workers were hired based on their knowledge of this theory. At case conferences, clients were assessed in terms of ego functioning. Group experiences were recommended when these were seen as enhancing such functioning.

Most agencies have preferences for particular theories, ideologies, and techniques. These are manifested in the way services are defined, people are interviewed for staff positions, assumptions are made about intake, consultants are recruited, and agency record forms are conceived. Such preferences govern the way workers are expected to act in groups.

Agency clarity regarding preferred treatment approaches can be supportive of workers and group members as the workers will know what is expected of them and will receive rewards for meeting these expectations. Clients will know what the available service is. In some instances, clients may even be informed of the effects and effectiveness of the approach through reserach evidence or case example.

Problems can arise when approaches to group work are utilized that are either ineffective, inappropriate, or not desired by workers, clients, or both. Under these mandatory circumstances, short of leaving the agency, workers can do the following: they can seek to hire staff trained in appropriate technologies; they can secure additional training for themselves; or, together with group members, they can creatively develop new group procedures.

The involvement of group members in the choice of service technologies presupposes that they have some knowledge of such matters. We believe that this information ought to be made routinely available and that, in addition, workers should find ways of explaining the nature of the services offered to group members.

How Intraorganizational Relationships Affect Groups

Example: The worker for a young boys' treatment group in the Community Mental Health Program was told by his supervisor that the group had been too noisy and rambunctious in recent meetings. The supervisor thought that the worker should exercise firmer controls. The worker, in turn, lectured the boys at the next meeting about their behavior.

Example: The morale of the staff in the school was low because a recent millage election had failed and many services were to be cut. The worker, in the next few meetings of the group, was lethargic, did not pursue new topics of importance to the members, and was not very empathic with the members.

Hasenfeld raises an important, yet subtle, issue when he states that "a process of 'isomorphism' occurs in which worker-group relations come to reflect the same structural properties of worker relations with staff members in the agency."[38] This phenomenon occurs because other agency personnel, particularly those in authority, provide models for the worker. Agency conditions affect the worker's emotional state, also, and set norms for what is and is not rewarded. Workers have several options in regard to this issue:

1. When problems arise in the group, the worker should analyze whether they parallel agencywide situations.

2. The worker can then consider whether action should be initiated at an agency or group level or both.

3. The worker, as agency concerns are discussed at a staff level, can consider their effect at a group level.

4. At times the worker can "buffer" the group from agency conditions by acting in ways that are at variance with these conditions. For example, workers should consult with group members on decisions even if they are not, themselves, consulted by administrators.

5. At times it becomes necessary to inform members about agency conditions that lead to undesirable consequences for the group; the members may then seek to initiate changes in such conditions, sometimes in concert with the group worker; they may try to isolate themselves from the effects of the conditions; or they may decide that the conditions are really not a problem for them or may even be constructive.

Thus far in this chapter we have outlined selected agency conditions that may have an effect on group work practice. We believe that all of these are relevant to group work in any agency but also that agencies with certain types of functions are likely to approach these in ways that differ from agencies with other functions. Some of these ways enhance group services; others hinder them. We shall now turn to an analysis of agency "types."

A TYPOLOGY OF AGENCY PURPOSES

In order to facilitate this analysis, as well as to illustrate the possible range of group work activities, we have developed a classification of agency purposes. To us, the phrase "agency purpose" means either the purpose the agency fulfills for the society, for the clientele, or both. Sometimes the agency purposes are directed toward societal objectives that are not, at least initially, sought by clients (for example, prisons). At other times, the purposes are mutual (a job

[38]Hasenfeld, "Organizational Factors," p. 303.

training agency established to reduce unemployment for clients who wish jobs). In presenting this classification, we draw the attention of the reader to several considerations:

1. It is rare, if not impossible, to find an agency whose services represent only one purpose. Thus all agencies have several purposes, but many are likely to emphasize some more than others.
2. An issue for any agency is the extent to which it has clarified for itself, if not for its clientele or the general public, what its purposes are.
3. When an agency seeks to fulfill a purpose, some of its activities may conflict with other activities because the agency has conflicting purposes. An example of this was found in a school program. Schools are society's way of socializing youngsters into roles by imparting skills as well as society's way of ensuring that behavior follows societal norms. Sometimes these two functions conflict, as when a youngster seeks a future role (for example, social radical) that some teachers believe is inconsistent with their value of maintaining the system.

Vinter[39] and Hasenfeld[40] describe the two major purposes of agencies as socialization and resocialization of the client. The former category involves helping persons viewed as "normal" and who are progressing from one status to another. Examples of this are assisting adolescents to assume adult responsibilities, middle-aged persons to plan for retirement, and school children to make better use of their learning environment. The latter category, resocialization, refers to helping people who are viewed as not experiencing "normal" phases of development or role transitions. Such people are often labeled "deviant," and who, by virtue of this position, experience conflict with others. Working with inmates of prisons and mental hospitals and some clients of mental health programs is an example of the resocialization category.

Subpurposes

Upon further consideration of these two categories, socialization and resocialization, we concluded that each category should be further subdivided. Under the heading of "socialization," one subpurpose is to help individuals who are having difficulty deciding on socialization goals. Because this is frequently, as Hartman states, due to *anomie*, which is "a state of societal demoralization—of normlessness—created by the disjunction of goals and norms for reaching these goals" we have termed this subpurpose *anomie reduction.*[41] One example of a client who required this type of service was a woman trying to raise her level of consciousness of emerging and changing women's roles so she could pursue them in a personally more satisfying way; another was a gay person who also sought to identify and follow newly emerging norms; and another was an adolescent confronted with the changing and conflicting patterns for youth. It is interesting that in our discussion of

[39]Robert D. Vinter, "Analysis of Treatment Organizations," *Social Work* 8 (1963), 3–15.
[40]Hasenfeld, "Organizational Factors," p. 296.
[41]Ann Hartman, "Anomie and Social Casework," *Social Casework* 50 (1969), 132.

this categorization with practitioners, they noted that almost all agencies have to deal with the problem of anomie to some degree; that is, clients frequently seek to understand and relate themselves to changing and conflicting norms. This may, therefore, be a highly significant phenomenon in our culture that always affects agency services.

Once people have decided on socialization goals and values, the next logical step is to achieve their goals. We have termed this subpurpose *role attainment*. This type of helping is in recognition of the fact that many people— citizens, employees, students, parents, and adults,—need help in meeting role requirements.

In considering the category of resocialization, we also recognized two subpurposes. The first refers to people who have not yet determined that they wish to fulfill a nondeviant, socially acceptable role. Because society establishes institutions such as courts to work to bring about resocialization, we have termed this subpurpose *social control*. Relevant to this is the issue of whether or not or to what degree social work as a profession is an instrument of social control. It is evident, however, that social workers frequently are employed in agencies with social control functions.

In a process similar to socialization, some clients who become group members do accept or come to accept resocialization goals. The purpose of helping such people, is called *alternative role attainment*; the types of people helped in this manner include many clients of outpatient psychiatric facilities, aftercare programs, and treatment-oriented correctional programs.

In the remainder of this chapter, we shall describe the kinds of agencies and groups that seek to fulfill each of these subpurposes. Longer examples are provided in Chapters 10–13. Again, the reader is reminded that there is no assumption that agencies fall into only one category. At any given moment, however, a worker should be able to identify which purpose an agency, a program, a group, or a group session is fulfilling. This framework, then, is a means to describe the range of group work activities so that later we can describe the different ways workers should act in relationship to the purposes appropriate to the situation.

Anomie Reduction

Example: A group of nine women in their twenties met together in a "Young Mothers' Club" in a community center. They had all been recently married and had either a young child or were pregnant. All had worked to supplement their family's income, most at occupations such as secretary, sales person, or waitress. They came together, originally, as a social club because several had gone to school or worked together. In the process of informal discussions, they discovered that they were all experiencing similar problems. These included the kinds of expectations their husbands held of them that denied them the equality they expected in their marriages. On the other hand, many did believe that mothers had more responsibilities than fathers for child rearing and they were uncertain how this related to the issue of equality. They asked each other for help in resolving some of these concerns and, when the Community Center was told of this, it offered them the services of a group worker.

In the first few meetings, the worker helped these young women to describe to each other how these issues were manifested in their own families. At times, they were embarrassed to describe some of their experiences, but the worker helped them through discussing norms of confidentiality and through sharing some details of her own life. The worker also used value clarification exercises to help the members decide what each believed most about her rights in her marriage. When it became apparent that most of the members had trouble explaining their beliefs to their husbands, the worker introduced some role plays to help them to practice a greater degree of assertiveness. The worker also assisted them in planning a joint meeting with their husbands to discuss the roles of each partner in a marriage.

Similar types of experiences to help members identify conflicting norms to which they are exposed are now offered in a number of agencies. Examples of organizations that have arisen to respond to these needs include teen "rap centers" associated with community mental health agencies and planned parenthood clinics, women's and minority groups' consciousness raising organizations, and many counseling programs associated with universities. In addition, a number of private organizations and institutes (some for profit) have formed to make this type of service available to the large number of people who desire it. Such clients are generally self-referred and highly motivated to participate, although they may not always be clear about the group experience they seek.

Several aspects of group work service focused on anomic situations are illustrated by the example of the "Young Mothers' Group." The group was formed around people who experienced similar normative problems. Because they quickly recognized that they were dealing with parallel issues, they were able to be supportive to and yet could also confront one another. They had somewhat different ideas about the resolution of value conflicts affecting young women today and, therefore, could help each other to examine alternative solutions. These characteristics made a group rather than an individual counseling experience a particularly valid one.

Role Attainment

Example: A high school was aware that a number of black students were motivated to complete their high school program but had various handicaps: (1) poor preparation, as they had been educated in less adequate grammar schools than other students; (2) insufficient support from families, as many had only one parent; and (3) hostility from school personnel who labeled them unmotivated and incompetent and failed to give them the help they needed.

One of several programs the school used to reverse this cycle of failure was group work on a voluntary basis; such individuals were invited to join a group conducted by a social worker that met on a weekly basis. In the first meetings, the students helped each other to choose short-term goals for themselves. These included regular completion of homework assignments, better quality of work as attested to by higher grades, and decisions regarding future employment and education. The members then each decided on "tasks" to help them reach their goals. Each member's goals were discussed by the entire group and suggestions were made as to appropriate tasks. For example, a young woman whose goal was better grades on tests chose as her tasks to study two hours a day after school and to complete two homework assignments during this period.

Members used their discussions at meetings to help each other accomplish their tasks. The student who wanted to improve grades spoke about interruptions from her family and friends while she was studying. The group members suggested how she could respond to these interruptions and she practiced their ideas in role plays at group meetings.

Organizations that emphasize role attainment include schools, settlement houses, family life and sex education agencies, nursery and preschool programs for children, and senior-citizens centers. The emphasis in this type of helping is not on giving up old attitudes, values, and behavior but on anticipatory socialization and building on already present knowledge and skills.

Adult clients who make use of these agencies tend to come voluntarily. Although children are required to participate in some programs, there is an overall assumption that client motivation is high and resistance to learning low. The focus of service is on career development providing as many opportunities for learning as possible. Ideally, agency rules are open and flexible, and there is opportunity for democratic decision making.

The preceding example of a role attainment group is illustrative of the fact that such groups usually consist of members who seek similar socialization goals and are striving to overcome similar barriers to such achievement. Members will, therefore, be prone to identify strongly with and give support to each other. The approach used in the example of picking tasks is only one of several that may be used. Such procedures, however, tend to focus on specific goals and means to attain them.

It is also common, in socialization-oriented groups, to discover barriers in the environment to such socialization (in this case, the attitudes of teachers). As we shall see later, there is a tendency for workers to focus on member behaviors rather than environmental conditions, thus leading members into activities in which their desires will be frustrated. Socialization-oriented groups should draw on the long tradition in community center and settlement house work with such groups that have strong social action components.

Social Control

Example: Group meetings were required of adolescent boys who were committed to the Training School. One such group consisted of ten boys between the ages of fifteen and seventeen. They had been sent to the institution for such offenses as repeated theft and destruction of property. In the second meeting of the group, the members sat in postures that showed their boredom and resentment. A few boys looked fearful. As the worker waited until all boys had arrived to begin the meeting, those present complained about the institution and about being required to attend the group. The worker began the discussion by empathizing with the boys' feelings. After a short period, however, he confronted the members with the statement that their complaints were "going nowhere" and that, perhaps, they could figure out something they could do to help themselves. In the discussion, he also commented that their difficulty in knowing what to do in tough situations may have landed them in the Training School. Many of the boys ridiculed this idea and said it was another example of the kind of preaching they always heard. One boy, however, did not join in this discussion and yet the worker knew that he was respected by the others. The worker sought to draw him out by commenting that maybe he saw things a little differently.

The social control purpose illustrated here is employed in an organization because society, usually through legislative and judicial processes, has sanctioned the agency to limit deviant behavior. Organizations that emphasize social control purposes include mental hospitals, residential treatment institutions, training schools for the delinquent and the retarded, drug centers, child guidance clinics, and community mental health facilities.

Behavioral change is central to social control goals for clients, that is, the diminution or elimination of behavior that led to the client's trouble with society. Service to clients is often involuntary, as the agency's control over its clientele is relatively high. The development of new and more functional modes of performance to replace the dysfunctional behavior should be, but is not always a focus of the agency's program. The rules of these organizations tend to be authoritarian and coercive, especially in closed settings, and clients are allowed relatively little option on a number of issues.

Clients recruited to social control organizations are often resistive to change and rebellious to the agency itself. This is sometimes fostered by the rigidity of agency rules and sanctions as well as by peer group pressure to engage in aggressive behavior. Thus the initial motivation for change among such clients may be low or even nonexistent. Further, it is usually necessary to deal with peer group resistance to change by seeking to change the norms and values of the group.

A major issue for the professional is the potential conflict between the social control purpose of the agency and the professional commitment to self-determination for clients. However the worker resolves the issue, it must be with honesty so that members know the limits of their situation as well as the worker's personal stands. Members must receive recognition for their desire to confront agency policies together with support to do this in a constructive manner; moreover, the agency must be helped to respond with understanding and flexibility.

Group treatment in these settings can be very effective because previous group forces often have molded the individual's norms, values, and behaviors. The opportunity afforded to individuals to change their behavior with the support of a benign group situation is invaluable.

The illustration beginning this section shows many of these issues—for example, the understandable resistance of the group members to the compulsory features of the situation. The worker empathizes with these feelings and yet does not deny the agency's power and its use to attain agency objectives. The worker uses confrontation more often than in other settings to point out the member's behavior and its possible effects. In this way the worker presents, none the less, the concept that the members have choices to make. Even though the worker may favor some choices as opposed to others, he employs the value of self-determination so that the members ultimately are responsible for their own decisions.

Alternative Role Attainment

Example: A psychiatric outpatient clinic has established a group composed of seven men and women who voluntarily came to the clinic. One was a man who had had a succession of relationships with women in which the woman had broken off with him for reasons he did not understand; another was a man who expressed a great deal of anxiety about starting relationships with either men or women; a third was a woman who was fired from a number of jobs with the charge she did not get along with co-workers; and others were a woman and man who were in the process of divorce from their respective spouses and expressed strong feelings of loss and sadness around this. All of these people had an interest in being members of a group conducted by a social worker on the staff. As part of the intake process into the group, the worker had explained to them that their problems appeared to be related to how they interacted with others and that in a group they could learn about, get feedback on, and modify such transactions.

At early meetings of the group, the members elaborated on the problems just described. In the way they presented their problems, some of the reasons for their difficulties can be seen. The man, for instance, with the succession of lovers backed off from discussions in the group as soon as another member expressed too much "caring." The woman who had been fired from her job asked very intimate questions of other group members and tended to ridicule their answers. Gradually, with the help of the worker, the members began to point out these kinds of patterns to each other. Some then began to try out other ways of responding in the group.

When alternative role attainment is the primary purpose, the focus in the group is on the development of new values, knowledge, and skills to replace outdated or dysfunctional ones. While the client is, or is likely to be, in trouble in his or her environment, there has not necessarily been a major violation of social norms with subsequent legal sanctions. While there may be considerable environmental pressure on clients to do something about their situation, they usually seek help voluntarily because of personal discomfort. Organizations serving these populations generally allow clients many more opportunites for choice than when social control functions are being exercised. An exception to this analysis is when inmates of correctional programs move voluntarily toward seeking rehabilitation. Under these circumstances, clients are rarely resistive to change, and their motivation to learn alternative roles is often high. However, they may find change difficult because of previous, even lifelong, patterns. The worker's efforts are directed at building on the motivation already present and increasing the client's comfort with this process. The peer group is used to increase client motivation by reinforcing individual change efforts. This type of group is also useful because clients' resocialization problems are intimately connected with the relationship patterns that they enact in group situations and which simulate life outside the group.

Groups that function as instruments of social control often proceed to become alternative role attainment groups. This occurs when group members identify a common ground between their needs and interests and those of the agency. Such a transition demands, however, that the agency be benign, have a therapeutic orientation, and be prepared to negotiate a common ground with groups and group members.

Other organizations that emphasize alternative role attainment purposes as part of resocialization include sheltered workshops and similar skill-development programs for the physically handicapped and the retarded, retraining programs for the unemployed, family service agencies, psychiatric clinics, medical social work departments, and family life education programs.

The preceding example illustrates how members in groups not only talk about their relationships but actually enact these behaviors *because* the group *is* a social situation. Members find that people in the group remind them of people outside. Members can also stereotype each other and hinder change as well as enhance it and this poses a problem to the group and the worker. Thus a wide range of learning possibilities occurs in an alternative role attainment group as members understand not only how to experiment with change but how to respond to people who seek to hinder it. This is especially true in experiences of resocialization as opposed to socialization, as new behaviors must replace old ones.

Because the group is, as stated, a social situation, members will also behave in socially conventional ways; they will resist commenting on each other's behaviors or revealing their own thoughts and feelings. As the previous example indicates, it takes a considerable amount of worker skill to help the members of such groups make good use of the group for change even when motivation is present; this is because the possibility is ever present that members will reinforce existing behaviors rather than new ones.

SUMMARY

This chapter began with a discussion of the importance of agency conditions in relation to group work practice—conditions that have evolved over more than half a century. An understanding of this would provide many insights into the current group work situation; therefore, an extensive offering of group work history was presented.

Following the section on group work history, the specific organizational conditions that can either enhance or hinder the group work experience were described. These conditions include purposes assigned to the group, the selection of members, the status of the group worker, and the agency allocation of resources to the group. A number of additional organizational conditions were also described.

The final section of the chapter included a discussion of the range of group services based on a typology of such purposes. This typology subdivides purposes into socialization (further split into anomie reduction and role attainment) and resocialization (further split into social control and alternative role attainment). Throughout this book, we shall use this set of categories to clarify the variations in group work practice that exist. A major emphasis shall be placed on this scheme in the third part of the book.

Exercise: ASSESSING AN AGENCY'S EFFECT ON GROUP WORK

The following questionnaire can be employed to help the reader assess the impact of agency conditions on group work services:

Purposes

1. What do agency documents state are the purposes of the agency?

2. What group purposes are compatible with agency purposes?

3. What types of clients are likely to come to the agency in view of its purposes? How will this affect group composition?

4. What will members perceive is expected of them in the light of agency purposes?

5. How will agency purposes affect activities of the group and the content of group deliberations?

Agency Referral Procedures

1. Are members recruited for or referred to groups before, during, or after agency intake?

2. Which agency staff are responsible for referral? How are people who work with groups in the agency involved in this process?

3. Is some service of the agency (for example, one-to-one casework) actually the preferred or predominant one?

4. Does the agency interact with its clients predominantly on a group, one-to-one, or family basis?

5. Is members' attendance at group meetings voluntary or compulsory?

6. How are potential members approached and prepared for the group?

7. What are the effects of this approach and preparation on (a) members' perceptions of the group, (b) members' attitudes toward the group, (c) the kinds of people likely to be referred to the group?

Status of the Group Worker

1. Does the group worker only work with groups? If not, what are his or her other tasks?

2. Are social workers who work with groups or who are highly knowledgeable about group work represented in supervisory and administrative positions to the same degree as social workers who are not?

3. What is the effect of the group worker's status on recruitment of group members, power to make decisions on ways of serving the group, and ability to secure resources for the group?

Resources Allocated by the Agency to the Group

1. What kind of room (that is, location, size, equipment) has the agency assigned to the group? To what other uses is it put? Is it regularly assigned? Are the group members allowed to alter the room in any way (for example, by putting up posters, shifting equipment)?

2. What kind of equipment is the group likely to require? Will it be readily available?

3. Will the group be likely to require other material resources (for example, transportation) and will the agency provide these?

4. Will the group require other human resources (for example, consultation) and will the agency provide this?

5. What are the effects of points 1–4 on group activities, morale, and climate?

Targets for Change Selected by the Agency

1. Does the agency perceive its groups as primarily directed at changing the members? If so, is this conceived of as changes in self-understanding, attitudes, knowledge, and/or behavior?

2. Does the agency perceive its group as seeking changes in the agency itself and/or in the environment outside the agency?

3. What are the effects of points 1 and 2 on the activities of the group and on the attitudes of the members to the group?

Interaction of the Group
with the Agency and Staff

1. With which staff members, in relation to the group worker, are members of the group likely to interact? What will be the nature and effect of this interaction on the member and on the group?

2. How is the agency decorated and how well is it maintained? What will be the effect of this on the group?

Interactions of the Agency
with the Group's Indigenous Leaders

1. Are group members involved in any way in agency decision making?

2. What are the effects of this involvement or lack of involvement on the group?

Agency's Preferred Service Technology

1. Does the agency have a preference regarding a theory or an approach to work with groups and/or individuals? What is it? How is it explained to members? What is the effect on the members?

2. How do the agency and the worker interact around preferred approaches (for example, consultation, training)?

3. Is the preferred approach consistent with approaches used in other services (for example, one-to-one, family, child care, custodial)? What is the effect on the group of this consistency or inconsistency?

Intraorganizational Relationships

1. How does the group worker interact with staff peers and administrators? How does this affect him/or her? How does this ultimately affect the group?

2. What is the morale of the staff? How does this affect the group?

3

The Pregroup Phase

In the first part of this book, we provided the reader with information on what group work is, how approaches to it vary, and how these approaches emerged historically. In Part Two, chapters 3 and 4 contain a detailed presentation of the principles and procedures that guide practice with groups. These are activities in which the worker is engaged prior to the first meeting of the group (this chapter) and the role of the worker during the first phase of group development, group formation (chapter 4).

We believe there are a number of tasks the worker should perform before the first group meeting that will make group experience more likely to be successful. In addition, there is research to show that the way these activities are performed will affect how rapidly and effectively the group moves forward to accomplish its goals. The reader should remember, however, that unpredicted events can always occur, as many group workers' diaries will attest. Sometimes even the most carefully laid plans must be cast aside. The intent of preplanning is not to eliminate uncertainty about group events, but to reduce it.

One of the first tasks of the worker is to conceptualize the purpose of the group, at least in a general sense. As we stated in Chapter 2, agencies often have purposes for sponsoring particular groups and the worker must take these into consideration or risk losing agency support. Sometimes agencies wish to relate their purposes to a needs assessment of clients, and we shall suggest means for accomplishing this. The reason for conceptualizing purpose before attempting other pregroup tasks is the relationship of purpose to other decisions such as those on composition and group size.

Because purpose is so closely allied to composition, we shall treat this topic next and shall discuss how to compose a group so that the selection of members will support the purposes for which the group was established. A topic that shall also be considered in relationship to composition is whether a group experience is appropriate for the individual concerned.

Another major topic that we shall discuss is how to prepare members for the group. This is often done in one or more sessions before the group begins. The worker seeks to understand the problems or concerns that brought the individuals to enter the agency and subsequently to contemplate a group experience. We shall describe ways in which the worker prepares other staff members to welcome the group as well as how the worker establishes physical conditions conducive to the group's beginning.

GROUP PURPOSES

By *group purposes,* we mean the specific reasons for which the group was established, usually expressed as the type of goals that the group will try to help its members attain. Group purposes may be conceived in different ways by the worker and the members; even each member may have a different perception of the purposes of the group. Thus group purposes affect and are affected by decisions on group composition, group program, worker interventions, number of meetings planned, and even choice of a worker for the group. An example should help to clarify these statements about group purposes.

Example: A welfare department formed a group composed of parents of high school students. The agency's reason *(agency purpose)* for establishing the group was to help to provide support to their children to remain in school. In order to compose a group for this purpose, the agency asked workers to refer to the group worker those parents who had expressed concern about this issue *(composition related to purpose).* Agency purpose thus became worker's purpose. The agency wanted the members to have the opportunity to describe their situation in detail. A small group—about five members—was decided on *(size related to purpose).* The worker believed that parents gathering for this purpose would want to focus on the issue quickly and learn how to deal with it. Thus, eight group meetings should be sufficient *(number of meetings related to purpose).*

When the group members were told about the group, several were of the opinion, privately, that the agency's "real" purpose was to check on how they were spending their welfare grant *(member's perception of purpose).* The worker anticipated that this might be what they thought and planned to discuss group purpose thoroughly at the first meeting to allay perceptions of purpose that would hinder the group's achievements.

At the first meeting, one member indicated a desire to be a member of a group that would help in making friends; the worker responded that, perhaps, another group could be formed for this purpose *(member's purpose)*. The members, by the end of the first meeting, agreed that they had problems with keeping their youngsters in school and they wanted to be in a group established for this reason *(members' consensus on purpose)*. In planning for the second meeting, they also decided that the purpose of that meeting would be to report on the difficulties their children had told them they were experiencing in school *(short-term purpose)*.

The reason for distinguishing among worker purpose, member purpose, consensus among members on purpose, and short-term and long-term purposes, is that a logical relationship surrounding these phenomena must exist in order for the group to progress smoothly toward its goals. If members and workers have different conceptions of group purpose, they are unlikely to find it very easy to work cooperatively together; similarly, if members do not agree on purpose, they are also unlikely to reach agreement on group goals or activities; if short-term purposes do not relate to the long-term ones, the group will not be able to build on its experiences to create significant accomplishments.

As reasons for discrepancies among purposes are discovered, these may suggest that purposes that were originally decided for the group should be changed. This is more valid than the idea that the members should forgo ideas they have about the group's purpose. While modifications in group purposes can and do occur, the process is time consuming and the potential for severe conflict is present. Much of this can be obviated by careful planning about group purposes prior to first meetings and it is to this that we shall now address ourselves.

Needs Assessment

One way of establishing purposes that will lead to viable groups is through assessing the needs of people who are, or might be, served by the agency. The following is a sample of a series of items developed for a family agency. Such questions can be raised in an interview, a questionnaire, or with other professionals who refer people to groups.

Group Needs Assessment Questionnaire: We plan to start a group to help people with a variety of concerns they may have, such as relationships with family and friends, job situations, and so forth. It will help us to set up groups that will be of interest if you will answer the following questions. If you wish to be notified about a group of interest to you, a place is provided for you to sign your name.

1. Please indicate your interest in being in a group:

    _____ very interested

    _____ somewhat interested

    _____ not interested at all

2. Please check any areas you might like to discuss in a group:

_____ relationship to husband/wife

_____ relationship to person with whom you live (specify

relationship) _____

_____ relationship to friends

_____ job concerns

_____ feelings of discomfort (sadness, fears, worrying)

_____ concerns about your future (job, schooling)

_____ concerns about making an important decision (where you will live; go to school; leave school or home)

3. Have you been in a group before to discuss personal concerns?

_____ yes   _____ no

4. If yes to question 3, what did you think of the experience?

5. Which of the following describes what you are like in groups?
   Check as many as apply.
   _____ I talk a lot.
   _____ I seldom say anything.
   _____ I make acquaintances easily.
   _____ It takes me a long time to get to know others.
   _____ My feelings get hurt easily.
   _____ I easily tell personal things about myself.
   _____ It is very hard for me to tell personal things about myself.
   _____ I think I have a good idea of what others think of me.
   _____ I like to stay on the subject.
   _____ I have little influence on others.
   _____ I can influence others a great deal.

At times, workers have little influence over the composition of the group and this makes it difficult or impossible prior to the first meetings to determine the purpose of the group. This is true when there are very few referrals to the group, when the group is already established (youth gangs), or when the group has been created for other purposes (cottage groups in a residential treatment center). In these cases, the question is reversed: Instead of "given a purpose, how shall the group be composed?" the worker asks "given group composition, what purposes can be achieved?" However, the worker can still use items such as those in the needs assessment instrument to help the group determine a purpose consistent with the purposes of the agency.

Organizational Functions and Group Purpose

To help the reader to understand the range of purposes, we present some examples in relationship to each of the types of organizational functions we described in the preceding chapter. In examining this list, it should be remembered that groups may also be composed of members with different needs; thus a group, on occasion, may serve several purposes.

Anomie Reduction Purposes

1. To decide what type of sexual life style is consistent with each member's current identity as well as future aspirations.
2. To select the kinds of roles in marriage that conform to each member's values and desires regarding marriage.
3. To clarify the meaning of masculinity (femininity) and what this implies for each member's behavior, life style, and crucial decisions, such as marriage, child rearing, and occupation.
4. To determine how to integrate the values of one's ethnic culture with one's personal aspirations.

Role Attainment Purposes

1. To learn how to fulfill the role of a parent.
2. To learn how to succeed in school by changing personal behavior and/or by changing school policies that may impede personal progress.
3. To learn the social skills necessary to function in adolescent (young adult, adult) situations.
4. For foster parents to learn to become better substitute parents.

Social Control Purposes

1. For individuals who are on parole to choose legitimate occupational careers.
2. For a student in primary school grades to learn cooperative rather than disruptive classroom behaviors.
3. For a patient in a mental hospital to cease behaviors that are disruptive of hospital routines and/or aversive to other patients.

Alternative Role Attainment Purposes

1. For mental patients, who have been socially isolated by virtue of unacceptable or bizarre behavior, to learn behaviors appropriate to the social roles they desire.
2. For child-abusing parents to learn to discipline their children in nonabusive ways.
3. For obese persons to learn eating habits that will lead to lower food intake and weight loss.

GROUP COMPOSITION

In situations where the purpose of the group is determined before it is created, the next step is to select the members. Some workers will have a large pool of people from whom to choose and will be able to consider many factors in this choice; in other situations, few prospective members are available and the worker may even conclude that a selection from this limited set of people cannot possibly lead to a viable group.

The worker, in considering group composition principles, must be aware that there are many unknowns regarding the combination of member characteristics that will produce optimal groups. Also, there are many forces that affect group outcomes (for example, techniques employed by the worker, available resources in the agency) so that attention should be paid to composition, but the worker should not become obsessed by compositional decisions. As Yalom states, "Time and energy spent on delicately casting and balancing a group is not justified given our current state of knowledge; the therapist does better to invest that time and energy in careful selection of patients for group therapy and in their pre-therapy preparation."[1] Nevertheless, we do not advocate inattention to group composition and we shall now discuss some major considerations for accomplishing this task. We also include an exercise at the end of this chapter so that readers may experience the application of the principles of composition.

Purpose and Group Composition

The central issue that workers should consider in composition is the purpose of the group. Some purposes cannot be addressed in groups composed in certain ways while for other purposes, composition may be less crucial. Some examples of compositional issues related to the major categories of group purposes are now given.

Anomie Reduction. A group in which members seek to determine or change their values should have members whose values are different enough to provide a range of ideas for each member to consider. One group for women seeking to clarify their female roles provided many models for the members because it included women who were career oriented, home oriented, as well as those who sought to combine both. The group also included women who were militant in their pursuit of their objectives as well as women who were not.

Role Attainment. In situations where groups are used to help members learn the necessary knowledge and skills to attain some role, it is best for members to have similar aspirations. Thus a group of adolescents, seeking to attain school success, provided a good deal of reinforcement to each other. Role attainment groups are also facilitated if, in addition to commonality of objectives, different knowledge and skills related to these objectives are possessed by each member. Members can thus help one another overcome personal as well as social obstacles to fulfill their roles.

[1]Irvin D. Yalom, *The Theory and Practice of Group Psychotherapy* (New York: Basic Books, 1975), p. 272.

Social Control. A group whose members hold similar values in regard to an antisocial behavior can provide reinforcement to maintain that behavior. Dissimilarity in this regard is often sought. An important principle can be demonstrated here; namely, that when composition cannot be varied (as is often true in institutions serving offenders) new approaches to intervention must be developed. Thus in fairly homogeneous social-control-oriented groups, workers use confrontive approaches and encourage members to confront each other regarding their attitudes and behaviors. A compositional technique to secure some heterogeneity in these groups is to "seed" them with people who have been members of other groups and have already begun the process of normative change.

Alternative Role Attainment. As in role attainment groups, similarity of resocialization objectives is sought so that members can help one another in that process. An example is that of a group of clients in a half-way house who had been previously diagnosed as schizophrenic and were now in the process of job training.

Ethnicity and Gender

There are many characteristics for the worker to evaluate when composing groups—age, social class, social skills, and how the individual is likely to act in the group. Two variables, crucial to consider under all circumstances, are the individual's gender and ethnicity. Under typical circumstances, it may not matter from which European country one's ancestors came, but it does matter whether one is a member of a group, such as blacks, Asians and Pacific Islanders, Hispanics, or Native Americans, that may be oppressed economically or socially.

A general principle to remember is not to compose a group in which a person, by virtue of such ethnicity or gender, represents a small minority of one or two within the group. Under those circumstances the person may experience little in common with other members. In addition, other members often see such individuals as representatives of their "group" rather than as individuals. The only woman or black in a group is often asked what all women or blacks think or feel. This is certainly an inappropriate and impossible burden.

At times it is appropriate and necessary to compose a group of people entirely of one gender or ethnic origin for the purpose of facilitating the resolution of identity issues or for providing social support. Thus, men's and women's consciousness-raising groups are increasingly being created and groups have been conducted with members of ethnic groups, often children or adolescents, to assist in the process of socialization.[2]

When identity and socialization are not the main purposes for forming the group, workers will often compose groups with members from several ethnic

---

[2]For example, see E.D. Edwards, M.E. Edwards, G.M. Daines, and F. Eddy, "Enhancing Self-Concept and Identification with 'Indianness' of American Indian Girls," *Social Work with Groups* I (1978), pp. 309–18; K. Hynes and J. Werbin, "Group Psychotherapy for Spanish Speaking Women," *Psychiatric Annals* VII (1977), 622–27.

backgrounds. Aside from avoiding "token" memberships, there are additional principles to consider. Davis, in an important review of these with regard to black Americans, draws a number of conclusions.[3] He notes that in one report, black members at first questioned the legitimacy of an all-black treatment group, but this concern gradually dissipated. At times, blacks have questioned the competency of their black worker. Blacks, particularly when militant, might question the competence of a white worker to work with blacks.

The proportion of blacks to whites within a group is also discussed by Davis. He explains that this topic is made more complex because blacks and whites interpret the meaning of proportions differently. As Davis states:

> Blacks, it appears, prefer groups that are 50 percent black and 50 percent white—numerical equality. Whites, on the other hand, appear to prefer groups that are approximately 20 percent black and 80 percent white, societal ratios of blacks and whites. Needless to say, the preferences of both groups cannot be simultaneously met. This difference in preference for racial balance has the potential to lead to member dissatisfaction, discomfort, and withdrawal. (p. 102)

Davis theorizes that whites "because of their customary numerical dominance, feel themselves to be psychologically in the minority, or outnumbered, if blacks are present in numbers greater than their societal proportions" (p. 102). He also notes that race is apt to be a more salient issue in situations that are intimate and that intimacy varies with group size and purpose.

Davis bases his propositions about racial composition on his own carefully conducted research. Similar studies should be conducted as to how ethnic composition situations other than black-white are experienced by the members. Short of that, we have to rely on the experiences of practitioners. Chu and Sue,[4] in their discussion of how composition affects Asian-Americans, describe how these members tend to react differently from others in a group.

> In a group of very verbose, articulate and aggressive non-Asians, the Asian member may be hesitant to speak up. In a confrontation, which inevitably happens at some point in a long-term group, the Asian may not know what to say, not being used to such interaction. (p. 30)

Chu and Sue conclude, therefore, that in at least the first stages of group experience, Asian-Americans should be grouped together. They assert that "Such a group can sense one another's communication and thus be more empathetic. Equal participation by Asians would also facilitate the development of leadership skills of some members within the group" (p. 30).

Ho[5] goes even further in recommending that members of Asian/Pacific American ethnic groups of a particular nationality and geographic location

[3]L.E. Davis, "Essential Components of Group Work with Black Americans," *Social Work with Groups* VII (1984), 97–109.

[4]J. Chu and S. Sue, "Asian/Pacific-Americans and Group Practice," *Social Work with Groups* VII (1984), 23–36.

[5]M.K. Ho, "Social Group Work with Asian/Pacific-Americans," *Social Work with Groups* VII (1984), 49–61.

should be grouped together. This is because of commonalities in sub-culture and language that are necessary for good group progress.

In contrast, in a discussion of group work with Hispanics, Acosta and Yamamoto[6] do not indicate that it is necessary to separate people whose origins are from different Hispanic backgrounds. They have experienced strong clashes between group members but believe this is due more to personality than variance in background.

Equally important in composition are gender issues. The worker must understand the processes that are likely to be created because a group is all of one gender, primarily of one gender, or about equally mixed. Martin and Shanahan, in a very thoughtful and comprehensive review of the relevant research, arrive at several conclusions.[7]

1. Even without interpersonal interaction (e.g., verbal exchanges) females are negatively "evaluated" in all-male groups and in groups in which they are tokens.
2. The quantity and content of verbal interaction in groups varies with sex composition of the group and by gender of the participant. For example, women talk less and are talked to less in mixed groups than in all-female groups; men in all-male groups tend to concentrate on competition and status topics while females in all-female groups focus on personal, home, and family topics. Both males and females are most likely to exhibit the greatest quantity of leader-like statements in same sex groups.
3. Females are perceived of less positively than males, even when equally influential.
4. "Solo" or "token" females in otherwise male groups tend to fare poorly.
5. The findings regarding women in all-female groups are inconsistent. Variations seem to be related to whether the study focused upon attraction to group, "growth" of members, inter-member influence, motivation for participation, or group effectiveness.

Martin and Shanahan make a number of suggestions related to these effects. These include actions to affirm the right of women to assume leadership and influential roles; ensuring that competence is equally rewarded in men and women; and ensuring balanced proportions of men and women in mixed groups. Additional issues, such as questioning the assumption that a division of labor and influence are undesirable features because they are found in men's groups, should be addressed in all-female groups so that women's groups can adapt these mechanisms when necessary.

In contrast to the many stresses that women have to cope with, men experience much that is valuable in mixed groups. Men are more likely to be "personal" and less competitive and disagreeable under these circumstances than when in all-male groups. Nevertheless, group leaders find that they have to discourage men from talking too much in mixed groups and from becoming overly competitive with one another.

[6]F.X. Acosta and J. Yamamoto, "The Utility of Group Work Practice for Hispanic Americans," *Social Work with Groups* VII (1984), 63–73.

[7]P.Y. Martin and K.A. Shanahan, "Transcending the Effects of Sex Composition in Small Groups," *Social Work with Groups* VII (1983), 19–32.

Finally, in all-male groups the worker must help the men to accept a greater degree of intimacy and self-disclosure than they might otherwise adopt. They must similarly be helped to deal with too much competition and conflict.

The above principles have been generated from an examination of a variety of groups, yet, there has been too limited an examination of gender issues in social work groups. We do not have good evidence as to whether some of these gender effects diminish over time or which approach to intervention is effective in changing stereotypical and undesirable reactions related to gender—reactions that limit the full development of the potential of group members. The preceding statements have to be taken, therefore, as hypotheses from which we may eventually create a sound approach to the role of group work in this aspect of human liberation.

Group Cohesiveness and Composition

In order for a group, certainly a voluntary one, to remain in existence, the members have to be motivated to attend, participate, and complete tasks. The concept that encompasses these variables is *cohesiveness,* usually defined as "the resultant of all the forces acting on all the members to remain in the group."[8]

Members can have many reasons to remain in a group, including attraction to other members, the worker, the goal, the activity, or the status associated with membership. Thibaut and Kelley have identified yet another variable, "the comparison level for alternatives," which is defined as "the standard that an individual uses to decide whether to remain in or to leave an interpersonal relationship."[9] This variable causes us to recognize that individuals not only choose to remain in groups because of what the group has to offer but also because of how these offerings compare with other opportunities.

The cohesiveness of a group is analogous to the concept of *relationship* in one-to-one interactions. According to research findings, it is one of the most important forces accounting for the effectiveness of a group.[10] In reference to this, Yalom states, "If an individual experienced little sense of belongingness or attraction to the group, even when measured early in the course of the sessions, there was little hope that he would benefit from the group and, in fact, a high likelihood that he would have a negative outcome."[11]

Although there are many bases of cohesiveness, the one that is most often studied, as well as sought after, is the attraction of members for each other. One way this attraction is enhanced is when members perceive each other as being similar to themselves. The worker can maximize cohesiveness, therefore, by composing groups of persons who are as similar as possible both on attributes (age, sex, race, socioeconomic status) as well as behaviors (types of problems, skills in problem solving, interests in the same activities).

[8]L. Festinger, "Informal Social Communication," *Psychological Review* LVII (1950), p. 274.
[9]J.W. Thibaut and H.H. Kelley, *The Social Psychology of Groups* (New York: John Wiley, 1959), p. 15.
[10]Yalom, *Group Psychotherapy,* pp. 49–52.
[11]Ibid., p. 52.

An issue that has troubled group workers is whether people will be reinforced for their dysfunctional ways of solving their problems if they are too similar in their behaviors. Many workers have argued that members should differ in their ways of coping. This will lead, presumably, to the kinds of constructive disagreements and tensions among members that will maintain interest in the group and stimulate members to consider new ideas and behaviors. Yalom has labeled this compositional model the "dissonance" one.[12]

Yalom concludes, based on his examination of both research and clinical experience, that "there is no evidence that deliberately heterogeneously composed groups facilitate therapy,"[13] and this has also been our experience. We, therefore, agree with Yalom's proposal that ". . . cohesiveness be our primary guideline in the composition of therapy groups."[14] This conclusion has been reached with the awareness that people differ considerably from one another and even the greatest efforts at matching will still produce an array of individuals with different experiences, ideas, and ways of responding to their environments.

Yalom asserts that cohesiveness should be emphasized in *therapy* groups. Thus he has a specific practice model in mind—one in which members are encouraged to remain in the group for a long period of time and treatment is accomplished through members' intensive examination of interpersonal processes in the group. Social workers often work with other kinds of groups. In these cases such an emphasis on homogeneity leading to cohesiveness may not be as necessary. Examples are:

1. Groups formed for a specific short-term purpose, such as preparation for discharge or orientation,[15]
2. groups employing a structured format, such as those for assertiveness training, and
3. groups with a strong educational component, such as parent training.

Deviance and Group Composition

Although we have stated that the worker should strive to select members who are similar when a cohesive group is sought, this is often not possible. The question then arises as to how dissimilar a member can be from others. The danger is that a member who is very different from others will be perceived as undesirable or, in sociological terms, deviant by the other members. When the difference is based on some attribute such as age or race, the members may avoid communicating with this person, thus creating a group isolate. When the difference is based on a behavior such as topics discussed, personal disclosure, or social skills, the members may become critical of the individual and then scapegoat the person, who will then develop negative feelings toward the group, avoid its influences, and eventually drop out. In some cases, the member will try

---

[12]Ibid., p. 270.
[13]Ibid.
[14]Ibid., p. 271.
[15]Recent discussions of this type of group include I.D. Yalom, *Inpatient Group Psychotherapy* (New York: Basic Books, 1983); and J.H. Schopler and M.J. Galinsky, "Meeting Practice Needs: Conceptualizing the Open-Ended Group," *Social Work with Groups* 7 (Summer, 1984), 3–21.

instead to modify his or her behavior so as to become more acceptable to others in the group but the risk still remains that such a person will become alienated from the group.

The worker must, therefore, avoid introducing someone who differs substantially from the other members in a way that group members consider salient to their interests. What constitutes such a salience must often be anticipated by the group worker based on experience with the population in question. For example, athletic skill may be an important consideration in an adolescent but not in an adult group; religious attitudes in a group to discuss child rearing but not in one to discuss employment; and types of sexual experience in a marital counseling group but not a preparation for retirement one.

There are several things the worker can do when there is a likelihood that group composition will lead to creating a deviant member. One is to seek to enroll another member who is either similar to the person in question or who is somewhere in the "middle," thus creating a continuum of member characteristics. This continuum then avoids the image and experience of a group that has extreme differences in attributes or behaviors between one person and the rest.

There are some situations where the worker may wish to constructively use the differences a member has from others. One example was that of a friendship group of adolescent boys in a community center. The worker asked them to accept a boy with cerebral palsy as a group member. After much discussion, this was accomplished. Some months later, when this boy had become well integrated into the group, another member mentioned that the boys will never again use the word "spastic" as a way of ridiculing someone.

One device used to compose groups and avoid creating a group isolate or deviant is to rate each member on a series of scales. Each scale represents an attribute or behavior deemed significant by the worker.[16] This graphic device, as illustrated in Table 3–1, has the property of making it easy to identify this type of

TABLE 3–1   Composition of an Adolescent Boys' Group

Name	Age	Race	Degree of Verbal Aggressiveness	Presenting Problem	Interest In Group
Sam	14	Black	Low	Severe conflict with teachers	Moderate
Bill	15	Black	Moderate	Theft from school	Moderate
Frank	15	White	Moderate	Runaway from family	Low
Carl	13	White	Moderate	Poor peer relations	High
Dick	17	Black	High	Frequent physical fights	Low

[16]For more details on this procedure, see Harvey J. Bertcher and Frank Maple, "Elements and Issues in Group Composition," in *Individual Change Through Small Groups,* eds. Martin Sundel, Paul Glasser, Rosemary Sarri, and Robert Vinter (New York: Free Press, 1985), pp. 180–202.

undesirable situation. The way that we have used such data is to examine each attribute or behavior to identify individuals who are "extreme" on that variable. Other variables are then examined to see if that person is also extreme with regard to these. If not, we assume that these other conditions will provide the bases for the commonality necessary for interpersonal attraction and group cohesiveness. When an individual is placed at an extreme on several scales in relationship to other group members, it is best to introduce others who are similar in some ways or to seek another group for him or her.

In our illustration (Table 3-1), Dick is older than the other boys; he is also verbally aggressive, engages in frequent physical fights, and is less interested in the group. His main area of identification is likely to be his race. On the other hand, he might serve as a model for the younger, particularly black members, in ways that are problematic. In this situation, the worker introduced two additional members to the group: another black 17-year-old who had been a runaway from his family and a 14-year-old white youth who had been involved in thefts—this latter member was not very aggressive, verbally or physically. The modified group composition, therefore, avoids the likely creation of an antisocial leader (Dick). It also avoids the equally likely creation of an isolate (Carl).

Program Activity and Group Composition

In most group situations, the major activity is group discussion, and verbal and cognitive approaches to treatment predominate. In group work, even before the advent of encounter and other groups that use nonverbal exercises, a variety of activities was used to achieve group purposes, including games, crafts, music, dance, and so forth. While many of these "programs" are chosen by groups after the group has been formed, the likelihood of their selection can often be predicted.

When the media likely to be used is anticipated, group composition is influenced. If discussion is to be employed, verbal skills must be assessed. Similarly, if the members are likely to communicate through drama, art, or athletics, the interest and level of skill in these must be rated.

Assessing Members in Relationship to Group Composition

The preceding discussion of factors to consider in composing groups is based on the idea that aspects of a person's behavior can be predicted. This is a difficult task because a person's behavior is determined both by personal characteristics and by the forces present in a situation.[17] For this reason, the best indicator of a person's behavior in a group is his or her actions in a similar group situation.[18] Some group-serving agencies, to secure this kind of information, have set up "waiting list" groups[19] or diagnostic groups.

[17]For a discussion of the point, see Marvin E. Shaw, *Group Dynamics: The Psychology of Small Group Behavior,* 3rd ed. (New York: McGraw-Hill, 1981), pp. 191–201.

[18]A. Goldstein, K. Heller, and L. Sechrest, *Psychotherapy and the Psychology of Behavior Change* (New York: John Wiley, 1966), p. 329.

[19]Yalom, *Group Psychotherapy,* p. 255.

Another possibility, suggested by Yalom, is an interpersonally oriented initial interview.[20] In this procedure, the worker assesses to what degree the clients can comment on the interpersonal process going on between them and the worker and how they assess and respond to the therapist's views of them. Also examined in such an interview is information about the clients' relationships with peers as well as the kinds of roles they have assumed in groups.

Various psychological instruments have been used to select members for groups, but probably the best known is Schutz's FIRO-B (Fundamental Interpersonal Relations Orientation) scales.[21] Schutz based his instrument on the proposition that everyone seeks to relate to others so as to satisfy three needs: *affection, control, and inclusion. Affection* pertains to close personal relationships, *control* to power over others, and *inclusion* to being with others. Everyone, according to Schutz, can be described as to the degree with which each of these is expressed and whether it is manifested toward others as well as expected from them.

One social work writer, William Shalinsky, utilized Schutz's scales to study the effects of different kinds of composition in children's groups. Shalinsky created some groups that were compatible and some that were not. Compatibility was defined as groupings consisting of people who were "similar to others in [their] total amount of expressed and wanted behavior in the need area of affection."[22] This researcher found that members of compatible groups liked each other more, found their group more attractive, and were even more cooperative. Also, compatible groups engaged in competitive tasks won significantly more often than incompatible ones.

The implication of Shalinsky's findings are that these interpersonal traits should be considered in composing groups and that homogeneity should be sought in this regard. This is also consistent with Yalom's emphasis on seeking cohesiveness in therapy groups and basing this on such measures as those devised by Shalinsky.

Selection of Worker or Co-Worker

When one views the small group as a system, then the group worker is as much a part of the system as the members, albeit with a different role. Therefore, compositional dynamics are created as much by the worker's characteristics as by those of the members. If the worker is the only male or female or black or white in the group, reactions will be the same as toward any group member with a characteristic that differs from others.

It is important, consequently, to consider the characteristics of the worker as carefully as those of members. The worker's characteristics can, for example, be used to "solve" some compositional problems such as "supplementing" the

---

[20]Ibid., pp. 257–58.
[21]William C. Schutz, *Firo: A Three Dimensional Theory of Interpersonal Orientations* (New York: Holt, Rinehart & Winston, 1958).
[22]William I. Shalinsky, "The Effects of Group Composition on Aspects of Group Functioning" (unpublished doctoral dissertation, Western Reserve University, 1967).

number of members who share some attribute. Thus, a mixed group of men and women, in which the number of referrals of women is small, might offset this with the appointment of a female worker.

Another question is whether there should be more than one worker assigned to the group, as in the co-worker situation. This device is sometimes used when the worker who is interested in facilitating the group differs from members in some important respect such as gender or ethnicity and it is important to provide a worker who is similar to members in these respects.

Usually there are reasons when workers desire to work in pairs other than composition. In work with multiple person systems, such as groups and families, this is a controversial topic. Some writers and practitioners strongly support co-worker models because they believe that the two workers can: bring different skills to the group; check each other's distortions about what is occurring in the group; constructively divide leadership roles such as those of task and social emotional facilitation; and model the ways that people can support each other and resolve differences. If the two workers are of different sexes, they can help members to deal with some family dynamics related to "mother" and "father."

Others seriously question the co-worker model. They think that it often provides an example of conflict rather than cooperation and that members become sidetracked from dealing with their own issues as they become interested in the interactions between the workers.

In our own experience, we have frequently found a co-worker model to be useful but not essential. On the other hand, we have observed it to be destructive when dysfunctional patterns emerge between the workers. This often happens when one worker operates as a more powerful figure than the other and this is associated with such attributes as race or gender—that is, the male worker dominates the female or the white worker dominates the non-white. This situation is often found when a male psychiatrist and female social worker or a white fully trained worker and a nonwhite paraprofessional join together.

Under any circumstance, co-workers must examine their own interactions throughout the life of the group. They must be sensitive to such patterns as the dominance of one over the other, the creation of coalitions between one worker and a group member, the assumption of less wanted activities by one worker such as cleaning up the meeting room after sessions, and so forth. This requires regular conferences between co-workers. Some workers have held such sessions in the presence of group members as a way of modeling the use of feedback to resolve differences between each other.[23]

Selection of Candidates for Groups

The process of composing groups consists of two stages: the first is to ascertain whether a group experience is an appropriate one at all; the second is to compose

---

[23] A comprehensive discussion of co-worker issues is provided in a special journal issue devoted to this topic. See *Social Work with Groups* 3 (1980).

groups of people who are both appropriate referrals to *any* group as well as to the one planned. In this respect we assume that both group and one-to-one helping are equally valid for a large proportion of people served by social work agencies.

Family Treatment. Probably the most important decisional issue is whether family treatment or other family involvement is required. Only after family approaches are rejected, should a worker consider whether casework or group work should be employed. It is, of course, possible to have a group composed of several families.[24] The decision to involve the family should be based on the following assessment:

1. Is the problem maintained by processes operating in the family as a system?
2. How will the family respond to changes the individual may choose to make and will these responses support or retard such changes?
3. Does the individual wish to involve the family and is the family amenable to such involvement?

If the family interaction maintains the problem or if the family opposes changes that the individual chooses to make, effective helping requires the worker to seek to involve other family members. Individual and group approaches should only be the worker's choice when these family considerations are lacking or minimal or when the client has rejected family involvement.

Client Preference. Another consideration is whether the potential group member wishes to be in a group. Clients usually come to agencies with expectations regarding the kinds of services they will receive and, often, this is for one-to-one help. The client's choice of individual, group, or family services should be an informed one based on information regarding different forms of interpersonal helping and what they are like. To impact such knowledge of group work, agencies have presented films, tapes, or even "comic books" that portray what happens in the agency's groups.

A group experience may be desirable for some clients, but is rejected because of some aspect of their situation. One example is a concern regarding confidentiality. In some cases, this problem is very "real" in that some information regarding clients might be harmful to them if publicized. On the other hand, all groups develop norms regarding confidentiality and breaches of this are almost nonexistent. Most clients who have such concerns are reassured by discussion of this issue prior to the group and during the first meetings.

Research Findings. Although workers should consider family issues, client attitudes, and confidentiality, they cannot draw from conclusive research findings to determine the efficacy of group as opposed to individual modalities of service. Yalom, however, presents an excellent discussion of therapy group

---

[24]H. Laqueur, H. Laburt, and G. Morong, "Multiple Family Therapy: Further Developments," *International Journal of Social Psychiatry* (1964) Congress Issue, 70–80.

member selection that does draw on research findings.[25] The problem of generalizing from his discussion is that it is based almost entirely on research and experience from either adult therapy groups or encounter groups. Group workers often work with children's, short term, and nonverbal activity groups, to name a few, where Yalom's conclusions may not hold.

For example, Yalom cites the "clinical consensus" that the following people are poor candidates for outpatient intensive group therapy: (1) brain damaged, (2) paranoid, (3) extremely narcissistic, (4) hypochondriacal, (5) suicidal, (6) addicted to drugs or alcohol, (7) acutely psychotic, or (8) sociopathic.[26] Group workers have worked with brain-damaged people; crisis groups have included suicidal people; groups patterned after Alcoholics Anonymous have been used with alcoholics; and confrontive group technologies such as Synanon games and guided group interaction have been used with people labeled sociopathic. At least anecdotal reports suggest some success with these populations through group methods other than traditional psychotherapy.

Yalom, while referring to groups that do not represent the full range of group work activities, took an imaginative approach to the issue of selecting appropriate members for groups. Since it is difficult to determine for whom groups are best suited, he examined, instead, the kinds of people who dropped out of therapy groups after twelve or fewer meetings.[27] Obviously, if people terminate early from a group, they are unlikely to have benefited from it. In the absence, therefore, of a replication of this study with social work groups, Yalom's findings should be considered in selecting members for such groups. The reasons, according to Yalom, for such premature termination were:

1. External Factors

These included conflicts between attending meetings and other events. Yalom implies the conflict may be a rationalization based on resistance to the group. Also, some people who present this kind of resistance to group attendance may be experiencing a crisis and wish to secure help on an immediate one-to-one basis.

2. Group Deviancy

People who are viewed by themselves and others in the group as different in attributes relevant to the group are likely to be harmed rather than helped through the group process. As Yalom states, "There is experimental evidence, then, that the group deviant derives less satisfaction from the group, experiences anxiety, is less valued by the group, is less prone to be influenced or benefited by the group, is more likely to be harmed by the group, and is far more prone than nondeviants to terminate membership."[28] Here Yalom is describing people who

[25] Yalom, *Group Psychotherapy*, pp. 221–43.
[26] Ibid., p. 221.
[27] Ibid, pp. 224–35.
[28] Ibid., p. 229.

are deviant in therapy groups because of their attitudes and behaviors, such as their strong use of denial and projection, their lack of interest in the intrapsychic, and their tendency to blame physical and health factors for their difficulties. From our group work experience, we conclude, also, that the worker's inability to find a group for a person in which other members have some similar attributes militates against offering group service to that person.

3. Problems of Intimacy

The people Yalom included in this category were those who manifested schizoid withdrawal, too rapid and intense self-disclosure, great fear of self-disclosure, and "unrealistic demands for instant intimacy."[29] Yalom recognizes that there is a paradox in the concept of problems with intimacy as these are the reasons people are often referred to groups. The implication here, is that some people are capable of working on these in group situations while others are overwhelmed in one way or another by the stimuli experienced in groups.

We remind the reader that Yalom is describing member problems with intimacy evoked in groups whose major focus is on the examination of relationship patterns. People with some severe intimacy problems have been helped with relationship issues in social work groups such as those where the programmatic emphasis is on activities requiring less verbal exchange and fewer demands for disclosure. Groups in mental health settings have utilized art, dramatics, and even games, and these have helped to shape social interaction behaviors and to desensitize people whose fears led to inappropriate behaviors regarding disclosure and intimacy. A subsequent experience may then appropriately be in a verbally oriented therapy group.

4. Fear of Emotional Contagion

This category of group dropouts includes people who "reported that they had been extremely adversely affected by hearing the problems of the other group members."[30] Yalom believes that such people may gradually be desensitized to this. In many groups in which the process is structured, such individuals may have less cause for anxiety as to how they will be affected by the behaviors and problems of others.

When Yalom's list of categories of people who drop out of groups is reviewed, the variable that seems the most pervasive for referral to any group is the likelihood that the person will find others to whom he or she can relate and who will reciprocate the desire for a relationship. In addition, expressions of difficulty in attending meetings, if not resolved, often indicate strong resistance to the group and militate against such a referral.

Yalom discusses "inclusion criteria," as those characteristics that most point to group therapy. He concludes that any person not excluded for the reasons just

[29]Ibid., p. 232.
[30]Ibid., p. 234.

listed can profit from group therapy. In one study, he found that those people who profitted the most were those who were most attracted to the group and introspective.[31] In another study specifically devoted to outcomes of encounter groups, the set of predictors of good outcomes included being valued by other members, being desirous of personal change, viewing oneself as deficient in understanding one's feelings, and having high expectations of the group.[32]

One problem with these studies is that they do not distinguish between those who benefited from group therapy and those who benefited from other group approaches. Another problem is that the findings may be confounded by therapist expectations that motivated, verbal, socially assertive persons will succeed in therapy. This also points to the strong need for research regarding the ways the many different types of groups conducted by social group workers are likely to affect their members.

PREPARING FOR GROUPS

Once candidates for the group have been selected, and prior to the first group meeting, the worker will accomplish a series of tasks. These tasks include preparing the individuals for the group, determining the optimum size of the group, and arranging the physical setting. Other people in the agency must also be prepared for the group so that they can support the arrangements that have been made. Careful attention to these details will do much to ensure the success of the group.

Preparing Members for the Group

The idea that members who are prepared for the group experience are more likely to benefit from it is receiving increased support. This has led to efforts to specify such systems of preparation sufficiently so that they can be tested. Northen, for example, recommends that the worker help the potential group member explore reactions to group placement and at the same time become acquainted with the worker. This, she asserts, will lead to a reduction in pre-group anxiety and confusion.[33]

Goldstein, Heller, and Sechrest present the following hypothesis: "Giving patients prior information about the nature of psychotherapy, the theories underlying it, and the techniques to be used will facilitate progress in psychotherapy."[34] Based on this type of prediction, a number of investigations have been conducted as to the effects of explanations given to clients in a "role induction" interview. In one study conducted as early as 1964, patients who were told how to behave in therapy rated higher on attendance, relationships, and other therapy-related behaviors, as well as outcome measures, than those not receiving such instruction.[35] Based on this

[31] Ibid., pp. 236–37.

[32] Morton A. Lieberman, Irvin Yalom, and M. Miles, *Encounter Groups: First Facts* (New York: Basic Books, 1973), pp. 315–55.

[33] Helen Northen, *Social Work with Groups* (New York: Columbia Univeristy Press, 1969), p. 108.

[34] Goldstein, Heller, and Sechrest, *Psychotherapy,* p. 245.

[35] R. Hoehn-Saric and others, "Systematic Preparation of Patients for Psychotherapy: Effects on Therapy Behavior and Outcome," *Journal of Psychiatry Research,* II (1964), 267–81.

finding, Goldstein and co-workers suggest that any such preparation present a theory relevant to the disorder, a rationale for the treatment, and a description of the treatment to follow.[36]

Yalom developed and tested a procedure for preparation of clients for groups that conforms to the preceding criteria.[37] In this approach, he includes the following information, which he tailors to the individual being interviewed:

1. All who enter psychotherapy have problems in relationships with others.
2. The therapy group is a place for "honest interpersonal exploration" but this will not be easy.
3. There will be a "carryover" from the working out of relationships in the group to relationships outside the group.
4. To accomplish this carryover, group members must be honest and direct with their feelings at the moment.
5. "Stumbling blocks," such as feeling discouraged in early meetings, will occur and members should not follow an inclination to leave during this period.
6. Treatment is gradual and long.

In addition, Yalom tells members about the history of group therapy, as well as the results of current outcome studies. They are also alerted to the issue of confidentiality. Finally, members are informed that if they develop relationships with other members outside the group, they should discuss this with the group.

In a test of this procedure with sixty people waiting for group psychotherapy, members of "prepared" groups had more faith in therapy and engaged in more group interaction than those in "unprepared" groups. This piece of research presents strong evidence for such preparation.

The task now is to develop analogous systems of preparation for the different types of groups served by group workers. One important step in this direction is the work of Diane Meadow.[38] She investigated the effects of pregroup preparation on time-limited groups led by M.S.W.'s practicing in community based, family-oriented agencies. In the experimental groups, members were prepared by discussing their expectations of the group, their perceptions of how to use the group, their reasons for joining the group (including any skepticism), their understanding of the referral to the group, their reservations about the experience (which they were assured were typical), their past experiences with groups, and the role of the group worker.

Meadow's findings were that members of the experimental groups, if they dropped out, were more likely to do so by discussing this decision with the worker than those in control groups; members of the experimental groups were less likely to miss meetings than those in control groups, although this was not statistically significant. In addition, members of the experimental groups were more likely than the controls to feel a greater sense of responsibility to the group and/or the group leader. They also had a clearer understanding of group

---

[36]Goldstein, Heller, and Sechrest, *Psychotherapy,* p. 250.

[37]Yalom, *Group Psychotherapy,* pp. 290–98.

[38]Diane Meadow, "Connecting Theory and Practice: The Effect of Pregroup Preparation on Individual and Group Behavior," No Date (Mimeographed).

purpose. Significant differences were not found between the experimental and control groups with reference to a number of group processes, but it is conceivable that as more work is done in preparing members for groups and examining group outcomes, these might also be affected.

Group Size

The size of the group should be determined in relationship to group purpose. The worker should also understand the kinds of processes that occur in groups of varying sizes. Small groups, such as those of about four to eight members, demand and produce more intimacy than larger groups. Such small groups are likely to bring pressure on members to participate. Larger groups, on the other hand, allow members to withdraw from active participation. The tendency in such groups is for a polarization to occur with some members talking a great deal while others seldom speak.

Writers on verbally oriented group psychotherapy have recommended that such groups have about seven members. This allows for a sufficient number to carry on the group when inevitable absences occur. Members have sufficient time for each to focus on his or her own issues, and withdrawal from participation and intermember hostility are quickly noted and discussed.

Usually children's groups should be of a smaller size. In general, children are unlikely to postpone attention to their concerns for any length of time. In addition, if there is any likelihood of destructive or aggressive behavior, the group will be small enough for the worker to respond to this while at the same time remaining in control of the overall group situation. The same may be true of adolescent groups. On the other hand, at times, adolescents want the comfort of withdrawing from a demand for participation and this can be accomplished in larger groups.

In large groups it is possible to employ some devices to produce greater intimacy. These include extending the length of meetings so that more members have time to receive group attention and dividing the group into subgroups, or even pairs, for discussion of issues, receipt of feedback, and reinforcement.

The following are some examples of ways of relating group size to group purpose. Groups devoted to helping members clarify their values can be large if similar sets of values are examined, otherwise such groups should be small. Role attainment groups where members face similar barriers to achieving socialization goals may be large, otherwise small. Social control groups, if large, may undesirably allow members to avoid confrontation which is usually employed in such groups. On the other hand, some individuals may be "turned off" by too early confrontation and also may profit from observing other people who are able to deal constructively with such confrontation in a large group. Alternative role attainment often requires attention to the conflicts each member experiences and should be small. However, people who are fearful of disclosure might initially benefit from a large group in which models for such behavior are available.

Preparing the Physical and Social Setting

Often neglected but important details in group beginnings are the selection of the group's meeting place and the preparation of other staff for the impact of the group. If at all possible, the group shoud have a permanent room. This facilitates the group member's sense of group identity and permanence. The room should have pictures or other symbols that indicate the agency's receptivity to the group. These might include pictures of scenes pleasurable to the members or of people with whom members might identify. Occasionally, abstract art is used as a way of eliciting members' projections.

Bruno Bettelheim, for example, has presented the epitome of thoughtfulness regarding a rationale for the selection of decoration and objects in a therapeutic setting.[39] He discusses in great detail the objects in his agency's (a residential treatment center for children) reception room—the "living room." These include an antique crib which communicates the belief that an infant's early experiences are important, a wall hanging showing a fairy tale, some furnishings suitable for adults and some for children, and an elaborately carved "throne," which easily supports a variety of images or fantasies.

The size of the room should also be planned with reference to the purposes of the group and its anticipated activities. Too large a space can give members the illusion that the group has no boundaries. Yet one worker "made do" in such a situation by structuring a fence of chairs across the width of a large room. This helped to set some limits for a large group of hyperactive children, otherwise likely to fan out beyond the worker's control. Too small a space, on the other hand, can cause anxiety in a group whose members are fearful of being prematurely forced into intimacy.

It has become a stereotype that a group worker arranges chairs into a circle at all meetings. Yet this face-to-face contact promotes more interaction than other arrangements. The distance between chairs can also be varied, although members will usually move chairs into positions in which they are comfortable and this will help the worker to assess the structure of interpersonal relationships. Groups with problems with interpersonal contact can, however, sit around a table as a sort of barrier.

The material objects in the room will also suggest activities to the members (for example, chalk and blackboard, games, sports equipment). For group therapy situations, either comfortable chairs or large cushions on a carpeted floor serve to communicate the idea that informal interaction is anticipated.

Other staff members should be aware of the beginning of the group. The receptionist should appear knowledgeable; attending a first meeting is anxiety-provoking enough without confusion beginning literally at the door of the agency. Members should be shown to the meeting room on arrival. The worker should be present early because the way members arrive and the timing of arrival will also disclose much about their attitudes to the group.

[39]Bruno Bettelheim, *A Home for the Heart* (New York: Knopf, 1974), pp. 104–58.

When other staff direct members to the room, their knowing about the group further communicates the agency's receptivity to the service. Staff, particularly those who have made referrals, will be asked questions by prospective members and, therefore, should be given information about the purpose of the group, frequency of meetings and their timing, as well as their location.

Part of the preparation for the first group meeting is the preparation of the worker, himself or herself. We all experience feelings and thoughts about beginnings—whether the experience will be what we anticipate, whether we will be able to cope with events, whether we will be liked by others, whether we will like them, whether the group will be a success. Some workers handle these concerns by overstructuring first meetings; others deny these feelings and present a facade to members; still others openly admit to members that they, like the members, have concerns about the beginning of the group but that together they can work to share and resolve these. Whatever the preferred style of beginning, the worker should be aware of what his or her style is, what it is a response to, and how it affects the members as they cope with the beginning of a new experience.

Type of Group

Prior to beginning the group, the worker will also determine the group's overall *format*. The alternatives include whether the group will be short term or long term; whether all members will be expected to begin and end at the same time or not (open ended versus closed ended groups); and whether the activities of the meetings will be predetermined or whether they will evolve from the immediate interaction among the members and the worker (structured and unstructured groups). We shall now discuss some of the criteria that workers use in making these decisions.

We think of groups as short term if, by plan, they will meet for two or three months or less. Long-term groups are those that will meet for more than six months. We conceive of a "grey area" (groups that meet from three to six months) that we hypothesize to incorporate some characteristics of each type. We find that most groups conducted by social workers, in view of client motivation and resources, are likely to be short term. This is likely to coincide with the idea of many clients that they are applying for or accepting services in order to resolve particular problem situations. We also find that some group members who continue in a group long after the original reason for joining the group has been resolved may either develop a dependency upon the group as a substitute for other social interactions or may even create problems in order to justify remaining in the group.

We recommend time-limited groups for most agency and client situations; however, there are several exceptions. One is that of the client who is not likely to function without continued support. An example of this is the long-term, chronic client (often diagnosed as *schizophrenic)* who is being maintained in the community. Even in this case, however, we hope that a range of self-help support groups will be made available when a professionally led group is no longer contributing substantially to the client's progress.

Another exception is long-term group therapy for people with severe disorders such as clients diagnosed as *borderline personality*. We recognize that psychiatric opinion is often in favor of individual therapy for such people. We, nevertheless, have seen some of these clients make progress in skillfully conducted groups that provide support, opportunities to develop social skills, feedback on relationship patterns, and considerable empathy.

We believe that groups with members who begin and end together have an advantage in terms of trust among members, knowledge members attain of each other, and the level of cohesiveness the group develops. Nevertheless, it is seldom feasible to form such groups. For example, social workers conduct groups in inpatient settings where patients are admitted daily and often remain for a few weeks or less. Another situation is one in which members enter a group, contract to work on a specific problem or problems, and terminate when their goals are attained. This group may consist of some members who are developing goals, some who are working on attaining them, and some who are terminating.

We have observed many open-ended groups and are strongly convinced that they "work." The main issue for the worker is to help members make use of their current interactions with others in the group in two crucial ways: (1) to gain support and feedback regarding their identification of and work toward attaining individual goals and (2) to examine their "here-and-now" experiences in the group as a means of identifying and assessing their problems in functioning with others.[40]

With reference to "structured" and "unstructured" groups, we believe that a continuum exists and may range from a minimum of interaction among members in some groups conducted primarily for imparting information, to a maximum in some psychotherapy groups in which workers and members react to processes as they emerge. We believe that the more structured end of the continuum should be used when the purpose of the group is primarily to help members acquire a very specific skill such as in communication, problem solving, assertiveness, or parenting training. The less structured end should be used when members are being helped to identify problems, to become aware of, or to modify, their characteristic ways of interacting with others, or to apply some of the skills they have acquired through more structured phases of the group.

SUMMARY

In this chapter, we have presented a rationale for preparing the group and have discussed its various aspects. Preplanning includes a determination of group purpose, a decision as to which persons can be helped in a group, a determination of the size and composition of the group, selection and preparation of the physical setting, and a determination of the group's format.

---

[40]See Yalom, *Inpatient Group Psychotherapy*, for an extensive discussion of how to work with such groups.

GROUP COMPOSITION EXERCISE

Goals

1. To learn to apply the principles of group composition.

2. To identify the steps involved in a group composition procedure.

3. To learn how to evaluate the adequacy of one's group composition procedure by assessing whether initial group processes are the ones intended by the way the group was composed.

Procedure

1. Prior to the exercise, trainees read about and discuss the principles of group composition described in this chapter.

2. Trainees (preferably about twenty, but the exercise can be done with sixteen) fill out the accompanying Assessment Form. This simulates a needs assessment and group referral process.

3. The instructor divides the group in half, and the halves exchange Assessment Forms. The two halves created in this way are instructed to compose a group consisting of about five persons from the other half. (If the halves are too small, they can supplement each other to form the group.) This task is to be completed by utilizing the principles of group composition that the trainees have discussed. The group may secure additional information to accomplish this task through delegating someone to go to the other half to arrange for a private "interview" with one or another prospective member.

There are two alternatives for the next step in the exercise:

a. Each half reports on the group it has composed and the rationale for believing it to be viable. The entire class discusses the issues this raises.

b. After composing a group, the trainees predict how the group is likely to begin (that is, topics likely to be discussed, initial exploration of commonalities, purposes which emerge, subgroupings). One or two members volunteer to be group workers and actually conduct a minisession (about twenty minutes) of the group. The trainees then present their rationale for composing the group, their predictions, and the initial group outcomes. The entire class discusses the issues posed by this.

Questions for Discussion

1. How was the initial purpose for the group determined?

2. How were individual reasons for wishing to be in a group related to group purpose?

3. What types of attributes were considered and why were they considered?

4. What types of member behaviors were considered and why were they considered?

5. How was motivation to be in a group considered?

6. How did the "workers" plan to begin the group in the light of the way it was composed? Did this plan involve some mechanism for dealing with some deficits in the composition (too great heterogeneity; insufficient basis for interpersonal attraction)?

ASSESSMENT FORM

Group Composition

Name_____

Sex _____   Age Group _____ 20–25 _____ 26–30 _____over 30

Briefly describe a question, concern, or issue you would like to discuss in a group.

If none, write NONE.

How active are you in groups?

_____ talk a great deal   _____ talk little
_____ talk somewhat   _____ say nothing or almost nothing

What are some of your hobbies or interests?

How do you feel about being in a group composed as part of this class?

_____ very interested   _____ somewhat opposed
_____ somewhat interested   _____ very opposed

_____ neutral

Notes for Group Composition Rater

4

Beginning A Group

In this chapter we shall describe the kinds of processes that occur in groups during their beginning phases and the activities of group workers to facilitate these processes. Group workers seek to understand the processes of group beginnings for several reasons.

1. All groups go through formation phases and the workers who understand these will not be overly concerned by inevitable events in the group. Rather, they will understand these as efforts of group members to cope with determining group purposes, selecting activities to achieve these purposes, and learning to trust and cooperate with each other.[1]

2. The worker can learn to differentiate between fairly typical patterns and those that require the worker and members to take special measures to save the group from inertia or destruction.

As we indicated in Chapter 3, the worker must learn to integrate knowledge of phases of group development with stages of the group work process. Chapter 4 seeks to enhance this integration with reference to group beginnings.

[1]Our discussion of group formation draws on such portrayals of group development as Rosemary C. Sarri and Maeda Galinsky, "A Conceptual Framework for Group Development," in *Individual Change Through Small Groups,* eds. Martin Sundel, Paul Glasser, Rosemary Sarri, and Robert Vinter (New York: Free Press, 1985), pp. 70–86; James A. Garland, Hubert E. Jones, and Ralph Kolodny, "A Model for Stages of Development in Social Work Groups," in *Explorations in Group Work,* ed. Saul Bernstein (Boston: Boston University School of Social Work, 1965), pp. 12–13; and Irvin D. Yalom, *The Theory and Practice of Group Psychotherapy* (New York: Basic Books, 1975), pp. 301–75.

In the first part of the chapter, we present the process of group formation as it may occur in any group. Following this general discussion of group formation, we present the tasks the worker must undertake in order to accomplish the purposes of the group. These tasks include assisting the members to decide on group purposes that will help them to achieve their goals as well as group rules that will govern behavior. Both the members and the worker will have to gather information in order to choose effective ways of accomplishing the group's goals. Usually, when the group is thought of as "treatment," this information gathering is conceived of as an *assessment*.

A number of issues regarding member emotions in beginning phases must also be understood. Members are often ambivalent because they are attracted to the group while also experiencing some anxiety about investing in it. The members will have feelings about the worker with which they must learn to cope.

We conclude the chapter with a discussion of how to resolve atypical formation difficulties. A group exercise based on enchancing one's understanding of group formation is also included.

PROCESS OF GROUP FORMATION

In the first meetings of groups, particularly those in which members have not known each other beforehand, there is little sharing of personal, intimate reactions and experiences. Rather, members will interact with one another in ways based on fairly superficial attributes or experiences. For example, members will comment on the similarities and differences of places they have lived and they will talk primarily with people who are similar in obvious ways such as age, race, and sex. Members may also seek out others in the group with common interests in sports, politics, religion, or leisure time activities.

In his discussion of group beginnings, Yalom notes that in groups defined as offering therapy, "symptom description is a favorite early issue, along with previous experiences, medications, and the like."[2] He sees this "stereotyped" activity as one way of coping with the anxiety posed by beginnings.

DECISIONS ON GROUP PURPOSE

In the process of becoming acquainted, members must determine group purpose(s). This may be simple, as when a group has been formed around some highly specific issue such as enhancing assertiveness or parenting. Members in these circumstances have joined the group to learn specific social skills or discipline techniques. The determination of group purpose may, however, be a more complex one when members have additional, alternative, or even covert reasons for joining the group.

One example of a covert reason for joining a group was that of a member of an assertiveness group who had hoped to make friends; another example was a

[2]Yalom, *Group Psychotherapy*, p. 305.

woman in a parent education group who sought encouragement to find employment outside her home. Another person joined a job placement group in order to recruit people for a social action project to promote a public service career program.

A thorough discussion of purposes in a group's formation period leads, in most circumstances, to a choice of group purpose that has the strongest commitment of all members. In some instances, however, individual issues that will broaden or change group purposes do not surface until the group progresses to the subsequent phase and activities to accomplish group purposes are determined. Problems that arise in making decisions on activities are often a result of lack of commitment to the group purpose by some or all members.

In some groups, the initial statement of purpose is vague. This is true of statements such as "enchancing interpersonal relationships." The group members in such groups must enter into further discussions of purpose in order to make the group purpose clear enough to serve as a basis for decisions regarding group activities.

ASSESSMENT IN GROUPS

Usually, in concert with determining purposes, members will find it necessary to gather various kinds of information. This activity can help members to specify group purposes in detail as they list problems that concern them individually or as a group. Such information gathering will also include securing details about individual or group problems. In groups devoted to achieving specific individual treatment goals, members will obtain data related to the causes of and solutions to individual behavior problems, thus forming an assessment of the member's individual behavior problems. In addition to or instead of a member-oriented assessment, the process of data gathering may focus on analyzing other systems, such as the schools, communities, or places of employment of members' families.

There are a number of useful guidelines for the assessment of individuals, groups, and larger systems, such as those provided by Siporin, Compton and Galaway, and Rose.[3] These frameworks can be used in individual, family, or group work. In all these contexts workers and clients should base their actions on an analysis of the systems that are relevant to the problem at hand.

Assessments of the problems of group members will employ the same concepts and theories as those used when working with people individually. There is no consensus, however, in social work regarding a theoretical framework for assessment, and group workers will use behavioral, ego psychological, role, or other theoretical systems in the same manner as other social workers. Group workers can draw upon the members, however, in the assessment process in several ways: first, members can be trained to participate in assessments of each

---

[3]Max Siporin, *Introduction to Social Work Practice* (New York: Macmillan, 1975), pp. 219–50; Beulah Compton and Burt Galaway, *Social Work Processes* (Homewood, Ill.: Dorsey Press, 1979), pp. 232–56; and Sheldon D. Rose, *Group Therapy: A Behavioral Approach* (Englewood Cliffs, N.J.: Prentice-Hall, Inc., 1977), pp. 25–40.

other; second, behavior in the group provides direct evidence regarding the member's interpersonal behavior that is not available through individual ways of helping.

Members, with or without a common conceptual framework, are likely to ask each other questions and to contribute information about their problems. Because of similarities in problems, cultures, and life experiences, members may have more insight into each other's difficulties than the worker has. This is a major advantage of the group context. In addition, members can be taught to utilize established frameworks for assessment.

Two examples of frameworks successfully taught to members of treatment groups are behavioral assessment and transactional analysis.[4] One applicable form of behavioral assessment involves explaining to members that behavior is *caused* by its antecedents and consequences.

There are two types of antecedents and consequences: overt and covert. Overt ones are those that occur in the environment; covert ones occur in the thoughts and feelings of the individual. A study of *antecedents* includes an examination of the thoughts and feelings of the person before the behavior occurs, the place where it occurs, who was present at the time, and what these people were doing. *Consequences* is a less technical expression than *reinforcement* and *punishment* but refers to both terms as well as to the likelihood that specified behaviors will be met with pleasurable or aversive responses, or none at all.

Members have been taught to recognize antecedents and consequences through explanation of these terms followed by examples and role plays, which are analyzed in this manner. Because of the member's familiarity with each other's circumstances, the group is an effective place to perform a behavioral assessment.

In a similar manner, members can be taught to use the principles of transactional analysis to help each other understand the sources of their difficulties. In this type of analysis, group members learn to recognize actions that stem from parent, adult, and child ego states. An ego state, as defined by Berne, is "a system of feelings which motivates a related set of behavior patterns."[5] The parent ego state derives from the individual's earlier experiences with parent figures and usually involves value positions and judgmental responses. The child ego state reflects one's childhood experiences and is reflected in responses to authority, playfulness, creativity, and dependence. The adult ego state represents rational, information processing approaches to situations and problems.

In utilizing a transactional approach, members identify how their behaviors relate to ego states and how their ego states are responded to by others—both in the group as well as outside of it. Members can seek to change their responses to others in ways that are related to their goals and to help others do the same. They can be trained to do this with similar procedures to those used in behavioral approaches, namely, discussion, role play, and analysis of actual life circumstances.

[4]For examples of the ways these are taught in groups, see Rose, *Group Therapy,* pp. 95-102.
[5]Eric Berne, *Transactional Analysis in Psychotherapy* (New York: Grove Press, 1961), p. 17.

The group, because it represents a small society in its own right, also provides direct information about the causes of member behaviors. The workers and members observe each other reacting to stress, nurturance, ambiguity, and other interpersonal circumstances. This use of the group for assessment purposes can be enhanced in several ways.

One method is role playing. Members can set up simulations of environmental situations or can replay intra-group ones. The members comment on these events, utilizing the variety of data provided. A member can even observe while another member plays his or her role and thus gain objectivity regarding the circumstances.

A second assessment device is provided by the use of activities. The worker can introduce crafts, dramatics, and games, to name a few, and through these media enable members to express their concerns and display responses to a variety of situations.[6]

A third device, usually referred to as the "fishbowl," requires part of the group to observe and give feedback to another part of the group. This procedure provides excellent training for members in the understanding of behavior. The observing subgroup, or even single members who are asked to observe the group, can be supplied with simple questionnaires or rating instruments to support this activity.

DETERMINATION OF NORMS

The formation period of the group is a crucial one in relationship to norm development. The norms that social workers seek to instill in groups are derived from the values of social work that we stated in Chapter 1, but are more specific indications of how members expect each other to behave. Glassman and Kates, in a paper on this subject, have done an excellent job of specifying the norms that are consistent with the humanistic orientation of most group workers.[7] The following draws substantially from their description of such norms.

In relationship to the value regarding the inherent worth of the individual, the norm that workers specify is for members to value the sanctity and rights of every other member. The worker helps this norm to develop by making statements about the value of each member's contribution to the work and direction of the group. The worker also facilitates this by explicitly recognizing the fact that members come from different cultures and backgrounds.

For the value of members assuming responsibility for one another, the worker specifies the norm that members should find ways to experience caring for one another. The worker facilitates this by helping members to explore their feelings for one another and by matching this to a criterion of caring. Related to

[6]Sallie R. Churchill, "Social Group Work: A Diagnostic Tool in Child Guidance," *American Journal of Orthopsychiatry* 35 (April, 1965), 581–88.

[7]Urania Glassman and Len Kates, "The Technical Development of the Democratic Humanistic Norms of the Social Work Group," Adelphi University School of Social Work, no date (mimeographed).

this value is the norm that members should seek ways of cooperating rather than competing with one another. The worker helps by identifying situations of non-cooperation and by support for the sharing of resources and the emergence of experiences through which members can work together.

Another value in group work is the right to be accepted unconditionally and, therefore, the right to be included in experiences that meet one's needs. A group norm that relates to this is that all members have an equal right to belong to the group. Clearly, all groups must have boundaries that define membership, but the worker insists that these be carefully determined, after which the individual's membership in the group is secure. This kind of security has extraordinary curative potential for the members.

Definitions of membership must be based on the needs of individuals and not on arbitrary ethnic, racial, class, or other lines that are used in a stereotypical manner. Based upon this, the group will not seek to exclude "difficult" members. As Glassman and Kates state, "It is a group that may choose to struggle with such a member and to develop fuller ways of coping with that individual, [that strengthens] itself as a collective."[8] The worker will often model this by himself or herself and struggle to accept and interact with difficult members. At times, members must be excluded for their own protection, but this step is taken only after careful consideration of the alternatives and with due recognition of the threat to their security.

The worth of every human being emphasizes the norm that "Everyone takes part and is helped to take part."[9] This leads the worker to encourage members with low participation rates and to subdue those who "overparticipate."

The value placed upon self-determination has many implications for group norms. These norms relate both to the self-determination of the individuals and self-determination issues for the group-as-a-whole. In supporting this norm, the worker will help the group to examine power issues relevant to how decisions are made in the group that affect the group itself and its individual members.

This norm relates to the topic of democracy in the group. Some groups will function with all of the democratic procedures that have been developed such as those in *Robert's Rules of Order*.[10] Members in some other groups are unable to feel secure without a great degree of worker control as in groups where members suffer from a psychosis, are very young, or have very limited mental abilities. The principle must be that workers help groups to develop as great a measure of democratic decision making as possible. Anything short of this must be justified to the members and to others in a position to safeguard their rights (such as the client's rights officer that has been created in many settings, the client's relatives, and sometimes the client's attorneys). Even in the latter instances, the worker will always try to help members move to a greater level of participation in decision making.

[8]Ibid., p. 14.
[9]Ibid., p. 16.
[10]H. Robert, *Robert's Rules of Order* (Glenview, Ill.: Scott, Foresman and Co., 1970).

Glassman and Kates also state the value that "The worker is accountable to the group."[11] This norm is implemented by encourging members to ask questions about the worker's actions and to evaluate the worker at periodic intervals.

A number of other values are cited by Glassman and Kates: the right to freedom of speech and expression, the belief that difference is enriching, and freedom of choice regarding whether to change or not. We believe that these are as important as the ones previously quoted, and in some sense may be an amplification of these values.

Although the worker seeks to instill values and norms while the group is being formed, a discussion of values and norms continues throughout its life. One of the most potent aspects of group process, as the group becomes more cohesive, is the pressure that emerges for conformity to norms. When these are therapeutic, by helping members achieve a personal goal of self-control, it is a valuable phenomenon. Otherwise the group can be a destructive experience and the worker should make this known to the group. An excellent discussion of such negatives that can emerge in groups is provided by Galinsky and Schopler.[12]

EMOTIONAL REACTIONS TO GROUP FORMATION

An emotional issue present in group beginnings is the conflict between being attracted to the group and simultaneously experiencing anxiety about the group.[13] This constitutes a form of approach–avoidance conflict for the members. The attraction to the group is attested to at least in voluntary groups by the members' presence. Members come because they hope that the group will help them attain their objectives. They may also look forward to the gratification of interacting with other members and/or with the worker. On the other hand, members often have apprehensions about the group. Will it help them to achieve their purposes or will it restrain them? Will other members be hostile, unaccepting, or unlikable? Will the costs of achieving goals be too great to pay? Will the members find some position in the group that will be familiar and comfortable?

If the group, in its first meetings, appears more on the positive side compared to other ways members might satisfy their wants, the members will remain and invest themselves in it. If the group, in the same period, is seen negatively, several members will discontinue, and this may be enough to destroy the group.

The worker should comment on these ambivalent feelings since this may help sustain the members through difficulties that are usually present in group beginnings. This action should have an empathic quality and may also enhance member-worker relationships. In addition, an empathic response invites the members to work on their feelings about the group's beginning and to cope with fears about the group. This type of discussion may also help members to approach formation issues in a more relaxed manner.

---

[11]Glassman and Kates, "The Technical Development of the Democratic Humanistic Norms," p. 21.

[12]M. Galinsky and J. Schopler, "Warning: Groups May be Dangerous," *Social Work* 22 (1977), 89–94.

[13]Garland, Jones, and Kolodny, in *Explorations in Group Work,* p. 21.

In the beginning of groups, as well as at other crucial times in their existence, members sometimes develop a tradition of a "round." This involves members, in turn, sharing their feelings at that moment. Since shared feelings often relate to common group themes, this procedure helps prepare the way for discussion.

RELATIONSHIP OF GROUP WORKER TO MEMBERS

Members, in an emotional sense, place the workers in a central position because of their presumed expertise and responsibility for the group. The members address a large proportion of their communications to the worker and may appear dependent on that person for solutions to individual and group problems. According to at least one writer, this early dependence on the group worker is the need for an omnipotent, omniscient, omnicaring parent.[14]

Too much dependence can be confronted at an appropriate stage in the development of the group. In the beginning, however, even though the worker risks dependence, he or she should nurture a relationship with each member. At the most elementary level, this includes addressing each member by name. To accentuate this expression of interest, the worker should seek occasions to single out each member for a comment, question, or encouraging remark. The worker also takes responsibility for opening the group meeting. This shows a readiness to take a share of responsibility for the group, even when the worker's plan and philosophy calls for the group's eventual assumption of responsibility for itself.

A large literature has demonstrated that the outcome of helping processes are strongly related to the degree to which the worker demonstrates three types of behaviors—empathy, genuineness, and warmth.[15] While much of the research on these variables has been done in the one-to-one counseling situation, some substantiation of their potency in group situations is available.[16]

Empathy

Empathy refers to the accuracy of the worker's feedback regarding the feelings the member experiences. Accuracy includes not only the feeling but the context in which the feeling was aroused. Some techniques, such as the exact repetition of members' statements, are often aversive to many people who view this as having a mocking quality. The worker must, therefore, choose a sincere and natural way of paraphrasing member feelings. An example of an empathic response of a worker

[14]See Yalom, *Group Psychotherapy,* Chapter 6.

[15]Morris B. Parloff, Irene Elkin Waskow, and Barry E. Wolfe, "Research on Therapist Variables in Relationship to Process and Outcome," in *Handbook of Psychotherapy and Behavior Change: An Empirical Analysis,* 2nd ed., eds. Sol L. Garfield and Allen E. Bergin (New York: John Wiley, 1978), pp. 242–52.

[16]C. B. Truax, R. R. Carkhuff, and I. Rodman, Jr., "Relationships Between Therapist Offered Conditions and Patient Change in Group Psychotherapy," *Journal of Clinical Psychology* XXI (1965), 327–29; C. B. Truax, J. Wittmer, and D. G. Wargo, "Effects of the Therapeutic Conditions of Accurate Empathy, Non-possessive Warmth, and Genuineness on Hospitalized Mental Patients During Group Therapy," *Journal of Clinical Psychology* XXVII (1971), 137–42.

to a member's statement that "I was frightened when I went home and found my wife had gone out," was "It was a scary feeling for you when you got back from work and found your wife wasn't home." The member then continued by saying "That's right and I didn't know what to do."

An important experience in a group is for members to offer and receive empathic responses from each other. This also increases the cohesiveness of the group. The worker increases the likelihood that members will be empathic with each other by the model he or she presents. In addition, the worker explains the value of empathy and trains members to make empathic responses to each other. This training can be done through calling attention to his or her own responses, role playing of empathic responses, or giving feedback to members when they naturally interact in this way.

The frequency of the total number of empathic responses in a group can be increased. This is accomplished by having a member or observer count the number of empathic acts. If the group believes this too low, an increase can become a group goal and the group can reward itself for achieving it. This type of self-monitoring is usually done in early stages of groups or when members are concerned about the group atmosphere.

Genuineness

Genuineness consists of the honesty and openness of the worker with the members. To be genuine the worker must have a substantial amount of self-awareness, otherwise he or she may unknowingly behave in inconsistent or covert ways. Genuine behavior will be devoid of contradictions in various aspects of the worker's behavior. The worker who is genuine, for example, will not deny being angry with members when this emotion is present. Similarly, when the worker feels warmly towards members, he or she will be free to say so. The worker will also engage in appropriate self-disclosure. While evidence exists of the value of the worker revealing aspects of his or her own experiences in order to model openness for members and provide useful data, a great deal of judgment must be exercised regarding when and how much disclosure should take place.[17]

In an extensive discussion of worker self-disclosure in groups, Weiner[18] points out that when members can observe the worker interact with other members it represents a degree of disclosure. In addition, members can help each other to deal with their reactions to worker disclosures.

Another aspect of genuineness is the willingness of the worker to provide feedback to members regarding perceptions of *their* behavior. The worker who withholds personal reactions to individuals in the group, as well as to the group itself, will not be evaluated by the members as having been honest with them. The worker must use judgment as to the way such reactions are shared and whether they are reflective of his or her biases in ways that are destructive to the members. Some examples of workers' reactions are given to illustrate this point.

[17]See Parloff, Waskow, and Wolfe, in *Handbook of Psychotherapy,* pp. 242–52.
[18]M.F. Weiner, *Therapist Disclosure: The Use of Self in Psychotherapy* (Boston: Butterworths, 1978), pp. 128–51.

Example: A worker told a group of young adults with socialization problems that they were wasting *their* time when they avoided discussions of their relationships to each other.

Example: A worker for a group of parents who sought better ways of raising their children pointed out to them the amount of time they spent complaining about their children rather than seeking better ways of responding in difficult encounters with them. The worker said they were doing some of the kinds of things they complained about their children doing.

At the same time the worker must help the members to behave more genuinely to each other. The following is an example of this.

Example: When Robert turned his back on Sam as the members were discussing Sam's problem, the worker pointed this out to him (helping Robert to be aware of the contradictory messages he presents to Sam). The worker then encouraged Robert to discuss what about Sam was upsetting him (helping Robert to engage in appropriate self-disclosure). In this discussion, the worker also supported Robert in telling Sam that whenever he (Robert) tried to help Sam, he (Sam) also turned away (helping Robert present his perceptions of Sam honestly to Sam).

Warmth

Warmth, usually referred to as non-possessive warmth, is somewhat harder to operationalize than empathy and genuineness because much of its expression is in the form of feelings. As Schulman points out also, "Several characteristics are included in the concept of warmth—equal worth, absence of blame, nondefensiveness, and closeness."[19] A rating scale Schulman uses divides warmth, for this reason, into two dimensions: positive regard and respect.[20]

Positive regard is the degree to which the worker shows interest in the group members and concern for his or her welfare. It also includes the acceptance, by the worker, of the members' freedom to be themselves. This does not preclude the worker's expectation that the members will seek to realize their fullest capacities.

Respect, on the other hand, is reflected in the way the worker appreciates the members' efforts. Even when they fail at these efforts or behave in some fashion that is unpleasant to others, the worker recognizes the fact that the members are trying to cope with difficult situations.

Example: When Mary reported to the group that she failed her examination, she was in tears as the worker placed her arm on Mary's shoulder. At this, Mary, even while crying, angrily attacked her teacher as a "mean old bitch." The worker, while her arm was still around Mary, said she could see why Mary felt this way. The worker also asked Mary how the group could help her. Mary said she knew

[19]Eveline D. Schulman, *Intervention in Human Services,* 2nd ed. (St. Louis, Mo.: C. V. Mosby, 1978), p. 225.
[20]Ibid., p. 231.

that Sue had had a "run in" with the same teacher and she asked Sue how she had handled it. The worker, in this way, facilitated Mary's securing expressions of warmth from other group members.

RELATIONSHIPS AMONG MEMBERS

The feelings members have toward one another, if primarily positive, will be the major reason they return to the group. The trust they develop in one another will also be the major determinant of their ability to help one another with personal difficulties or with tasks.

Seeking Similarities

The worker seeks to develop relationships among the members by helping them to discover similarities in their life experiences, their difficulties, and their ways of responding to situations. This is initiated by encouraging the members to tell about themselves, while seeing to it that a few members do not monopolize the first sessions, thus causing other members to lose interest in the group. One relevant question could be how they came to join the group. In a child guidance clinic, children in a group used small dolls to describe their family composition; in a group of handicapped people undergoing physical and occupational rehabilitation, members described the kinds of rehabilitation programs in which they had participated.

In some groups where the intent is for the group to continue for a long period and complex interactional patterns are likely to be discussed, the worker may draw attention to more subtle similarities. In a group of people served by an out-patient psychiatric clinic, one member spoke of his difficulties in setting out for the group meeting that evening; another spoke of problems in starting school; and a third talked of how difficult it had been in the beginning of her marriage. The worker noted the common theme of feelings about difficult beginnings and stated this.

Talking to Each Other

One of the major issues in first meetings is the tendency for members to talk to the worker rather than each other. This may be inevitable when the worker offers information to orient members. On the other hand, members must be encouraged to talk to each other and in the group's beginning this should be raised as an issue. The worker can draw attention to this in several ways: first, by redirecting questions, placed to him or her, back to group members; second, by directly pointing out the value of members helping each other; third, by identifying commonalities among the members. The worker may also choose to raise the issue of overdependency on the worker for discussion.

Reducing Distortions

Members should be helped to separate perceptions of each other from realities. While this process continues over the life of the group, it is important to begin early. Some workers accelerate the process by asking members to select a member who reminds them of someone. Members then discuss this either in pairs or with the whole group. A less direct form of this exercise is to ask members in rotation to focus on one member at a time and associate colors, animals, and so forth, with that member. This experience is then discussed and can lead to an awareness of the kinds of emotions and meanings members project onto each other.

During these kinds of early processes, the worker should be aware that closeness among members, or for that matter among any human beings, is not easy to attain and may be particularly difficult for the types of people served by social workers. The worker should acknowledge this in as empathic a manner as possible.

Careful Listening

One of the techniques to facilitate closeness is to enhance the way members listen to each other. Some of the approaches mentioned in this chapter are likely to encourage such careful listening. Thus identifying one's fantasies about other members helps in being more attentive to the actual rather than imagined statements of the other people. Being sensitive to common concerns also has this effect. One technique directly related to this issue is to help members to be aware of times when they are not listening and out of this awareness to commit themselves to practice listening.

For training in listening, some workers use the exercise of asking members, for a limited period, to repeat the previous comment before continuing on with their own. Another is for members to rotate the role of "summarizer." The group will then be asked to turn to the "summarizer" whenever it wishes to examine its recent process.

When the members who have failed to listen are confronted by the worker, they can be asked to talk about feelings they had at such times. Members, particularly children who are being taught group discussion skills, can be rewarded with tokens by other members of the group when such other members feel understood.

GROUP STRUCTURE DURING FORMATION

Another task of the worker in the beginning of a group is to enable the group to have the kinds of structures conducive to further group development. Group structures consist of the patterns of relationships among members. We shall deal here with group structure issues relevant to group beginnings; in the next chapter, we shall elaborate on stuctural issues occurring in groups at later stages.

Types of Structures

Some of the major group structures are the following:

1. Communications structure: who speaks to whom about what and under what circumstances;[21]
2. Sociometric structure: who likes or dislikes whom in the group (These emotional patterns contribute to the creation of subgroups. Groups are often subdivided into cliques of members who interact with each other more frequently than they do with others outside of the subgroup);[22]
3. Power structure: who influences whom in the group and in what manner;[23]
4. Leadership structure: who contributes most to the determination and accomplishment of group tasks as well as who contributes most to reducing tensions, enhancing group cohesiveness, and securing compliance with formal and informal rules;[24]
5. Role structure: who occupies formally recognized positions, such as chairpersons, secretaries, and so forth, who fills positions created by group activities (for example, pitcher, expert in sewing), and who fulfills categories growing out of even more informal group interactions (for example, mediator, clown, rebel).[25]

Structural Changes

The worker should examine each of the types of structure just listed in terms of their effects on group beginnings. The communications structure should become one in which the maximum number of members participate and in which members respond to each other. Rose, for example, suggests a number of devices to measure communication patterns,[26] including simple tallies of the number of times each member talks. We have also used a form of recording (see Figure 4-1) that captures who is spoken to as well as the people speaking. Rose also uses behavioral approaches to change these patterns such as the person on the speaker's right reinforcing low-frequency speakers with tokens and restraining high-frequency speakers with a hand on their shoulder.

Sociometric structures in which members are new to each other early in the group's life are not likely to be defined rigidly. The exception may be when members have some definite cleavages determined by race, age, or sex. The worker's role is to use activities or encourage participation so that members have as much contact as possible with those who differ from themselves. These activities may include games, discussions in dyads or triads, and role plays that require various types of subgroups for execcution.

---

[21]Margaret E. Hartford, *Groups in Social Work: Applications of Small Group Theory and Research to Social Work Practice* (New York: Columbia University Press, 1972), pp. 218–27.
[22]Ibid., p. 196.
[23]Ibid., pp. 261–69.
[24]Ibid., pp. 264–67.
[25]Ibid., pp. 216–18.
[26]Rose, *Group Therapy,* pp. 133–40.

Person Spoken To

Person Speaking	John	Bill	Sam	Frank	Several	All	O
John		|||					
Bill	||||						
Sam										
Frank						||	||

FIGURE 4–1   Communication Structure Rating Form

Similarly, some members may appear to have more power than other members by virtue of their expertise, control over resources (for example, a car, sports equipment), ability to punish (for example, use of sarcasm), or ability to inflict physical harm. The worker strives to help members to use power in ways that help them attain treatment goals without interfering with other members' attainment of goals.

Some individuals who experience themselves as relatively powerless should be helped to gain a share of influence in the group. This can be done through helping such members assume useful roles in the group, coaching members on ways of being more assertive in the group, and also giving support to the contributions made by these members during group meetings.

In reference to leadership structure, Sarri and Galinsky have pointed out that the beginning phase is characterized by "leadership roles played by the more assertive and aggressive individuals."[27] This may be functional at the early stage in group development but the group must have the flexibility, as purposes and tasks are clarified, to allow inputs from other people. The worker, consequently, should try to keep the leadership structure fluid by emphasizing temporary assignments to group tasks and rotation of any influential positions.

Finally, in regard to role structure, the worker must examine how all of the roles just described are performed. In the situation where members have joined the group to solve problems through discussion, the group is unlikely to choose "officers" in any formal sense. On the other hand, in anomie reduction and role attainment group situations, the members' assumption of group leadership positions may be an important type of experience. In groups with formal leadership roles, the worker in the group formation stage helps the members to determine the nature of such positions, the ways in which members will be chosen to fill them, and the attributes that members should possess in order to be chosen for positions.

A broader issue, in terms of role structure, is how to fill positions created by group activities. For example, when the group utilizes role play, members should be selected for the roles consistent with their goals. Similarly, in a game, members

[27]Sarri and Galinsky, in *Individual Change*, p. 74.

may have different tasks and the worker should try to match people to positions in constructive ways.

During the process of group formation, the worker will utilize the role structure of the group to help members become committed to the group and deal with ambivalence about the group. The worker can also use role assignments to obtain information about the problems of members. The following are a few examples of this use of role structure.

Example. In the second meeting of a parents' group, the worker suggested that the members take turns summarizing the discussion taking place. The worker did this because she thought it would help members to think about and take more responsibility for the problem-solving activity of the group.

Example. In the third meeting of a group of ten-year-old boys who had problems in following school rules, the worker introduced a game in which the group was divided into two teams. He asked a boy who had been rebellious against rules to be the scorekeeper. The worker was interested in seeing how this boy handled rules when he had some responsibility for their execution.

The worker watches to see what kinds of informal positions members enter through various transactions among themselves. Some of these will be conducive to the further development of the group while some will not. Some members will function as tension relievers through humor (group "clowns"), through compromise (group "diplomats"), or through promoting social activities ("social directors"). The group will turn to these individuals when such needs arise and the ability of some members to function in this way is beneficial to the group and should be supported by the worker.

On the other hand, some members are placed in positions that are likely to be harmful to themselves or the group. This includes scapegoats and *overactive deviants*—a term used by Bales to describe people who are verbally very active yet do not contribute positively to resolving task or social-emotional issues.[28] The worker should quickly identify the emergence of these phenomena so that their causes can be assessed and coped with.

In regard to scapegoating and deviance, the worker should try to prevent some members from becoming locked into such roles in early meetings as it is difficult to remove a deviant label once it has been affixed. It is even possible that such members will either be pushed out of the group or leave voluntarily. These issues are complex and often difficult to manage. We shall, therefore, discuss management of deviance in group situations in more detail in later chapters devoted to middle phases of the group's evolution.

In early stages, one activity of the worker with regard to such issues as scape-goating is to promote the group norm that members should take responsibility for

---

[28]Robert F. Bales, "Task Roles and Social Roles in Problem Solving Groups," in *Readings in Social Psychology,* 3rd ed., eds. Eleanor E. Maccoby, Theodore M. Newcomb, and Eugene L. Hartley (New York: Holt, Rinehart & Winston, 1958), pp. 427–46.

their actions toward each other and they should seek to help one another. This means that members should be confronted with the consequences of their behavior.

The worker should also initiate a group norm that the group will *examine* how it responds to deviant members. Each member should, in this way, take responsibility for his or her role in this process.

INDIVIDUAL AND GROUP GOALS

Research evidence is strong that clarity of goals elicits actions to achieve these goals and clarity regarding such intended actions helps to secure their enactment.[29] While this principle is sound, there are many ways that workers and members can select goals and means to achieve them.

Frequently members in early meetings are not ready to select and agree on goals stated in specific terms. In these cases, the worker should attempt to secure agreement that one of the "goals" of early interactions is to identify and agree on individual and group goals. According to Croxton, this is often "no more than agreement to try out the process."[30] This can include an agreement to attend a few meetings, explore whether goals that can be met through the group experience exist, and sample the types of activities and interactions that will occur in the group.

The group worker considers several orders of goals. This is a complex matter because both goals for individuals and goals for the group exist and must be related to each other. Individual goals are the changes that the members would like to achieve in themselves, their situations, or both, as a result of participation in the group; group goals are the changes that the group agrees to seek to achieve in its members, itself, or its environment as a result of the group activity. An example of an individual goal is a desire of a group member to act more assertively with fellow students. The same group chose the group goal that all of the members should act more assertively in their social situations. This was a group of high school students and they chose another group goal: to change school conditions that punished assertive behavior.

Our approach to group work[31] is oriented toward describing goals as specifically and as early as possible. We characterize a well-formulated goal statement as including a specific description of the behavior desired in oneself or others, the conditions under which the behavior will occur, and the criterion of successful performance. Rose gives an example of such a goal statement: "By the end of treatment, George will carry on conversation with his friends while main-

[29]Janice H. Schopler, Maeda Galinsky, and Mark Alicke, "Goals in Social Group Work Practice: Formulation, Implementation, and Evaluation," in *Individual Change Through Small Groups,* eds. Sundel, Glasser, Sarri, and Vinter (New York: Free Press, 1985), pp. 140–58.

[30]Tom A. Croxton, "The Therapeutic Contract in Social Treatment," in *Individual Change Through Small Groups,* eds. Sundel, Glasser, Sarri, and Vinter (New York: Free Press, 1985), p. 172.

[31]Robert D. Vinter, "The Essential Components of Social Work Practice," in *Individual Change Through Small Groups,* eds. Sundel, Glasser, Sarri, and Vinter (New York: Free Press, 1985), pp. 15–17.

taining eye contact with them at least 50 percent of the time.''[32] This statement meets the requirements of a goal statement as it specifies the behavior (carrying on a conversation while maintaining eye contact), the circumstances (with friends), and the criterion of successful performance (50 percent of the time).

Other group work approaches place less emphasis on specific individual goals as an outcome of the group work experience. These tend to see this goal-oriented approach as false to their view of reality that individuals continuously modify their aspirations on the basis of current experience. Adherents of that view argue that too much of a future orientation prevents the fullest and finest involvement in and acquisition of benefits from contemporary ("here-and-now") events. Some emphasis on future outcomes is necessary in any approach. Schwartz, for example, speaks of "valued outcomes" during different phases of the group's work.[33]

Our view incorporates both positions and conforms to our perception of how people cope effectively with their situations. People often seek to fulfill their wants through a choice of future goals that have been selected by thoughtful appraisal of personal and social realities. In pursuing such goals, however, a great deal may be learned about their realities and as a result these goals may need to be altered. The group work process, therefore, can operate both with a goal orientation and a withdrawal of commitment to such goals when they are determined to be inappropriate, unattainable, or no longer relevant because of the changing nature of the situation.

THE GROUP WORK CONTRACT

The idea of a group work contract draws on ethical as well as research considerations. The ethical issue is that the dimensions of the group work experience are agreed to by the group members and not imposed on them by the worker. These include goals, means of achieving goals, and actions to maintain the group such as helping other members, attending meetings, and paying fees. The research considerations relate to the finding, noted in the discussion of goals, that clarity of goals, as well as means of attaining them, enhances the effectiveness of the group experience.

Contracts in group work are of five types:

1. Between the group-as-a-whole and the agency;
2. Between the group and the worker;
3. Between a group member and the worker;
4. Between one member and another;
5. Between a member and the group.

---

[32]Rose, *Group Therapy,* p. 76.
[33]William Schwartz, "Social Group Work: The Interactionist Approach," in *Encyclopedia of Social Work* II (New York: National Association of Social Workers, 1971), 1260.

The term *contract* has been used to describe an actual written document signed by the separate parties; it has also been used to describe verbal agreements that are specific as to the terms; finally it has been used to describe agreements that are not as formalized as the former types but are acknowledged as operative by the group members and the worker.

We believe all of these contracts to be valid under different circumstances. Schwartz, for example, refers to a contract between the group-as-a-whole and the agency when he states that the worker asks both to "reach some consensus about the members' needs and the agency's stake in offering the service." He seems, however, to be addressing the group-worker contract when he writes of a "contracting phase" in which a consensus is sought on "purposes, roles, and procedures." Finally, Schwartz sees the worker monitoring the terms of the contract and asking the group and agency to "renegotiate" when this becomes necessary.[34]

Garvin and Glasser in their discussion of contract refer to an agreement between the members and the worker regarding the problems to be dealt with by each individual and the means that will be employed to attain these ends.[35] Neither Garvin and Glasser's nor Schwartz's conceptions refer to written documents and, in fact, Garvin and Glasser specifically write that "the group work contract, in contrast to the legal contract, is not a fixed document; rather it is a process with many subtle components." Modifications, therefore, can occur from session to session or "even during a given interaction."[36]

Sheldon Rose, in contrast, favors a written instrument. An example he presents includes commitments of the member regarding fees, attendance, punctuality, completion of homework assignments, attention during meetings, and participation in research. The workers commit themselves to the time of meetings, the clarification of member problems, the facilitation of members' use of resources, the provision of effective procedures, respect for confidentiality, and the refund of fees under specified circumstances.[37]

At times workers will become even more specific about aspects of the contract. These include goal statements, procedures to be used, reasons for believing in the procedures' effectiveness (for example, research studies), and potential "side effects" (possible negative effects of participation in the group).

Member-to-member contracts are often used in phases of the group that occur after formation when members attempt to attain individual goals. These contracts are commitments of members to reward other members for an activity or the completion of a task. One such procedure, for example, is for two nonverbal members to agree to reward each other with money they have put into a common pool if a specified increase in group participation takes place. This type of reinforcement can also take place with the group-as-a-whole giving a reward for the accomplishments of members.

[34]Ibid., p. 1260.
[35]Charles D. Garvin and Paul H. Glasser, "Social Group Work: The Preventive and Rehabilitative Approach," *Individual Change Through Small Groups,* eds. Sundel, Glasser, Sarri, and Vinter (New York: Free Press, 1985), p. 38.
[36]Ibid.
[37]Rose, *Group Therapy,* p. 23.

PROBLEMS IN GROUP BEGINNINGS

The preceding material may appear to suggest that beginnings of groups are easy. Actually, beginnings are always somewhat difficult because of the risks people think they are taking in entering any new enterprise. For some people, however, their mistrust of others and their fears of the unknown are so great that the worker must put forth great efforts to accomplish the tasks associated with formation.

One such situation occurs when the members are highly resistant in the beginning. This resistance can be manifested in refusal to participate verbally, in direct expressions of hostility, or in indirect expressions such as disagreeing with the purposes of the group in ways that do not appear sincere. The worker, in these circumstances, does not deny the reality of what is happening; rather the worker poses it as a problem for solution.

Above all, however, the worker does not make the mistake of thinking the group can move ahead before this kind of resistance is diminished. Workers must not convey, on the other hand, that they are paralyzed by expressions of resistance for this can communicate that "something dreadful" exists that justifies all the self-protection the members can muster. Workers use a variety of program tools to help overcome the difficulties experienced in group beginnings. These include "ice-breakers" such as games in which members have to guess "who they are" with reference to names that are pinned to the back of their clothes. Or, members interview each other in pairs and take turns introducing each other. Under some circumstances, to reinforce coming to the first meeting, workers will offer something to eat as soon as members arrive.

At times, the worker can diminish initial resistance by reducing members' anxiety. Ways of doing this include relaxation training[38] as well as introducing activities that are fun. Direct discussions of feelings can also be promoted. Finally, the relaxing way the worker handles the stresses of beginning the group is also important.

Another problem that can confront the group worker is the group that seems to remain too long in its formation phase. Such a group will continue to argue about, question, or frequently shift its goals; the same members do not attend consecutive meetings and group cohesiveness remains low. This state may be a result of agency conditions, such as those prevailing in some residential settings where persons do not remain very long. It may also be a result of group composition factors, incorrectly chosen group purposes, a truncated process of negotiating group goals, or a group norm of resistance to the agency or worker. When formation is prolonged, all of these as well as other possible contributing factors should be examined so that barriers to the further development of the group may be removed.

It is possible, also, that a group that never goes beyond formation can also be intentionally established. Some groups formed to provide a moderate amount

---

[38]Douglas A. Bernstein and Thomas D. Borkovec, *Progressive Relaxation Training: A Manual for the Helping Professions* (Champaign, Illinois: Research Press, 1973).

of support to people leaving a program fall into this category. Some very short-term groups (five sessions or less) may move quickly beyond formation if they are carefully composed and have clear yet modest objectives.

Other groups may continue with frequent additions or departures of members. Schopler and Galinsky indicate that there is a wide range of groups of this type to be found in general and psychiatric hospitals, social service departments, mental health centers, family service agencies, drug and alcohol rehabilitation centers, residential treatment facilities, nursing and maternity homes, and prisons.[39]

These groups, according to Schopler and Galinsky, meet a great variety of needs such as immediate availability of service, prompt offering and obtaining of information, and screening for other services. They state more specific purposes as follows:

> The specific purposes identified in open-ended groups can be categorized as: (1) helping clients cope with transitions and crises; (2) providing other types of short- and long-term therapy; (3) offering support to clients with common problems; (4) assessing or screening clients; (5) orienting and educating clients; (6) training and supervising staff and students; and (7) facilitating outreach efforts.[40]

Schopler and Galinsky summarize several reports regarding the impact of a new member on group development in such groups. New members appear to have the least impact during the formation stage itself since the group is still forming. During the "power and control stage" when conflict is high, a new member might heighten the conflict. Several writers agree that during a "differentiation" stage, when members are seeking to develop a greater balance between interdependence and autonomy, there may be a resentment of new members.[41] From this discussion, it can be seen that contrary to some views, such open-ended groups are not locked into perpetual formation. Intimacy and interaction do increase as members become familiar with group norms even with an ever changing membership.

A distinguishing feature of many of these groups is the focus of their work on the "present." This leads to a rapidity with which decisions are reached and attachments to the group are developed. According to Schopler and Galinsky, the group also "profits from the constant reminders of reality and the broader frame of reference offered by new members."[42] Adopting a positive view of such groups, they state:

> Every session involves preparation or "tuning in" to the particular demands of change. New members may need to be introduced or departing members may need to deal with separation; and, the work of the group must go on. Since change may be an almost constant phenomenon, the leader must help the group establish mechanisms for dealing with turnover, adapt a leadership style appropriate to the group's development, and create a supportive environment.[43]

[39]J.H. Schopler and M.J. Galinsky, "Meeting Practice Needs: Conceptualizing the Open-Ended Group," *Social Work with Groups* 7 (1984), 3–21.

[40]Ibid., p. 5.

[41]Ibid., pp. 8–9.

[42]Ibid., p. 11.

[43]Ibid., p. 12.

SUMMARY

In this chapter we reviewed the events that occur in a group during its formation phase. This includes deciding on group purposes, formulating individual and group goals, gathering information that will be necessary to achieve these purposes and goals, and determining norms. During this phase, the worker helps the member with emotional reactions to beginnings as well as with relationships among themselves and with the worker. The latter relationship is enhanced by the worker's empathy, genuineness, and nonpossessive warmth. The worker is aided in facilitating the group's development by an understanding of structures and processes as they occur when the group is forming. A contract is often developed between the worker and group as well as among the members as to expectations of each other. Problems can occur in formation that will affect group development. These were also discussed.

GROUP FORMATION EXERCISE

Goals

1. To understand group tasks during the group formation stage.

2. To identify ways of helping a group accomplish formation tasks.

3. To learn to assess the degree to which the group has accomplished group formation.

Procedure

1. Prior to the exercise, trainees read about and discuss the principles of group formation described in this chapter.

2. Five trainees are asked to volunteer to form a group which will hold a short meeting in the center of the class. An interest in a common topic is desirable (for example, how group members will apply this course to their work; finding better housing; dealing with "burn out").

3. Members of the group are centered in the front of the class and instructed to act as if they are having a first meeting of a group related to the issue selected in step 2. No group worker is present.

4. After about 10 to 15 minutes, the group discussion is suspended. The accompanying Group Formation Assessment Form is utilized to discuss how well the group is handling the tasks of formation. Ways of helping the group with formation tasks are also discussed. (Depending on time, the trainer may choose to emphasize some but not all items on the form.)

5. Another member of the class (or two members if co-workers are desired) is asked to volunteer to be a group worker to help the group in the ways suggested in step 4.

6. After 10 to 15 minutes of the group meeting with a group worker, the group stops and the class, utilizing the Group Formation Assessment Form, discusses further progress in group formation and the role of the worker in this.

GROUP FORMATION ASSESSMENT FORM

Group Purposes

1. For each member, utilize the following table to indicate the purpose the number expresses for being in the group and the degree of relationship to the stated purpose of the group.

Member's Name	Member's Purpose	Relationship to stated purpose[a]

[a]Code: A for highly related; B for moderately related; C for slightly related or not related at all.

2. Which of the following should a worker do in light of 1?

_____ Because purposes are clear and a consensus exists, move to plan activities related to purpose.

_____ Because there is dissent on purpose, renegotiate either purpose or composition.

_____ Purpose of members in relationships to group purposes are not yet clear; continue discussing purpose.

_____ Other (specify) _____

_____

Gathering Relevant Information

3 . Has the group decided on the type of information it needs to plan activities to accomplish purpose?

_____ yes   _____ no

Specify the type of information to be sought.

4. Has the group decided how it will secure this information? Specify how the group will secure this information.

5. What should a worker do to initiate or enhance the collection of information? (More than one of these activities can be listed.)

_____ Suggest the type and source of information.

_____ Instruct the group about an individual assessment procedure (behavioral analysis; transactional analysis; kinds of motivation, capacity, opportunity, and so on.).

_____ Instruct the group about an environmental assessment procedure.

_____ Other (specify) _____

Determination of Norms

6. Check which norms are relevant and rate the degree of agreement.

	Relevant		Agreement[a]
	Yes	No	
Confidentiality			
Attendance			
Honesty with each other			
Help each other			
Other (specify)			

[a] Code: A for all or most; B for some; C for few or none.

7. What should the worker do in light of step 6?

_____ Ask for discussion of norm.

_____ State his or her position on norm.

_____ Other (specify) _____

Emotional Reactions to Group Formation

8. Rate the percentage of members who are strongly experiencing the emotion and indicate how the worker might respond to this.

Emotion	Percentage Strongly Experiencing	Suggested Worker Response[a]
Attraction to group		
Fear		
Anger		
Mixed attraction to & rejection of group		
Other (specify)		

[a] Code: A for discussion of emotion; B for utilization of relaxation procedure; C for offering of self or others as models; D for other (specify).

Relationship to Group Worker

9. Which of the following characterizes the reaction of some members to the worker? Indicate how the worker should respond to this.

Reaction of Some Member to Worker	Suggestions for Worker Response
Dependency	
Anger	
Liking	
Fear	
Rejection	
No visible reaction	

Relationship Among Members

10. Have members sought for and found similarities among one another?

11. For a 5-minute interval, evaluate the pattern of member and worker communications by writing "m" each time a member speaks and "w" each time the worker speaks (for example, w m m w m m m m).

How would you characterize the member communication pattern in the group?

_____ Primarily member to member.

_____ About evenly mixed between members talking to each other and to the worker.

_____ Members talk primarily to worker.

12. How frequently are expressings of warmth or caring expressed by a member to a member?

_____ Frequently.

_____ Occasionally.

_____ Seldom.

_____ Never.

Goals

13. Have any members stated goals for themselves? (specify)

14. Has the group set any goals for itself? (specify)

Emergence of Group Structures

15. Which members seek to exert the most influence? Is that helpful or harmful to others?

16. Do members volunteer for tasks? What is the effect of this or other member roles on group development?

17. Are any members seen as deviant by other members? What is the effect on the member(s) in question?

Contract

18. What kinds of agreements have been reached on the following procedures and processes? (specify)

Attendance _____

_____

Punctuality _____

_____

Participation _____

_____

Helping each other _____

_____

Helping specific others in group _____

_____

Expectations of worker _____

_____

Expectations of agency _____

_____

5

Achieving Group Purposes Through Changes In Group Conditions

In the previous chapter, we considered how the worker interacts with individuals and the group-as-a-whole during the group's formation period. In this and the next two chapters, we shall consider how the worker assesses and works with the group, its members, and the environment during the "middle" phases of the group's life. We shall assume, therefore, that we are presenting material relevant to both a group and its members who have determined their purposes and selected their initial goals. The members have developed some attraction to each other as well as sufficient cohesiveness so that they are motivated to choose and pursue activities to attain group and individual goals. The group has also developed an initial structure and some group rules regarding procedures to be followed.

ACTIONS OF THE GROUP WORKER

Group work writers generally assert that the value of group experience, as contrasted with one-to-one helping, centers on the ways that group conditions can help members attain their goals. As we have discussed earlier, some workers seek to bring this about by specifying such benefits specifically and uniquely for each individual. Others seek the creation of a group which, by virtue of circumstances such as norms of honesty, broad participation, and democratic decision making, is assumed to be beneficial to members.

In any case, the worker will interact with individual members, several members, the entire group, and people and institutions outside the group in order to help create desired group conditions. All of these entities interact and affect one another. A worker, consequently, to achieve changes in the group-as-a-whole, may initiate this change process through transactions with any one or more of these four components, and, in fact, different workers may achieve the same needs with different approaches. Whether one of these types of transactions is more appropriate or effective than the others has not been established. The "practice wisdom" is undoubtedly that it depends on the circumstances. The group worker must be able, therefore, to employ skills relevant to interacting with members, subgroups, groups, and group environments. In any group the worker is likely to do all of these. Sometimes this is a planned sequence such as in the following example.

Example. The group worker sought a volunteer from the group to describe a problem she was having in social relationships. Agnes volunteered and the worker asked her to describe an example (*interaction with an individual*).

Agnes later agreed to role play a family situation about which she was concerned. The worker and Agnes secured several volunteers to role play Agnes's family and she helped them to set up the role play (*interaction with a subgroup*).

After the role play, the worker asked the group to give feedback to Agnes on her handling of the situation (*interaction with the entire group*).

The worker, at Agnes's request, agreed to interview her husband to help him to deal with his concerns about her participation in the group (*interaction with person outside the group on behalf of a group member*).

At other times, the worker interacts first with one of the various systems related to a member's concern and then makes decisions about subsequent interactions based on the flow of events. This is seen in the next illustration.

Example. The worker discussed with the boys in the group home the destructive events that took place on "Devil's Night." Several of the boys had thrown an egg at an elderly man on the street near the home (*interaction with entire group*). Jim denied any part in the affair although the other boys said he had been with them. The worker, at one point in the discussion, asked Jim what his feelings would be if his participation in something like this were known (*interaction with individual*). Jim said that Bill always tried to put him on the spot and the worker encouraged Jim and Bill to discuss this (*interaction with subgroup*). The worker also told the group about his discussion with the man who had been assaulted when he had come to the home to complain (*interaction with person outside the group*).

The worker is aware that talking with one or several members in the group will have an effect on the other members. This effect can be on their own problem solving as well as on their interactions with each other. During a group meeting, in a sense, it is impossible to interact with only some members. Nevertheless, the worker may, at times, have a compelling reason to single out a member. The effect on other members may or may not be a major consideration.

At other times, when the worker speaks to some members, he or she may desire an effect on other members. Still again, when effects on other members are anticipated and are undesirable, the worker will refrain from individual attention. Similarly, when workers intervene in processes of the group-as-a-whole, they must consider how the process affects each individual member. Sometimes this is predictable. At other times, the effects of group processes on members is not known until they have occurred. The worker must quickly decide what to do next in view of such effects. An example of this occurred when a worker with a group of youngsters in a residential treatment center participated in a discussion of feelings about holidays. He did not realize that two of the members had been very depressed a few weeks previously on Thanksgiving because their parents had not visited them. When the discussion began, these two members became emotionally withdrawn. The worker asked them about this behavior and learned about their parents. The worker expressed his understanding of their feelings, thus shifting his attention from the group-as-a-whole to the individual members.

As the preceding shows, it is impossible to affect one level of the individual-group-environment set without affecting all levels. Workers, nevertheless, frequently focus their attention on one level or another. Even though in practice the worker recognizes the interrelatedness of such parts, we shall consider separately in this and the following two chapters how the worker might use one or another system when the target is the group, or the individual, or the environment. In this chapter, we shall focus on the group.

This way of approaching the activities of the worker is similar to that of Pincus and Minahan who distinguish between action and target systems.[1] *Action systems* are those with which the worker directly interacts; *target systems* are those that are to be changed as a result of these interactions. These two systems can, of course, coincide, such as when the worker helps the group (*action system*) change its methods of problem solving (*target system*). These two systems can be different, as when the worker helps the group (*action system*) plan a strategy for changing an agency rule (*target system*).

When the target system is the group, the worker should involve the members in deciding what aspects of the group need to be changed and how this should be brought about. We believe that the following is a logical way of dealing with this situation:

1. Help the group to identify a problem in its functioning. This can often be accomplished by asking members whether they think there is something standing in the way of the group accomplishing its purposes.
2. Help the group to assess which group conditions serve to maintain the group problem. A typology of group conditions will be presented shortly.
3. Help the group to measure the group condition using some of the approaches described throughout this book, and in Chapter 8, in particular.

[1]Allen Pincus and Anne Minahan, *Social Work Practice: Model and Method* (Itasca, Illinois: F. E. Peacock, 1973).

4. Help the group to choose a way of modifying the group condition. The first decision to be made is whether the action system used to promote this change will be a member, a subgroup, the group-as-a-whole, or some person or system outside of the group. The second decision involves the specific strategy to be utilized with the action system and will be described throughout this chapter. We shall then summarize this material with a table in which we suggest linkages between the group-level problem and the choice of action system and strategy to ameliorate it.

5. Help the group to evaluate the effectiveness of the approach it has chosen to modify a group condition. This can be done by using the measure selected at step 3.

6. If the outcome is less than satisfactory, help the group to return to (4) and seek to change group conditions by using another approach.

ASSESSMENT OF GROUP CONDITIONS

The worker will continuously assess the conditions that exist in the group and will seek to help the members modify the conditions that impede the attainment of individual and group goals. By *group conditions,* we mean some phenomenon that is characteristic of the group, either a way that the members are acting, thinking, or feeling or a situation that is present in the particular group.

Admittedly, this assessment is a complex task and beginning group workers can feel overwhelmed by a discussion of group conditions. Eventually they will understand these conditions so well that they will be able to identify and focus on them quickly. Our classification of group conditions follows:

1. Stage of group development
2. Group structure
3. Group process
4. Group culture
5. Group resources
6. Extragroup transactions
7. Group boundaries
8. Group climate

We shall now describe each of these conditions more fully so that the reader may identify them when working with a group. We shall then identify ways in which the worker can help the members have an impact on conditions present in their group.

Middle Phases of Group Development

In the preceding chapter, we described the formation phase of group development. At this point we shall focus on "middle" phases. Most authorities agree that during this period group members' energies are invested in initiating and carrying out activities related to their purposes.[2] While doing this, members develop new or more complex structures related to leadership and group tasks. They also develop processes for goal attainment such as how to approach problem solving, how to deal with differences of opinion, and how to respond to members who represent a minority on issues. By this time groups have also developed some spoken or unspoken rules (norms) regarding such behaviors as attendance at and behavior during meetings.

After an initial period of considerable agreement, however, groups usually enter into a period of conflict. Garland, Jones, and Kolodny refer to this as a "power and control" phase while Sarri and Galinsky term it a "revision" phase.[3] At this time, leadership (either indigenous or that of the worker) is challenged and goals and activities are questioned. This is due to the larger number of members who now feel free to express their sentiments as well as a reaction against the initial leadership often held by the more aggressive individuals. Early experiences with pursuing goals may also produce new information or disclose unknown barriers that require new procedures, leadership, and so forth.

During this phase the worker must be supportive when cohesiveness declines because of conflict in the group creating anxiety for the members. It is hoped that the worker and the members will be able to resolve conflicts in such a way as to lead to leadership patterns and reformulated goals to which members are even more committed than before. The experience of resolving conflicts can also lead to a feeling of closeness among members as well as a conviction that conflicts can be constructively coped with in the group.

After "revision" phases, the group resumes its activities with even more cohesiveness, commitment to goals, and appropriateness of structure. The members, however, with increased feelings of closeness to each other may stress their commonalities rather than their differences. This can lead to a degree of dependency that is not as conducive to pursuing individual goals as might be desirable. The worker should then support efforts of members to stress their individuality as well as commonality, thus creating a phase referred to by Garland and his colleagues as "differentiation."[4] In this phase, members reinforce each other's uniqueness.

During these middle phase processes, the worker examines specific group conditions to determine if they enhance or hinder goal-directed activities. We shall turn, therefore, to a closer description of such group conditions as they emerge in the group's middle phases.

[2]Our discussion of group development draws upon such authors as Rosemary C. Sarri and Maeda Galinsky, "A Conceptual Framework for Group Development," in *Individual Change Through Small Groups,* eds. Martin Sundel, Paul Glasser, Rosemary Sarri, and Robert Vinter (New York: Free Press, 1985), pp. 70–86; James A. Garland, Hubert E. Jones, and Ralph Kolodny, "A Model for Stages of Development in Social Work Groups," in *Explorations in Group Work,* ed. Saul Bernstein (Boston: Boston University School of Social Work, 1965), p. 113; and Irvin D. Yalom, *The Theory and Practice of Group Psychotherapy,* 2nd ed. (New York: Basic Books, 1975), pp. 301–75.

[3]Garland, Jones, and Kolodny, in *Explorations in Group Work,* pp. 30–34; Sarri and Galinsky, in *Individual Change,* p. 76.

[4]Garland, Jones, and Kolodny, in *Explorations in Group Work,* pp. 37–41.

Group Structures

In the previous chapter, concepts frequently used to characterize group structures were defined and illustrated for the period of group formation. In this chapter we shall use the same concepts to describe group conditions that occur during middle phases.

Communications Structure. During the formation period, members tend to direct many of their remarks to the worker. By the middle phases, the members have developed more familiarity with each other and they should have developed a commitment to helping one another. For these reasons, communication among members increases and between members and the worker decreases. Patterns of communication emerge that are characteristic of the way members communicate in their life situations; and these may also have contributed to the problems that led to their seeking group services.

These patterns include dominating discussion, talking primarily to the worker, or withdrawing from interaction. Such patterns may vary with the content of the discussion; some members will only talk about certain topics to selected other members. This can relate to a desire to secure reinforcement for behavior, a perceived similarity of the other member to a significant figure in one's history, or a wish to evoke a particular emotional response. Members may be willing to participate in discussions on some topics but not others. The worker should try to identify communication issues such as these. Depending on the relationship of the members' communication patterns to the members' problems, the worker will seek to change such patterns. Ways to do this will be described later in this chapter.

Sociometric Structure. The worker should assess the nature of the subgroups formed in the group. This can be done by observing who chooses to interact with whom, who comes or leaves meetings with whom, and the expressions of caring and affection exchanged among members. The sociometric questionnaire is not a device generally used by the worker to ask members about feelings of closeness within the group. Such questionnaires are experienced by members as very threatening, and fear of being excluded or rejected can cause anxieties. A sociometric analysis can usually be achieved through observation.

Some of the problems in middle phases of groups that are illuminated through sociometric analysis include the existence of dyads in which members reinforce each other's problematic behaviors, subgroups that compete with each other in destructive ways for control of the group, isolate members who may become scapegoats, and intermember conflicts that reduce the overall cohesiveness of the group.

Power Structure. In the middle phases of the group, various members often seek to have more influence on group decisions and processes than they possessed in the beginning. This can be desirable if members use this influence to make the group responsive to them and also to help one another. At times, this is not the case and members challenge the authority of the worker in destructive ways or seek to manipulate other members in directions that do not correspond to such members' goals. These actions may represent the types of uses of power outside of the group that have created the problems for which the members seek help.

Other kinds of power issues are: members' attempts to coerce others into deviant activity; worker's inability to limit behavior that is destructive to individuals or even the whole group; outsiders' (teacher, parents, spouse) use of power over the group members in a negative way.

Therefore, the worker analyzes the sources of power (stemming from expertise, control over resources, ability to punish, functioning as a role model) possessed by the worker, the members, and the people outside the group. The ways power must be used to help accomplish individual and group tasks is determined. When detrimental uses of power exist, the worker must seek to change this.

Role Structure. A role consideration during middle phases of the group is whether the members possess the skills to carry out their responsibilities during this period. If there is a formal leadership structure, members may not be able to perform leadership functions because of behavioral deficits related to leadership. In any group when problem solving occurs, members should be able to give and ask for information and suggestions. If not, then the worker have to train members in such skills.

In later phases of the group, also, members might become locked into roles that are dysfunctional for them. The "clown" may wish to behave more seriously, the "mediator" to take sides, and passive people to function assertively. The worker, being cognizant of roles that are created out of group interactions, will attend to those that impede either the attainment of individual goals or the creation of an effective group. In any case, the middle phase of the group should provide many opportunities for members to experiment with new roles and to consider employing these outside of the group in their natural systems.

Group Processes

As commonly defined, "process" is a continuous action, operation, or series of changes taking place in a definite manner. A group continuously changes over a period of time and the nature of these changes constitutes *group process.*[5] Group process is a more difficult concept to operationalize than group structure, perhaps because it is easier to think about a phenomenon as if it were unchanging. Also, group workers have often thought of process as one or another single aspect of the range of variables that change in groups. When Yalom defines process as the

---

[5]For an extended discussion of group process, see Charles D. Garvin, "Group Process: Usage and Uses in Social Work Practice," in *Individual Change Through Small Groups,* 2nd ed., eds. Martin Sundel, Paul Glasser, Rosemary Sarri, and Robert Vinter (New York: Free Press, 1985), pp. 203–25.

"relationship implications of interpersonal transactions" (a very important *aspect* of process), he is discussing a process component, but not the only one.[6]

For this reason, in another discussion, we defined process as "changes that take place in group conditions."[7] Again, as with group structure, we must recognize that changes are in *the group as an entity* and that their subdivision is only for analytical purposes. In fact, there are many valid ways for workers and members to examine their group's *process:* one important way is to consider some dimension of process, such as stages of problem solving. Another is to examine the specific sequence of events in a group session in order to investigate some pattern, causal event, or consequence of the sequence.

We have conceptualized a classification of dimensions of group process that we believe incorporates all of the sequences of events that might occur in the group. As shown in Table 5-1, these dimensions are the (1) goal oriented *activities* of the group, and the (2) quality of the *interactions* among the members. The former largely corresponds to the goal attainment and the latter to the group maintenance functions referred to in the small group literature.[8]

We have further subdivided these two dimensions of process into those that occur at the *overt* levels and those that occur at the *covert* levels. Overt refers to those events that are observable, as in the actions and communications of group members. Covert refers to the feelings and thoughts of members as these are reported by them and as these relate to activities and interactions.

Our definitions of these dimensions of group process follows. Goal determination (1) consists of all of the actions of members as they seek to determine group goals. Goal pursuit (2) consists of everything members do to attain these goals. The covert goal oriented activity is the evolution of agreed upon values (3) related to the group's goals and the ways the group acts to attain them.

Role differentiation (4) refers to the evolution of the group's role structure. Such a structure consists of the perceptions and expectations of members regarding how each will behave because of his or her position in the group.

TABLE 5-1   Aspects of Group Process

	Goal-Oriented Activities	*Quality of Interactions*
OVERT	1. Goal determination 2. Goal pursuit	4. Role differentiation 5. Communication–interaction 6. Conflict resolution and behavior control
COVERT	3. Values and norms	7. Emotions

[6]Irving D. Yalom, *The Theory and Practice of Group Psychotherapy*, 2nd ed. (New York: Basic Books, 1975), p. 122.

[7]Garvin, "Group Process," p. 203.

[8]Robert F. Bales, "Task Roles and Social-Emotional Roles in Problem-Solving Groups," in *Readings in Social Psychology*, 3rd ed., eds. E.E. Maccoby, T.M. Newcomb, and E.T. Hartley (New York: Holt, Rinehart and Winston, 1958), pp. 437–47.

Communication–interaction (5) refers to the messages members send to one another as they define and enact their roles. Conflict resolution–behavior control (6) refers to the interactions that occur among members as they seek to perpetuate the group through controlling tension-inducing behavior. The covert interaction oriented activity is that of emotions (7) including caring as well as hostile affects that members experience toward one another.

Because it is highly important for workers to be able to identify the dimensions of group process that may be causing problems to members, we shall describe each dimension in more detail. In a later portion of the chapter, we shall describe ways that workers and members may work together to modify such problematic situations.

1. Goal determination. This dimension of process occurs as members interact to determine the desired end-state to be achieved by the group. This interaction often takes place in stages related to short- and long-range goals. Thus a long-range group goal of helping members to develop social skills might be coupled with short-range goals of learning how to approach others, carry on conversations, and act assertively.

An example of the process of goal determination is a discussion of the kinds of personal difficulties to be worked on in the group. This discussion included whether the group would seek to change some aspects of the members' environments or how the members were able to cope with those environments.

2. Goal pursuit. McGrath has generated a comprehensive typology of the kinds of activities in which groups can engage in order to attain their goals.[9] His presentation is very useful in that it summarizes all of the major research efforts related to each type of activity. We believe that it would be a very useful intellectual effort for a group work theoretician to develop practice principles derived from McGrath's work. This cannot be done within the limits of this book, but we believe it will be valuable for practitioners to consider the following list of the activities identified by McGrath when they help groups to choose ways to pursue goals.

McGrath indicates four types of activities that he calls *tasks.* Each task is subdivided into two sub-tasks.[10]

Generating tasks

Planning Tasks: Generating plans as to how the group will undertake some activity.
Creativity Tasks: Generating ideas as in "brainstorming."

Choosing Tasks

Intellective Tasks: Solving problems in which there exists an answer whose "correctness" will be clearly evident.

[9]Joseph E. McGrath, *Groups: Interaction and Performance* (Englewood Cliffs, N.J.: Prentice-Hall, 1984).
[10]Ibid., p. 62.

Decision-Making Tasks: Solving problems about which some ambiguity exists as to how members will agree upon the "correctness" of the answer.

Negotiating Tasks

Cognitive-Conflict Tasks: Resolving conflicts of viewpoints, that is, members do not agree as to how the issue to be resolved is to be understood or evaluated.

Mixed-Motive Tasks: Members have a conflict of interests, that is, gains may be made by some members at the expense of others.

Executing Tasks

Contests/Battles: Activities in which members are pitted against one another as in competitive sports.

Performances: Psychomotor tasks performed against objective or absolute standards of excellence such as in executing a painting or a dance step.

In traditional group work terminology, the activities undertaken by the group to achieve its goals are termed *programs.* Analytic methods for planning and assessing programs have not been extensively dealt with, however, in the group work literature. An important contribution to this need is the work of Vinter.[11] We shall discuss his work later in this chapter, as well as a range of ways in which program (task) is used in group work to modify group conditions.

A type of task, referred to in McGrath's typology as "choosing," is often referred to by group workers simply as *problem-solving.*[12] We shall discuss this process in more detail at a later point in this chapter.

The goal pursuit dimension of process usually involves several of the types of tasks defined by McGrath. For example, a group session began in a prison with members discussing how, when seeking employment, they could overcome the stigma of having been in jail. Several members indicated they wished, instead, to discuss a complaint they had against a guard. Several minutes were spent determining which issue would be discussed that day (negotiating task, probably a mixed-motive type). The majority was in favor of discussing the employment-related topic and this was the one they pursued.

This discussion began with sharing information about actual job-seeking experiences. Questions were raised as to the availability of jobs and the resources to help ex-offenders. Several members were able to supply enough information to satisfy the others (intellective task). Several suggestions were made for ways to find jobs. These were evaluated and members helped each other to determine which suggestions to implement (decision-making task).

During this discussion, it was evident that the men were apprehensive about talking with potential employers. A script was created (creativity task) from some of the ideas offered during the discussion. Various members used the script to role

[11]Robert D. Vinter, "Program Activities: An Analysis of Their Effects on Participant Behavior," in *Individual Change Through Small Groups,* eds. Martin Sundel, Paul Glasser, Rosemary Sarri, and Robert Vinter (New York: Free Press, 1985), pp. 226–36.

[12]For a presentation of the extensive research on problem-solving, see Harold H. Kelley and John W. Thibaut, "Group Problem Solving," in *The Handbook of Social Psychology,* 2nd ed. (Reading, Mass.: Addison-Wesley, 1969), Vol. IV, eds. Gardner Lindzey and Elliot Aronson, pp. 1–101.

play both the applicants and the employers (performance task). After each role play, members gave feedback to each other regarding how each had handled the "interview"; they also gave suggestions to each other as to how to improve their interviewing behavior.

3. Values and norms. In the preceding chapter, we described the norms that the worker helps the group to develop in order to attain goals within the value framework accepted by most group workers. Group norms, however, continue to develop and change throughout the life of the group. We discuss norms as the covert level of the activity dimension of group process because they strongly influence the members' choice of goals as well as how they will be pursued. Admittedly, norms influence interactions, but this ultimately refers back to which interactions are required for the group to accomplish its purposes.

The kinds of norms that the group members focus upon are related to the developmental phase of the group. During the revision phase, when conflict is often heightened, social control mechanisms are developed further and deviation from norms are more pronounced. Pressures toward uniformity and consensus are clearly apparent.

In the revision phase, the group's norms may also change. The revision stage is likely to be ending when the group develops a stronger consensus regarding its norms as well as sanctions related to them. In later phases of group life, norms become even more clearly enunciated and deviation will certainly be noted.

4. Role Differentiation. This dimension of process involves a change from (1) an undifferentiated condition to one in which roles are clearly defined or (2) a change in the group from the presence of one set of roles to the presence of another. The latter occurs when a group undertakes a new project that requires interactions that were not needed previously.

Role differentiation also becomes more elaborate as the group develops. In the formation stage, for example, leadership roles are often unclear, shifting, and likely to be assumed by the more aggressive members. During the revision phase, the leadership of these individuals is likely to be challenged. In later stages, the identity of members who most frequently play task and social-emotional leadership roles is much clearer and more likely to be accepted.

In group treatment situations, members go through a role differentiation process when they clarify and assume the role of "client"; and when they demonstrate helping behaviors toward each other, the group becomes a mutual-aid system. This process also is evident as workers help members assume roles in activities to further the members' attainment of their treatment goals.

5. Communication-interaction. This process dimension refers to communications among members with regard to existing or emerging differentiation of roles. It fulfills the function of helping members coordinate their roles with each other. We referred earlier to a communications structure of "who speaks to whom about what." The process dimension involves how the pattern of communication evolves and shifts as both the group and its members develop.

During group formation, the communication-interaction process occurs as members seek out their commonalities. In the next stages, members communicate with each other in ways that are necessary for them to develop and carry out their tasks. When conflicts arise, members are likely to interact intensively and frequently in order to reduce the related stress.

Maintenance of the group requires that members test out how far they can trust each other before sharing sensitive information. In this process, members will express emotions regarding role assignments and will react to each other's emotional expression. This may include expressions of fear or anger regarding the role of the worker, as well as of other members.

Some examples of communication-interaction are: questions addressed to workers to determine their expertise, attitudes, and expectations; questions members direct to other members about expectations they hold for each other; and statements members make about how they hope other members will be of help to them. We shall discuss in the next chapter devoted to individual change a type of intervention into communication process called *process commentary.* This intervention can have major effects upon the way all group members communicate with one another as well as upon the competence of each individual to interact with others.

6. Conflict resolution and behavior control. Some of the processes that relate to this dimension are: (1) struggles for power among members, (2) struggles for power between members and the group worker, and (3) efforts to control behavior that deviates from group norms. None of these events are intrinsically good or bad and the worker's judgments regarding them will depend on the purposes and goals of the group. For example, some power struggles can occur between those members who are committed to the goals of the group and those who are not.

At other times, power conflicts may be provoked by some members who have problems in finding a role in the group. In a group of adolescents, for example, an influential member supported the goal of "making it" in school. Another member sought the recognition of others in the group and thought the only way he could do this was to rebel against the idea that it is desirable to secure additional education. The worker undertook to help the members understand this process so that they could choose alternative means of gaining status that were consistent with the group's purpose to support educational attainment.

When the behavior control process is directed at a member who is violating a norm, several stages are often observed. Members are likely to first draw attention to the deviant behavior after which they will increase their communications to that person. If the deviant behavior does not cease, the members will gradually withdraw their attention from the deviant individual and may then seek to avoid or even to eject him or her from the group. In view of the group and individual goals in the specific situation, the worker may support either the group or the individual but in most cases will prohibit expelling the individual. Workers will strive to limit any excessive sanction imposed by the group. Groups can become punitive in the pursuit of their legitimate ends and, in this way, defeat them (the proverbial means-ends question).

7. Emotions. This aspect of process refers to changes in the positive and negative feelings members have about each other as well as the group. Members, as we indicated in the previous chapter, will usually enter the group with mixed feelings about the group and with few feelings about other members except those they might have known. There can be an immediate emotional reaction to others in the group if members see others as similar to people who are not in the group. In therapy group situations, workers will often help members to state their first impressions as a way of helping them to recognize the ways they distort the "here and now."

During the revision phase of the group, members will tend to polarize their feelings as they show support for those with whom they agree and act negatively toward those with whom they are in conflict. A resolution of the conflict, typical of this phase, will often lead to warm feelings toward those for whom members previously felt hostility.

Some of the emotions members experience may have erotic overtones and the worker can help the members to feel safe with these, whether directed at the worker or at other members. As sexuality is an inevitable part of life, so it is of group experience.

Group Culture

The group's culture consists of the ways members believe they should behave, think, or feel. These views sometimes stem from the group members' ethnic, religious, or other cultural backgrounds. When we find a group beginning a meeting, for example, with a prayer or other ritual, this is frequently because the members are accustomed to doing this in other groups to which they belong. The worker is well advised, therefore, to learn as much as possible about the members' cultural backgrounds.

In addition, groups will develop rituals that grow out of the group experience, particularly if they become cohesive. In a similar vein, members may come to hold common views about their social realities. This phenomenon will further add to the attraction members feel toward their group.

In social work groups, shared views may be problematic; for example, members may believe in the superiority of certain social classes, or races, or of one sex over another. They may hold the view that it is not possible to succeed in life, or they may reinforce in each other dysfunctional attributions about the causes of their problems. On the other hand, such shared attributions may enhance the achievement of the members' goals; for example, members may come to accept the value of analyzing the antecedents and consequences of their behaviors or they may adopt the view that all human beings are potent and capable of modifying their destinies.

Whitaker and Lieberman[13] have developed a model of group therapy based upon the way members evolve a view of group conditions in similar ways. These authors conceptualize group events as embodying a *group focal conflict* between a wish that they term a *disturbing motive* and an associated fear that they term a *reactive motive*. These wishes and fears come to be held by many or most of the members as they associate with and influence each other's views.

An example of a focal group conflict occurred in a group of adolescent girls who *wished* to discuss some of their questions about sexual behavior (disturbing motive). They feared that this discussion would cause them to be rejected by the worker (reactive motive). The conflict between this wish and this fear led the girls to attack the worker "before she can attack us." This behavior is a "solution" to the conflict that will not help the girls to reach their goal. The worker, therefore, sought to help them to understand their views, how they emerged, and the consequences of holding such views. This process resulted in the girls being able to satisfy their wishes for a meaningful discussion.

Group Resources

To exist, groups require many types of resources. One that often comes to mind is the physical setting for the group, such as the type of room (or outdoor space), the size of the room, and the existing equipment and furniture as well as those that are potentially available to the group. Program supplies such as sports, craft, music, or other equipment are needed resources, too. Since group members may wish to serve refreshments, these are resources that are sometimes required. Other supplies may be sought for use as rewards in a behavioral reinforcement program.

In addition to material resources, members may require human ones such as experts who bring knowledge or skill not possessed by the group worker. These may be speakers on health issues, teachers of program skills, group process observers, or individuals who have the power to bring about environmental changes sought by the members.

Many events within the group are dictated by the presence or absence of resources and must be assessed by the worker in terms of the purposes of the group. Some groups cannot attain their goals at all if a particular resource is not supplied, but this is a rare event. A very positive consequence is often the result when the members, with the help of the worker, struggle successfully (or even unsuccessfully) to secure a resource. The lesson learned in the former case relates to resourcefulness in the face of scarcity. The lesson in the latter one is how to survive without a needed resource—something that is a frequent challenge to the people served by group workers.

---

[13] Dorothy S. Whitaker and Morton A. Lieberman, *Psychotherapy Through the Group Process* (New York: Lieber-Atherton, Inc., 1964).

Extragroup Transactions

Groups served by group workers do not exist in isolation but may interact with other groups in the agency, the agency as an entity, and with groups and institutions outside of the agency as well as the families of the members. These interactions include the following types of activities:

> The group has a joint event with another system.
>
> The group asks for support from another system.
>
> Another system makes a demand or request of the group for resources, support, or compliance.
>
> The group (or its representative) cooperates with other systems to attain mutual benefits.
>
> Members receive treatment from other systems in addition to the group and these systems interact with one or more members of the group.

The worker will seek to assess these transactions in order to evaluate their impact on the group. The worker, as we shall describe in this chapter and the succeeding ones that discuss environmental change, will mediate between the group and other systems, will advocate for the group, or will help the group members to become more competent in dealing with the environment.

Group Boundaries

The group members frequently have to make or respond to decisions about the addition and deletion of members. These decisions may be made by the group-as-a-whole, by individual members, by the worker, or by the agency. This issue of who is in the group or not is defined as one of boundaries. At times the boundary of the group can be a rigid one in which members take every step they can to prevent an old member from leaving or a new one from joining. At other times, the boundary may be a very loose one in which it is difficult to tell who is a member and who is not, and little attention is paid to this issue.

The kinds of issues that arise in groups around boundaries are illustrated by the following questions: Should a person who has missed a number of meetings, or violated an important group norm, or resigned be considered a member? Can people join the group for a short period? Does a person become a member immediately or is there a probationary period at first?

The worker seeks to understand the way the group members define boundaries by observing their reactions when individuals enter or leave the group, miss meetings, or express a desire to join the group. The very act of asking members questions about these events will have an impact upon the group's boundaries. In any case, the nature of the group's boundaries should be examined in the light of the group's purposes. If strong cohesiveness is desired, for example, clear boundaries are usually important. On the other hand, the open-ended groups we described earlier required a much looser set of group boundaries.

Group Climate

It is frequently possible to identify the emotional climate that is present in a group at a specified time. The members may appear happy, energetic, depressed, apathetic, or subdued—to cite a few of the emotions one may find. It is also possible to find different subgroups within the group displaying different emotions.

The fact that several or all of the members exhibit the same emotion may be due to the fact that they are reacting to a common event or to the fact that the emotions experienced by some members are "causing" those of others as a type of "contagion." These emotions can have strong effects on how the group accomplishes its purposes. The worker will seek to assess these emotional states by making observations of members' non-verbal expressions or by asking members directly about their feelings. A "projective" approach can be used by asking members to associate colors or adjectives to the group. In ways that we shall discuss later in this chapter, the worker will seek to have an impact on the emotional character of the group.

THE MODIFICATION OF GROUP CONDITIONS

The preceding discussion presents the way we assess group conditions. We shall now turn to the ways group workers *act* so as to influence or to facilitate the members' efforts to change such group conditions.

One way we categorize ways of changing group conditions is related to the type of action system utilized. The worker can influence group conditions, by interacting with (1) one member (in front of others or privately), (2) several members, (3) the entire group, or (4) people outside the group. Needless to say, this decision can be and is often made as a result of group discussion. We shall describe various approaches used to modify group conditions. Then we shall relate these approaches to the group conditions listed previously.

Modifying Group Conditions through Individuals

One way of influencing the group is for the worker to interact with one member of the group. Single members can have significant affects on group conditions when they (1) have tasks to perform for the group, (2) when they have considerable power in the group, or (3) when they fulfill critical functions in the group.

Some examples of the first category, *tasks to perform,* are: members who arrange for group activities, secure resources for the group (information, equipment), or fulfill roles such as observer, chairperson, secretary, or referee. The allocation of the tasks constitutes part of the structure of the group. The worker usually is active in decisions as to who will fulfill these roles. The worker, when necessary, will facilitate the way the members perform in these roles, thus contributing to the process of goal attainment.

One of the ways the worker facilitates role performance is by "coaching" the member. This term is analogous to coaching in athletics: the worker gives support to such members as well as feedback on their effectiveness and "tips" on how to do the job.

The worker may use behavior modification techniques to help members with their roles, such as offering to tell or to show the member how to perform the role (modeling); the worker can also reinforce the member for his or her actions. Members may be anxious about the way they are carrying out group responsibilities and the worker can help the members to reduce some of their tension through relaxation techniques.[14]

In the second circumstance, when the member fulfills a leadership function for the group (for example, chairperson or committee member), in addition to the preceding techniques, the worker can also provide leadership training. This consists of sessions with some or all of the members on such leadership skills as moderating a discussion or facilitating participation.[15]

At times the worker interacts with a member in relationship to the power structure of the group. This occurs most often when there is an imbalance of power that hinders the effective functioning of the group. For example, some members may dominate group decision making and exclude others from this process. The worker can involve the entire group in an examination of this problem but may interact instead with the individuals concerned. These individuals may be ones who are powerless and whom the worker seeks to empower by assertiveness training or by appointing them to roles that carry power in the group.

At other times, the worker helps more powerful individuals to relinquish power or to use it sparingly in the interests of other members as well as the quality of relationships among all members. This can be done by helping to develop values of concern of one member for another as well as helping them to see the way that domination of others can be destructive to themselves.

The third circumstance, when workers interact with individuals to modify group conditions, is when the individual's behavior has the function of maintaining problematic group structures or processes. Such circumstances are maintained *both* by the behavior of the individual concerned and by the responses of other group members. A good example of this is a scapegoating process. This occurs, according to Northen, when the members "turn their aggressions on to one who becomes a symbol of some tendency or characteristic they dislike in themselves and on whom they project their hostility, thus protecting themselves from recognition of their own unacceptable tendencies and freeing themselves from guilty feelings."[16]

---

[14]Douglas A. Bernstein and Thomas D. Borkovec, *Progressive Relaxation Training: A Manual for the Helping Professions* (Champaign, Ill.: Research Press, 1973).

[15]Harvey Bertcher, *Group Participation Techniques for Leaders and Members* (Beverly Hills, Calif.: Sage Publications, Inc., 1979).

[16]Helen Northen, *Social Work With Groups* (New York: Columbia University Press, 1969), pp. 165–66.

The worker responds to scapegoating situations by calling the member's attention to his or her own behavior and also the other group members' attention to the reasons for their response to it. Both "parties" should examine their contribution to the maintenance of a scapegoating situation. Shulman warns the worker against "preempting" this encounter between member and group as both attempt to cope with the scapegoating process.[17] The worker can do this by too rapid a defense of the scapegoat or condemnation of the other members. As the worker helps the group members to take common responsibility for a scapegoating process, they may each then be supported in finding ways to behave differently.

Sometimes scapegoating is a dysfunctional response to a stress from outside the group, such as stigma placed on group membership. The worker will then help members to redirect their efforts so as to cope directly with these sources of tension.

Modifying Group Conditions through Subgroups

Group conditions are also changed by the worker's interactions with subgroups. The following are some examples of occasions when attention to a subgroup is an appropriate way of changing a group condition.

A subgroup may form and sabotage the whole group. The subgroup can do this by opposing group purposes or activities or by rebelling against the actions of the worker. The underlying cause of this process often is that the subgroup members seek a "place in the group" and recognition of their uniqueness and they cannot find this through acceptable behavior. This happens when relevant roles have been preempted by other members. Members of such a subgroup also want an opportunity to influence the group and they may even experience the worker as undercutting this.

Based on the worker's assessment of such issues as these, he or she can discuss legitimate desires for influence on the group with the subgroup members concerned. The worker can also act to create useful roles for members of such subgroups by helping them to accomplish tasks for the group, thus attaining more influence in the group. Instead of responding to a tendency to "fight back," the worker looks for ways to "connect" with dissident subgroups and to demonstrate a concern for their wants.

Subgroups can be helped to take responsibility for planning activities for the whole group, can gather information for the group, and can provide feedback to the group through observing other subgroups in a "fishbowl" format.

Members of a subgroup may be motivated to help the group as a unit to change in ways that are desirable, which for one reason or another, the group as

---

[17]Lawrence Shulman, "Scapegoats, Group Workers, and Preemptive Intervention," *Social Work* XII, no. 2 (1967), 37–43.

a unit is unable or unwilling to accomplish. The idea of using a subsystem to change a larger system of which it is part (and vice-versa) is an important one in group work practice.

Modifying Group Conditions through the Whole Group

Workers can interact with the group-as-a-whole to help members change group conditions by seeking to have an impact on the members' attributions, behaviors, tasks and activities, norms, ways of problem solving, and emotions. We shall discuss each of these in turn.

Altering Member Attributions. The group members can become aware of group conditions that exist and plan a different way of structuring the group, engaging in a process, and so forth. This can occur when workers help members to examine group conditions and make a decision to change them. This usually occurs when members develop a new picture of the group by gathering data about some aspect of their group's operation. We shall discuss this type of data collection in Chapter 8. In addition to the types of quantitative measures to be discussed in Chapter 8, members can be taught a conceptual framework to aid them in understanding group phenomena. For example, Bion's concepts of basic assumption groups can be taught to members.[18] Another example of such a framework is transactional analysis.[19]

A device that has been used to motivate members to examine their attributions is to assign the group the responsibility of making important decisions affecting the members, such as granting "passes" to leave the residential institution, of which the group is a part.[20] Poor decisions can be rejected by staff or administration. The group is expected, however, to examine the processes that led to its decisions.

Modifying Members' Behavior. In the preceding section, we noted that group conditions can sometimes be changed through modifying one member's behavior. It is also possible to change the group by modifying the interpersonal behavior of many members through a single procedure. The following are a series of examples of how this has been done in groups.

Example. A group of boys had a low rate of participation in group discussions. When the worker gave each boy a peanut every time he spoke, the overall rate increased. Subsequently, to increase the amount of conversations devoted to the group's purpose, peanuts were only awarded for that type of contribution. The boys, in this case, were not only affected by being given rewards but by observing

[18]W.R. Bion, *Experiences in Groups* (New York: Basic Books, 1959).
[19]Berne, *Transactional Analysis,* pp. 90–97.
[20]See George W. Fairweather, ed., *Social Psychology in Treating Mental Illness: An Experimental Approach* (New York: John Wiley, 1964).

the entire process and by vicariously experiencing each other's rewards. This type of procedure can be used to change any class of behavior in the group such as statements about feelings, personal statements, and so forth[21] and is an example of the use of positive reinforcement.

Example. As we stated earlier, Rose reported on changing a pattern in which some members talked too much and others too little. Low participants were reinforced by people on their right whenever they spoke, while high participants received a restraining hand on their shoulders whenever they spoke.[22] This is another example of the use of positive reinforcement.

Example. Another example provided by Rose was of a group in which members spoke more frequently to the worker than they did to each other, thus limiting many of the ways they could help one another. This pattern was shown to exist by the input of an observer who recorded the sequence of member and worker contributions in a simple manner: L M L M M L M L. The group discussed this pattern and decided that the person sitting next to the worker will remind him of his behavior by holding a card up to him which reads "pause."[23]

Example. One group, also reported by Rose, was composed of mothers. Their problem—frequent deviation from their planned agenda—was dealt with in the following manner:

> . . . the trainer showed a video tape of a segment of the previous week's meeting. She pointed out how the off-task discussion prevented the members from achieving the agreed upon goals. However, she noted that social contact with each other was an important part of coming to the group. She wondered how the members could meet both aims—the achievement of the task goals and the satisfaction of informal discussion. One member suggested that they plan to stay a few minutes longer after the formal session to discuss their children. The trainer agreed to increase the break between the first and second hours to 15 minutes. The group members then tried to define task-oriented discussion. They decided that it referred to any verbal contribution related to the agenda item being handled at any given point in time. If it was not related, it was off-task. One member agreed to review the tapes with the trainer to monitor the off-task behavior. They then decided that each person would remind her buddy if she were off-task. The trainer suggested that if the agenda items were finished early, the meeting could be ended early, which would give them more time for socializing.[24]

Example. A final behavioral technique, also reported by Rose, was used in a group where members made too many critical and unpleasant remarks to one another. Each time members felt abused, they placed a white poker chip in a large

---

[21]For an extensive discussion of such procedures, see Rose, *Group Therapy,* pp. 86–102.
[22]Ibid., p. 137.
[23]Ibid., p. 139.
[24]Ibid., p. 141.

can in the center of the group; a red chip signified a feeling of reinforcement. This simple procedure immediately led to a modification of the type of comments made in the direction of more reinforcing responses.[25]

Utilizing Tasks and Activities. One of the most creative contributions group workers bring to their work is their use of activities. This use is based on their understanding of the effects of program activities on both group conditions and member goal attainment. Virtually every group-work text describes the use of media such as crafts, games, dramatics, cooking, nature study, and dance. One of the earliest and best of these efforts and one that stands as a classic is the work of Wilson and Ryland. The authors describe each of these media in great detail and how they can be used to enhance the purposes of group work.[26] Another very important contribution, and also a classic, is the work done by Middleman in her thorough analysis of this subject.[27]

Along with these authors, we consider program activities to be more than simply another set of techniques for enchancing group experience. Through such activities, individuals can express their creativity, approach situations in a manner that generates new perspectives on themselves and their environments, communicate with others on more levels than those available in strictly verbal interactions, and develop new interests and talents. It is possible for people to reveal much to each other in group discussion, but it is also possible to conceal a great deal. When people engage in activities with each other, such as a game or a dramatic enactment, they "tell" a good deal about how they react to situations. They can also experiment with new ways of responding to such situations.

Program activities make it possible for group workers to be involved with many individuals who are not accessible to standard forms of group psychotherapy in which they are expected to *talk* to others about their problems. This includes children (group workers understood many of the ideas of "play therapy" before that term was ever used), adults who by virtue of their mental status are relatively inarticulate, people of any age who are not motivated to approach problems verbally but seek help in interacting with others, and those who can benefit from social contacts but who are not ready to sustain such contacts without a good deal of structure and support.

We shall describe briefly some of the major types of activities used by group workers as well as a conceptual framework for assessing the way activities can be adapted to the needs of particular group members. Some of the most common activities employed by group workers are *games*. Games include those in which an element of competition is present (some board games, sports, "low organized" games such as "tag"); those in which there is no "winner" (games that elicit some response such as a series of cards that are drawn from a deck with "personal"

[25]Ibid., p. 142.

[26]Gertrude Wilson and Gladys Ryland, *Social Group Work Practice* (Boston: Houghton-Mifflin, 1949).

[27]Ruth Middleman, *The Non-Verbal Method in Working with Groups* (New York: Association Press, 1968).

questions—favorite food, music, and so forth); those that elicit some emotional reaction such as laughter or surprise (supplying words to fill in the blanks in a story without "hearing" the story until afterwards). Games can create many structural patterns in the group such as pairs, triads, leaders, competitors, and so forth.

Workers use games to "break the ice" in the beginning phases of a group, to promote more interactions or to change existing interactional patterns. Games are used to generate immediate reactions to events such as winning, losing, cooperating, leading, or following. They are also used to alter the emotional climate of the group, to help members discharge tensions, or even to create situations in which members explore new ways to handle tensions.

Another activity that workers or members may introduce is *arts or crafts* where members may engage singly in drawing, making a ceramic object, or sewing a shirt. Or, they may participate cooperatively with a group to create a mural or construct something for all to use, such as a game.

Workers promote arts or crafts projects to help members communicate with one another in nonverbal ways, experience a sense of their own creativity or competence, or cooperate. These types of projects can also help members to express emotions that are difficult to put into words but can be conveyed through the use of color, through the way a medium is used (such as clay, finger paints, hammer and nails), or through abstract images.

Workers and members may also utilize *drama* activities—role plays, skits, improvisations, play readings, charades, as well as full dramatic productions.

Role plays have many different purposes: they may help a member prepare for the utilization of a behavior outside of the group (behavioral rehearsal); they may be used for diagnostic purposes in which the member demonstrates how he or she responds to a problem situation; they may be employed to help the member understand the reaction of others through "playing the part" of a "significant other"; they may be created so that some other members or the worker can model a behavior for a member; finally, they may facilitate decision making as the member experiments with different responses to a situation.

The other types of dramatic activities can fulfill the same functions as role plays but can also accomplish others. The content of the drama may raise value or other questions that members may become motivated to think about and to discuss because of their involvement in the drama. Members may develop the ability to express emotions or act in ways they previously refrained from because they have "tried it out" in a "make believe" situation. The group may become more cohesive because the members have cooperated together in a highly interactive activity.

Members in social work groups can also benefit from engaging in activities that draw upon *music*. These include singing, writing songs, playing musical instruments, and moving rhythmically through clapping and dancing. Some of the benefits of these activities are the creation of a feeling of unity by engaging in simultaneous actions, the release of emotions, the stimulation of happy feelings when the music is spirited, and the opportunity to lead or to follow others. Dance provides the additional benefit of helping participants express themselves through bodily movement in ways that transcend the verbal.

Members may also listen to music. By associating thoughts and feelings to what they hear, they often become aware of aspects of themselves and their experiences that were previously not accessible. Music can be combined with another medium as when members are encouraged to paint abstractly while listening to music.

Another activity often used in groups is *cooking* and then eating what was prepared. Simple refreshments (such as coffee for adults and punch for children) may be served to help members relax or even to provide reinforcement for attendance and participation. Cooking elaborate refreshments, because of the meaning food has to people, will motivate members to cooperate with others in the group when no other activity is likely to initiate this. Thus, food preparation very frequently has been used with children and adolescents, the developmentally disabled, and low-functioning clients.

Food preparation has also been used to teach the skill of cooking in its own right. Low-income people have been taught how to prepare nutritious yet inexpensive and tasty dishes, and people with limited social skills have been taught how to entertain others through the medium of food.

At times, social work groups will take *trips.* These may be used for a variety of purposes. Some low-functioning members travel to restaurants, stores, or places of amusement in order to learn behaviors that are appropriate to those places; other groups go to places that will expand knowledge or aspirations such as a group of adolescents who travelled to a variety of workplaces as part of a discussion of careers.

The use of camping by group workers is almost legendary. The camping experience has often provided a crucial turning point for delinquents, people with limited social skills, and people with physical handicaps. The experiences of living together, sharing a full round of daily activities, overcoming hardships such as bad weather or getting lost when on a group hike, improvising necessities, and enjoying a campfire and stories on a starry night have come close to performing miracles with severely troubled members.

A final item in this list of activities is the use of *fantasy.* Members will sometimes be asked to imagine a specified type of event and, for those who wish, to share the experience afterwards. Small groups of members can also be asked to create a fantasy together. This kind of activity serves several purposes. When members are tense, they can be helped to relax by imagining a peaceful scene. When members appear to be wishing they were elsewhere, they can "leave" the meeting in fantasy and then "return," thus identifying some sources of resistance to group participation.

Another version of this activity is a "continuation" story in which each member does an "add on" to the events described by another member. This and other devices help members to express, albeit indirectly, wishes, concerns, and other aspects of their mental lives.

When the worker selects or helps the members to select an activity, he or she must anticipate the specific effects the activity will have on the group and its members. Vinter has developed a way for workers to analyze programmatic components to make this possible.[28] A description of this framework follows, and we shall provide an exercise at the end of the chapter to enable the reader to develop proficiency in its use.

Vinter's analysis begins with the idea that all activities take place in a *physical field*. This "refers to the physical space and terrain, and the physical and social objects characteristic of each activity." Group workers learn to predict the positive and negative effects of items in the physical field. It does not take much experience, for example, to forecast what happens when a person of the other sex enters the meeting room of a group of adolescents. Group workers interacting with children, also, never forget such experiences as bringing a group of hyperactive boys into a room with lumps of clay on the table—the clay soon flies. A positive example is that of a worker who wished to stimulate a group of youths to consider occupational career issues and, therefore, placed a number of colorful career pamphlets in the meeting room.

All activities also consist of *constituent performances* which are "behaviors that are essential to the activity and thus are required of participants." For example, a discussion requires members to listen to each other and to respond appropriately and a baseball game requires participants to learn a set of rules and follow them in accomplishing such actions as running bases, catching the ball, and batting.

Vinter states that the physical field and the constituent performances constitute the *activity-setting*. The activity-setting produces the *respondent behaviors,* which are "individual participant actions evoked by, but not essential to, participation in the activity." Thus, in a game, group members may cheer, express feelings of disappointment on losing, or embrace each other. These are respondent behaviors occurring through that activity. Group workers will choose or help the members to choose activities that require constituent performances or elicit respondent behaviors that are relevant to the member's individual goals.

An example of this type of planning is a group worker who introduced a simple craft project into a group of mildly retarded children. The project necessitated that the children learn some construction skills and cooperate with each other (constituent performances). The worker's conviction was that these skills would be useful to the children; cooperative behavior was also a treatment goal. In the process of accomplishing the activity, the members struck up conversations with one another (respondent behaviors) which also was consistent with the worker's goals of helping the members to acquire social skills.

The worker who is planning an activity or predicting the effect of an activity on the group can utilize Vinter's scheme for assessment of the dimensions of activity-settings. These dimensions consist of six factors.

[28]Vinter, *Individual Change,* pp. 226–36.

The first factor, the *prescriptiveness of the pattern of constituent perform-ances,* denotes "the degree and range of rules or other guides for conduct." Thus baseball is more prescriptive than tag and painting a portrait that is an accurate likeness is more prescriptive than creating an abstract drawing.

The second factor, the *institutionalized controls governing participant acti-vity,* consists of the "form and source or agent of controls that are exercised over participants during the activity." The controls might be exerted by the group worker or by members of the group on each other or might stem from norms that have been internalized by the members. A group discussion or project in which the rules or procedures are maintained by the worker through the use of rewards places the worker as the source of controls. In many activities chosen by the members and known to them, such as a basketball game selected by adolescents, the members will enforce the rules on each other and the group will be the source of controls. If the activity has been engaged in frequently by members, they are likely to have internalized the rules to such an extent that very little control is exerted actively by either the worker or other members.

The source of controls has great implications for the power structure of the group. Workers should be aware that activities that force them to exert most of the controls are likely to produce hostility toward the worker. Thus workers will choose or support activities, particularly in early stages of the group, that produce controls from within the group and even within each member. A worker, for example, who was planning a first meeting with a group of aggressive, hyperactive youngsters included a tag game that they all knew. The game had the dual function of releasing energy and drawing on rules members were likely to follow without external pressure.

The *provision for physical movement,* the third factor, involves "the extent to which participants are required or permitted to move their bodies in the activity-setting." A discussion is obviously more restricted in movement than a ball game. Even within a discussion, however, members may have opportunities to move around or may be restrained from such movement. These physical move-ment options will have such effects on the members as allowing or limiting dis-charge of tension, encouraging or discouraging interactions, or increasing or decreasing the ability of the worker or the members to exert controls.

Fourth, the *competence required for performance,* is "the minimum level of ability required to participate in the activity." The level of ability is usually determined by the worker and/or the members and is not primarily a product of impersonal and remote decisions of "authorities." Thus the members of a group or the worker will decide whether a person is "good enough" to play ball or take part in discussions or join in a song.

Norms regarding competence will also have many effects on group condi-tions: they will determine whether a member is regarded as deviant because he or she is much more or much less competent than others; whether a member has much or little power because of degrees of expertise; and whether subgroups will form because of similarities and differences in competence for group activities.

Provision for participant interactiveness is the fifth factor. The definition of this dimension is "the way the activity-setting locates and engages participants so that interaction among them is required or provoked." A group discussion, for example, in which members direct most comments to the worker is less interactive than one in which members are reinforced for responding to each other. An art project involving a group mural is likely to be more interactive than an art project in which each member makes a separate drawing. Thus, this dimension has many implications for the kinds of group structures and processes that emerge.

The final dimension, the *reward structure,* consists of "the types of rewards available, their abundance or scarcity, and the manner in which they are distributed." Some aspects of the reward structure are easier to assess than others because a full assessment of rewards must include the intrinsic gratifications that members receive from participation (for example, feelings of worth, release of emotions) as well as the extrinsic ones such as tokens, food, or being a "winner." The importance of the reward structure is severalfold: whether or not members will enter the activity at all or stay with it; whether members will tolerate a large number of rules, a restriction in movement, or a demand to increase competence; and whether members will modify previously acquired structures or processes are all affected by the availability of rewards. Within limits, therefore, a change in any dimension can be enhanced by appropriate rewards.

Vinter's approach to analyzing program activities and their effects has been used to generate many hypotheses about differential use of programs. Vinter, himself, indicated the likely effects on respondent behaviors of variations in each of the activity-setting dimensions.[29] For example, he predicted that high prescriptiveness is associated with high fatigue, high physical movement with aggressiveness, and scarcity of rewards with competiveness.

Whitaker, utilizing Vinter's format, makes highly specific recommendations for programs that might meet the needs of various kinds of children as group members.[30] He utilizes the member variables of skill, motivation, and internal controls to define eight categories of children out of the various permutations possible for high or low ratings on these three attributes. Thus one child may have high skills, motivation, and control; another may be low on all three of these; a third may have high control but have low skill and motivation, and so on.

His example of the latter child who is low on skill and motivation but high on control is stated as follows: "This child is poorly motivated and unskilled but presents no great control problem. He is probably a shy, withdrawing youngster who feels rebuffed by his peers and has a very low self-image. He too needs immediate successes and uncomplicated games and projects. Lots of help and praise will enhance his development; the rest of the group could help in this respect."[31] Whitaker proceeds to indicate the kinds of activity-setting dimensions that each of these types of children will require. He selects "programs" such as swimming,

[29]Ibid., pp. 239–41.

[30]James K. Whitaker, "Program Activities: Their Selection and Use in a Therapeutic Milieu," in *Individual Change Through Small Groups,* eds., Martin Sundel, Paul Glasser, Rosemary Sarri, and Robert Vinter (New York: Free Press, 1985), pp. 237–50.

[31]Ibid., p. 241.

finger painting, copper enameling, kickball, and Simon Says and rates them with regard to such dimensions. This then leads to specific prescriptions of such activities for each type of child.

Such an analysis has not been made for programs used primarily in adult groups but Whitaker's approach could be extended in this way. This is an important area: one which could easily be researched and to which more attention should be paid. Even without research validation, however, the knowledge of how to analyze the dimensions of programs is very useful to practitioners.

Altering Group Norms. Group conditions are, in part, maintained by group norms. These are beliefs about what such conditions ought to be. Group workers will use a number of approaches to help members alter their norms in order to modify group conditions.

One set of techniques for altering group norms is *value clarification exercises,* which can be used to help members identify and change their individual beliefs and can be used to alter beliefs that are collectively held by all or most group members and which serve, therefore, to maintain group conditions. Value clarification exercises usually help members to become aware of values they hold in specified situations or on specified topics. The following are a few examples of such value clarification experiences.

Example. A Values Auction. In a value auction, members are given a set amount of play money. An "auction" is then held for such "values" as friendship, health, a guarantee of a good job, and a good marriage. Members keep an account of how much they bid on each of these items. On the bases of this, a discussion is held in the group as to how and why values differ. Members discover others in the group who hold similar as well as different values and they seek these people out to discuss how they wish to realize their values.

Example: Alligator River. The group worker reads the group a story about a woman who wishes to cross a river to meet her lover. She consulted one friend who refused to be involved. A boatman then agreed to take her across at the price of sexual relations. When she had thus crossed, her lover found out the "price she paid" and deserted her. She told another friend about this and he did harm to the lover. The story thus ends. The members of the group are asked to rank these characters in terms of the most harmful and the most harmed individuals. Afterwards members share and discuss their ratings. The exercise illuminates values associated with sex roles and loyalties. Members, as in the first example, seek others in the group for further clarification of similarities and differences on these issues.

Because group workers can come to have a great deal of emotional meaning to group members, statements of their own values can affect the values of group members. Workers can express their points of view on what constitutes respect, how human beings ought to treat one another, what constitutes a "good" society, or what are desirable norms on sexuality, economic honesty, or cheating on examinations. Workers will avoid stating their values when this will interfere with members' exploration of their own values or when worker statements will be regarded as "preachy" by members. Another important set of norms has to do with openness among group members and the kinds of self-disclosure that should take place.

For many normative issues, the worker will be careful to indicate what his or her beliefs are and will state that members must examine and take responsibility for their own beliefs. Some workers take the position, in addition, that some beliefs are so essential to human dignity that the workers should present these vigorously and conclusively. These include, for example, nonuse of violence (for example, sexual assault) to achieve one's objectives.

Some values are relevant immediately to group processes, such as requiring full consensus on some issues and at least majority rule on others. The full consensus rule is employed when a decision could harm a member; an agreement not to discuss sensitive issues without full agreement in a group of very anxious persons is an example of this. These kinds of decisional roles are included in what Vinter calls "operating and governing procedures." Such procedures can also include standardized ways of opening and closing meetings, expressing opinions on topics, serving refreshments, notifying the group about absences or tardinesses, and so on. These procedures, then, are supported by group norms. They also serve to provide members with a sense of structure which, for many, is associated with security. It also serves to define the group as different from others, a fact that can also enhance the members' sense of the group as an entity with which they can identify themselves.

Another norm related to group processes is that a member should not be pressured to give personal information or to take part in an exercise. The worker should assess the need for all of these kinds of norms as part of creating a safe group atmosphere.

The worker also has the responsibility to set limits in the group. This is more often required in some groups, such as children's groups, than in others. The worker, in these groups, may be required to restrain members from physical attacks on one another and this can extend also to destructive use of property. Children may run in and out of the room disturbing other activities in the agency or they may use obscene language which, at times, is anxiety provoking to themselves or others.

The worker faced with such behavior as that just described has several options. A statement regarding permissible behavior and group discussion and support of such rules will help to prevent some antisocial behavior. Additional prevention is possible when workers are aware of and respond to tensions that are building in groups before they reach the point where the members with the poorest controls begin to act aggressively. The major tool the worker will use is *program* which can help to discharge tension or to control behavior because the rules intrinsic to the activity lead to rewards which are also part of it.

Fritz Redl and David Wineman have described a number of techniques that are useful in group situations to control behavior.[32] These include "planned ignoring," "tension decontamination through humor," "direct appeal," "antiseptic bouncing," "physical restraint," and "permission and authoritative verbot."

Control issues can also be present in adult groups. They arise more frequently in groups of adults who are psychotic or seriously retarded. However, in any adult group in which interpersonal relationship issues are intensively examined, strong emotions may be aroused. Emotions such as crying or expressions of caring and affection are not usually inhibited by the worker but aggressive expressions likely to lead to physical attack will be. In this latter case, in some encounter-type groups, members are encouraged to express physical competition in such controlled ways as arm wrestling.

Even minor physical encounters are controversial as a group therapeutic device although some therapists have written favorably about personal issues that have been brought to awareness and dealt with in this manner.[33] The determining criterion should be that no actual physical harm is likely and that no psychological harm befalls participants or observers. This certainly places a heavy burden of proof on the worker.

Enhancing Group Problem Solving.   In most groups, a good deal of time is spent in seeking solutions to problems through a rational and orderly discussion. Even though a problem-solving discussion is a type of group task (or what we have termed program activity), it is such an important component of group work that we provide a separate discussion of it. In social work groups, the problem discussed may involve a decision to be made by one individual affecting himself or herself or may involve a decision to be made by the group members affecting them all. It is also possible that the decision may be one that involves a problem that is a common one for several or all of the members. We recommend the following steps be taken by the group, with help from the worker, in any problem-solving process:[34]

1. The problem is specified in detail.   This specification includes the details of the problematic situation such as who does what to whom, under what conditions, and with what response; how frequently this occurs; how much harm is done; how motivated the person is to do something to ameliorate the problem.

2. The group members determine whether a group problem solving process should occur.   The members must decide whether this problem takes precedence over others and how much group time will be allocated to the process. The worker

[32]Fritz Redl and David Wineman, *Controls From Within* (New York: Free Press, 1956), pp. 153–45.

[33]William C. Schutz, *Here Comes Everybody* (New York: Harper & Row, Pub., 1971).

[34]The following discussion draws heavily from Charles Garvin and Brett Seabury, *Interpersonal Practice in Social Work: Processes and Procedures* (Englewood Cliffs, N.J.: Prentice-Hall, 1984), pp. 244–46.

must help the members to become motivated to invest themselves in the process such as becoming involved in the problem specification process (by asking questions) or by seeing how problem-solving is relevant to their own concerns. As Toseland and Rivas point out, the members must decide that the subject is a legitimate one for the group to consider and that it is likely to be resolved successfully.[35]

3. The group members are oriented to problem solving. If the group members have had little experience in engaging in a systematic problem-solving effort, they should be taught its components by having information presented to them. There is a tendency in groups for members to jump from problem specification to solution without taking the necessary steps; there is another tendency to adopt the first solution presented. These "errors" can be avoided when members are made aware of the disadvantages of acting in such a manner.

4. Goals to be attained through problem solving are specified. The members are helped to develop an idea of what the situation will be like when the problem is solved. This will help the members to determine when the problem-solving process has been completed. Some problems may actually be resolved in part of a group session while others may be discussed over a number of sessions. It may be possible to subdivide a problem and make it easier to resolve by developing a series of subgoals that are worked on in sequence. If the group establishes a time schedule for this, it will also help the member or members concerned to engage in tasks that are required.

5. Information is sought to help the group members generate possible solutions as well as to evaluate such solutions. Such information includes what the member has done before, other data about the member's personality, the situation, and the resources that are available to carry out each solution. The worker will use a number of techniques to help members approach the task of generating solutions in an open manner. One such technique is "brainstorming": a rule is agreed to that any and all ideas can be stated with no criticism or discussion of any one until a sufficient list of ideas is generated. Another technique is to introduce an analogy that will help members to view their problem in a new manner. An example of this in one group was a problem provided by a member who had been unsuccessful in a series of job interviews. The worker asked, "How is seeking a job like selling a new type of radio?" The members gave answers such as, "The radio must appear to be different and better than other radios," and "The purchasers must believe that they are receiving more for their money." The worker then asked how these principles might be used by the member in her job interviews. Toseland and Rivas refer to this type of approach as "lateral thinking" which they describe as follows:

[35]Ronald W. Toseland and Robert F. Rivas, *An Introduction to Group Work Practice* (New York: Macmillan, 1984), p. 269.

Lateral thinking processes are particularly useful in problematic situations when vertical thinking processes have not yielded a creative solution. Lateral thinking helps to free ideas that have been blocked by stale, routine ways of conceptualizing a problem and its potential solutions. Instead of relying on an orderly, linear combination of facts, lateral thinking is characterized by the use of analogies, metaphors, similarities, contrasts, and paradoxes.[36]

6. Alternative solutions are evaluated. The criteria that should be employed for evalution are what the benefits to the group member, as well as others, will be if the solution is chosen and what negative consequences may result. In addition, the values of the member as well as those of significant others should be considered.

7. One alternative is chosen. In accomplishing this task, the members first review the alternatives so that they are clear to each one. This activity sometimes leads to a combination of several alternatives in order to maximize the benefits. The choice of an alternative should be based on such criteria as feasibility, length of time to enact, costs, benefits, impact on others, value considerations, long-term as well as short-term consequences, and the resources and other supports available. If the problem is that of a single member, he or she will make the final choice of alternatives. If the problem is one that the group has identified, the group will have to decide what decisional rule (majority, consensus, two-thirds) to employ.

8. Planning the details for carrying out the chosen alternative. Simply choosing an alternative is not sufficient. The member or members will usually need help in planning how and when to enact the alternative. This may involve role playing, rehearsing the action in words, anticipating the reaction of others, identifying barriers, planning how to evaluate the consequences of the action, and determining the future role of the group and its members with reference to the problem and its solution.

Altering Group Emotional States. Another set of techniques for modifying group conditions through direct interactions with the group are those directed at the emotions of group members. Some of these are employed when the group climate is tense because of the anxiety of all or many group members. Under these circumstances, workers may simply discuss the fact that members are tense and then explore the sources of such tension. An example from one group was a discussion of an untrue rumor that the agency would close.

Group workers, to reduce tensions, also introduce procedures to enhance coping with an issue that all members face, such as the termination of the group. The ability of the worker to be a model of relaxation in the face of such stresses is useful in this process.

[36]Ibid., p. 276.

At other times, the worker will choose to deal with the group members' tension level through a relaxation procedure. This can range from encouraging members to be more conscious of their breathing to a progressive relaxation exercise. The latter requires that the worker develop skills in the use of relaxation training. One way of providing this training involves, according to Rose, "the alternation of tension of the muscles in each large muscle group, with the release of that tension..."[37] The member must receive feedback on the appropriate actions and Rose accomplishes this through pairing the members, with one member being the coach and the other the relaxer. The coach can call the worker over when uncertainties as to the proper instruction arise. Rose cautions the worker to bring members out of a relaxation procedure gradually by slow movements of various body segments. He also warns that the procedure is not to be rushed and that part of several sessions should be used to learn the entire procedure. Members must also try, if possible, to practice relaxation outside of group sessions.[38]

Another technique for relaxation involves the use of fantasy. Each member is encouraged to imagine a peaceful scene. Some members have chosen listening to music or sitting by a slowly moving river. The members picture themselves as present at such scenes. Members are than gradually encouraged to "return" to the group.

Sometimes the emotional condition that the worker seeks to alter is the lack of positive emotional expression among the members when members feel it but do not communicate it. Lange and Jakubowski describe an exercise they call "giving and receiving compliments" that helps to instill more skill in expressing and receiving this sentiment.[39] The exercise involves pointing out behavior that discourages compliments, such as denying their validity or behavior that is a negative way of giving a compliment, such as depreciating one's self in the process. A demonstration and practice of brief, unqualified compliments follows. In the experiential part of the exercise, members stand in a circle, give a compliment to the person to their right, and receive an appropriate response. In a second "go round" each "giver" expresses to the receiver something which he or she specifically *liked* about how the "receiver" responded to his or her compliment.

A host of other emotional conditions arise in groups and may be idiosyncratic to some members or widely shared. These include competitiveness, sadness, jealousy, and elation. The worker on occasion desires members to become more aware of these affects and to examine their effects on behavior. This can often be secured through process illumination, that is asking members to discuss the implications of their communications to one another. At other times workers will

[37]Rose, *Group Therapy*, p. 121.
[38]Ibid., p. 122.
[39]Arthur J. Lange and Patricia Jakubowski, *Responsible Assertive Behavior* (Champaign, Ill.: Research Press, 1976), pp. 74–76.

introduce an exercise to elicit already present emotions. Thus a game might reveal some competitive feelings, an art project, feelings of elation or depression, and a discussion of positives members see in each other, feelings of jealousy.

Modifying Group Conditions through Influences from the Environment

The Agency. In Chapter 2, we discussed the ways that the agency can affect group work. Several of these can be utilized by the worker who wishes to use the agency to change some internal condition of the group. The worker can do this either through making the agency's input more visible or by approaching others in the agency in an effort to *change* the organizational input.

One of the agency conditions that can be made more visible is the agency's purpose for the group. A group that avoids working on members' problems can be reminded of this purpose by the worker, or the agency can act, for instance, by asking the group to evaluate how well it is responding to its purposes.

The agency can also affect group conditions by referring more members to the group, thus modifying composition. Some of the occasions when the worker might ask the agency to do this are when the group is overloaded with antisocial members, when the group members lack expertise to carry out the group's purposes, or when some members of the group have become isolated because of the degree to which they differ from other members.

Another way the agency can modify the group is through the resources allocated to the group. The room in which the group meets can be changed to another more conducive to desired activities and equipment can be supplied to the group for prescribed programs. Expertise, in addition to that of the worker, can also be made available so as to affect group conditions. An example of this could be a speaker on contraception for an adolescent group, a "process observer" for a social skills group, and an expert on value clarification for a group of probationers.

The agency can also affect the group through interacting with indigenous leaders or other group members. Some agencies will form either a council of representatives of groups or will include members and other consumers of services on advisory committees or boards, where issues of importance to the agency will be reported to the group and discussed. This may have effects on the group's goals, activities, and values. An example of this was a discussion an agency had with such an advisory committee regarding the fact that the agency, a settlement house, was underused by the Chicano members of the community. Following this discussion, several of the youth groups in the agency sought out Chicanos and invited them to join their groups.

Agencies have a major effect on group conditions through their preferences for the techniques workers should use with groups. One agency, for example, wished to facilitate the use of behavior modification. It solicited items that could be offered to members in exchange for tokens, made various counting devices available for determining the frequency of behaviors, and issued brochures to members explaining a behavioral approach to group work. This had a major influence on the discussions and approaches that were utilized by these members.

Lastly, it is important to remember that groups are likely to interact with other staff and other clients of the agency. The agency, therefore, can use these actions purposefully to modify group conditions. Groups can be brought together in the agency when the interaction between them can prove beneficial; members of one group can visit another to describe to the host group how their own group dealt with selected issues; a few members from each of several groups can be brought together around a common issue and still return to their "own" group; group members may receive one-to-one services from staff members other than their group worker and this may have influence on the group.

In all of these examples of how an agency might affect conditions within the group, the group worker should have had a role in initiating the agency input or in approving it. The worker's subsequent role within the group then becomes a different one than when he or she sought the change by interventions within the group. The worker can become the person who helps the group members to consider their response to the agency input. This places the worker in a mediating rather than directive role and this can be important in work with some resistant groups.

The Family. Group conditions can be modified by other forces in the environment outside of the agency and the worker may decide to utilize these. The families of the group members are one important possibility. Workers who form groups for children in agencies such as child guidance clinics will usually meet with the parents, often in a group. Joint meetings can also be arranged between the parents' and the children's groups. The parents can discuss such issues as how to reinforce the children's progress and commitment to their group and how to deal with issues that the children might bring home about their group. The parents can also encourage the childen to raise their concerns in their own group.

Another example of the impact of relatives on a group was presented in a report of work done with a group of husbands who assaulted their wives.[40] The agency was one that provided a shelter for abused wives and it continued to provide a range of services to these women. It supported the husbands in moving toward meeting with the wives present and helped the wives make use of this meeting. Ultimately the agency helped form a new group in which both the husbands and wives were members.

The Community. Workers also seek to influence group conditions through the impact of other agencies in the community. For example, a group service agency formed groups of children who were referred by the local school because of difficulties they were having in the classroom. The worker acted to set goals with each child concerning what the child hoped to achieve through group

[40] Janet A. Geller, "Reaching the Battering Husband," *Social Work With Groups* I (Spring, 1978), pp. 27–38.

participation. In many cases this involved securing better classroom grades. The grading period, however, was too far off to provide the kind of immediate reinforcement each child needed. The worker, therefore, secured agreements from the teachers to provide more immediate feedback and encouragement to the children than might otherwise have been the case.

Workers also seek the cooperation of indigenous community groups because of their impact on group conditions. Spergel, for example, presents an extended discussion of work with adolescent gangs.[41] An intrinsic part of his approach is the worker's activity with community groups because of their impact on the adolescents. This type of effort can include helping the group members find jobs, cope with the restrictions of probation, and learn new skills.

A very important part, also, of the environmental impact on the group relates to culture and ethnicity. One of the ways that this is manifested, for example, is on the structuring of group meetings. In some cultures, group meetings begin and end with a prayer or a song. Quaker groups are accustomed to silent periods in which members reflect quietly before speaking. Some cultures have values regarding what may be addressed in public gatherings and what must be restricted to intrafamilial deliberations.

The worker can utilize knowledge of cultural inputs into the group in several other ways. A group's utilization of cultural forms can enhance its cohesiveness through the members awareness of their common heritage. The worker can also help the larger cultural system interpret its values to group members. A case of the latter was when a worker suggested the group invite members of the Southern Christian Leadership Conference (SCLC) to speak about the SCLC and its goals for social change in reference to black people. This presentation provided inspiration to group members when they discussed their personal goals.

At times the worker will target cultural conditions that have negative impacts on group processes for change. In one ethnic community, there was little encouragement for higher education yet many members of a group meeting in a community center wished to consider this career option. The worker held several meetings with parents and other community leaders to discuss and try to change their antipathy to education. She felt that only in this way might the youths in the group secure the support or at least acceptance they needed.

Employing the Model for Changing Group Conditions

At the beginning of the chapter, we presented a six step model for working with the group's members to help them create a group that will be conducive to their goal attainment. The model prescribes that when the worker and members identify a group level problem, they should determine the group condition that maintains the problem and then choose a means of altering that condition. While it is impossible for us to indicate all the types of group problems workers may

[41]Irving Spergel, *Street Gang Work: Theory and Practice* (Reading, Mass.: Addison-Wesley, 1966).

encounter and all the combinations of assessments and change plans that are appropriate to these problems, we shall now offer a series of examples of these relationships. We hope that these examples will help workers to understand better how to make use of the ideas in this chapter.

Group Problem: Members are not sufficiently attracted to the group. Some of the group conditions related to this problem are that the group may be at an early *stage of development* when members are ambivalent about membership; the *group climate* may be an angry or fearful one; or the *boundaries* of the group that define group membership might be unclear. Some of the approaches for change the worker might introduce are at the *group* level. The worker might introduce a *program* activity in which members deal with such formation issues as determining group purpose, developing relationships with other members, and expressing feelings about the group. The worker might initiate a *problem solving* process in which the members select a solution to the group's lack of attractiveness. The worker might introduce an activity that will have an impact on climate, if the problem is with group climate; or the worker might help the members to find ways to relax, if they are anxious about the group; or to ventilate their feelings, if they are angry. If the relevant group condition is a boundary issue, the worker might intervene at the *environmental* level. This might involve negotiations with systems in the environment that have an effect on the group's boundaries.

Group Problem: Members think group is not helping them to achieve their goals. Some conditions that contribute to this type of problem are the *stage of development* of the group, because the group might still be in formation; the aspect of *group process* that we have labeled *goal pursuit* may be faulty in that an inappropriate task has been chosen; or the group may lack *resources* to attain the goals chosen by the members. A *group level* intervention is often used to resolve this type of problem. The worker, if this is a stage of development issue, might move more quickly to help the members select the type of activities that will be conducive to goal attainment or the worker may remind the members that they have not yet clarified their group goals. If inappropriate activities have been chosen, the worker might employ the framework we referred to earlier in this chapter to help the group modify the current activity or to choose a new one altogether. If the group lacks resources the worker may help them to engage in *problem solving* in order to find a way to secure resources, or the worker may help them to interact with institutions in the environment capable of providing these resources.

Group Problem: The members are in conflict with or hostile to one another. The group conditions that might contribute to this problem are a *group structure* in which the *power* component is dysfunctional; the group's *stage of development* in which power and control issues are foremost (revision phase); or the *group process* in which the group task promotes competitiveness among members. The worker might intervene at the *individual* level by helping a member to assume the role of mediator between the conflicting members. The worker, alternatively, might act at the *subgroup* level by encouraging the members involved in the conflict to talk to each other and resolve it while other members remain in the background. The worker might intervene at the group level by helping the members to consider normative issues that underlie their conflicts, by helping the members to engage in problem solving, or by discussing the stage of development issue with the members, if that is the source of the conflict. This last approach requires the worker to provide emotional support to the members as they cope with inevitable leadership and power shifts within the group.

Group Problem: Some members oppose the agency purposes that led to the agency's creation or sponsorship of the group. The conditions that might contribute to this problem are that the group might be in the formation *stage of development;* its *extra-group transactions* with other groups that have an impact on member attitudes might be problematic; or the group's culture might incorporate values that are in opposition to those of the agency. If the problem is related to group formation, the worker will likely intervene at the *group* level by helping the members to consider their purposes and how they may or may not relate to agency purposes. If the problem relates to the impact of other systems, the worker might act at the *environmental* level by mediating between the group and such environmental systems as the agency, the members' families, or the members' peers. If the group's culture creates tension between it and the agency, the worker might also intervene at the *environmental* level by mediating between the group and the agency. The worker might alternatively intervene at the *group* level by helping the members consider how their norms might be hindering the attainment of their goals.

The contents of this chapter illustrate how practitioners should help groups to resolve their problems. We urge readers to develop ways of recording and communicating to others how they have assessed group problems and worked with groups to resolve them. The field of group practice will become a more effective one as its practitioners use a common framework to evaluate their practice and disseminate their findings.

SUMMARY

In this chapter we presented a model for facilitating the development of groups to help members accomplish their purposes, and described a set of variables for assessing group conditions relevant to this. These variables were the stage of group development, group structure, group process, group culture, group resources, extra-group transactions, group boundaries, and group climate. We subsequently described how workers can intervene to help the members modify such group conditions. These interventions can occur with individuals, sub-groups, the group-as-a-whole, or systems in the environment.

Workers help members as individuals to modify group conditions through performing tasks for the group, utilizing power in a responsible manner, and examining the critical functions they fulfill for the group. They help subgroups modify group conditions by using their influence constructively or by performing tasks for the group also.

Workers intervene with the group-as-a-whole by having an impact on members' attributions, behaviors, tasks and activities, norms, ways of problem solving, and emotions. They can intervene in the environment by making environmental inputs more visible, by changing some aspect of the agency, by interacting with members' families, by treating some aspect of the community as an action system, and by focusing on some aspect of the members' ethnicity and culture.

In the next chapter, we shall focus our attention on changing the behavior of the individual member. We shall describe the types of goals that members seek to achieve through group experience. These, also, may be attained through the worker's interactions with the group members themselves, the group-as-a-whole, and people outside the group.

GROUP DEVELOPMENT EXERCISE

Goals

1. To be able to identify the stage of development of the group.

2. To understand the means of helping a group achieve group conditions conducive to accomplishing group purposes.

Procedure

1. Prior to the exercise, trainees read about and discuss the nature of group conditions during its middle phases and means for modifying such group conditions.

2. One of the problems in experiential learning around middle phases is that role plays and simulations, however characterized, are "new experiences" and participants usually respond in ways appropriate to formation process. The accompanying observation questions should be used with a genuine middle phase. Several options are available to the trainee to accomplish this.

(a) Have observers respond to a discussion in the classroom itself, as the group. This can be the discussion called for in step (1).

(b) Have a student bring in a tape of an actual group that has completed the process of formation.

(c) Have a group of students, for whatever purpose, agree early in the course to meet several times outside of the class and to hold a "later" meeting in a "fishbowl" format in the class. This can be a brief meeting (about fifteen minutes).

(d) Have the trainees "as a last resort" attempt to role play a group in its middle phases. The best way to do this is to have a class member describe to the role players the behaviors at a meeting of a group he or she has participated in that was in its middle phases. The players try, as much as possible, to simulate that meeting.

Assessment of Phase

1. Is the group, "in fact," post formation? (The answer is probably "yes" if several of the following items below are present.)

_____Group is more invested in carrying out an activity (including discussion) than in deciding what activities are relevant. If an activity or discussion topic is picked, this occurs easily and with considerable consensus.

_____If there is disagreement about choosing or carrying out the activity, there exists considerable consensus among at least one set of group members and this is opposed by another subgroup or a member or members. (This may be true in a so called "revision" or "power and control" phase.)

_____References are made to agreed-upon group norms or rules.

_____Members talk as much or more to each other than they do to group worker.

_____A pattern exists as to who talks to whom, and/or where persons sit and/or who has most influence and/or who carries out which tasks.

_____Group purposes and/or goals are clear.

Group Structure Observation

2. Using a "sociogram" format, [for example,] sketch who seems to be most attracted to whom.

Is this conducive to attainment of group goals?

3. Who appears to have the most influence on members?

Is this conducive to attainment of group goals?

Group Process Observation

Select some comments members' made to others in the meeting.

4. What implications did these comments have for the relationship among the members concerned?

5. What kinds of discussion, if any, took place regarding the relationship implications of these interactions?

6. What was the impact of the discussion referred to in Question 5 on the achievement of group goals?

For any problem-solving discussion(s) during the session, use the following scale.

7 . By the end of the problem-solving discussion, what was the status of the problem?

_____Completely resolved: all aspects of the situation were decided on to the complete satisfaction of the group [and the member(s) concerned] so that no further work was necessary in this area.

_____There has been movement on the direction of resolution but the group [and member(s) concerned] could have moved further toward resolution, given the time and resources available.

_____No change took place toward resolving the probem yet the problem was not worsened in the process.

_____There has been movement away from resolution during this episode in that greater verbal differences were produced and/or more "friction" occurred.

_____The movement was completely away from the problem in that the issue was abandoned either due to frustration or the immediate attraction of an alternate issue.

8. Did a member or members speak or act in any way that was substantially different from most others in the group?

How did other members respond to this?

After a group response, did the member change his or her "deviant" behavior?

Shared Attribution Observation
9. Indicate an example in which the members appeared to agree on the "causes" of a situation.

Was this shared perception of cause facilitative or hindering of the group achieving its goal?

Worker's Effects to Change Structures, Processes, or Attribution
Choose one of the preceding group conditions that the worker sought to modify.

10. Which of the following ways characterized the worker's intervention to change the group condition:

Modifying group conditions through individuals.

_____ Assigning an individual a task.

_____ Assigning an individual a role.

_____ Coaching or training an individual.

_____ Reinforcing an individual.

_____ Modifying the influence of an individual.

_____ Other (specify).

Modifying group conditions through subgroups

_____ Modifying the influence of a subgroup.

_____ Assigning the subgroup a task.

_____ Helping a subgroup to study its process.

_____ Other (specify).

Modifying good conditions through interacting with the group-as-a-whole

_____ Altering member cognitions of these group conditions.

_____ Modifying the behavior of many members.

_____ Use of program (task, activity).

_____ Altering norms.

_____ Other (specify).

Modifying group conditions through the environment

_____ Use of agency purpose for group.

_____ Secure change in agency allocation of resources.

_____ Establishing or changing linkage between some group members and external people or systems.

_____ Change interactions between group or group members and people or systems outside of agency.

_____ Use norms and traditions coming from a reference group of the members (for example, ethnic groups).

_____ Other (specify).

PROGRAM EXERCISE

(Adapted from an exercise originally developed by Harvey Bertcher for classroom use.)

Goals

1. To be able to analyze a "program" in terms of its physical field, constituent performances, respondent behaviors, and activity dimensions.

2. To be able to plan a modification in the activity dimensions of a "program" in order to better attain the group's purposes.

Procedures

1. Prior to the exercise, trainees read about and discuss ways of analyzing a "program."

2. Trainees are divided into three groups. Each group is assigned one of the accompanying program problems. The group will follow the instructions for choosing, role playing, and analyzing a "program" to solve the problem.

3. After completion of the entire exercise, trainees can discuss program problems from their own practice as a way of learning more about this approach to programming.

The Program Problems

Group A. The Mental Health Association has decided to sponsor the formation of a social club for ex-psychiatric hospital patients, and has employed you on a part-time basis to direct its activities. The purpose of this club is to assist members with reality problems such as finding employment, developing friendships, becoming involved in community activities with people who are not ex-patients and so forth, rather than treatment of their psychological problems. You have had three meetings with the group and are still having trouble helping the members interact. You have to use a game for this purpose.

1. Select one game and *demonstrate* your use of it with such a group. (Read the General Instructions before proceeding.)

Group B. You have been assigned to work with a group in one ward of a psychiatric hospital. Most of the patients on this ward have been in the hospital for several years and are extremely withdrawn. While a long-range goal is to help patients improve sufficiently so that they can leave the hospital, you are primarily concerned at this time with getting them to communicate with one another—something they generally avoid. Since several of the members seem to enjoy music, you have decided to introduce a *musical activity.*

2. Select a musical activity and demonstrate your use of it with such a group. (Read the General Instructions before proceeding.)

Group C. You are working with a group of college students who are having difficulty focusing on their reason for attending the group which is that they are having difficulties in interpersonal relationships. You have decided that an exercise involving *fantasy* might help them with this avoidance of facing the reason they have joined the group. The group is meeting in the Counseling Services of the University.

3. Select an activity involving fantasy and *demonstrate* your use of it with such a group. (Read the General Instructions before proceeding.)

General Instructions—All Groups

You will be expected to present an analysis of the activity or task you have been assigned with regard to the following, using Vinter's "Program" paper as a guide:

A . *Identify*

1. The physical field

2. The constituent performance

3. The respondent behaviors

B. Rate the activity according to Vinter's six "activity-setting dimensions."

C. Select a particular respondent behavior you might like to have seen increased or decreased. Indicate which of the activity's dimensions can be altered or decreased. Indicate which of the activity's dimensions can be altered to secure the desired change. Also indicate how this alteration would affect all of the other dimensions. (Obviously, this will be based on the respondent behaviors observed in class during your presentation.)

6

Achieving
Individual Change
Through Groups

Some group workers may assume that creating a set of desirable conditions in a group will benefit all or most members. There is no strong evidence to support this proposition that conditions such as democratic processes, maximum participation, norms of self-disclosure, or any combination of such group events will inevitably lead to an achievement of the goals members have set for themselves. These conditions may be sought by members and may even be necessary to achieve individual change but they are not sufficient. This chapter will consider a variety of approaches and procedures that may be required, in addition to creating a supportive group, for members to attain their goals. An application of these approaches is available to the reader through an individual change exercise at the end of the chapter.

In a broad sense, many individuals who seek help from group participation do so in order to accomplish one or more of the following types of goals:

1. To improve one's ability to create and sustain intimate relationships.
2. To improve one's ability, in an intimate relationship, to maintain an appropriate level of separateness. This allows the individual to take responsibility for his or her own actions, to fulfill his or her needs, and to act in a manner consistent with his or her values.
3. To acquire skills in social interactions such as initiating relationships, communicating effectively, resolving conflicts, working cooperatively, and giving and receiving feedback from others.

4. To learn to cope with the stress of changing roles associated with new phases in life or into other types of social roles such as divorcee, widower, employee, or parent and to be able to give and receive support from others in this process.
5. To solve specific problems by utilizing the experiences of others as well as by learning more effective means of problem solving.
6. To change oppressive social situations by joining with others who also seek such change and who agree to work together collectively to accomplish this.
7. To develop new interests and skills in social activities.

In achieving these goals, members will at times interact with the worker, with a few members (a subgroup), with all members, and with others in the environment. The worker may also interact with individuals in the environment on behalf of the members. The process of changing one's self and one's social situation will involve the members' awareness of themselves and others, their understanding of how and why things occur, their feelings, attitudes, and behaviors.

Throughout the members' experiences in the group, they can benefit from increasing their awareness of how their methods of interacting with other group members may parallel their problems in interacting with people in the environment outside of the group. Particularly in groups viewed as "treatment" focused, this awareness will frequently be facilitated through a method known as "process commentary" in which members give and receive feedback on the way they experience intragroup interactions. We shall describe this later in the chapter. Members will use the information to experiment with new ways of relating to others, first in the group and later in the environment.

As the above discussion implies, we shall present ways of facilitating individual change through worker intervention at various systematic levels, namely the one-to-one (often in the presence of other group members), the group, and the outside of group environment. These interventions should be based on an assessment of the problems of members and individualized goals and plans.

Even though we are presenting the change process in an orderly manner, it is often less orderly in the actual group situation. Individual, subgroup, and whole group processes occur simultaneously or in rapid succession and the worker is certainly not in the position of controlling all of this even if he or she wishes to do so.

Our intent, therefore, is to present the worker with a way of identifying individual change potential in the situation and being able to act with self-awareness of what he or she is seeking to accomplish and through what means. The group situation is always one where many events occur, each with the possibility of being used by individuals to create change. No one group aspect is the *only* source of change and workers should not be dismayed by missed opportunities. There is always another one around the proverbial corner. The experienced worker, consequently, will be able to see the vast array of possibilities. It is this array that we hope to illustrate in the material that follows.

ONE-TO-ONE INTERACTIONS

A central issue for some group workers is whether or not there should even be any significant amount of one-to-one interaction between the worker and an individual member. Some group workers believe that this can undermine the mutual aid contract that members should help one another and that they should receive what they need through participation in group processes. We believe that this is an extreme position and one based more on ideology than research.

In contrast, we believe that the decision to help a member through a one-to-one transaction or through affecting a group process that, in turn, will benefit the member is a question to be decided through an examination of the specific situation. The following are criteria that should be used in making a decision on this issue:

1. Is the group ready to act in ways that will benefit the member? The group may be preoccupied with initial organizational tasks; the number of members requiring individual attention at a particular meeting may be too great; the group may have an attitude toward the member that will not be therapeutic, as in the case of members seen as deviant by others. In these situations, the worker will often interact directly with the member.

2. Is the member's problem of such a crisis nature that a lack of immediate help will have serious consequences? The worker can try to change some of the group conditions mentioned in criterion 1 if the member can wait for help. The worker, therefore, is frequently in the position of weighing the costs of waiting until the group is ready to help against the costs of "jumping in" instead of relying on the group. Such an issue can be discussed with some groups as a way of helping the group to become more aware of the changes it should make in itself in order to be more helpful to members. Such a discussion may even aid the group to move more quickly to help members.

3. Will there be negative consequences, in the long run, for members helped on a one-to-one basis? We are all familiar with the "teacher's pet" phenomenon. This is only one of several negative consequences of giving attention to one person in a group that is not given to others. The members may become hostile to the person the worker helps the most or, in contrast, may join in helping this person to such a degree that he or she is permanently labeled as needy and maintained always in a dependent position in the group.

4. Will there be negative consequences, in the long run, for the group when the worker helps members on a one-to-one basis? As described in the preceding chapter, the rationale for group work is that the group does provide resources that are not available in one-to-one approaches. The objective of the worker, therefore, should be to help the group to help the members and, whenever possible, to strengthen the group's commitment to this. One-to-one helping by group workers should be used but not as the preferred mode. Too frequent use of it will create the expectation that the only or major help to individuals is from the worker, a perception that often exists early in the group's life and can be hard to overcome. Group workers have always been highly critical of practitioners who establish communication structures in which members speak primarily to the worker rather than to each other and this has been disparaged as "casework in the group."

5. Will the group's help to one member harm other members? A member may have a problem that, if dealt with in or by the group, may be harmful to another member. An example of this occurred in a group of patients in a mental hospital. A member had a great deal of anxiety about sexual fantasies. The worker believed that the group's discussion of sexual problems would provoke anxiety in other members that they could not handle at that time. He, therefore, offered to talk with the member outside of the group.

6. Are there legitimate reasons for one-to-one confidentiality? A member's presentation of an issue may require the member to reveal information to the group that violates

commitments made to others. On the other hand, members do illegitimately confide in the worker rather than the group. Their desire may be to occupy a special position vis-a-vis the worker, or they may be avoiding efforts to develop more trust between themselves and other members. These latter problems will be discussed with the member in terms of the implicit or covert intent of the member so that appropriate solutions may be found.

7. Which form of help—individual or group—will be the most potent for solving the problem? In most cases, when the group is prepared to consider the problem, the influence of other members will be greater than the influence of the worker alone. Exceptions may be when the group has a great deal of dissension or conflict regarding the ends sought by the member (and the member is made insecure by this), when the group has little or no expertise or experience with the issue, or when the member is an isolate in the group. Thus, when an analysis of all other factors is not conclusive for the worker's decision as to how to help, the most effective and efficient approach should be used. Even in the examples just given, however, if the situation is not an emergency, the worker may rely on the group's processes. Helping the member in areas in which the group lacks knowledge may lead to all members acquiring more information. Seeking to help an isolate may lead to less isolation for the individual.

After considering the preceding criteria, the worker must still decide whether an interaction with the member should take place outside of the group meeting or in the presence of other group members. When interaction takes place other than in group sessions, workers will employ the same techniques as those used in individual sessions. These include problem-solving approaches, interpretation, confrontation, support, and offering advice. All group workers must be skillful in individual interviewing and must be able to engage effectively in this activity during intake periods, in an auxiliary way after the group is formed, and for follow-up and transfer of learning purposes after the group has terminated.

Several of the preceding criteria are also relevant to the choice of either talking with the member during or after a meeting: the first when there is no time to deal with a crisis issue during a meeting, the fifth when the discussion will harm another, and the sixth when confidentiality is essential. These are the main reasons for extra-group sessions with individuals. The other criteria suggest reasons for employing group processes or worker-member communications *during* a meeting.

In addition to these criteria, there are some additional considerations when a one-to-one session is to occur outside of a meeting. The worker must consider whether the one-to-one session afterward will diminish the member's investment in the group: this should be discussed with the member. The worker should also assume that the member may make reference to the session, and even its content, to other group members publicly and privately and this will affect group processes.

An example of the latter was a discussion by a worker when a member approached her after the meeting of a group formed to help socially isolated adolescents. The worker held this discussion because the member was very anxious about an invitation to a party that was prior to the next group meeting. At the meeting, the member told of his party experience and of the suggestions the worker had made. Because the other members envied the social success of their peer, they deprecated the worker's suggestions as well as the value of the member's experience. The worker recognized the necessity of discussing this response with the members.

Another consideration is that the member's concern may involve relationships with other group members. In this case, the worker should postpone the discussion until all relevant members are present. At the very least, it may be necessary to report the content of the discussion to the other members because they may resent the fact that the worker discussed material relevant to them when they were absent.

When workers talk with one member during a group meeting, they use all of the techniques social workers employ when working with a single client. The difference is that the worker must consider the effect of the technique in view of the fact that others are "listening in"; this may cause the intervention to have a different impact on the member in question than when it is used privately. In addition, the intervention may affect members in addition to the one at whom it is directed. Although this is not a book devoted to one-on-one helping, we shall briefly describe the major types of one-to-one interventions as used by group workers.

Changing Thoughts and Beliefs: Members may make statements that are irrational and that lead to negative judgments of themselves. Some of these are: one must be loved or respected by everyone; it is easier to avoid responsibilities than to face them; one must be extraordinarily competent in order to achieve; and, one will find it impossible to control one's emotions. Ellis and Harper have developed a set of techniques workers use to help members modify such statements.[1] These include instructing them in the importance of identifying and modifying such beliefs, pointing out such beliefs when they are explicitly or implicitly expressed, and suggesting alternative and more rational beliefs to members.

Enhancing Awareness: One technique for enhancing the member's awareness of aspects of themselves or others is *confrontation*. This takes the form of a firm statement to the member about the feeling, thought, or behavior that he or she is blocking from awareness. Because the individual often blocks perceptions in this manner (not to do so may be uncomfortable), the confrontation may lead to an expression of anxiety or anger and the worker has to be prepared to respond to such feelings. The worker is most likely to be able to do this if he or she has a relationship with the client. The confrontation is then viewed as a helpful rather than a hostile act. The member must be secure enough with the worker and with other group members in order to reflect on the implications of the information presented through the confrontation without becoming defensive.

Another technique for enhancing the member's awareness is *interpretation*. As we use the term, an interpretation is a process rather than a single statement of the worker whereby the member becomes aware of the relationship between two

---

[1] A. Ellis and R.A. Harper, *A New Guide to Rational Living* (North Hollywood, Calif.: Wilshire, 1975).

sets of events. An example of such awareness occurred when a member discovered that she was reacting toward another group member (one set of events) in the same dependent manner she had used with her sister (another set of events). The process begins when the member becomes aware of one set of events, then the other, and finally the connection between the two. This usually happens through an extended period of time during which the member reflects on each series of events and the possible relationships between them.

A third technique for enhancing the member's awareness is to alter the members *attributions*. These consist of the beliefs members have about the nature of and the causes of events from within themselves and from their environments. Workers will modify such attributions by stating their own beliefs and their reasons for them. This is sometimes referred to as "reframing." An example occurred in a group situation when one member accused another of expressing too much criticism of him. The worker pointed out that this was one way in which the critical member expressed her caring. This opened up a fruitful discussion of better ways of expressing caring.

Offering Reinforcement: Workers can help members to sustain a desirable behavior by rewarding the member. This reward acts as reinforcement if the result is, in fact, that the member continues to behave in the way desired. Reinforcement can be the following: verbal, as in praise; physical, as a touch on the arm; or material, when presenting a "token" that can be exchanged for something of value. Another behavioral technique involves the use of an aversive act to decrease a behavior. In view of social work ethics, the most frequently used aversive act of a worker is to express disapproval or criticism.

Offering a Model: Workers also help members to learn desirable behaviors by modeling them. The worker may do this implicitly by talking softly when a member is shouting; explicitly when asking a member to observe the worker as he or she "plays a role" that the client must enact; or verbally as the worker describes how an act may be performed.

Helping with Feelings: One of the things workers do to help members with their feelings is to encourage their expression. Another way is to help the member to relax. This can be done by training all members in progressive muscle relaxation[2] and then encouraging a member to use this procedure when he or she is tense. An individual can also be instructed to take a series of deep breaths as a means of reducing tension.

Modifying Attitudes: The worker will help members to modify attitudes that are barriers to their attaining their goals or using the aid available from the group. Workers can suggest reasons members should change their attitude. They

---

[2]See J. Fisher, *Effective Casework Practice: An Eclectic Approach* (New York: McGraw-Hill, 1978), pp. 298–99.

can also urge the members to act in some way that is inconsistent with their attitudes. An example of the former is a member who held negative attitudes toward blacks. The worker offered the member evidence that his beliefs were faulty. An example of the latter occurred when the worker urged the member to share a personal experience with a black member of the group even though he believed that the black member would not understand the experience.

Utilizing Role Assignments: In group situations, a worker has an additional tool for affecting members' behaviors that is not easily used in one-to-one situations—the opportunity to affect the roles that the member assumes in group activities. A worker can ask a member to chair a committee, distribute refreshments, play first base, become "it" in a tag game, or lead a discussion. All of these types of assignments carry with them the opportunity to learn new behaviors, change the views others have of one's self, express new feelings, and see things from a different perspective.

When the worker communicates with an individual during a group session, the effect on others must be assessed. For purposes of analysis, this can be sequentially divided into events prior to, during, and subsequent to the worker's action.

Prior to such one-to-one encounters in a group, the worker considers the following:

1. Are other members likely to act with similar intent to the worker's? If not, can they be helped to do so?
2. Should the entire group be asked to discuss the issue?
3. Does the member in question prefer the worker to help, other members to help, or no one to interfere?
4. Will the worker's action facilitate or hinder subsequent helping behavior by others in the group?
5. How will the worker's action affect other group conditions such as group cohesiveness, group norms, or group attributions?

During the worker's interaction with a single member, he or she observes the immediate effects on other members. Some of these effects may be as follows:

1. Other members observe the worker's intent and join in to support it by imitating the worker's actions, agreeing with them, or praising them.
2. Other members react negatively to the worker's actions and seek to sabotage them by disagreement and ridicule.
3. The worker's actions initiate a group process in which the actions, their intent, or their content are discussed or reacted to in some other way. For example, in a group of 10- and 11-year-old boys, some members reacted to the worker's discussions with a boy about the quality of his work by adding that the important thing was not whether anyone else thought your work was good but how you felt about it yourself. As the boys worked on their project, they continued to discuss times when work of their own, that they liked, had been criticized by others.

After the worker interacts with a member, he or she observes the subsequent and longer-term effects on others. These can include the following:

1. Members continue efforts to help the member initially helped by the worker.
2. Members utilize the worker as a model and seek to help others in ways demonstrated by the worker.
3. Members withdraw from or react to the member in negative ways.
4. Members become more dependent on the worker for help.
5. The worker's words and actions affect group norms, group structures, group processes, or group attributions.

Example: In a group of ten- and eleven-year-old boys in a child guidance clinic, the activity at one session included a project in which the boys worked on decorative plaques to take home. Jim, who was of low status in the group, complained that he did not have the skill. The worker said that he would teach him to do the things he did not know how to do. The worker also expressed his understanding that Jim was worried about how his plaque would look *(helping with feelings)*. As Jim worked on his plaque, Bob made some critical remarks about it. The worker reminded Bob about the group's rule that when a boy said something about another, it should be with an effort to be helpful *(modifying attitudes)*. A little later on, Jim appeared to be discouraged about his work even though it was clearly as good as that of the other boys. The worker reminded Jim of discussions they had had about how heavily Jim criticized himself and the reasons for this *(changing thoughts and beliefs)*. Toward the end of the session, Bill said that he did not know how to apply shellac and the worker asked Jim to show him as Jim had done this very well *(utilizing role assignments)*.

In each of these interventions, the worker could have turned to the group. He did not do so in this series of events primarily because he thought the group was not ready and the consequences of inaction might be costly for the boys. The worker planned, as the group continued, to help the group members to take these kinds of responsibilities for each other.

THE INDIVIDUAL AS TARGET OF GROUP INTERVENTIONS

In the previous chapter, we described ways in which the worker seeks to modify group conditions so as to create a group beneficial to all members as well as a group conducive to facilitating individual goal attainment. At this point, we shall describe how the worker intervenes in group processes to benefit *specific individuals*.

Factors Affecting Use of Group

Time. In this discussion of enhancing individual change through group processes, we elaborate on several factors affecting the worker's intervention plan. The first of these is the time frame, that is, whether the worker asks the group to allocate a substantial amount of time to a member or whether the attention paid to the member by the group is brief. The second is the specific approach used in the group to help the individual (for example, problem solving, role allocation, feedback). The third is the intent of the group's attention to the member, whether it is to help the member to understand himself or herself or the situation, to set personal goals, to change some aspect of self or situation, or to evaluate and maintain a change. With regard to each of these issues, we shall discuss the worker's actions and the criteria for employing them.

An issue, when the group is focusing on a member, is how much time the group will invest. The range can be from briefly commenting on member's problem or behavior to devoting an entire meeting to it. Brief comments on a member's behavior by other group members are appropriate under several circumstances. One is when the group has a good understanding of the goals of a member and how the member hopes to achieve them. Such brief attention is then for giving praise or feedback, or even for confronting the member with some aspect of behavior. The following is an example from a weight reduction group.

Example: When members reported on their progress the preceding week, one member said that she had attended a dinner party and had not asked for second helpings; she was praised by several members. Another member briefly illustrated how she had refused an offer of food and, in this case, it was pointed out to her that she did not sound very convincing. Another member told of an effort she had made to find a job and she was confronted with the fact that, in her reports, she avoided telling of her efforts to diet. The worker had previously discussed with the group the usefulness of these types of comments.

Brief comments made by group members to one another do not present as many issues for the group worker as spending most or all of a meeting on the problem of one member. Obviously, under those circumstances, the worker must seriously consider how this attention will affect other members. If their concerns are very similar, they will not grow impatient or uninterested, and they may learn vicariously. In any case, a group should not be expected to use its time in this way during group formation, except under crisis conditions for one member. When members have developed concern for one another and have learned that each person's needs for group attention will be met, such use of a meeting will be more acceptable.

Size. The size of the group will be a major factor in how much time a group can comfortably give a member. A small group, of five to seven members, will usually be willing to spend time in this way because in a few meetings all who desire this experience can receive it. Members of a larger group will frequently not be willing to devote an entire meeting to one member but may focus on one member's problems if several persons receive such help at each meeting. This type of group usually has two or two and a half hour sessions. It is possible, in larger groups, to subdivide the group into pairs to give feedback to all or most members.

Theoretical Issues. There are major differences of opinion as to the validity of focusing extensively on one member. Yalom, for example, in his emphasis on group process has the group focus on relationships among members rather than on one member as such.[3] Members who seek to spend a great deal of time on their "story" are described in Yalom's chapter on problem patients as "monopolists."[4]

Several approaches do focus on individuals. In one gestalt technique, the "hot seat," the worker directs attention to one individual, often asking that person to take roles representing parts of self, significant individuals, or people and objects in a dream.[5] The rest of the group remains passive during this procedure unless called on to give the member feedback or to provide the person with an opportunity to experience some emotion or thought by repeating it to others. Several people, but not everyone, may take the hot seat at a session. The exception is a marathon session, often lasting six to eight hours, in which each person is likely to "work" in this way.

In gestalt groups also—and increasingly in any group—members may do a "round." The procedure is for members, usually in rotation, to speak for a few minutes about their current thoughts and feelings. This may be used to open a meeting, when the meeting has reached some impasse or plateau, and at its end. Members are not expected to react to each other's statements; however, content that emerges may be used either for "hot seat" work or general group discussion and new and important material is often uncovered in this way.

Another example of focusing on one individual, is from positive peer culture groups utilized to help delinquent adolescents. Members will declare problems they have had since the last session using agreed upon terms to characterize such problems. Members then state whether or not they wish to be "awarded the meeting." The group decides this based on a consensus as to who most needs help that day.[6]

Many group workers will not use the gestalt and positive peer culture approaches because of their emphasis on one individual receiving help for a sustained period and, in traditional gestalt groups, more from the worker than from other members. The emphasis in group work is on helping members to help one another through group discussions and other activities. In the latter, one member may, in view of the circumstances, become the focus of attention for most or all of a meeting but this is not standard practice.

We agree with this group work norm and do not recommend, as a group work procedure, the standard "hot seat" technique or even an award of an entire meeting to a member. These remove attention from the current interactions among members and what is learned from these. Nevertheless, there are occasions

---

[3]Irving D. Yalom, *The Theory and Practice of Group Psychotherapy,* 2nd ed. (New York: Basic Books, 1975), pp. 121–63.

[4]Ibid., pp. 376–81.

[5]F.S. Perls, R.F. Hefferline, and P. Goodman, *Gestalt Therapy* (New York: Julian Press, 1965), pp. 146–61.

[6]Harry H. Vorrath and Larry K. Brendtro, *Positive Peer Culture* (Chicago: Aldine, 1974), pp. 100–101.

when only such sustained attention can affect strong yet maladaptive defenses and workers and members can allocate their meeting time in these situations accordingly.

More research should be done on such issues. The effects of sustained attention to one member should be compared to briefer process comments to the same or other members. The immediate and long-range effects of such interventions should be examined both in terms of the actual behavior in question as well as on group cohesiveness, the individual's attitude to the group, and the ways the individual is perceived by others.

An important distinction is whether the group's change strategy is *active* or *passive*. By "active" we mean that the group, with intent and planning, participates in the change effort; for example, the members of one group agreed to praise Don for assertive behaviors. By "passive" we recognize that a group may modify the behavior of a member without intentionally seeking to do so; for example, Don observed assertive behaviors of other group members and sought to emulate them. The passive effects are very important and powerful and constitute one of the main reasons for referring people to groups. Other reasons are opportunities to imitate other members, to learn vicariously from the efforts of others, to identify with group norms, and to behave in such a way as to secure status in the group. Nevertheless, these influences are more nebulous than the active and so we shall give the latter the most attention here.

Active forces that the worker helps the group to mobilize are used to (1) change the perceptions, cognitions, affects, and actions, and (2) to facilitate the problem solving of the member. These efforts take place through interactional processes between the member and the group and through the ways the member's role is structured by the group. The worker's role in each of these efforts will now be described.

Techniques For Changing Individual Perceptions

One of the best-established propositions about groups is that they are influential in modifying a member's perception of reality.[7] This principle, of course, can work in opposite ways: either to move the individual's perceptions closer to "reality" or away from it. Nevertheless, the idea of reliability rests on the argument that when several people see the same thing, it is more likely to be so than when only one person sees it. The group worker operates on this principle in several ways: When there is some question as to the accuracy of the member's views, the worker will ask others to give information to a member on their perceptions of the member's behavior as well as other people's actions toward the member.

---

[7]M.A. Deutsch and A.B. Gerard, "A Study of Normative and Informational Social Influences upon Individual Judgment." *Journal of Abnormal and Social Psychology* 51 (1955), pp. 629–36.

Example: A group of socially inadequate young adults had recently gone to a restaurant. A member was convinced that she had been singled out by the waitress for poor service. She attributed this to her lack of attractiveness. The other group members, when asked by the worker, had all noticed that the waitress was very busy and she had not given any of the members enough attention.

Another example, related to the same member, occurred at a meeting when she again referred to her physical appearance. The worker suggested that members report to her what they "saw." One commented on her attractive eyes, another on her pleasant smile, and a third on the way she managed to convey a sense of personal energy in her movements. These comments were very helpful in changing this woman's image of herself.

Techniques for Changing Individual Cognitions

Members' problems are often related to what they think as well as what they perceive about their situations. One crucial type of cognition is *attributions;* namely, what members believe about the causes of their behavior or that of others.[8] The reason for the importance of attributions is that people will strive to change circumstances they believe cause their difficulties. Some people are likely to attribute their difficulties to the environment and others to themselves. Still others can, of course, attribute problems to both.

The group can affect attributions in several ways. As Strong states in reference to clients in general, "If the client believes his behavior is due to a specific circumstance, event, or person, showing him a consistent pattern of similar actions over a wide spectrum of other persons or events would free the act for stable personal attribution." When the opposite occurs and the individual in some inappropriate way attributes something to self, "information that suggests he responds in that way only to a particular individual or circumstance, or that he has never behaved that way before or since, leads to external or circumstantial attribution."[9]

The process of determining attributions, as described by Strong, is very likely to occur in groups. Members can observe one another's behavior and provide feedback to each other. The worker can use this feedback to help each member to choose suitable change targets, whether internally, in the environment, or both.

When the behavior has occurred in a great variety of circumstances and is pointed out to the member, the member is likely to attribute negative outcomes to self. The member is then likely to seek to change his or her behavior so as to secure better outcomes in those situations. When the behavior, on the other hand, as

---

[8] For some important clinical applications of attributional concepts, see S.R. Strong and R.P. Matross, "A Study of Attribution Techniques in the Interview," *Office for Student Affairs Research Bulletin, University of Minnesota* 15, No. 2 (1974).

[9] Stanley R. Strong, "Social Psychological Approach to Psychotherapy Research," in *Handbook of Psychotherapy of Behavior Change: An Empirical Analysis,* 2nd ed., eds. Sol L. Garfield and Allen E. Bergin (New York: John Wiley, 1978), p. 126.

pointed out in the group, typically occurs only in one situation, the member is likely to attribute problematic outcomes to that situation and consequently will try to change the situation.

Example: In a group of adult parolees, one of the members complained that his employer did not listen to "his side" of an argument. The worker asked the group if they recalled other similar complaints from this member. Several members pointed out that he had made such complaints about his wife and even about other members of the group. The member then moved to a personal attribution of the causes of the problem and was open to the worker's observation that it may have had something to do with how he presented his "side."

Example. In contrast, in a group composed of couples working on marital problems, a wife stated that she believed her problem was due to the fact that she was not as intelligent or articulate as her husband. The members pointed out to her the many occasions in the group when she made well-stated and insightful comments. This led to a change in her attributions in the direction of considering her husband's attitude to her rather than her sense of personal inadequacy. She and her husband became more open to considering the sexist roots of their troubles rather than blame them on the wife.

One of the major techniques used in treatment groups to enhance members' understanding of the effects of their behavior on others is *process commentary.* Workers introduce this intervention by directing the members' attention to an interaction that has just occurred in the group. This is often referred to as a "here and now" focus. This is a very powerful technique because the members cannot easily disguise the behavior they had demonstrated in full view of all the others. This type of reflection in the group ultimately assists members in resolving problems outside of the group because of the relationship that is likely to exist between actions and reactions in both places. Members also learn from this experience how to examine interactions in situations of which they are a part outside of the group. As a consequence of the awareness promoted by a process discussion, the member will experiment with ways of interacting with others that are more likely to meet his or her needs than the previous way of behaving.

Workers may draw attention to processes by questions such as the following:

> How did you feel when X said that to you?
> What did you think Y was saying?
> What did X remind you of when she/he said that?
> Why did X attack Y?
> Why was X attacked when he said that?
> Why are you not saying anything now?
> Why did you laugh when X said that?
> Each time I said something tonight, you disagreed with me.
> Even though you argue with me, you always sit next to me.

Techniques for Changing Individual Affects

This section should be more appropriately labeled "expressing affects" as, aside from learning to be relaxed rather than tense in some situations, a major effect of the group on member feelings is to help the member to become more aware of or more able to express them. This can be facilitated by the worker in several ways. One way is to ask the members to provide information to the individual as to the kind of emotion he or she communicates, verbally and nonverbally.

Example: In a group of recently divorced people, one member, Jack, denied that he was angry when another member criticized him. Several members then told him that he had said this with clenched teeth, loudly, and while "jabbing his finger" at the group. Jack smiled and said that "I guess I have a hard time admitting what I feel."

A technique the worker can use to help members to express feelings is to set up practice opportunities in the group.

Example: Sarah, a member of an assertiveness group, said that she had difficulty letting people know that she felt good about them or what they did. The worker asked her to pick out another member who had done something that she liked and to tell her about it. Sarah told Jane that she liked the way she accepted the ideas of others without becoming defensive. The worker asked Jane to give Sarah feedback on Sarah's compliment. Jane said that Sarah looked very sincere when she said this and that it was also said in a warm manner.

Techniques for Changing Individual Actions

Members can have direct effects on each other's actions as well as their thoughts, perceptions, and feelings. As discussed in this book, members, by plan, can increase or decrease behaviors by applying reinforcement principles. This can be in the form of a reward for desirable actions or an aversive stimulus for undesirable ones. The reward can be in a verbal form (for example, praise) or a nonverbal one (for example, tokens, candy, money). The aversive stimulus can also be in either form. The verbal one can range from extended criticism to a simple "no." The nonverbal one can include a token whose color is designated as "criticism" (red for criticism, blue for reward) or can consist of taking back tokens that already have been awarded. In any of these cases, the worker will help the member to contract with some or all of the other members to provide these stimuli.

Example: In a group of school-age boys in a child guidance clinic, Bob frequently hit other boys in the group when he felt angry with them. He indicated that he wanted to decrease this behavior and instead tell the other boy what was bothering him. A contract was established, with the agreement of all concerned, that Bob would receive a token each time he initiated a conversation about his feelings and would relinquish one each time he threatened to or actually hit another. The tokens were exchangeable for items in the group's "store."

Another way members can influence each other's behavior is by various forms of modeling. A verbal form of modeling is for one member to describe to another member how he or she could act in a given circumstance. The member can either try this out through a role play in the group, with appropriate coaching and feedback, or in the real life situation. In the latter case, the member will report back to the group.

A behavioral form of modeling involves one member demonstrating to another member how the latter might act in a specified situation. As with verbal modeling, the member can rehearse the behavior in the group, execute it in the environment, or both.

A "trial-and-error" approach can also be used when the members do not have behavioral suggestions or when the member does not want them. The member tries out a behavior in a role play or describes a potential behavior and other members join the member in evaluating the effects of the behavior.

In all these ways of affecting an individual's behavior, the group is analogous to a rich "smorgasbord." Members usually possess a great variety of experience among them and they each can draw on this to broaden their behavioral options and to become more socially adequate and effective.

Techniques for Helping Individuals Solve Problems

The ways just described in which the group can help the members are, in a sense, forms of problem solving where changes are sought in order to solve problems. As we indicated in the previous chapter, we use the term *problem solving* to mean the rational and cognitive process of identifying, evaluating, choosing, and implementing of a solution from among a range of alternatives. Problem solving can be used to determine a course of action for the group, a solution to a problem affecting several members, or a solution to the problem of one member.

Subject to the considerations regarding the amount of time consumed by one member, the group may agree to engage in a process of finding a solution to one member's problem. A major difference between this and problem solving in respect to a group problem is in whose hands the final decision rests. In the former case, the decision ultimately is made either under a consensus or a majority rule. In the latter, since it is the individual's "life," he or she must be the final arbiter. This can be frustrating to the group if the individual rejects the solution that the other members support. This is not likely to happen, however, when the individual is part of the process of problem solving rather than a bystander. When it does occur, it may be an example of a game transactional analysts call "yes, but," in which the individual invites suggestions and then finds a basis for rejecting each suggestion that is offered.

Under the right circumstances, a group problem-solving process related to a member's problem can be a very valuable experience for the member and can employ all of the procedures previously discussed in this chapter. The member's perception of what the problem is can become clearer when various members describe the problem as they see it or ask the member questions about it. Sometimes members, even more than the worker, can be helpful in assessing the problem because of the similarity between them and the person presenting the problem—a similarity that often extends to common problems, ages, social backgrounds, and environmental circumstances.

Similarly, the members will use their life experience to help the individual evaluate solutions to the problem. Again, they may know better than the worker does which suggestions are feasible in terms of both the capacities of the member as well as the responses of the environment. When the individual, with the help of the group, has determined a course of action, the members can reinforce the member's behavior as well as engage in further problem solving as new problems arise.

Techniques for Structuring the Member's Role

The preceding group procedures are all based on the idea that the members may affect each other through direct interactions among themselves. In addition, the group, as facilitated by the worker, can seek to change a member through assigning the member particular roles in the group. The expectations of the member as he or she seeks to perform the role are then instrumental in producing the changes the member desires. The worker can, with the concurrence of the group, make such role assignments or the group can, with the help of the worker, make its own decisions in this respect.

One set of roles about which the group makes decisions are "officers," in groups that are structured in this way. Whatever type of role is being considered, the group should be helped by the worker to assess both the needs of the group and the needs of the members considered for various positions.

Example: A group of teenagers, meeting in a community center, selected as its treasurer a boy who felt that he was not accepted by the others because he was the only Chicano. The boys said that they wanted to show Carlos that they liked him and wanted him to feel part of the group. The worker had been active in helping the boys and Carlos to discuss how they felt about their cultural differences and the decision was an outcome of this discussion.

Some roles are specific to particular activities. Thus there are playing positions in a baseball game, "teacher" of a song, "designer" of an art project, and "creator" of a fantasy to be acted out by the group. The people who perform each of these roles will have their behavior affected by that performance. No "cook book" exists regarding this use of roles but even beginning workers, out of their own experience, can analyze such positional effects. These effects include following sets of rules, expressing repressed aspects of one's self, developing skills, learning to control impulsive behavior, and changing a self-image.

A third set of roles grows out of the interactions among members. These roles are very informal, sometimes to the degree that they exist but are not recognized. These roles may sometimes be harmful to the member, such as the group scapegoat or deviant. Others can be constructive, if consistent with the individual's goals, such as the group "mediator," "tension breaker," or "most objective" of the group members.

The existence of such "interactive" roles can be identified by the worker when one member is consistently called on by the group to perform the same task or to be the recipient of either negative or positive emotions. When the role is beneficial to the member, the worker can reinforce the members for responding in the way they do. When the role is not beneficial, it usually takes many discussions with the member and the whole group to get the member "off the hook."

The worker can even create such roles. Thus, in a difficult situation for the group, the worker might say, "Let's see what Sue thinks about this. She's usually pretty sound in her ideas on this subject." Or, when the group is in need of some tension release, the worker can turn to a member who has provided the appropriate light touch before and even with a nod communicate an expectation that this type of help from the member will be useful at that point.

PHASES OF INDIVIDUAL CHANGE

Many changes that individuals achieve through group participation take place in ways that are not specifically planned. We do not wish to minimize the sudden insight, the accidental discovery of a skill or an interest, or a leap that may take place in a member's sense of self. Nevertheless, many changes can be and should be the result of a process moving through problem identification, assessment, goal determination, creation and implementation of a change plan, and assessment and stabilization of change. This sequence, in more or less orderly fashion, can take place through group experience as well as one-to-one counseling. The ways that groups, with the help of the worker, facilitate individual change are employed in all of these phases of change. Each, however, is more pertinent to some change tasks than others.

Problem identification can be enhanced through expansion of the member's perception of the situation. As previously described, this can be accomplished through other members sharing their perceptions of the member, particularly the member's behavior in the group. Assessment is affected by the member's attributions regarding the problem and are determined, in part, by the way the group helps the member to identify the occasions when he or she behaves in specified ways. Goals are determined by the member in terms of what is realistic, given the member's capacities and the environmental opportunities. Other members' perceptions of these realities are useful information. In addition, the individual must be aware of and be able to express his or her feelings about the problem and the individuals related to the problem—and the group, as we have shown, facilitates this.

The change plan, under some circumstances, is a matter of choosing the right change procedure. Depending on the nature of the problem, this may be a choice to change a perception, feeling, attribution, or action. The group can help the member to do this in any of the ways described in this chapter. Under some circumstances, the change plan must be chosen from a range of alternatives whose appropriateness can only be determined as a result of a problem-solving process. The group can help the individual to identify various actions, evaluate them on the basis of appropriateness and effectiveness, and choose one for application to the problem.

The group, subsequently, can help the member in a variety of ways to implement the change plan. The members can rehearse various parts of the plan by either discussing or role playing their behaviors in the group. The members reinforce with praise, for example, the member's efforts. They can provide him or her with feedback on how well the plan is being carried out. They can suggest modifications of the plan to take new information into consideration. A buddy "system" can be employed in which the member calls others in the group for support when the group is not in session.

When the change involves the member acting differently, this new behavior must be stabilized and maintained in the member's actual environment. The group can help with this in the following ways:[10]

1. The group can afford the member a continuing opportunity to practice the behavior, so as to strengthen it.
2. The group can provide the member with an opportunity to practice the behavior under a variety of cirumstances. This principle also contributes to the member's ability to behave in the desired way. This variety can be provided by role playing the behavior as it may occur in many different circumstances. It can also be provided through the program of the group. For example, a group of adult mental patients in a half-way house were taken on weekly trips by the worker. The members had been learning effective ways of making requests. The trips were to a restaurant, a vocational training program, a department store, and a community center. With regard to each of these institutions, the members planned ways of expressing requests. The worker helped the group to list how to make effective requests such as knowing what you want, describing what you want specifically, deciding what alternatives you will settle for, and so on. Members then evaluated each other's behavior on the trips in terms of these criteria.
3. The group can help the member to think of "natural reinforcers." This means that some sort of gratification, reward, or support must be found in the member's environment to help to maintain the change. Because members are likely to be familiar with each other's life circumstances, they are in good positions to suggest realistic natural reinforcers to each other. These may include encouragement from a friend or family member or membership in a "support group." Members may have to learn how to ask for encouragement and this behavior can also be practiced in the group.

[10]This section draws on a similar discussion in Sheldon D. Rose, *Group Therapy: A Behavioral Approach* (Englewood Cliffs, N.J.: Prentice-Hall, Inc., 1977), pp. 154–63.

4. It is difficult to think of an example of a change sought through group experience, either in one's self or others, that will continue without problems or "setbacks." The worker initiates a discussion of this for several reasons: Members will be less likely to become discouraged when this occurs, also they can be prepared with coping strategies for at least some contingencies. The worker can help the members to help each other, particularly around the latter issue. Members, again because of the frequent similarity in their circumstances, can predict some of the setbacks for each other. Some may have already struggled with these setbacks and can describe what they did and how this worked for them.

Rose gives a number of very specific suggestions for dealing with setbacks:[11]

1. Members can be helped to create lists of what they can and cannot control in relationship to maintaining their progress. Members can then help each other to work out plans for influencing those situations that can be modified. For others that cannot be influenced, the members can at least discuss ways of dealing with the resulting feelings of inadequacy and frustration.
2. Members can help each other create lists of potential resources, particularly social service agencies, together with notations on the types of services rendered and the way one applies for service. Members may discuss their previous experiences with these resources so that members can approach them with concrete knowledge rather than the general information that is provided in informational bulletins.
3. Members, with suggestions from the worker, can role play some situations where setbacks are likely to take place. Rose suggests that an element of surprise can be introduced by the workers from their knowledge of previous occasions for setback. Members will then give feedback to each other on how they coped with these unexpected occasions.

A generalized reason for setbacks stems from what Rose refers to as an "unsympathetic environment."[12] Anyone who has been in or worked with groups oriented to the personal growth of their members has experienced the kind of almost utopian group atmosphere that can emerge. The group can be a place in which members are accepting and supportive and in which they can take risks through sharing personal experiences and experimenting with new behaviors. This leads to two types of stress. One is that others in the environment must adapt to changes that have taken place in the member and this can be a major source of setback. It is, in fact, the major argument for a "systems" perspective in which others are involved in one way or another in the change process rather than having to adapt to its "results." Another type of stress occurs when group members sometimes experience a "halo effect" in which they "expect" people outside the group to be as understanding and supportive as the group has been. Members should discuss this with each other so that they can cope with the transition between group and environment; they may also seek to make their families and work places and other environments more like the group, that is, more honest and supportive.

[11]Ibid., pp. 158–59.
[12]Ibid., pp. 159–60.

ENVIRONMENTAL INTERACTIONS

In this chapter we have considered how people may be helped to change and to cope more effectively with their environments through the worker's one-to-one interactions with each member and through the worker's facilitation of the group's attention to members as individuals. Effective individual help may require, however, a third level of worker intervention: the worker's activity in the environment on behalf of individual members. In the next chapter, we shall elaborate on how individuals and groups attempt to change their environment. At this point we shall consider how and when the worker acts on *behalf of* members to change the environment so as to promote individual change.

The term "environment" is a very nonspecific one. Operationally, in group work, the aspects of the environment that are targeted for change are likely to be the agency itself, the members' families, other social institutions (schools, welfare departments, and various social agencies), law enforcement and criminal justice agencies, and peer groups.

Examples of worker interventions in this category are a worker's actions to have the agency obtain a Big Brother for a member of a boy's group; a discussion with a child's parents as to how they can support the behavioral changes sought in the group; a conference with a probation officer to ask for reinforcement for a probationer's participation in the group; and a meeting with a public assistance worker to back a group member's appeal for additional funds because of the cost of attending the group.

The worker will target the environment as part of the plan to help the members attain their goals. Such plans almost always include modifying some aspect of one's self as well as of the environment. The worker will directly intervene in the member's environment under the following circumstances:

1. The environmental change is a prerequisite to individual change and the member lacks the skill or the power to accomplish the change. Workers will try to help members to acquire such skill and power, and this shall be discussed in the next chapter. Sometimes this is not possible within the time frame of the group, or the consequences of waiting until the member can acquire these resources may be too great. In the example in which the worker consulted with the member's parents, the member was a retarded youngster, whose parents overprotected him. The member in this case will not be able to point this out to them until much more work is done both in the group as well as in other training environments.

2. The members should be fully apprised of the choice between changing their own environments or having the worker do so. Their wishes in this matter will be the main factor in the worker's decision. The worker, however, should seek to understand the members' reasons for this preference. Some members are too dependent and may seek inappropriately to have the worker act in their behalf outside the group as well as in. Equally inappropriate, other members may tell the worker to refrain from acting in their behalf in the environment. This may be due to a dysfunctional desire to avoid seeking any help from others; it may also be due to fears that the worker's actions will lead to punishment of the member.

3. When the members cannot act in their own behalf, the worker must determine that the appropriate agency of change is the worker and not the group. The group, as we shall see in the next chapter, can also take actions in the environment on behalf of

individual members. This is most likely to be appropriate when the "environment" that is targeted is a large system, such as the service agency itself or another institution or agency. The group may represent more power by virtue of its numbers and, therefore, may be more potent than the worker acting alone. The other members might also have had similar problems with the organization in question.

On the other hand, the worker will be more likely to act alone with smaller systems such as the family and the peer group. In these cases, group action might be overwhelming. Confidentiality can also be a concern in these situations.

Example: In a group formed to help mothers receiving Aid to Families of Dependent Children Grants, the members had concerns about helping their children achieve in school. One of the mothers was concerned with the rules of the school that made it impossible for her child to receive extra help that he needed. The entire group composed a petition and asked to meet with the principal as a way of seeking a change in the rule. Their reason was that several of their children had had trouble with the same rule in the past *(group takes action for change on behalf of individual).* The group was successful in having the rule changed. The son was reluctant to take advantage of the new rule as he was embarrassed by the group's action. The worker met with him on a one-to-one basis to help him to overcome this feeling. In this instance, the boy represented part of the "environment" of the mother in the group.

Worker's Roles

When the worker intervenes in the environment in order to accomplish a change in group member behavior, the worker takes on one of four roles and each role is associated with specific techniques. We shall not give extensive detail on these roles here as they are generic skills of all social workers, not only group workers, and they are dealt with extensively in most practice texts.[13] We shall, however, briefly describe them.

Advocate. The first worker role is that of the *advocate.* As Grosser points out, the social work client is often in conflict with social institutions.[14] When workers function as advocates, they become partisans in such conflict. They will "argue, debate, bargain, negotiate, and manipulate the environment on behalf of the client."[15]

The role of advocate is appropriate in many circumstances to group workers. Examples of these include a group worker urging a judge to grant probation to a member of an adolescent group; pressuring a housing agency to grant a

---

[13]See Compton and Galaway, *Social Work Processes,* pp. 337–44; Ruth R. Middleman and Gale Goldberg, *Social Service Delivery: A Structural Approach to Social Work Practice* (New York: Columbia University Press, 1974), pp. 54–82.

[14]Charles F. Grosser, "Community Development Programs Serving the Urban Poor," in *Social Work Processes,* rev. ed., eds. B.R. Compton and B. Galaway (Homewood, Ill.: Dorsey Press, 1979), p. 348.

[15]Compton and Galaway, *Social Work Processes,* p. 342.

priority to a member of a group of welfare recipients; requesting a manpower training program to respond better to the career aspirations of a member of a rehabilitation group; insisting that the agency reevaluate the basis for calculating the service fee that the worker believed was too high for a member of a therapy group.

Several cautions have been raised regarding fulfillment of the advocacy role. One is that some workers serve as the client's advocate when the client has not clearly agreed to this. The other is that the client may suffer retribution for having used the worker as an advocate. A consensus on this should clearly be sought as part of the member-worker contract.

Mediator.   The second role is that of *mediator.* In this role the worker seeks to resolve disputes between members and others. This includes helping the parties to negotiate together and to find the common ground for their respective interests. The worker's techniques include facilitating listening and communication, maintaining engagement, focusing on the issue at hand, persuading, and conciliating.

Examples of group workers using mediation include a worker mediating between some members of an abused wives' group and their husbands, between some members of a foster children's group and their foster parents, and between some members of a school group and their teachers.

The caution to be observed in fulfilling this role is to avoid taking sides inappropriately. The group members must not perceive the group worker as turning against them. The people in the environment must, on the other hand, also perceive the worker as empathizing with their feelings and concerns.

Broker.   The third role is that of *broker.* In this role the worker focuses on helping members to select social resources that they require and then helping them use the necessary resources. The environmental change aspect of this is to help the environmental component to provide information to the client and facilitate the client's entry. Worker techniques include information gathering, clarification of organizational requirements, communicating how intake procedures should change to meet the needs of particular clients, and securing support from the agency for the client's entry.

Some examples of this from group work include securing marital counseling for a member of a job training support group, tutoring for a member of a child guidance group and medical care for a member of a group of older persons.

The caution that the worker must observe is to be well enough acquainted with the services offered in the community to be sure that the referral is an appropriate one. The intake procedures of those agencies must also be familiar to the worker; frequently these are problematic to group members and this can lead to either an advocacy or a mediation role for the worker.

Conferee.   The final role is that of *conferee.* Middelman and Goldberg describe this role as fulfilled when "two or more persons consult together, compare opinions, deliberate, and devise actions to be taken after the conference."[16] Unlike the advocacy role, there is no assumption that the worker and client have determined in advance their expectations of the system in question. Rather, the assumption is that something is amiss in service to the client and this will be worked out in a collaborative way, usually involving the client in the process. The primary skills in this activity are problem solving and enhancing communication. An example of this role was a meeting held with a member of a hospital group and her doctor.

Group workers who have assumed the role of conferee have been those in agencies offering a variety of services to the group member and those in which several agencies have agreed to cooperate in offering a service to the group member and to seek a consensus on compatible ways of offering services.

The major caution here is for the worker to refrain from placing agency needs for conflict-free service ahead of client needs. Another concern is to prevent major decision making without client involvement.

SUMMARY

This chapter has been devoted to presenting ways the group worker acts so as to facilitate change in individual group members. The worker's activity can be with the member in question, the group, and the environment. The worker must decide which of these, singly or in combination, should be utilized for such facilitation. The complexity present in groups is that such decisions must be made in ways that consider the effects on other group members as individuals as well as the group-as-a-whole. This is difficult and often all the worker can do is to monitor such effects rather than to know and to consider them prior to an intervention.

The worker's activity on behalf of individuals can draw from many techniques, depending on whether the action system is the individual, the group, or people outside of the group. The special skills of the group worker, when interacting with individuals in the group, is related to knowledge of the effects on other individuals and how this will also affect the member in question. The group worker possesses skills in applying knowledge to the different ways groups can impact on individuals. Finally, the group worker, along with all social workers, must be skillful in affecting the environment on behalf of clients. These environmental techniques were summarized in terms of the roles of advocate, broker, mediator, and conferee.

Chapters 5 and 6 have considered the activities of the worker when the target system is the group and the individual. In the next chapter, we shall consider the activities of the worker when the target system is the environment.

[16]Middleman and Goldberg, *Social Service Delivery*, p. 73.

INDIVIDUAL CHANGE THROUGH GROUPS EXERCISES

EXERCISE I

Objective

1. To identify group effects on individual behavior.

Procedure

1. Trainees read and discuss the section of Chapter 6 which represents group effects on individual behavior (pp. 156 to pp. 159).

2. Trainees observe a group for fifteen to thirty minutes while taking notes of the effects on individual behavior utilizing the accompanying observation form.

3. The trainer leads a discussion drawing upon feedback from the Group Effects On Individual Members Observation Form.

EXERCISE II

Objective

1. To identify worker's efforts to facilitate change in a member.

Procedure

1. Trainees read and discuss the sections of Chapter 6 in which worker's actions to change members' behavior (through one-to-one, group, and extra-group interventions) are presented (pp. 159 to pp. 165).

2. Trainees observe a group (or read a group record).

3. Each trainee selects a behavior of a member in the group that the member wishes, or would be likely to wish, to change.

4. Trainees complete the accompanying Planning and Assessment Form.

5. The trainer leads a discussion based on this form.

GROUP EFFECTS ON INDIVIDUAL MEMBERS OBSERVATION FORM

Select one member in the group and observe the following:

Name _____Sex _____Age _____

Passive Effects

In which of the following is this member like other members? Describe.

1. Style of dress (formal, informal).

2. Posture (erect, slumped).

3. Use of language (slang, repeats terms).

4. Expresses support of goal, value, or activity as stated by others.

5. Acts toward a member and to others in the group in ways that are similar.

Active Effects

Describe each of the following, including the effects on the member observed.

6. Do others tell this member how they expect him or her to perceive something?

7. Do others give an explanation of an event to this member and expect him or her to accept this?

8. Do members ask or tell this person how he or she feels or seek to change his or her affects?

9. Do members seek to reward or punish this person's behavior?

10. Do members seek to instruct this person in how to perform tasks?

11. Do members seek to help this person go through a problem-solving process in relation to his or her "own issue"?

12. Do members assign this person to a "role"?

13. Do members seek to secure a commitment of this member to change himself or herself?

INDIVIDUAL CHANGE PLANNING AND ASSESSMENT FORM

1. Describe the behavior of an individual in the group as *it occurs in a specific situation* and what the target of change might be.

2. Describe the behavior as it should occur at the end of a planned intervention.

3. To change this behavior, check any of the following worker (with member) interventions which would be likely to help achieve the change as described in 2.

_____ Encouragement/reinforcement.

_____ Relating to feelings.

_____ Modeling behavior.

_____ Describe a rule, policy, or value.

_____ Warn of consequences of behavior.

_____ Interpret behavior.

_____ Homework, task, behavioral, assignment.

_____ Orient and assign member to role.

4. Check any of the following worker (with group) interventions which would be likely to help achieve the change as described in 2.

_____ Help the group discuss their perceptions of the nature of the member's behavior, or other forms of process commentary.

_____ Help the group discuss their perceptions of the causes of the member's behavior.

_____ Help the group to discuss the member's feelings.

_____ Help other members to reward the member's behavior.

_____ Help other members to criticize the member's behavior.

_____ Help other members to model behavior for the member.

5. Check any of the following worker (with environment) roles which would be likely to help achieve the change as described in 2.

(First indicate the person or system in the environment to be contacted:

_____)

_____ Broker.

_____ Advocate.

_____ Mediator.

_____ Conferee.

6. Which of the preceding approaches that you have checked will be the most appropriate given the member's attitudes and capacities, group conditions, and environmental realities?

7

Group Work
And
Environmental
Change

Throughout this book we have asserted the principle that all social work activity should be directed at understanding the impact on individuals of their own behavior, their environments, and the interactions between the two. Worker interventions can be directed, as required, at changes in any one of these. In this chapter, our focus shall be on occasions requiring changes in the environment and ways of achieving these changes through group services. Such changes may be sought and achieved by the individual (often with the help of the group), by the group (on behalf of one or all members), or by the worker. The worker's activities in the environment were dealt with in the last chapter; the way workers help members to change their own environments shall be presented now.

We shall begin with a discussion of the rationale for environmental change. This shall be followed by an analysis of ways in which the "environment" can be assessed so as to facilitate the development of effective plans for environmental change. Actual procedures for changing the environment as employed by members, by individuals, and by the group-as-a-whole shall comprise the final section of the chapter. An environmental change exercise follows the chapter.

RATIONALE FOR ENVIRONMENTAL CHANGE

Interaction with Environment

The proposition that the individual's behavior is a consequence of his or her interaction with the environment is the first reason for the group worker's attention to environmental change. Vinter has termed this type of analysis "an interactional view of deviance," which he clarifies as follows:

> All behavior amenable to change is regarded as socially induced, acquired through learning and related processes; it is exhibited, evoked, or constrained within the context of specific social situations. The sources of behavior lie both within the individual (in terms of his enduring attributes and acquired capabilities) and within the social situation (in terms of opportunities, demands, and inducements). Behavior, moreover, is judged, encouraged or sanctioned by others within the person's immediate social situation. These actions between persons constitute a series of interactions which shape and sustain behavioral patterns. The judgments and responses of others must be regarded as crucial features of all behavioral patterns. Social definitions of deviance are necessarily relative, and those who define behavior as problematic often refer to specialized standards of conduct. In this view, therefore, the targets of intervention include not only the individual whose behavior is judged to be inadequate or deviant, but also the judgments and interactional responses of individuals and groups whom he contacts regularly or frequently at the time.[1]

The "interactional view of deviance," therefore, means that those environmental transactions and forces that maintain problems of group members must be identified and changed. At issue is the degree to which environmental forces that initially created such problems must be examined when they no longer exist.

Those who argue for some historical reconstruction believe that the members' understanding of such forces is necessary for individual change, particularly as they may be unable to free themselves from their memories of the past. Furthermore, an uncovering of the history and initial causes of problems may provide clues to forces that may be operating in the current situation. Those who oppose attention to history believe that this may obstruct a focus on current conditions and that it is the current conditions that must be understood and changed; furthermore, behavior *can* be changed through modification in the current situation with little or no attention to historical causes.

Our position is the moderate one. We do not find that attention to history is always required and such attention can obstruct efforts to change the contemporary situation. Nevertheless, the individual sometimes must be freed from "unfinished business" in the form of an obsession with the past; the past also provides clues to present patterns in functioning. The worker must help the members to assess, then, in the group how their reflections on the past are used.

Labeling Process

Another reason for attention to the environment is that, as Vinter also suggested in the preceding quotation, it is the environment that has "observed, evaluated,

---

[1] Robert D. Vinter, "An Approach to Group Work Practice," in *Individual Change Through Small Groups*, 2nd ed., eds. Martin Sundel, Paul Glasser, Rosemary Sarri, and Robert Vinter (New York: Free Press, 1985), pp. 5–6.

and officially labeled the behavior."[2] Changes in this evaluation and labeling process are often required for the group members to be able to function in desired ways.

Example: In a group of boys with problems in associating with peers, one member, John, fought a great deal with other children. The initial causes of his behavior stemmed from the abusive ways his parents had disciplined him. Currently, however, he is labeled as a "bad" boy by the neighbors who keep their children away from him. He also was under the frequent scrutiny of the police who had been contacted by a neighbor; the police often made remarks to John to "stay out of trouble" and this served to lead John to feel stigmatized and rejected. The worker concluded that it was necessary, consequently, to target the neighbors and the police for change.

Choosing New Environments and Transactions

A third reason for attention to the environment is that, as a solution to their problems, members may wish to function in new environments or in different ways in the environment. The environment may not provide opportunities for this, thus requiring an analysis of and change in environmental opportunity structures.[3]

Example: A deficient opportunity structure was observed relevant to group work in an elementary school. The group worker recognized that several members of the group needed tutoring in order to compensate for educational deficits. This service was not available; the worker, therefore, joined with a group of parents to lobby for it.

Example: In a group of welfare recipients, most of the members were from black and Chicano groups. They experienced discrimination in employment from several of the employers in the area. In this case, necessary opportunity structures were closed to them because of racism. They decided, with the aid of the worker, to seek the help of a union to challenge this discrimination.

One issue raised by some workers is the appropriateness of any environmental targets at all. These workers argue that focusing on the environment can be a type of member "projection" and abdication of personal responsibility for one's life. These workers, furthermore, are only willing to contract with members to facilitate individual change. We are strongly opposed to this position as many of the problems brought by members to social work groups are maintained by

---

[2]Robert D. Vinter with Malda J. Galinsky, "Extragroup Relations and Approaches," in *Individual Change Through Small Groups,* 2nd ed., eds. Martin Sundel, Paul Glasser, Rosemary Sarri, and Robert Vinter (New York: Free Press, 1985), p. 268.

[3]A more extended discussion of the importance of opportunity structures is found in Richard A. Cloward and Lloyd E. Ohlin, *Delinquency and Opportunity* (Glencoe, Ill.: Free Press, 1969).

dysfunctional environments and can only be solved by changes in those social conditions.

Furthermore, we have found that even when the member's behavior constitutes a major component of the problem, many members would not accept help if a recognition of this were demanded prematurely. A good example of this principle is found in a report of group work with husbands who physically abused their wives.[4] In the first sessions of the group, the men blamed their wives for "making them do it." After they had developed sufficient trust and cohesiveness, they were able to look at their own contributions to the violence in their marriages. In addition, when a member states that something is entirely the fault of other people or systems, the worker can ask, "What do you want to do about it?" This immediately involves the members in examining their own behavior as well as that of others.

SELECTION OF ENVIRONMENTAL TARGETS

Choosing the System

The first task confronting workers and members is the selection of those systems in which change is necessary in order for members to achieve their goals. The following are some examples of the major types of targets that are likely to be chosen.

Family Targets. In a group of adolescents, the members discussed such issues as the rules established by their parents, the kinds of support they received in their families for achievement, and conflicts between their parents that were deflected on to them. They discussed strategies for helping their parents to change, including joint meetings with the parents.

Peer Targets. A group of men preparing themselves for discharge from a prison discussed many ways that peers had influenced them, thus contributing to their lack of adjustment prior to committing their offenses. This included pressures to go to bars as well as to join in illegal activities. The men discussed ways of being more assertive in rejecting such pressures as well as, on occasion, seeking to change the behavior of friends with regard to such destructive acts.

Organizational Targets. A group of youths in a residential treatment center discussed the rules of the institution. They believed that some of these rules were arbitrary and were more for the convenience of the staff than for the benefit of the youths. This point of view was reinforced by thoughtful discussion in the group. The members began to explore ways in which they have input into consideration of agency rules. The youths also attended a local public high school. Their

---

[4]Janet A. Geller, "Reaching the Battering Husband," *Social Work with Groups* 1 (Spring, 1978), 27–38.

discussion of rules turned to the ways that the high school maintained discipline. The members thought that some of the methods to be used in affecting their agency's rules could also be used to change the high school's rules.

Societal Targets. A group worker met with a group of welfare recipients who were enrolled in a program for training and employment. They learned that new legislation was being considered by the Congress to restrict the amount of training the program could offer. The members resolved to contact the local welfare rights organization to see if they could do anything to oppose this legislation.

Choosing the "Level"

The second task for the group and the worker is to consider the "level" of the chosen environmental system that should be targeted. The levels include one individual within the system (for example, mother in the family, teacher in the school, co-worker in the factory); a set of people with similar roles in the system (for example, all teachers, both parents, all fellow employees); the entire system (for example, all members of the family, the entire school, the business or factory); or finally the system's authority structure (for example, the board of directors of the agency).

The following criteria will help the worker and the group decide which level to target:[5]

1. The members must decide the degree to which the behavior of some individual external to the group is determined by idiosyncratic factors or organizational ones. For example, is the individual following "orders" or creating them? This is sometimes a difficult assessment to make because people can perform in ways condoned by the "system" but not part of its official rules. Thus a teacher might discriminate against some group of students when this is unofficially supported by the school yet is not part of its "official rules."

   When the behavior of the individual is idiosyncratic, the member should seek to have an effect on that individual's behavior. An exception to this is when the individual is intransigent; the member may then seek to have the larger organization exert influence on this person or remove him or her. Thus a teacher who was prejudiced against members of a minority group and who would not change was replaced after an appeal to school authorities.

2. The members should also assess the aspects of the external system that are most amenable to change. In some school situations, for example, the teacher concerned might be most responsive; in others it may be the principal, the teacher's union, or the superintendent. As a general rule, it may be easier to change an individual or a few individuals than the whole system, unless such individuals are acting in clear conformity with the rules and procedures of their organization.

When seeking to change a system, rather than a few individuals within it, consideration should be given to which aspect of the system to change. The reader

---

[5]For a more extended discussion of organizational change in social work, see Edward J. Pawlak, "Organization Tinkering," in *Social Work Processes,* rev. ed., eds. Beulah Roberts Compton and Burt Galaway (Homewood, Ill.: Dorsey Press, 1979), pp. 498–504.

can utilize the list of group dimensions we presented in Chapter 5 to analyze aspects of other systems also. These dimensions consisted of the system's stage of development, structure, process, culture, resources, extra-system transactions, boundaries, and climate. Examples of some of these as targets of environmental change are the following:

1. *The culture of the system.* A youth group sought to change the rules regarding smoking in the high school so that areas will be designated for smoking to be allowed.
2. *The structure of the system.* Members of a group sought to change the channels of communication in a school system so that they will be permitted to express their grievances to the Board of Education without first consulting the principal; another group wanted to alter the decisional structure in a hospital through the establishment of an advisory group of patients; another wanted to modify the division of labor in a residential treatment center so that paraprofessional workers, with whom they felt secure, will be allowed to sponsor "support" groups.
3. *The allocation of resources in the system.* In a residential treatment center, some rooms that were appropriate for group meetings were reserved, even after school hours, for the use of the agency's school. The members of a group sought to change this allocation of space.

STRATEGIES FOR ENVIRONMENTAL CHANGE

Before a specific strategy is chosen, a decision must be made as to whether the major instrument of change is the individual, the group, or the worker. Since the choice of the worker was described in the preceding chapter, the decision regarding individual or group shall be presented here. As we stated elsewhere, "clients should be maximally involved in securing changes in the environments which affect them, so that ultimately they will be able to act on their own behalf without professional help."[6] Constraints on this are suggested by an evaluation of the following factors:

1. Member Motivation. The member must have a desire to act to attain environmental change. This desire will be a product of previous experiences with efforts to change the environment. Such experiences may have met with reinforcement either in terms of actual success or other rewards for having made the effort. On the other hand, the member may have experienced failure or may have been otherwise punished for such activity. The members may also have identified other reasons for anticipating their success or failure in modifying social conditions and situations such as knowledge of the experiences of others and assessments of the actual situation.

2. Member Capacity. The member's willingness to seek environmental change or the worker's judgment that this is appropriate will be related to the skills

---

[6]Charles Garvin and others, "Group Work Intervention in the Social Environment," in *Individual Change Through Small Groups,* 2nd ed., eds. Martin Sundel, Paul Glasser, Rosemary Sarri, and Robert Vinter (New York: Free Press, 1985), p. 282. The discussion that follows draws extensively from this work.

the member possesses. These skills, as we have stated elsewhere, include the member's ability "to understand the intent of the change effort, perform the actions required, and withstand the anxiety and stress which may be engendered by the effort."[7] We concluded in that discussion that young children, psychotics, or the retarded will not be able to contribute a great deal to environmental change, especially beyond the immediate social situation, but that public welfare recipients, inmates of correctional institutions, and parents of school children will have the capacity for such activity.

3. *Other Criteria.* In our previous discussion of factors to be considered in selecting the agent for environmental change, we also listed the likely effectiveness of any strategy, the risks to which the group member will be exposed, the effect of the effort on such group conditions as cohesiveness and group structure, and its relationship to the members' goals.

Based on the preceding criteria, the individual and the group should consider whether the group will help the individual to plan his or her own strategy for environmental change or whether the entire group will take action on behalf of one or more members. The following are some examples of such decisions.

Example: In a group of high school students experiencing school difficulties, a member complained about one of his teachers, who did not give him adequate explanations when he asked questions. The member discussed with the group how to explain his needs to the teacher. He was helped to role play appropriate assertive responses that will make his needs known and will not be experienced by the teacher as an attack. In this case, an individual change effort was appropriate because it was likely to be effective, the client wished to take responsibility, and it was consistent with the members' goal to become more assertive with people in authority.

In the same group, several members concluded that they received less help from their teachers than other students because they were not judged to be "college material." In this case, the members planned to invite their teachers to a group meeting in which they would discuss their own ambitions and the role of a high school education in achieving these. The group meeting was deemed to be more appropriate than individual appeals because the worker and group believed this would be the most effective strategy. Also the members were better able *(capacity)* to present their case collectively. They were not as highly motivated as the student in the previous case who acted as an individual, and they needed the group's reinforcement to present their case. Moreover, they were still acting on their own behalf and this was a step toward developing motivation and capacity to act as an individual when necessary.

We shall now present the strategies that can be employed for environmental change.[8] Some of these are most appropriately used by individuals, others by the

---

[7]Ibid., p. 282.

[8]These categories of environmental change activities are a modification of one presented in Garvin and others, in *Individual Change*, pp. 286-92.

group. In any case, our assumption is that the choice of strategy should be a product of group problem-solving activity.

One important consideration in selecting an environmental change strategy is the level of conflict induced with the system being changed. In some cases, the environment can be changed in ways that are regarded as benign; that is, the environmental system may regard the change as being in its own best interests; in other cases, the environmental system is only amenable to change when forced to do so in ways that it regards as unpleasant or punitive. We propose that the best strategy is the least conflictual one that can attain the desired objective. This is usually the least costly in terms of energy and resources; it has the fewest side effects in terms of future retaliation; and it still permits an escalation of conflict when this is deemed necessary. Finally, the least conflictual approach is also viewed by observers as a just one. We shall, therefore, present and rank strategies in an ascending order of conflict.

A second consideration underlying any environmental change is that such efforts require the members to be *assertive*. An extensive literature exists on means of acquiring assertive behavior.[9] Such behavior is defined as acts that secure a person his or her rights without denying the rights of others. It is distinguished from *nonassertive* behavior which fails to assert one's rights and *aggressive* behavior which attains one's rights while denying those of others. Assertiveness is related also to a philosophy that leads people to value themselves and to believe that they have the right to actualize themselves and to prevent others from infringing on this right.

Assertive responses can be increased through training. Such training, usually done in groups, begins with helping members to understand and apply an assertive philosophy. Members then are taught the differences among assertive, nonassertive, and aggressive behaviors. Situations are subsequently identified in which members have not behaved assertively. With the facilitation of the worker, the members help each other to identify the nonassertive or aggressive components of their responses and how these can be made assertive. Members practice such assertive responses through role playing them in the group with other members. The members try these responses out in the environment and report back to the group on the result. This may require further modification of member responses if the member's objectives have not been adequately achieved because the response was inadequately assertive. An escalation in the degree of conflict may also be justifiable when the member's rights are still denied.

Environmental Change Activities Solely for Individuals

Some environmental change activities can only be employed by the group members as individuals because they involve immediate ways of interacting with environments.

[9]See, for example, Arthur J. Lange and Patricia Jakubowski, *Responsible Assertive Behavior* (Champaign, Illinois: Research Press, 1976).

Avoidance. In the avoidance approach, the member changes the environment *as it affects him or her* by staying away from it. An example of this is adolescents who avoid peers who elicit behavior that will get them into trouble. The group can help the youth to find alternative peer groups as well as resist invitations to associate with the problematic group.

Alternate Reactions. In employing alternate reactions, the member changes his or her own behavior without making any overt demand on the other person. This change, however, is presumed to lead to a change in the other. An example of this is a husband who resolves to respond to his wife's aggressive responses with assertive ones although he had been aggressive before. He hopes that his wife will use his newly acquired behaviors as a model for her own behavior.

Manipulation of the Social and/or Physical Situation. An example of manipulation occurred in a group meeting in a children's residential treatment center. A member of the group lived in a cottage consisting of several bedrooms. The other boys in his room were older than he and tended to reinforce his dependence on others. With the help of the other members of the group, he resolved to ask for a change to a room with younger boys.

Environmental Change Activities Employed by Individuals and Groups

Interpretation. One action that can be used either by members in their own interests or by the group on behalf of members is *interpretation;* that is, to explain to others the causes or consequences of either the member's behavior or their own. One example is a group that helped a member to explain to the teacher that his sleepiness in class was due to his new medication to prevent seizures. In another youth group, the members decided to explain to an agency that assigning them the meeting room occupied by the Alcoholics Anonymous program was leading to ridicule from other groups.

Education. Another approach is *education,* as the actions of others may be due to incorrect or missing knowledge. A group of former prisoners, for example, discussed their difficulties in securing employment. They realized that many employers were unaware of the excellent work performance of rehabilitated offenders. The group drew up a fact book indicating research findings that members will use to better inform themselves as well as prospective employers.

Evaluation. The action involved in evaluation is to gather information on the behavior of individuals or organizations. Such data may relate to either the extent of the behavior itself or its effects. A wife, for example, complained that her husband seldom showed her affection. The group suggested to her that she talk to her husband about keeping a chart of the frequency of this behavior. She later reported to the group that his demonstrations of affection increased when he became aware of their low frequency. In another group, the sponsoring agency decided to raise the fees for service, arguing that increased revenues were necessary and this raise would not have an effect on members' use of the agency. The group members discussed this and suggested that the agency keep a record of attendance and continuance. After three months, this information was compared to the experience during the three months prior to the new policy. The agency discovered that the members who were of the lowest income began to use services less; this led the agency to reexamine the policy.

Use of Influentials. The strategy of using influentials is one in which the member or the group asks a person with power to change a person or system. A group of patients in a hospital, for example, were concerned about some of the actions of the nursing staff. They had originally tried interpretive and educational approaches without success and now believed that an escalation in the use of power was legitimate even if this led to the possibility of conflict. They invited the director of nursing to meet with them so they could try to convince her of the justice of their cause. They hoped she would use her influence to change the actions of the nurses. In another example a college student in a group sponsored by the university's counseling services complained about unfair grading policies of an instructor. He had been helped previously by the group to explain the results of his policies to the instructor *(interpretation)*. He had also urged the instructor to ask for feedback from the students on the policy *(evaluation)*. Since neither approach was acceptable to the instructor, the student was helped by the group to plan how to present his case to the department chairperson.

Bargaining. Either the member or the group can use *bargaining* by doing something in exchange for a desired environmental modification. A group wanted a meeting room of its own. It agreed to clean out a room, now used for storage, if it was made available to the group. The woman in the previous illustration who did not receive the affection she wished from her husband considered the possibility of offering to cook his favorite meals more frequently for him in exchange for more attention.

Confrontation. The strategy of confrontation can lead to more conflict than the other strategies because it forces people to face the ways in which their behavior or attitudes are problematic and demanding of some change. This type of action can also be taken by the group. A member of an adolescent group was concernced about the fact that he was usually the one singled out for blame whenever the classroom became noisy or was disrupted in any other way. The group, many of whose members were in the same classroom, confirmed his perception that he was a scapegoat in that situation. The member was supported in his plan to tell the teacher to stop scapegoating him and to find a better way of affixing the blame. In another group of welfare recipients, several of the members had the same Assistance Payments Worker. This worker, they believed, was lax in submitting legitimate requests for more funds for his clients. The group members drew up a list of occasions when the worker had been negligent and submitted this to him. He was told that his actions would be reviewed in a month and if better service were not received, charges against him would be filed with the director of the agency.

Mass Media. Groups will also resort, on occasion, to uses of the *mass media,* such as newspapers. Individuals in the group, as well as the group-as-a-whole, can submit documentation on injustice to the mass media. For this purpose members have used the "letters to the editor" column as well as contacts with feature reporters. Members of an adolescent group in a residential treatment center asked a reporter to investigate charges that the agency overlooked drug use in the agency and failed to protect members who were suicidal. This process induces a great deal of conflict with the agency because of the repercussions the agency faces from legislators and other funding sources.

Resistance. The two most extreme strategies for change are *passive* and *active resistance.* Both have the intent of causing a major disruption in the system at which they are directed. The former accomplishes this through non-cooperation with key authorities. Members engaging in passive resistance will refuse to perform tasks or, in a more extreme way, will obstruct other activities by "sit-ins." People in groups that use this device have refused to do homework that was regarded as excessive or "make work" chores in residential centers or at places of employment. Members, operating singly, have been reluctant to use this strategy because they usually perceive themselves as powerless and likely to lose more than they gain when confronting the full power of social institutions. Nevertheless, constant frustration of legitimate demands often leaves few other choices when the demands are serious enough.

Passive resistance must be part of a long-term, complex strategy with structures for maintaining such a strategy when the immediate retaliation, likely to ensue, erupts. For example, a group of welfare mothers who "sat in" in a local welfare department to demand clothing allowances were arrested and jailed. The group was so demoralized by this experience that it was completely destroyed.

Admittedly, these forms of resistance are more often used when the group is viewed as part of a community organization effort. Nevertheless, with poor or otherwise oppressed people it is difficult to separate the need for personal change from social change as both are so interwoven and so necessary to improve their lot. Some agencies, such as the Mobilization for Youth program in New York, in the 1960s, employed teams of treatment-oriented as well as community-oriented workers to work with individuals and groups.[10] This method of service, while at its peak in the 1960s, may yet have its day again.

---

[10]For a case study of this combination of individual, group, and community services see Francis P. Purcell and Harry Specht, "The House on Sixth Street," *Social Work* 10, no. 4 (October, 1965), 69–76.

Active resistance involves taking an action that is likely to be unpleasant or disruptive to a system. Actions that fall in this category are picketing and marching. More extreme forms include destruction of property or depriving people, even temporarily, of their freedom. The more extreme forms are not considered by most social workers to be professionally acceptable.[11] Nevertheless, social workers should be cognizant of the extremely cruel conditions that have led some clients to engage in prison riots, university disruptions, or industrial actions. In these circumstances, attention should clearly be drawn also to the systems that are inhumane and self-seeking.

Whenever any escalation of conflict is contemplated, even short of active and passive resistance, group members must be helped to consider whether less conflictual strategies are likely to be effective. Some people, because of the kinds of neglect and abuse they have suffered in their lives, believe that they are justified in responding in destructive ways. This type of characterological problem requires expert and sensitive handling by workers so that members will not persist in ultimately self-destructive responses. Some such members are found in groups meeting in correctional settings where confronting this behavior is not easy because of the support the behavior may receive from other clients as well as the reality support it will encounter whenever injustices reoccur.

Environmental Change Activities Employed by Groups

The preceding list is composed of strategies that may be used by individuals or groups; there are also two procedures that require a group in order to be executed.

Cooptation. Cooptation involves the interaction of the people to be influenced with the group. This is accomplished in such a way that the group becomes a reference group for the person, helping to define his or her values and perceptions. An example of this is provided by Klein in his discussion of a youth group's efforts to cope with police officers who harrassed the members when they used the local park. The members' strategy included inviting members of the police force to visit some of their meetings to become better acquainted with them and their activities.[12]

Alliance. In the alliance strategy the group joins together with other groups to attain a common environmental change goal. An example provided by Glasser and co-workers is stated as follows: "A psychiatric orderly consistently brings the ward patients to the dining room late. As a result they must eat hurriedly and sometimes do not get a full meal. Treatment group patients may enlist the support of the other groups on the ward or organize other patients into a larger group, to put pressure on the attendant to change his pattern."[13]

[11]For an extended discussion of the ethical issues involved, see Harry Specht, "Disruptive Tactics," *Social Work* 14 (April, 1969), 5–15.
[12]Alan Klein, *Society, Democracy and the Group* (New York: Woman's Press and William Morrow, 1953), pp. 329–30.
[13]Garvin and others, in *Individual Change*, p. 288.

SUMMARY

In accomplishing group work goals, the targets of change at any given time may be the individual, the group, or some aspect of the environment. This chapter was devoted to procedures used when the latter is the target. The instrument of such change can be the individual member, as influenced by the worker and/or the group, the group itself, or the worker. When the worker tries to change the member's environment, it is usually to affect some subsequent change in the member and, therefore, we dealt with worker efforts to change the environment in the previous chapter.

This chapter presented a rationale for environmental change followed by procedures to accomplish this as used by members acting alone, either by members as individuals or the group-as-a-whole, and finally by group action. Each procedure was defined and examples from group work practice were provided.

ENVIRONMENTAL CHANGE EXERCISE

Goals

1. To identify occasions for environmental changes.

2. To discriminate among occasions when the members, the worker, or the members and worker together seek to change the environment.

3. To choose the appropriate strategy for environmental change.

Procedure

1. Prior to the exercise, trainees read about and discuss reasons for environmental change and strategies for accomplishing this.

2. Five trainees are asked to volunteer to form a group which will hold a short meeting in front of the class. The topic of the meeting is to be "Concerns I have about learning to be a group worker." One member is chosen as worker for the group.

3. After the meeting, the entire training group or class uses the environmental change planning form as a means of analyzing the group meeting.

ENVIRONMENTAL CHANGE PLANNING FORM

1. Briefly describe a problem one or more members have in attaining a goal.

2. Will a person or persons outside of the group hinder the member from attaining the goal? If so, describe.

3. Is this hindrance a product of one of the following? (check any that apply):

_____ stage of development of the system

_____ structure of the system

_____ process of the system

_____ culture

_____ extra-system transactions

_____ system boundaries

_____ system climate

_____ the way the system allocates resources

4. Describe motivation of member(s) to seek changes in the environment through his or her own efforts.

5. Describe capacity of member(s) to seek changes in the environment.

6. What risks will the member(s) incur by seeking changes in the environment?

7. In view of 4, 5, and 6, should the member be helped to plan to achieve changes in the environment alone or with the help of the worker, or should the worker become the main instrument of change?

8. Which of the following change strategies will be used:

_____ avoidance

_____ alternative reactions

_____ manipulation of situation

_____ interpretation

_____ education

_____ evaluation

_____ use of influentials

_____ bargaining

_____ confrontation

_____ mass media

_____ passive resistance

9. Describe in detail the way the strategy will be used.

10. How will the effectiveness of the strategy be evaluated? (Trainees can consult Chapter 8, Evaluation of Environmental Changes, for help in answering this question.)

8

The Evaluation
Of Group Work
Practice

A growing idea in social work is that the "practitioner" should become a "practitioner-researcher." One reason for this is political—the current emphasis on accountability. Funding sources and legislative bodies have raised questions about whether the funds for social programs are well spent, which has led to the requirement that workers collect and report data on the outcome of their activities. While the purpose of this is to ensure that funds are routed to activities that are the most effective, thus benefiting more people, this unfortunately is not always the result of evaluative efforts.

A reason for difficulties in performing an evaluation is the current state of knowledge regarding measurement of the outcomes of social work intervention. An exception is the rapid development of the field of behavior modification, one that has led to many reliable devices for the measurement of behavioral change. However, not all intervention goals are conceptualized as changes in discrete behaviors. Goals are sometimes described in terms of emotions, attitudes, self-evaluations, the qualities of decisions that one may make, as well as institutional changes. While practitioners and researchers are working to create valid and reliable measures of *all* phenomena related to social work objectives, there are still weaknesses in their products as well as disagreements among practitioners as to appropriate types of measurement.

Another problem with the current approach to accountability is that the type of data to be collected is often imposed by the agency upon the worker, at times with little regard for the worker's concerns regarding the types of variations that exist among clients. Workers, therefore, do not always take seriously data collection for purposes of program evaluation. Many group workers known to the author record data on agency forms with little thought because of their lack of identification with the purposes and methods of evaluation required by the agency.

Group workers, like all social workers, experience the difficulties with current evaluative technologies that we have described. This does not militate against our conviction that workers' evaluation of their practice should be an essential component of their activity and that all workers must struggle to overcome some of the barriers to such practice that exist through inadequacies in evaluative technology and approaches inappropriately imposed by the agency. The reasons for such evaluation go beyond the concern that resources should be allocated to programs that are effective. The worker also has an obligation to the group members. They have a right to examine whether or not their investment in the group work process has attained the goals they have established for themselves.

Furthermore, the worker has a responsibility to practice in ways that are effective. Workers, consequently, must know which of the procedures they employ to facilitate individual change are the most effective and efficient. When workers apply procedures to change group and environmental conditions to attain individual goals, they must also know whether those "work." Thus the requirement we place on workers, as professionals, is that they must employ the interventions that are the most likely to help members with the least investment of time and energy by all parties.

In the term "practitioner-researcher," we have purposely placed the word "practitioner" first. The interests of practitioners must be in serving the members of the group. If taking responsibility for the effectiveness of that service leads to a better understanding of the procedures employed—and in some instances to insights into human behavior—that is valuable but secondary to offering service in a responsible and accountable way. Thus the practitioner should not employ questionnaires or other instruments or subject members to any stress unless these are required to serve those members. When practitioners desire to do research, as such, members should be informed about this as a separate issue which they can accept or reject on its own merits.

It follows from these comments that all relevant parties should be involved in determining the nature and extent of an evaluative procedure. First and foremost, the group members should be helped to determine what they wish to know about the effects of group services. Second, the workers themselves should consider what kinds of information will help them to be responsible to the members as well as to lead to better practice. Agency requests for information from workers or even members should not conflict with or impede these requirements.

In determining how to evaluate group work practice, the worker must decide (with proper involvement of members and significant others) on the design of the evaluation and on the instruments to be used. Furthermore, the worker must gather evaluative information not only in relationship to the members but to the group and to the environment when these systems are targets of intervention. We will, therefore, separately consider issues of design and measurement as these apply to individual members, the group, and systems outside of the group.

EVALUATION OF INDIVIDUAL CHANGE
OF GROUP MEMBERS

Evaluation Design

The design of an evaluation consists of plans as to when and from whom information will be collected, as well as the type of information that will be sought. These plans, in turn, are based on the way in which the information will be analyzed to determine the effects of service.

To identify whether individuals have benefited from group work service, a measurement must be made of their relevant circumstances and behaviors prior to the group work experience and after it. In addition, depending on the situation, additional measurements must be made during the group work process as well as some time after it has terminated.

The measurement of the status of a member's problems or concerns prior to group work service is referred to as a *baseline*. The member, then, seeks an improvement in this measure as a result of group participation. An appropriate baseline requires a process in which members decide what they wish to change as a result of group experience and what their change goals are. Examples of some ways used by group members to establish individual baselines are as follows.

Example. A member of a group of college students measured, for three classes, how anxious he felt when he spoke out. He used a scale in which zero represented complete calm and 100 the most anxiety he has felt.[1]

Example. A member of a parent's group counted how many times she criticized her son for each of three consecutive days.

Example. A member of an assertiveness group measured his degree of assertiveness using the Rathus scale.[2]

Example. A member of a career decision group indicated that twice previously he thought he had made the right career decision but had withdrawn from training programs before they started because of doubts about his decision.

---

[1]This is referred to as a "subjective units of disturbance scale." For details, see Joseph Wolpe, *The Practice of Behavior Therapy,* 2nd ed. (Elmsford, N.Y.: Pergamon Press, 1973), p. 120.

[2]S.A. Rathus, "A 30-item Schedule for Assessing Assertive Behavior," *Behavior Research and Therapy* 11 (1973), 398–406.

Example. A member of a gay "coming-out" group said that he had gone home twice in the past month to tell his parents about his "gayness" and left without accomplishing this.

Technical issues regarding baseline measurements are beyond the scope of this text. A major technical issue relates to the number of baseline measurements that should be made in order to ensure that the measure represents the *typical* behavior of the group member. The reader can consult several texts that explain, in detail, the criteria for an appropriate baseline.[3]

In addition to the frequency of measurements, another decision must be made as to whether effectiveness will be evaluated in terms of each individual separately or whether it will be evaluated for the group as a whole. There is a long tradition of evaluating group and individual treatments by examining their effects on individuals. The presentation of case studies are instances of this. In such case studies, the practitioner asserts the value of his or her approach by showing that it has helped specific persons. This method, without a doubt, advanced knowledge about many techniques and will continue to do so. The measures were qualitative in that they described the situation of the person before and after treatment.

One of the newest designs for evaluating change efforts is also focused on the individual case but quantitative rather than qualitative measures are employed. These are usually referred to as "single subject designs" and include a baseline measure as well as subsequent measurements. Because of the quantitative nature of the measurements, statistical procedures are usually employed to rule out some of the causes of the change that lie in events other than the group experience. For example, an anxious member may, without treatment, experience a gradual lessening of anxiety. During treatment, this progress may occur more rapidly. Relatively simple statistical procedures can be used to determine the likelihood that a change in the rate of progress is due to something other than the group intervention.[4]

There are a number of different kinds of single case designs, each with a rationale for its use.[5] One of the most common designs is the AB design in which a baseline measurement is made followed by a measurement after (and sometimes during) the intervention. Another is a multiple baseline design in which baseline measures are made on some behaviors while treatments occur for others. Variations of this latter design include measuring baselines and changes that involve different members in the group or different situations for the same member. Another common design involves obtaining a baseline followed by

---

[3]See, for example, D.M. Gottman and S.R. Leiblum, *How to do Psychotherapy and How to Evaluate It* (New York: Holt, Rinehart & Winston, 1974), pp. 38–41.

[4]For a discussion of statistical procedures that can be applied by practitioners with little knowledge of statistics, see S. Jayaratne, "Analytic Procedures for Single Subject Designs," *Social Work Research and Abstracts* 14 (Fall, 1978), 30–40. For an analysis of technical issues in the use of such designs in social work, see Joel Fischer, *Effective Casework Practice* (New York: McGraw-Hill, 1978), pp. 88–102. The same author also discusses what he terms "objectified case studies," on pages 102 to 108.

[5]For a comprehensive presentation of single case designs, see M. Hersen and D.H. Barlow, *Single Case Experimental Designs* (Elmsford, N.Y.: Pergamon Press, 1976).

several types of interventions with measurements secured after each intervention. This last design helps to identify the relative potency of different interventions especially if one utilizes them with different members and in different sequences.

A problem for group workers with some of the designs is that what is done with one member will affect others. It is, therefore, difficult to separate the effects of an intervention in the group from the effects members have on each other. Nevertheless, it is still valuable to know if members are making progress, even when the variable responsible for the progress cannot be determined with certainty.

A major issue for group workers who utilize a variety of techniques, not primarily behavioral, is how to measure baselines and changes that are not thought of in terms of specific behaviors that can be counted. These include the quality of one's communications, decisions, satisfactions with self, and perceptions of self. Measures exist for all of these phenomena and new ones are now being created. The lack of measures, therefore, cannot be a reason for failing to evaluate individual progress.[6] Rose provides a number of examples of measurements of changes in group members that were examined through single subject designs. These included leadership behaviors, emotional responses, and information-giving responses.[7]

Practitioners will occasionally use control group designs,[8] in which the worker compares a number of members who received a particular form of service with those who received an alternative form or no service at all. The value of this approach is that reasons for change, other than the specific intervention, can be ruled out. The practitioner's problem with such designs is that they require procedures that are time consuming and sometimes difficult to achieve, such as random assignment of members to experimental and control group. In addition, data analysis problems are caused by premature termination of members from groups and the influences of members on each other.

In rating individual behaviors to evaluate the effects of group work, the worker has a number of different data sources that can be utilized. One is the member's *self report*. In this instance, the members count their own behaviors or rate their own feelings or attitudes or indicate the situations in which they experience some form of difficulty. Another is the *worker's observation* or *judgment*. The worker, or other group members, can count how often the member speaks, rate the degree of assertiveness of the member's statements, or whether the member speaks of personal material in the group. *Outside observers'* ratings can be employed for the same purpose and these observers, with the permission of the

---

[6]For a recent and authoritative discussion of the measurement of individual change as a result of treatment, see Allen E. Bergin and Michael J. Lambert, "The Evaluation of Therapeutic Outcomes," in *Handbook of Psychotherapy and Behavior Change,* 2nd ed., eds. Sol L. Garfield and Allen E. Bergin (New York: John Wiley, 1978), pp. 139–89.

[7]Sheldon Rose, *Group Therapy: A Behavioral Approach* (Englewood Cliffs, N.J.: Prentice-Hall, Inc., 1977), pp. 66–72.

[8]Readers interested in applying such designs should consult texts on the subject such as D.T. Campbell and J.C. Stanley, *Experimental and Quasi-Experimental Designs for Research* (Skokie, Ill.: Rand McNally, 1963).

members, can either sit in on meetings or review tape recordings. The worker can also use records kept by others such as school teachers, parents, or employers, with permission of the member.

Measurement Techniques

Workers must be familiar with a variety of measures, including the following:[9]

Behavioral Counts. Behavioral counts include the number of times a member engages in a desired act such as completion of homework assignments, absences from school, initiation of conversation with acquaintances, or expressions of affection. Many devices have been developed to facilitate counts such as mechanical counters and charts.[10]

Goal Attainment Scaling. Goal attainment scaling is a procedure for measuring clients' progress in attaining goals.[11] As can be seen in the completed form in Table 8-1, a scale is developed for all goals of each client. The scale consists of five levels ranging from the most favorable to the most unfavorable outcome with relationship to the goal. The midpoint of the scale represents the "expected" level of success. When this approach is used in groups, the group members can help each other to define each level and to rate outcomes in terms of these levels.

Kiresuk and Garwick have developed statistical procedures that create goal attainment scores for clients.[12] These scores can be used to help the group worker to identify which types of groups are the most helpful to their members. Workers can examine the conditions found in successful and unsuccessful groups as a way of developing a better understanding of the most effective sets of group experiences in relationship to members' attributes, problems, and so forth.

We have also used goal attainment scales to evaluate members' achievements when the members were very low functioning and capable only minimally of participating in creating scale points. We worked with the members to help them identify their "expected level of success" and created the other levels without full member participation. We recognize the limitations of this but have yet to devise another solution to such problems in developing the scale.

---

[9]For an excellent discussion of the training of practitioners who can utilize appropriate outcome measures, see Martin Bloom, "Incorporating Objective Outcome Measures into Competency Training," in *The Pursuit of Competence in Social Work,* eds. Frank W. Clark and others (San Francisco: Jossey-Bass, 1979), pp. 111–22.

[10]For a comprehensive discussion of counts used in group work, see Rose, *Group Therapy,* pp. 43–46.

[11]For further details on this approach, see Thomas J. Kiresuk and Geoffrey Garwick, "Basic Goal Attainment Procedures," in *Social Work Processes,* 2nd ed., eds. Beulah Roberts Compton and Burt Galaway (Homewood, Ill.: Dorsey Press, 1979), pp. 412–21.

[12]Ibid.

TABLE 8–1 Goal Attainment Follow-up Grid [a]

Program using GAS __Intercity__ __Head Start__

Client __Mrs. B__

Date of scale construction __8-1-73__

Follow-up date __9-1-73__

Scale Headings And Scale Weights

Levels of predicted attainments	Scale 1	Scale 2	Scale 3	Scale 4
Most unfavorable outcome thought likely.	Mrs. B. reports angrily yelling at Jimmy daily or oftener during last week in August.	No action on or discussion of Mrs. B's loneliness.	No discussion or action about returning to clinic.	
Less than expected success.	Mrs. B reports angrily yelling at Jimmy more than three times but less than daily during last week in August.	Mrs. B discusses her loneliness but cannot make plans to deal with it.	Mrs. B is discussing her reaction to the clinic but has not formulated plans to return.	

TABLE 8-1 (continued)

Levels of predicted attainments	Scale 1	Scale 2	Scale 3	Scale 4
Expected level of success.	Mrs. B. reports angrily yelling at Jimmy no more than three times during last week in August.	Mrs. B is discussing her loneliness and making plans to join a group.	Mrs. B has discussed her reaction to the clinic and plans to secure a return appointment.	
More than expected success.	Mrs. B has discontinued angrily yelling at Jimmy but has not discovered another way to discipline him.	Mrs. B has initiated contacts with a group.	Mrs. B has telephoned the clinic for a return appointment.	
Most favorable outcome thought likely.	Above, and Mrs. B is using another form of discipline before becoming angry with Jimmy.	Mrs. B has attended one group meeting.	Mrs. B has been into the clinic for a return appointment.	

[a] These are examples of scales that might have been developed with Mrs. B. Taken from Beulah R. Compton and Burt Galaway, *Social Work Processes*, rev. ed. (Homewood, Illinois: The Dorsey Press, 1979), p. 410. ©1979 by The Dorsey Press.

Self Ratings on Emotional States. One of the emotions for which members often seek help is anxiety. This type of discomfort is experienced by members with phobias or problems when performing such tasks as asking a person for a date or answering questions posed by a teacher. As we reported, practitioners have found considerable reliability in asking members to rate their own degrees of anxiety on a scale of 0 to 100.[13] Such scales have also been used for irritation, anger, and congeniality.[14]

Value Clarification Ratings. Members often seek to clarify and affirm their values as a result of group experience. Some of the instruments utilized for value clarification exercises can also be used to determine baselines as well as changes in the values of members. One example of this is the "values grid" (see Table 8-2). The members place the value issues relevant to them in the issue column. For example, in one adolescent group, the members listed "declaring pride in being black," "what it means to be a man or woman," and "how honest I should be with people I am close to." Members check the seven columns in terms of the following questions:

1. Are you *proud* of (do you prize or cherish) your position?
2. Have you *publicly affirmed* your position?
3. Have you chosen your position from *alternatives?*
4. Have you chosen your position after *thoughtful consideration* of the pros and cons and consequences?
5. Have you chosen your position *freely?*
6. Have you *acted* on or done anything about your beliefs?
7. Have you acted with *repetition,* pattern, or consistency on this issue?[15]

[13]Wolpe, *The Practice of Behavior Therapy,* p. 100.
[14]T.M. Sherman and W.H. Cormier, "The Use of Subjective Scales for Measuring Interpersonal Reactions," *Journal of Behavior Therapy and Experimental Psychiatry* 3 (1972), 279–80.
[15]For many such instruments, see Sidney B. Simon, Leland W. Howe, and Howard Kirschenbaum, *Values Clarification: A Handbook of Practical Strategies for Teachers and Students* (New York: Hart Publishing Co., Inc., 1972).

TABLE 8-2   Value Grid[a]

Issue	1	2	3	4	5	6	7
1							
2							
3							
4							
5							

[a]Taken from Sydney B. Simon, Leland W. Howe, and Howard Kirschenbaum, *Values Clarification: A Handbook of Practical Strategies for Students and Teachers* (New York: Hart Publishing Company, Inc., 1972), p. 35.

Ratings on Skills in Understanding Self and Situation. A goal of group services for members may be to help them to learn how to understand and make rational decisions regarding behavior or situations. After the group experience is over, their improved ability to analyze situations and make decisions will help the members to cope better with problem situations. A number of approaches previously discussed present the members with ways of accomplishing this, including problem solving, behavioral analysis, and transactional analysis. Scales can be used to evaluate the ability of the member to use any of these approaches. The member can apply the scale to his or her own process or other members can use it as a basis for interviewing the members to assess their cognitive effort. Some questions, for example, that can be used to assess members' skills in problem solving are the following:

1. Has the member sought information relevant to the problem? For example, if the problem is finding a job, has the member found out about the types of jobs most available for persons with his or her training and abilities?
2. Has the member identified the alternatives available to him or her? Do these alternatives include all the most important or relevant ones? Has the individual used the information generated in question 1 to identify alternatives?
3. Has the member evaluated the alternatives using criteria such as the following?
   the alternative with the most likelihood of helping the member achieve his or her goal
   the alternative with the fewest disadvantages or costs
   the alternative most consistent with the member's values
4. Has the member chosen the alternative which he or she evaluated most favorably?
5. Has the member developed or begun to develop a plan to implement the alternative?

These questions can be answered either with a "yes" or "no" or they can be rated on a zero to five scale with zero standing for absence of the behavior and five representing its presence to the fullest degree. Admittedly such a scale does not represent the kind of specificity that is used in formal research but it does present information that will help the members and the worker to judge whether a rational approach to problem solving has been utilized and is, therefore, likely to be a part of the way members will now approach problems.

Task Accomplishment. In many groups, including task-centered ones, the member seeks to attain goals by accomplishing tasks. We have slightly modified the instruments developed by Reid and Epstein for use with such groups.[16] To evaluate client task completion, we developed a form to be completed after each session. Within each space allocated on the form for each group member, the following information is requested: the task or the subtask to be completed by that session; the obstacles encountered by the member in accomplishing the task; the plan that the member has devised at that session to overcome the obstacles;

---

[16]William Reid and Laura Epstein, *Task Centered Practice* (New York: Columbia University Press, 1977), p. 288.

who suggested the task (worker, member, other members); and ratings of the member's commitment to the task and the degree to which the task was accomplished.

Reid has also developed an instrument to measure progress made by clients in solving problems.[17] This instrument allows the client and the worker to choose from among six types of scales the one most appropriate for the client's situation. The scales differ in the types of measurements that are required from fully quantitative to fully qualitative. The instrument can also be used to measure members' problem reduction in groups.

Psychological Instruments. Many instruments developed by psychologists and other behavioral scientists, as well as social workers, can be used by social work practitioners. Their use does not require highly specialized training. Increasingly, in fact, social workers themselves are developing evaluation and assessment instruments that are compatible with social work objectives and methods. The Rathus scale for measuring assertiveness, referred to previously, can be used when social workers seek to help members become more assertive. Examples of other instruments of similar availability are Thomas's[18] and Hops and co-workers[19] for assessing marital communication, Rose's and co-workers' for interpersonal competence,[20] Derogatis's and co-workers' for psychiatric symptoms,[21] Fitts's for self concept,[22] McNair's and co-workers' for moods,[23] and Hudson's for marital satisfaction, generalized contentment, self-esteem, sexual satisfaction, parent attitudes toward children, and child's attitude to either mother or father.[24]

EVALUATION OF CHANGES IN GROUP CONDITIONS

As discussed in Chapter 5, the group worker seeks to modify group conditions and to help the members to do so also in order to create a group conducive to attaining members' goals. A variety of procedures were presented for the worker to accomplish this. Workers, therefore, should seek to evaluate whether their

[17]William Reid, *The Task Centered System* (New York: Columbia University Press, 1978), pp. 272–93. In this book Reid presents an early version of the scales. The elaboration of these scales referred to here is in an, as yet, unpublished document.

[18]Edwin Thomas, *Marital Communication and Decision Making: Analysis, Assessment and Change* (New York: Free Press, 1977).

[19]H. Hops, T. Wills, G.R. Patterson, and R.L. Weiss, *The Marital Interaction Coding System* (unpublished manuscript, University of Oregon and Oregon Research Institute, 1972).

[20]S.D. Rose, J.J. Gayner, and J.L. Edleson, "Measuring Interpersonal Competence," *Social Work* 22 (1977), 125–29.

[21]L.R. Derogatis, R.S. Lipman, and L. Covi, "SCL-90: An Outpatient Psychiatric Rating Scale (Preliminary Report)," *Psychopharmacology Bulletin* 9 (1973), 13–27.

[22]W.F. Fitts, *Tennessee Self-Concept Scale Manual* (Nashville, Tenn.: Counsellor Recordings and Tests, 1965).

[23]D.M. McNair, M. Lorr, and L.F. Dopplemen, *Manual for the Profile of Mood States* (San Diego: Educational and Industrial Testing Service, 1971).

[24]All these scales are printed in Fischer, *Effective Casework Practice,* pp. 110–15.

activities lead to desired changes in the group. Often these group changes will be self-evident. At other times, the worker will seek a reliable means of measuring group changes so as to evaluate the effectiveness of group work techniques and to reinforce members for cooperating in their use.

Measurement Techniques

We shall now discuss some of the approaches that should become familiar to group workers for measuring changes in group conditions.

Group Recording. Group workers, as part of responsible practice, will write a record after each meeting. Sometimes, when the worker wishes to engage in a thorough analysis of factors that contributed to a particular group outcome, she or he will write a *process record.* In this record, the worker presents the most significant events that occurred during the meeting. It is almost impossible (in terms of time spent, if nothing else) to record every word that is spoken. Instead, the worker selects the statements made by members and workers that most reveal the role played by each in determining the direction taken during the session, how the individuals coped with events, or how group conditions evolved. Inevitably, the worker will have to form a judgment as to relevant statements. If workers wish consultation based on more "objective" data, they often seek permission of the group members to electronically record the session.

The following is an example of a segment of a process record from a group of adults whose goals related to improving their interpersonal relationships:

> The group members were discussing the idea that many of them did not know how to be assertive. Sam said that he had been left behind when this colleagues at work went out together for lunch. Mary asked him what he was doing at the time. He said that he was doing some filing. She asked him to pretend that she was one of his co-workers and to act the way he had been behaving at the time. He did this and afterwards I (the worker) asked the group to give him feedback. Jill said that he seemed to be avoiding eye contact with the others in the office. Bob noted that when Mary walked past him, be bent over even farther. The worker asked Sam what kind of message he may have been sending to others. Before Sam could answer, Barbara said that she had similar problems and she didn't know why Sam was getting all of the attention. I wondered why Barbara raised that issue right now.

A less time-consuming type of recording is of *critical incidents.* This requires the worker to write a process record but only of an incident that happened during the full group session. The worker believes such an incident should be closely examined for the information it offers about an event that either affects the whole group or some part of it.

Most frequently, the worker engages in *summary recording.* Through this format the worker summarizes the main events occurring during the session and includes few direct quotes from members or workers. Toseland and Rivas present a typical form for such recording.[25] This form consists of the following items: group name; dates of beginning and ending of group; worker's name; session number; members present and absent; purpose of group; goals of session; activities at session; worker's analysis of meeting; and future plans.

We have devised a form to be used when workers are seeking to develop new group work technologies. Prior to the meeting, the worker prepares a list of the activities he or she has planned for the session with details as to the techniques he or she plans to use. Each activity is numbered, as well as the group work recording form. The worker is asked to record after the appropriate number whether the activity was conducted as planned, how the activity was modified, and how successful the activity was in terms of its purpose. The form also has a place to record critical incidents related to the use of the technology as well as issues that were encountered in this use.

Still another type of group recording makes use of codes to describe the sequence of events in a group meeting. An example of this type of instrument follows:

GROUP WORK RECORDING FORM

Practitioner's Name: _____ Group Name: _____ Session#: _____

Date of Meeting: _____ Time of Meeting: From ____ To ____

Members Present:

1. Practitioner's goals for group session (Comment as to whether these are acknowledged by members):

2. Practitioner's goals for individuals during session (Comment as to whether these are acknowledged by members):

3. Practitioner's agenda for session (Comment on how this relates to members' agenda):

4. Process

[25]Ronald Toseland and Robert Rivas, *An Introduction to Group Work Practice* (New York: Macmillan, 1984), p. 310.

Codes[a]	Episode 1 Time:	Episode 2 Time:	Episode 3 Time:	Episode 4 Time:	Episode 5 Time:
Content Code					
Intervention Codes					
Type of Process Code					

[a] Codes will be created by the agency; the following are illustrative: content = individual's problem behavior, group condition, group planning, nonverbal program; interventions = interpretations, facilitate problem solving, reinforcement, modeling; type of program = discussion, presentation, game, creative project, exercise, problem solving, role play.

In space below, briefly describe incidents, significant interactions among members or between members and worker and indicate in which episodes interaction took place:

5. Major obstacles, if any, to attaining goals during meeting:

6. Report of evaluative data collected during meeting:

7. Plans for next meeting:

8. Overall assessment of session

The major objectives of the session were accomplished *for* the following proportion of members

____ Completely   ____ All

____ Almost completely   ____ Most

____ Partially   ____ About half

____ To a slight degree   ____ A few

____ Not at all   ____ None

Behavioral Counts. We began our discussion of evaluating individual changes with behavioral counts, largely because of the simplicity of this form of measurement. For similar reasons, such counts can also often be used to assess changes in group conditions. Many changes that group workers seek to achieve in groups are manifested in specific behaviors of members that can be defined and counted on a tally sheet. For example, the workers and the group may seek to increase certain classes of member behaviors for all members, such as, expressions of feelings, self-disclosure statements, requests for help from others, arrivals on time to the meetings, declarations regarding one's values, or verbal reinforcements to others. Either the worker, an outside observer, or a member can keep a record of all such acts and can report the results to the group. This represents a group condition in that such behaviors are partially under the control of group norms that call for either expressing or inhibiting them. Group members and workers, when evaluating their groups, will often seek to change the frequency with which certain behaviors are expressed so that the effectiveness of the group will be enhanced.

Measurements of Group Structures. Since the basic tool in group work is the communication among members and between members and the worker, the communication structure—who talks to whom about what—is often the target of change. In Chapter 5 we presented a number of examples of ways to assess communications structures and these can be used to evaluate whether efforts to change such structures are effective. One of the simplest techniques, which was described in that chapter, was a tabulation of the sequence of member and worker statements (M M M W M W M M M W). This can be used to indicate whether there is an increase in member-to-member as compared to member-to-worker interactions simply by dividing the number of Ms by the number of Ws.

Some devices that are used to change group conditions can also be used to measure changes. Rose, for example, described a procedure to help a group become more aware of its pattern of offering reinforcing remarks as compared to punishing remarks.[26] Members placed poker chips in a can using one color to indicate feeling reinforced and another to indicate feeling punished. While the chips were used to signal subjective experience, they can be counted to evaluate a change in this type of communication in the group.

Rose has also developed a system for assessing content expressed by one member to another. He developed the following content categories: suggestion-opinion-giving response; questions; responses to questions; self-suggestion responses; negative affect; positive affect; and information giving.[27] The observer coded each remark in terms of who said it, who it was directed to, and the category into which it fit. This allowed the worker to tabulate who spoke most frequently, who was spoken to most often, and the most frequent types of comments. Depending on member and worker concerns, any one of these as well as other potential tabulations might be used to select goals for changes in group conditions and then to monitor changes.

To assess changes in a group's sociometric structure, some workers rely on observations of subgroups while others have used standard sociometric questionnaires in which members are asked with whom they chose to work or to whom

---

[26]Rose, *Group Therapy,* p. 142.
[27]Ibid., pp. 50–51. These categories are similar to those used by Bales to study group interactions; see Robert F. Bales, *Interactive Process Analysis: A Method for the Study of Small Groups* (Reading, Mass.: Addison-Wesley, 1950).

they felt closest. Such questionnaires can provoke a great deal of anxiety, however. Yalom reports, nevertheless, asking each member to rate all members of the group in popularity, apparently without serious harm to the members.[28] These approaches can be used to assess changes in the number of isolates and the composition of subgroups.

Workers may also wish to monitor changes in the power structure of the group, particularly when members are influenced by others in the group in dysfunctional ways. Some members, also, may have had little influence on the group, causing damage to their self-esteem as well as hindering their integration into group activities. One way to assess changes in this pattern is to record responses to members' ideas or suggestions. These responses can be coded as (1) support or agreement; (2) disagreement; or (3) not relevant (for example, changed subject or ignored statement). All responses are not coded; only those that are made in relationship to directions, suggestions, or new ideas. Some members do not contribute any of these and, at least by this measure, are low in this manifestation of power.

Measurement of Group Processes. One of the most important group processes is problem solving and workers will seek to assess changes in the group's problem-solving capacity. We previously presented a means of evaluating the group's handling of problem-solving incidents as an exercise (see exercise at end of Chapter 5). The instrument presented there was utilized as follows: tape recordings were made of group meetings and were replayed in order to identify problem-solving episodes. The scale was used to rate each of these episodes. Changes in problem-solving processes were examined from both within the meetings and over several meetings. Occasionally, a group which engages in effective problem solving regresses. The worker in these situations will examine the content of the problem as well as other events in the group in order to diagnose the source of the difficulty.

Another crucial type of process, also a form of problem solving, is the process illumination activity discussed in Chapter 5. Although this is an essential part of most approaches to group psychotherapy, we have not found any literature regarding an evaluation of its impact as a specific and discrete tool. We do have several suggestions, however, for an evaluation of this procedure. Members whose interpersonal processes have been examined in this way can be asked, after the procedure has been utilized, to note in a personal journal what they have learned about their responses to the other person and about the other's responses also. Subsequent "processing" of their interactions can also be noted in the journal. The worker or an observer can also make notes on the types of learning they assumed took place. Periodically workers can examine the log, with the permission of the member, to assess the kind of learning that was accomplished. Hopefully, this kind of exploratory work might help workers to develop more systematic ways of studying the effects of process illumination.

---

[28] Irvin D. Yalom, *The Theory and Practice of Group Psychotherapy,* 2nd ed. (New York: Basic Books, 1975), p. 51.

The process of changes in attraction of members to each other and to the group, a major component of cohesiveness, is a very essential one. A successful group depends on the members' attendance and investment. The workers should, therefore, obtain feedback from members as to their reactions to the group at specific meetings as well as over longer periods of time. A two- or three-question instrument can be completed just before members leave in which they record how strongly they desire to return (for example, on a 7-point scale from "not at all" to "very much") and the activities or discussions during the meeting they found most and least useful. Yalom describes a cohesiveness scale that he and his colleagues used on which members rated the following items (on five-point scales).[29]

1. How often do you think your group should meet?
2. How well do you like the group you are in?
3. If most of the members of your group decided to dissolve the group by leaving, how would you like an opportunity to dissuade them?
4. Do you feel that working with the group you are in will enable you to attain most of the goals in therapy?
5. If you could replace members of your group with other "ideal group members," how many would you exchange (exclusive of group therapists)?
6. To what degree do you feel you are included by the group in the group's activities?
7. How do you feel about your participation in, and contribution to, the group work?
8. How do you feel about the length of the group meeting?
9. How do you feel about the group therapists?
10. Are you ashamed of being in group therapy?
11. Compared to other therapy groups, how well would you imagine your group works together?

This scale can then be totaled for each person and a group average computed. The worker should calculate the group median rather than mean so than the statistic is not strongly affected by a small number of members who may be extremely positive or negative. Changes in group cohesiveness over time can be examined to identify the need for or the consequences of interventions aimed at this phenomenon.

Workers should also assess the phase of development of the group. This is usually done through the examination of one's impressions of a variety of group conditions. In Chapter 5 we presented an instrument for collecting data about group development. It can be used by workers to confirm their impressions as well as to identify aspects of the group that are impeding development such as ambiguity of purpose, antagonisms among members, dysfunctional structures, or inappropriate choices of activities.

Rose has developed another way of measuring group processes.[30] At the end of the session he presents members with a questionnaire with items that the members can respond to by circling a point on a scale. The following are examples

---

[29]Yalom, *Group Psychotherapy,* p. 51.
[30]Sheldon D. Rose, "Use of Data in Identifying and Resolving Group Problems in Goal Oriented Treatment Groups," *Social Work with Groups* 7, no. 2 (Summer, 1984), 23–36.

of such items: How useful was today's session for you? Describe your involvement in today's session; rate the extent of your self-disclosure of relevant information about yourself or your problem; how important to you were the problems or situations you discussed (others discussed) in the group today? Circle the number on the scale which best describes the interrelationships among group members and leaders in this group. Circle all the words which best describes you at today's session (e.g., excited, bored, depressed, interested, comfortable); how satisfied were you with today's session?

Measurement of Shared Attributions. As discussed in Chapter 5, the group affects the way members view events. The worker cannot assume, however, that a group discussion of the cause of some event accurately reflects how each individual views it. A number of members, for example, may have remained out of the conversation. Do they agree with what is being said? Are they afraid to voice disagreement? Are they suspending judgment to hear what others think? Consequently, workers will sometimes ask members privately to write their perceptions of the causes of an event or their values regarding it. If the worker has asked the group to discuss its understanding of the event, this can be compared to members' individual responses. Similarities and differences in what individuals say privately and in the presence of others will tell a great deal about group conditions, such as willingness of members to honestly share opinions and ability of some members to control the opinions held by others.

Social-Psychological Instruments. Instruments that have been developed by social scientists can also be used, with some adaptation, by practitioners for evaluation of group changes. The practitioner who desires to measure change in some group dimension can usually locate such instruments by consulting one of the standard texts on the sociology of groups.[31] Some examples of instruments that can be used are Bales's for observing interactions,[32] Byrne's for assessing member's similarity of activity preferences,[33] and Crosbie's for charting members' statuses (for example, power and prestige).[34]

EVALUATION OF ENVIRONMENTAL CHANGES

The basis for evaluating an environmental change, when the aspect of the environment that is targeted is some specific policy or resource, may be self-evident. Evidence that the policy has been changed can easily be secured. For example, the

[31]See, for example, Howard L. Nixon II, *The Small Group* (Englewood Cliffs, N.J.: Prentice-Hall, Inc., 1979); and Stephen Wilson, *Informal Groups: An Introduction* (Englewood Cliffs, N.J.: Prentice-Hall, Inc., 1978).

[32]Bales, *Interaction Process Analysis.*

[33]D. Byrne, *The Attraction Paradigm* (New York: Academic Press, 1971.)

[34]Paul V. Crosbie, "Effects of Status Inconsistency: Negative Evidence From Small Groups," *Social Psychological Quarterly* no. 2 (June, 1979), 110–25.

member has had a welfare grant increased or a school has established a new curriculum. At other times, the environmental change the members are seeking may be harder to identify because it relates to attitudes of organizational participants or patterns of interaction within the system.

Measurement Techniques

Some ways to assess environmental changes are to draw upon official reports, member's experiences, and interviews with informants, or to administer appropriate instruments. We shall describe each of these sources.

Official Reports. Some reasons to examine these are to determine if policies have changed, if resources are being used differently, or if the way services are being delivered has been altered. Such documents include annual reports, budgets, service descriptions, and statistical reports.

Member experiences. Members who are involved in the same organization can compare their experiences. This is appropriate if the change sought is in the behavior of the organization toward these members, such as the amount of reinforcement for students provided by a teacher. Another example of this occurred in a group in a hospital setting. The members sought more courteous attention from the nursing staff. Members agreed to keep records of the responses of nurses. This was subsequently shared at a meeting between the group members and representatives of the nursing staff when it was decided to present this data at a meeting of all of the nurses.

Interviews. Some organizational manifestations can best be examined through sensitive interviews with key personnel by trained observers. An example of a phenomenon that was measured this way was the imposition of destructive labels on group members, a form of negatively stereotyping them. Another type of occasion requiring such interviews is when individuals in the environment act in undesirable ways toward group members and are able to continue this through informal support from others in their system. An example of this was when a school counselor advised all black students not to consider going to college. A student brought this issue to the attention of her group and the members decided to interview their teachers to find out how aware they were of this advice. At a later time, they interviewed the teachers again to find out if any actions had been taken to prevent this type of discrimination.

Structured Instruments. The group, the worker, or both can choose to use an already developed instrument to measure changes in environmental conditions. For example, Moos has developed a number of scales to measure environmental conditions that impact on participants.[35] These conditions, which include

[35]Rudolf H. Moos, *Evaluating Treatment Environments: A Social Ecological Approach* (New York: John Wiley, 1974).

such dimensions as the degee of structure, the freedom to express one's beliefs, and the presence of conflict, are examined by asking organization members to rate items on a questionnaire. Group members can use this instrument to evaluate changes in such environments as school rooms, hospital wards, residential treatment milieux, or even communities.

Guerney, in a training program for use in groups to enhance relationships, developed a number of scales to measure changes in relationships such as an "interpersonal relationship scale" and a "relationship change scale."[36] Items in these scales can be used to assess changes in the quality of relationships, even when the specific procedure developed by Guerney is not utilized. These changes, because they are interactional, reflect not only the behavior of the group member, but the responses of significant others. Such measures may be used when these others are part of the group work process as in couples' groups or when a member of the group is working on relationship issues that involve people not in the group.

Example. Members in a group of high school students were being helped to stay in school and to be more successful. For baseline data, the worker utilized the school grades of the members during the previous semester; responses to a brief questionnaire developed by the worker regarding their attitudes toward school; and the proportion of homework assignments they had completed the first two weeks the group met. During these first weeks, the worker helped the members to become more acquainted with each other and did not attempt any actions to modify the members' school behaviors. The worker asked the members to record their assignments on a daily basis and to check those that were finished. These same measures were utilized when the group had met for two months and when the group terminated at the end of four months. Several group process issues emerged during these four months. One was the attendance of members during the first meetings. Several times during these months the worker distributed a modification of the cohesiveness scale previously described. The worker discovered an increase in cohesiveness as the members became more committed to the group's goals and as changes were made in the group's program to make the group more attractive. At one point, also, some members who were less committed to the group's goals heavily influenced others. The worker asked the members separately to list the members of the group who most influenced them. The results of the survey were presented to the group and this led to a very thoughtful discussion on how and why members were influenced by peers. The same questionnaire submitted later showed a number of changes in who influenced whom that the worker believed were conducive to the member's attaining their goals. The means of helping the members included securing the teachers' support. A few teachers had negatively labeled the members and their lack of encouragement was demoralizing. The group invited these teachers to sit in on several meetings in order to learn about members' efforts. Afterward, members

---

[36]Bernard G. Guerney, Jr. *Relationship Enhancement* (San Francisco: Jossey-Bass, 1977).

who encountered these teachers in classes kept a "log" of transactions. The logs were presented in group meetings to help the members assess changes brought about by these interventions with the teachers.

SUMMARY

This chapter began with a general discussion of the current emphasis on accountability in social work. While some undesirable consequences of this emphasis were described, we favor the concept of the practitioner–researcher. In group work this requires the worker to be able, with the cooperation of the members, to assess changes in individuals, group conditions, and the environment of the group. The chapter, therefore, included a discussion of some of the types of measures that the group worker should be able to employ to evaluate changes in each of these entities. In addition, some form of recording should be maintained for each group session. A sample recording form was presented.

GROUP WORK RECORDING EXERCISE

Goals

1. To understand the components of group work practice recordings.
2. To develop accuracy in recording group sessions.

Procedure

1. Trainees review and discuss Recording of Group Sessions in this chapter.

2. Trainees observe an example of a group session. This can be a role play, a tape, a film or a written, detailed account of a group work session. (For the latter purpose, the extended examples in Chapter 10–15 can be utilized.)

3. Each trainee completes the group work recording form presented in this chapter.

4. The teacher or trainer leads a discussion in the training group or class based on how each person has responded to each item on the form. Differences in responses are noted and discussed as a means of increasing members' skills in utilizing the form.

9

The Group
And Endings

What the end of a group experience means to participants is something that must be understood by workers so that they can be helpful. Much of the future impact of the experience is determined at this stage. If the termination process is a successful one, members will be more likely to transfer the learning in the group to other life situations, to enter into other group experiences when the need arises, and to remember the group with positive feelings rather than with guilt or anger. In this chapter we shall discuss the group termination phenomena that workers must understand and the tasks they must undertake in order to achieve the beneficial results of a "good" termination experience.

MEANINGS OF ENDINGS

In many ways all endings have some things in common. This is true whether the ending is of a relationship with a single person or a group; whether the ending is the termination of a relationship in which all parties simply separate or one in which someone has died. Some have even speculated on similarities with occasions when one loses a treasured possession or even part of one's self as in surgery or disability. In all of these events, the person has invested energy in the situation, may have expressed affection, and has participated in an ongoing experience with the other person or object.

After the loss, the individual has the task of withdrawing this energy investment, of engaging in mourning for the lost person or object, and of establishing a new equilibrium in which the person, group, or object no longer plays the same role except in memory. From the earliest days of life, people must cope with the experience of loss. Young children who see their parents leave their field of vision are uncertain of the parent's return until this has been repeated a number of times. When a parent leaves for work, this is experienced as a loss at least until the child understands the reasons for this absence. Playmates move away, teachers change, and sooner or later—often first with pets—the permanency of death must be dealt with.

Thus coping with loss is an essential part of life, perhaps one that creates some sense of tragedy, and life cannot be lived to its fullest until one comes to some terms with the inevitability of endings. The ability of the group worker to *understand* these issues and to use the ending of the group as an occasion to help the members add to *their understanding* is essential.

Somewhat different processes will take place, depending on the plan as to when the group will end. Some groups do not have a fixed time for ending. In these, various members may leave while the group goes on—either because they have accomplished their purposes or because they have given up hope of doing so. Some groups may end at the same time for all members when it is agreed that optimum benefits have been attained. Probably the majority of groups conducted by social workers have a fixed number of sessions whether these be short-term groups of a few months or long-term groups that last, for example, for a school year.

Unless there are strong reasons to the contrary, such as uncertainty as to group purpose or the complexities of the length of time it takes to achieve personality change, we prefer a time limit to groups—whether it is short or long term. This is because of our belief that time limits serve to mobilize the energy and the planning of activities by participants to achieve their goals—if the time limits are reasonable.[1] Other things being equal, we also favor a short period of time rather than a long one because of such ideas as those advanced by Reid and Epstein to the effect that people are most motivated to receive help when they experience disequilibrium in their lives and are most likely to terminate when equilibrium has been restored.[2]

Groups that have time limits, particularly short-term groups of eight to twelve sessions, start the termination process early, perhaps from their beginning. Members know the date of the last meeting, even if (as frequently happens) they

[1]The author has always been interested in the ideas regarding the meaning of time in the helping process developed by the "functional" approach to social work. See Ruth Elizabeth Smalley, *Theory for Social Work Practice* (New York: Columbia University Press, 1967), pp. 142–51. Another approach to the time dimension may be found in Arnold P. Goldstein, Kenneth Heller, and Lee B. Sechrest, *Psychotherapy and the Psychology of Behavior Change* (New York: John Wiley, 1966), pp. 280–86.

[2]William Reid and Laura Epstein, *Task Centered Casework* (New York: Columbia University Press, 1977), p. 28.

deny this or try to negotiate an extension. Plans are made for activities with an awareness of the time frame available to the group. The depth of relationships is affected, also, by this awareness. Thus any discussions of relationships or choice of member goals are held with an implicit or explicit sense of the available time. Since the date of the ending is known in advance, members are not surprised when the worker raises issues around planning for the last sessions.

Groups which have no advance determination of the length and which are terminating because the goals have been attained pose a different issue. Members are more likely to deny that they are ready for termination and they will raise questions as to why the worker has decided to terminate. They must adjust to an event whose timing was, at least initially, ambiguous or unknown.

As we have seen, there are differences between the termination of groups with established time periods and those in which the ending was determined later. Nevertheless, if the experiences have been positive and members have accomplished many of their goals, there is more in common in the way the worker facilitates the termination process in these two situations than there is with situations when the group was unsuccessful. Another dissimilar event is when termination was imposed by unanticipated circumstances such as the loss of the worker from the agency. Another termination is when members enter and leave at different times, although planned, as in so-called "open groups."

WORKER TASKS

First we shall discuss the worker's tasks in groups when the group experience was generally viewed as positive and when all members terminate simultaneously. We shall return, at the end of the chapter, to a discussion of termination tasks under a variety of other circumstances. In the former circumstances the worker helps the members as follows:

> To evaluate the group in relationship to achievement of its goals
> To understand and cope with their feelings regarding termination
> To maintain the beneficial changes that have resulted from the group experience
> To utilize the skills, attitudes, and knowledge gained through the group in a variety of circumstances
> To seek out and utilize new services when this is appropriate.

There is no established order to any of these tasks. In each group the nature of the members' experiences will determine whether accomplishing one task will naturally lead to another. For example, in an evaluation of one group, as criticisms were offered, angry feelings were expressed. On the other hand, a discussion of new situations in which acquired skills will be appropriately used led to positive expressions. The worker, therefore, will usually plan with the members, for accomplishing each of these tasks in an order and in a way that makes sense to the group in question. Even after this process has begun, changes will take place in the termination plan because of unanticipated issues that arise. To help the reader apply the principles of termination planning, we have included a termination exercise at the end of this chapter.

In groups that have only met for a few months, a major emphasis on termination tasks will usually occur during the last two or three meetings. Long-term groups may devote part of several more sessions to termination issues.

EVALUATION

The last chapter was devoted to a presentation of many of the ways that changes in individuals, groups, and the environment can be measured. Of concern here is the way these or other instruments and procedures will be used by workers as part of the termination process. One aspect of this process is a decision as to which formal sources of information will be utilized in the group as part of termination. The evaluative instruments and design, for purposes of accountability, will already have been determined. The issue here is which findings will be examined *by the group members* and how this will take place.

Members' Evaluation of the Group

The worker should review the types of instruments that have been in use and their purposes. The members, on the basis of the issues they have decided are relevant for their termination concerns, will select, from the data available, the specific information to discuss. This discussion will emphasize the meaning of the information to the members and the reasons they perceive for their successes and failures in the group. These reasons are seldom produced by the questionnaires and instruments themselves.

Example. In an assertiveness training group the members discussed the changes in each member (on an assertiveness scale); all of these changes constituted an improvement but some member's gains were greater than others. One member with a small increment talked about the severe criticism he still receives from his employer when he asserts himself. Another member with a much greater gain spoke of the encouragement she had received from her friends as she became more assertive with her family.

An important part of the evaluative process is the free and unstructured discussion of their personal changes in which members are likely to engage. This includes things they liked and did not like about the group. Such discussion is invaluable to the worker as many dimensions of change can be identified that have not been included in any instrument and that can help the worker to plan for subsequent groups. The aspects of the experience that members believe caused their changes also will suggest potent aspects of the group experience that were not part of the worker's strategy.

A worker, for example, who attributed most of the members' changes to the kinds of techniques he used, such as role plays and demonstrations, was surprised to learn that the members thought many of their gains were due to his acceptance, liking, and concern for them. In a contrasting way, another worker attributed change to the supportive atmosphere of the group and was equally surprised to hear the members' assertion that the most helpful thing to them was the specific advice they received as to how to train their children. There is no certain way of knowing whether the members' or the worker's perceptions of why changes took place were most correct but the ideas of the members should be seriously considered.

Similarly, when the members discuss what they liked and disliked about the group, they will frequently comment on dimensions that have not been formally measured and that may even have been unpredicted. Thus one group discussed at length an experience they had when a severe blizzard prevented their leaving the agency and they had to "camp out" there overnight: the things they learned about each other when discussion was unstructured; the small ways they helped each other with such problems as making plans for children and spouses; and the stronger identification they had with the group after the experience was over demonstrated a great deal to the worker about the "causes" of the excellent outcomes of that group. While the worker cannot "program" blizzards, he did decide to consider a "marathon" session in similar groups in the future.

Members' Evaluation of the Worker

An important component to evaluation, not considered yet, is an evaluation of the worker. Workers should not wait until the termination of the group to ask for feedback from members on their activities and in long-term groups workers should ask for this several times. Most workers do not yet do this directly, but it is our conviction that this is a requirement for responsible practice and workers should be trained to include this with other evaluative activities. Asking for a personal evaluation is, of course, anxiety provoking for most, if not all, workers because of the desire to be regarded highly, a fear of negative criticism, and a concern that undesirable traits unknown even to the workers may be uncovered. Workers, however, who face these concerns and ask for an evaluation will demonstrate that they can take feedback in the same way as they expect members to. Workers also have an opportunity to model constructive ways of handling both criticism and praise.

The problem is how to ask for an evaluation by members. Ideally, the kind of trust that has built up between members and the worker will allow members to take responsibility for their critique and still be free to offer it sincerely. They can respond to written questions and discuss their answers openly. There will be times, however, even in effective groups, when the worker and the members will decide together that the most useful responses will be anonymous ones.

Some questions that workers can ask to receive feedback on their work are the following:

1. What are some of my actions you find most and least helpful?
2. What actions would you like me to take that are not being taken?

3. Are there personal qualities of mine you find helpful or not helpful (for example, ways of speaking, timing of interventions, sense of humor, ways of expressing self)?
4. How well do you think I understand what you are thinking and feeling? How do I communicate that?
5. How honest do you believe I am with you?
6. Do you experience me as supportive and caring?
7. How do you think I respond to members of a sex or ethnic culture different from my own?

An important thing for workers to remember is that members will find offering this type of feedback difficult. There are many social conventions against giving honest responses to these kinds of questions and this is compounded by the emotional meaning workers usually have for members. This makes it particularly difficult for members to express criticism. Thus in such discussions the topic can subtly shift to a discussion of the group's program, the agency's inputs, or the general type of service offered. This shift can also be a response to a sense of the worker's discomfort. When the worker, however, clearly and honestly asks for evaluation, it is likely to be forthcoming.

UNDERSTAND AND COPE WITH FEELINGS

As indicated in the opening paragraphs of this chapter, people have many feelings with which they find it difficult to deal during endings. They must learn to handle these feelings for several reasons. One is that each time a person copes with feelings regarding endings, he or she will undoubtedly acquire strengths that will be useful in coping with the endings yet to come. Second, unresolved feelings about an experience such as group work can hinder the member's ability to remember and utilize the learning acquired through that experience.

All losses engender similar feelings although these feelings may vary in sequence and in intensity. Kübler-Ross, for example, in her seminal work on death and dying describes the sequence of reactions that she observed to occur when one learns of impending death.[3] We believe that these feelings are present to some degree whenever any ending is faced. The first response she notes is that of denial and this almost always occurs when the worker broaches the subject of the groups' ending. Members may not deny that the group will end but they frequently do deny the feelings they have about this. They manifest this by continuing to engage in whatever activities were before them when the subject of termination was raised or they may state that they do not have feelings about the group's ending or that they have already dealt with these feelings. Another manifestation of such denial is seen in members who miss meetings after termination is first discussed or who diminish in their degree of group participation. Workers, particularly in short-term group or groups they deem less successful, may join in this denial and underestimate the meaning of the relationships, the activities, and the identification of members with the group.

[3]Elisabeth Kübler-Ross, *On Death and Dying* (New York: Macmillan, 1969).

In dealing with denial, workers can acknowledge to the members that endings are difficult and that feelings about them are also hard to express. They can ask the members to recall other endings of relationships and since those were more distant, members may be initially more able to express feelings experienced in those situations. Some workers have introduced a period in which members mill about the meeting room saying goodbye to other members as well as to the worker; a variation of this is to rotate around the group asking members to formulate a farewell statement. This type of experience elicits expressions, on verbal and nonverbal levels, of feelings that can be explored.

Kübler-Ross describes another reaction, one which is also present in group terminations, that of anger. In groups this is often expressed at the agency which may have established time limits, at the group (and indirectly the worker) for not having accomplished more, and even at one's self for not having fully achieved one's goals. Anger can also be shown by members who become overly critical of the worker thus rejecting him or her before they are rejected. This emotion at termination is difficult for members and workers. Workers may feel guilt because of their sense of responsibility for what happened in the group; members will fear that positive aspects of the experience will be lost because of their anger. Nevertheless, a group that has encouraged an honest expression of feeling throughout its existence cannot do an "about face" at this point. The legitimacy of the feelings must be acknowledged through the worker admitting that imperfections of the group or one's self or both do make one angry. The important question is what the members will "do" with the anger. Ultimately, the anger must be channeled so that the member works to make future situations more responsive to the member's needs and the member more effective on his or her own behalf.

The third reaction described by Kübler-Ross is "bargaining." In groups, members who react this way seek to postpone the endings of the group or to create new experiences that may not be appropriate. In a sense, this may be one way the member channels anger and thus is a first step in coping effectively with it. The worker should continue to empathize with the members' desires to continue the group and the feelings that have elicited that solution. If the worker continues to be firm on plans for ending, however, more effective means of coping with anger over termination are likely to emerge.

Depression, according to Kübler-Ross, is another stage of this process. While we do not find that these stages appear discretely or consecutively in groups, depression often occurs after a phase of denial and bargaining. It is manifested in a lack of energy for the final activities of the group, a recounting of sad events or failures that occurred earlier, and even in direct emotional expression such as tears. We believe that this is a period of withdrawal of energy from the group and of mourning and is a psychological necessity. When it is not denied but is allowed full expression, it usually leads to a return of energy to perform the other tasks that are necessary for termination. The members invest energy in these tasks in a phase analogous to the one Kübler-Ross describes as "acceptance."

One way some members respond to the feelings about termination is through regression. They will behave in ways that they did earlier in the life of the group. Members in one group, for example, began to manifest relationship problems that had presumably been resolved. Members of a children's group increased their quarreling and cooperated less in activities than they had at the meeting before termination was discussed. While regression is a defense that some people use in times of stress, in groups it has the added function of demonstrating that members still need each other, the worker, and the group.

In a sense, this discussion of some of the feelings at termination suggest that they are all "negative" or "painful." If the group has been successful, there are also several positive feelings manifested. Members will experience pleasures at having attained their goals, mastered obstacles, and remained in the group through the difficulties. Members also inevitably experience some relief that the time investment and expense of attending meetings will end. They may feel some guilt for this latter emotion yet in the continuing spirit of disclosure they can also assert pleasure that these costs will cease.

As can be seen, the feelings toward endings are ambivalent ones and this typifies any change. During the group, it is hoped that members have come to understand ambivalence and this can be deepened as they explore their feelings toward termination. An ability to work through ambivalence is necessary during all transitions and this may be one of the most significant learnings that occur at the group's end.

Much of the "dual" nature of termination responses is reflected in Garland, Jones, and Kolodny's discussion of "flight" during the termination phase.[4] This can be a "nihilistic flight" or "destructive reaction to separation" such as "rejecting and rejection-provoking behaviors" or "positive flight" such as when "constructive moves are made toward 'self-weaning' from the group." The latter "includes finding new groups, activities, work interests, friends, etc., outside the group while continuing as a member."

MAINTAIN CHANGES

The problem of helping the client to maintain changes after the end of the helping process is a general one. Research into all forms of change efforts shows that a significant proportion of the people participating in the effort do not maintain their changes. This has led to an increasing amount of attention to maintenance of change.[5] A major barrier to this is that members' ability to hold on to changes is not only a function of how the change was produced, as the strongest reverses often result from the negative impact of the environment. Friends and relatives

---

[4]James A. Garland, Hubert E. Jones, and Ralph Kolodny, "A Model for Stages of Development in Social Work Groups," in *Explorations in Group Work,* ed. Saul Bernstein (Boston: Boston University School of Social Work, 1965), p. 44.

[5]For a recent, extensive treatment of this topic see Arnold P. Goldstein and Frederick H. Kanfer, eds., *Maximizing Treatment Gains: Transfer Enhancement in Psychotherapy* (New York: Academic Press, 1979).

may seek to reinforce older ways of behaving. Formal organizations such as schools and places of employment may punish the new behaviors. Even without these negative forces, the members may still be uncertain of acting in new ways.

The worker, therefore, as termination approaches, must apply techniques to help the members deal with those forces that can undo the beneficial effects of the group. Some of these have been discussed already but bear repetition here. One principle for accomplishing this is *overlearning*. This means that members have the opportunity to test out a number of times what they have learned before the group ends. If the termination plan includes a reduction of the frequency of meetings, members can assign themselves to a number of "trials" of new behaviors between these meetings.

Workers will also discuss the resistance members may meet in the environment and other members, familiar with each other's situations, can do the same. This has several effects: members will be less likely to become discouraged when "backsliding" takes place. They also should engage in problem solving as to how they will deal with these barriers. Such warnings are analogous to "paradoxical instructions," also. Some members have a tendency, for psychological reasons, to undermine their own progress, particularly if it has been recognized by others. It is harder to revert to this kind of negativism when both continued progress *as well as* regression are predicted.

Approaches to helping that involve work with representatives of all of the member's relevant systems are emphasized by "network" theorists who are most concerned about the kinds of environmental issues just discussed.[6] While there is much to commend total "network" approaches, research does not clearly indicate when they are required, especially if environmental issues have been extensively considered by group members.

Some group members' problems are precisely that they do not have supportive networks that can be drawn on to help sustain changes. In these cases, the best way to help members maintain their gains is to facilitate their forming or joining support groups after the group work experience has ended. Sometimes the professionally led group itself will be continued without such leadership by the members for the same reasons. Some criticize these efforts on the grounds that group work has created a dependency on itself rather than on autonomy. We do not agree with this criticism. Most well-functioning people are able to draw on supportive and reinforcing networks consisting of family, peers, colleagues, or fellow members of church and other community groups. Many "graduates" of the group work experience do not have these social assets and there is nothing intrinsically demeaning for them in seeking support from self-help groups. Increasingly, group-based programs have responded to this principle.[7]

---

[6]R.V. Speck and C.L. Attneave, *Family Networks* (New York: Pantheon, 1973).

[7]Examples are the Synanon communities, the community-based programs developed by agencies using positive peer culture, and the types of services developed by Fairweather. For the latter, see George W. Fairweather and others, *Community Life for the Mentally Ill: An Alternative to Institutional Care* (Chicago: Aldine, 1969).

The concept underlying this section is that maintaining progress often depends on securing continuing reinforcement for it. Hopefully, this will come from the members' natural environment. They will often have to deliberately ask for reinforcement, however, even if this *is* a sad commentary on how unlikely we often are to express praise to each other. One of the final exercises in the group can be to help members role play ways of asking for recognition from significant others. The anxiety such requests often cause and the assumption that one is then devoid of humility can be overcome and can enable the members to make a small contribution to the creation of a society in which norms favoring positive statements properly outnumber those favoring negative ones.

UTILIZE SKILLS IN A VARIETY OF CIRCUMSTANCES

Helping the members to utilize what they have learned in the group in a variety of situations will also help them maintain their gains. This process of generalization begins within the group itself. Members who have relationship problems, for example, often begin to try out new ways of interacting with other group members. Nevertheless, the purpose of joining a group is not to learn to adapt to the group or even to learn how to secure changes in it but to acquire personal and social changes in one's natural environment. Therefore, the worker must help the members to transfer what they have learned to other appropriate situations.

There are several ways the worker can help the members in this regard. One way is to vary, even within the group, the contexts in which members use their skills. This can be done by taking trips with the group into environments, when this is possible, and when it is not, by simulating such environments through role plays and similar devices.

Example.   In a group of retarded youths meeting under the auspices of a community mental health program, members had been learning the skill of asking for information and clarifying information that was not clear. During the final meetings of the group, the members took trips to a job program, a health service, a vocational school, and a department store. Before these trips, the group members discussed the types of information they would seek in each setting. Afterward, the members returned to their group meetings to discuss their experiences and to identify the common elements in their responses to each situation.

Since each environment in which a member uses a skill is in some respects unique, members must be able to solve the problems posed by these differences. Therefore, there is scarcely a group in which it is not appropriate to seek to enhance the members' problem-solving skills.

In addition, members must not only be able to "act"; they must also understand how to analyze situations and to explain why each situation calls for the solution that it does. Thus in some way all groups must seek to add to the members' understanding of human behavior. If members understand the principles that govern their actions, they will be able to apply these actions in the broadest range of circumstances. This ability to understand behavior has even broader ramifications, as Yalom points out:

> In part, however, explanation and clarification function as effective curative agents in their own right. Man has always abhorred uncertainty and through the ages has sought to order his universe by providing explanations, primarily religious or scientific. Similarly with psychiatric patients: fear and anxiety which stem from uncertainty of the source, meaning, and seriousness of psychiatric symptoms may so compound the total dysphoria that effective exploration becomes vastly more difficult. Thus, didactic instruction, through its provision of structure and explanation, has intrinsic value and deserves a place in our repertoire of therapeutic instruments.[8]

The worker will utilize this principle of cognitive understanding thoughout the group but the ending is a good time to reinforce it so as to prepare members to apply broadly what they have learned. There are a number of therapeutic systems we have described in this book that explicitly provide for teaching a causal framework to members; these include transactional analysis, positive peer culture, and some approaches to behavior modification. In another sense, this is also true for ego psychological and other cognitively oriented systems whose goal is to enable the member to develop insight.

UTILIZE NEW SERVICES

Members will often seek out new services after the group ends as a logial sequel to their participation in the group. Thus in a group to help unwed mothers to make some decisions regarding raising their children or placing them for adoption, some members sought services to help them acquire child rearing skills; others wished services to help them resume their vocational and educational careers. In the last meetings of the group, the resources to meet these needs were discussed. The worker as well as members shared their knowledge of the agencies providing these services.

Giving knowledge about resources should be more than a simple presentation of information. In the group of unwed mothers just referred to, each member discussed her specific needs in relation to available services. She also was helped to present her expectations of the service, her fears regarding it, and any barriers she anticipated in its use. The members and worker presented their ideas as to the likelihood that these expectations would be met. Ways were also sought to alleviate anxiety about the service and to overcome the barriers. In some cases the worker and in other cases the "buddies" within the group, offered to provide support and additional information as the member coped with applying for and making use of the projected resource.

---

[8]Irvin D. Yalom, *The Theory and Practice of Group Psychotherapy,* 2nd ed. (New York: Basic Books, 1975), p. 11.

REDUCE COHESION

During the first phases of the group, the worker seeks to increase the cohesiveness of the group and this process is reversed during the termination phase. Members must be helped to become less attracted to the group and, when appropriate, more attracted to alternative relationships. The worker, therefore, also reverses the application of principles for attaining group cohesion. For example, instead of increasing the frequency with which members have contact with one another, this may be reduced by having meetings less often and/or for a shorter time. Some groups will taper off with a meeting every other week or once a month. The worker may place less emphasis on resolving conflicts within the group and may not call attention to commonalities of experiences or attitudes except as these relate to ways of coping with termination. This may not be true in group psychotherapy, when this type of process is maintained until the very end.

CEREMONIES

Transitions in social institutions are often marked with ceremonies. These include graduations, weddings, farewell parties, and even funerals. The function of these events is to clearly demarcate one status from another, to express aspirations, to give final rewards, to allow for the expression of sentiment, to provide group support for change, and to emphasize the positives even of sad occasions. The last meeting of the group, consequently, is often the occasion for a ceremony.

The elements that have been used in ceremonies when social work groups have ended include special refreshments, gift giving, "mock" diplomas, opportunities for members to say "last words," taking a group picture, short speeches by the worker, "rituals," or singing a beloved song together. All of these fulfill one or more of the functions just listed.

To be most meaningful, the ceremony should be planned by some or all of the group members together with the worker. This does not preclude some "surprise" elements, such as "diplomas," injected by the worker or a special planning committee. Members may also add spontaneously to these final events as the ceremony is in progress.

SPECIAL TERMINATION ISSUES

The discussion of termination presumed that the entire group ended; alternatively, one member may leave and the group still continues. This occurs in groups that meet indefinitely although members join for periods that coincide with their needs—so called *open-ended* groups. Another example of this is a time-limited group in which a member leaves for personal reasons such as a geographical move or even dissatisfaction with the group.

A modified termination process occurs, even when one member leaves. Unless this termination is appropriately responded to, the results can be negative for the same reasons as if the entire group ended without dealing with termination. This includes reinforcement of what the member has learned in the group, work with feelings about leaving, transfer of the learning to new situations, and movement toward new resources if this is necessary. For these reasons, the worker will encourage the member to attend at least two meetings after he or she decides to leave. The first of these sessions usually is devoted to feelings about leaving and the second to the reinforcement and transfer issues.

In addition to the value accruing to the member who leaves, there are benefits to all the other members. When a termination process does not occur, all members may worry about whether they are really valued by their peers and if their departure will be ignored. Members, moreover, need an opportunity to express their feelings of loss of the departing member. Finally, each member who leaves provides a preparation and a rehearsal for how other members will deal with their departures from the group.

Nevertheless, times may occur when a member does leave abruptly. Members should be given an opportunity to discuss their feelings of rejection. They may also wish to contact that person, perhaps by phone, to express some of their thoughts and feelings about the termination.

A special case of the single person leaving is the departure of the worker, usually because he or she is also terminating from the agency. Members will often experience this as as rejection or as a punitive response to ways they have behaved in the group, even when they know rationally that this is not the case. Members, therefore, will need several sessions to discuss their reaction to the worker's leaving and at least some of these sessions should involve the new worker. This is because, even after the worker leaves, responses to that departure are likely to be discussed by the members. Depending on the nature of the group and the quality of the relationship with the worker, this ending will include an evaluation of the worker, expressions of appreciation, and even a ceremony.

Terminations are particularly difficult when the members and/or the worker view the group as unsuccessful in achieving its major objectives. Nevertheless, an absence of appropriate processes around that kind of termination can also compound the negative effects on the group by exaggerating them, by confusing responsibility, and by making it difficult for members to seek out group experiences that will be beneficial to them.

When the group is unsuccessful, members should still evaluate it so that specific reasons for failure are identified. Members can then seek group experiences devoid of those dimensions. Some reasons for failures that are frequently found are poor group composition, lack of readiness or commitment of members, lack of resources from the agency, negative responses from the environment, unrealistic or inappropriate goals, and poor leadership from the group worker. Reasons for lack of success are seldom any one of these singly and the task of the worker is to prevent a displacement of all the blame onto a single variable.

After discussing the issues just described, members will usually discover some positive elements that have been overlooked in the group and that can be reinforced. This will allow members, also, to express, without either guilt or over-statement, feelings regarding leaving individuals they have liked in the group as well as relief that the group has ended. Such an approach to ending even successful groups, allows for a rational approach to be taken to selecting alternative experiences that will obtain better outcomes for the members.

Sometimes, a group "peters out" with fewer and fewer members attending. In this case, the worker should ask the members to attend a formal ending to the group. This accomplishes all of the goals just described for unsuccessful groups; it is clear that the group has ended, feelings of members are responded to, reasons for failure of the group are clarified, and members are helped to make alternative plans. In some rare cases, the reasons for the group's failure are identified in ways that allow for these to be overcome and the group starts again with more likelihood of success.

Another special issue is posed by "open ended" groups, such as those in hospitals, in which members may only be present for a few meetings. These should be treated as "one session" groups in which each session concludes with a brief termination discussion in which members evaluate the session, comment on what they did or did not "get" from it, and, if they know they are leaving, say goodbyes.

SUMMARY

This chapter began with a discussion of the meaning of endings and an application of this to group situations. Specific tasks of the worker were described as these apply to the endings of relatively successful groups; these include dealing with feelings, evaluating the group, reinforcing gains, promoting transfer of learning, and making appropriate referrals to new resources. General issues in termination were also discussed as reducing cohesiveness and planning ceremonies. In conclusion, this chapter presented ideas on termination of individuals when the group continues as well as termination processes in unsuccessful groups.

TERMINATION EXERCISE

Goals

1. To learn to identify member responses to group termination.

2. To acquire skills in helping group members cope with termination.

Procedure

(This exercise is most effective when utilized with a training group that is actually terminating. Others must simulate this.)

1. Participants review this chapter and discuss it.

2. Participants divide into four subgroups. Each subgroup is assigned a task as follows: Subgroup A plans an evaluation procedure for the entire group; this can apply to the group thus far, or if the group only convened for this exercise, for this session only. Subgroup B plans a procedure to help the group members to deal with feelings about termination. Subgroup C plans a procedure(s) to help the group to maintain and transfer something that the members have learned thus far. Subgroup D plans a ceremony for the group to utilize as a termination ceremony.

3. Each subgroup facilitates the group's participation in the procedures it has devised. The order can be determined by the trainer, by negotiation among the subgroups, or by the group as a whole.

4. This termination process is assessed utilizing the accompanying termination assessment form.

5. The group discusses how the termination process they have experienced might be used in some way with other groups as well as what modifications might be required with such groups.

TERMINATION ASSESSMENT FORM

Evaluating the Group Experience

1. Check whether the following dimensions were discussed.

_____ Whether the activities were appropriate to goals.

_____ Whether the interpersonal relationships in the group were conducive to attaining goals.

_____ Whether the members' investment in the group was conducive to attaining goals.

_____ The relationship of the worker's performance to goal attainment.

_____ A summary of the individual member's goal attainments.

_____ Relationship of agency conditions to goal attainment.

2. Discuss each of these dimensions of assessment in terms of the adequacy of the process.

Dealing with Feelings

3. Was denial of feelings about termination present and how was it dealt with?

4. Were there feelings of sadness and how were they dealt with?

5. Were there feelings of anger? At whom were they directed? How were these dealt with?

6. Were there feelings of pleasure regarding the ending of the group? How were these responded to?

7. If ambivalence was present, how was it dealt with?

Maintenance of Change

8. Check which of the following were employed.

_____ Overlearning.

_____ How to cope with a negative environment.

_____ How to develop a supportive environment.

_____ Other (specify).

9. Discuss how well each was employed and with what likely effects.

Generalization

10. Check which of the following were employed.

_____ Varying the context of the group experience.

_____ Enchancing understanding of general principles.

_____ Assignments to practice skills outside the group.

_____ Other (specify).

11. Discuss how well each was employed and with what likely effects.

Referral

12. Were suggestions made for future experiences that will be appropriate to the member's needs? (Specify.)

13. Were members helped to examine how they will apply for such experiences? (Specify.)

14. Were members helped to anticipate any barriers to the use of such experiences?

15. Were members offered any support from the worker or other group members in gaining access to such experience or overcoming barriers to their use?

10

Working
With Groups
To Reduce Anomie

In Chapter 2 we discussed the purposes that were assigned by agencies to the groups they serve. To assist in this analysis, we utilized a typography that consisted of (1) anomie reduction; (2) role attainment; (3) social control; and (4) alternative role attainment.

This was followed by Chapters 3 to 9, where we presented general principles and procedures, along with some variations, for working with groups. To elaborate more fully on these variations, we now present the next six chapters—the first four are devoted to the four categories in our typology. One chapter deals with work with oppressed groups and one with task-oriented groups such as committees. Each chapter will conclude with an extended practice example to offer the reader additional insights on how groups with different purposes are conducted.

In this chapter, we shall present ways of working with groups when the purpose of reducing anomie is at the forefront, such as when the worker wishes to help the members to determine their values, norms, and aspirations in situations where these are in flux, in conflict, or largely absent.

When we first conceptualized anomie reduction as one of the major functions of group service, we did not realize how pervasive this function was. In subsequent use of this material in teaching, the students were able to identify aspects of anomie reduction in their practice with all groups. This is probably because, as one writer states,

All societal roles and practices are open to suspicion. Conventional sex roles are questioned for the limitations they place on individual expressiveness. The Anglo's domination of industry and education is questioned for racist practices and elitist control. Government and the courts are suspect. Formulas and principles of welfare and taxation are challenged. No longer are conventional marriages and single careers the norm; private medicine doesn't work; the environment is deteriorating at an unacceptable rate; and all hidden forms of influence, whether from the private sector or from the government, are being viewed for the limitations they pose to individual freedom and democratic values.[1]

No wonder that members of groups struggle with normative issues.

Beyond the fact that the material in this chapter pertains, to some degree, to all groups, as we indicated in Chapter 2, some groups are established primarily to resolve normative concerns. These groups are most likely to focus on people who, at a particular time, have become strongly aware, for political or social reasons, of their anomic state. As of this writing, related groups with which we have had contact have been devoted to men's, women's, homosexuals', youth's, and ethnic minority concerns. In addition, some of the approaches have been adapted for groups of expectant fathers, employees, students, the elderly, the handicapped, and the socially militant. Thus, for purposes of semantic simplicity, we shall use the phrase *anomie reduction group* to refer to groups specifically formed for this purpose as well as all groups that at some stages of their development focus on this purpose.

Many of the techniques used by such groups have come from "consciousness raising" and "values clarification" programs and, to a lesser degree, from the encounter movement. While we shall discuss a range of approaches to anomie reduction, we shall draw heavily from these programs.

In this, as well as the following chapters, we have organized our presentation around the basic tasks of work with groups, namely those occurring before the group meets (for example, selection of members, composition of the group), during group formation (for example, clarification of purpose, choice of strategy), when the group acts to attain its objectives (for example, choice of techniques and targets for change), and when the group is evaluated and terminated (for example, planning for next experiences, choice of evaluation instrument).

PREGROUP TASKS

As Culbert states, the people in a consciousness-raising group—and we believe in all anomie reduction groups—"should have a common relationship to the social system or structure serving as the focus of their discussion."[2] He gives, as an

---

[1]Samuel A. Culbert, "Consciousness-Raising: A Five Stage Model for Social and Organizational Change," in *The Planning of Change*, 3rd ed., eds. Warren G. Bennis and others (New York: Holt, Rinehart & Winston, 1976), p. 231.
[2]Ibid., p. 233. Because of the relevance of consciousness-raising activities for anomie reduction groups, we shall be making many references to the consciousness-raising experience.

example of this, a group in which married women discussed their family roles. In this group all members were married and he argues that if the group included single women or men, this would have diffused its focus.

Workers, therefore, recruiting for such groups have a conception of the type of consciousness-raising purpose of the group and members are screened for their compatibility with this. We have found, beyond this compatibility, that heterogeneity in the way the members have defined their relationship to the role is valuable. Thus a group of men seeking to cope with changing masculine roles found it beneficial to enroll some members who were "gay" and some who were "straight." When members discussed their experiences as males at different stages of their lives, the similarities as well as differences between the "gay" and "straight" men helped each to clarify many of their conceptions of masculinity. Furthermore, this group was composed of men of different ages—the youngest being 19 and the oldest 50—and different statuses—ranging from cook to college professor. Because of this compositional range, the similarities and differences in their experiences helped to illuminate many of the issues they discussed.

The fact that the men's group just described "worked" was, in part, due to the fact that they broadly defined their consciousness-raising purpose as dealing with men's roles. Had they initially, or later, decided the primary focus was narrower (for example, the role of husband or of gay person), the most desirable composition would have been of persons with the same role.

When anomie reduction activities occur in groups primarily established for other purposes, how well they are handled will depend on the composition of the group. If the members seeking to clarify their roles and values share role and value concerns with some other members, these can be dealt with in the group—if opposition to such consideration is absent. Opposition may arise if the others find this process threatening or irrelevant.

Thus, in one social skills group of university students, a gay woman worked on some of her beliefs about her role because several other women in the group identified as lesbians and from their experiences were able to help her clarify some of her issues. The other members of the group, whose life styles were different, were not too naive, hostile, or uninterested to impede this process. On the other hand, a gay man in another group, when he dealt with analogous issues, had to respond to the curiosity of some members and the discomfort of others. The worker subsequently helped him to find another group that was more supportive when he dealt with his sexual orientation.

Anomie reduction activities are best conducted in groups containing between eight and twelve members. A smaller group, while providing for a great deal of intimacy, is impeded when one or two members have to miss a meeting because a few absences in a group of this size are strongly felt. On the other hand, larger groups prevent members from receiving support from each other as they relate a general topic to individual experiences.

The anomie reduction group should begin with a clear idea as to the number of sessions it will hold. Two patterns are possible: either a short term or an indefinite term. The short-term (six to twelve sessions) experience is typical of a group whose focus is on a circumscribed role such as "working mother," "coming out gay," or "expectant father." The long, indefinite-term group is one in which the focus is so broad as to incorporate the whole range of men's or women's roles. In the latter type of group, the members should agree after the second or third meeting to evaluate how satisfactory the composition is, that is, whether they have sufficient compatibility, homogeneity, heterogeneity, and size for their purposes. When there are major problems in these aspects of composition, the worker should help the group to terminate and reform or seek changes in membership.

Group workers have organized and facilitated anomie reduction groups, particularly of the short-term variety. Long-term groups frequently arise in the community out of the needs of their members or are recruited as part of the development of social movements. In the latter case, group workers are called on as consultants by all or some of the members. Long-term groups can also be the outgrowth of short-term, worker-led groups that decide to continue (on a leaderless basis) with occasional consultation. In that event, the group will have to choose members to fulfill coordinator and recorder functions and these should rotate so no one is overly burdened with these tasks or uses them to avoid a more intensive involvement in the group.

GROUP FORMATION TASKS

Some assessment and screening is usually accomplished prior to the beginning of the group. This process ascertains whether the person can function as a group member; that is, reveal aspects of self to others, engage in problem-solving efforts in a group, and accept help from others. The commitment of the individual to clarifying the role(s) relevant to the group's purpose is also examined as well as personal values in relationship to the role. This initial assessment is essential in determining whether the individuals have been appropriately referred to the group and how they will affect and be affected by its composition.

During group formation, the process of assessing the members' anomic concerns will continue. In this type of group, particularly, efforts to understand internal barriers to defining one's values and roles as well as barriers from the environment will be undertaken in the formation phase and will continue throughout the life of the group. The ability to look at both of these dimensions is important. Culbert found, in his examination of consciousness-raising groups, that the duality in assessment can be approached through a general discussion of what members feel is "off" in their interaction with some system. This discussion is facilitated by asking questions such as the following: "In what ways could this feeling be a clue that the system expects something from me that does not seem natural or consistent with my self-interests? In what ways could this feeling be a clue that something which seems natural enough to me is considered inappropriate or inadequate by the system?"[3]

---

[3]Ibid., p. 236.

Culbert further noted that many people are reluctant to identify the way the "system" has contributed to their problem and they will, consequently, blame themselves and their inadequacies for their role-related problems. He recommends confronting this issue and suggests an exercise in which members relate instances "where they accepted the blame or reponsibility for something that went wrong only to receive a later indication that they were not at fault."[4]

It has been our experience that the opposite also occurs. Members project the blame onto the environment rather than seeing that they compounded their problems when they failed to take moral stands and avoided experiences that would help them make moral decisions.

Another major aspect of assessment in these types of groups is the sort of personal identity the person has as well as the one he or she may be seeking. These identity issues have often been suppressed or confused by environmental forces. To "uncover" identity processes, members will often relate their "life stories" with relationship to the role in question.

Example. In a men's consciousness-raising group, each member told how he had viewed himself at various stages of his life in regard to the concept of "maleness" and how this self-presentation was viewed by family, friends, and others. The men reflected on such issues as how they wanted to express emotions, how some of them wanted to engage in activities not usually defined as "masculine," and how they experienced friendships with other men. They asked each other questions that helped to open some long "forgotten" hopes and experiences. Because they shared a common cultural heritage, as men in our society, their questions to each other brought out highly relevant material.

The type of discussion just described adds to an assessment of how each member had made important role choices previously and whether such choices led to satisfaction or frustration. Value conflicts that still should be resolved can also be uncovered in this way. An examination of previous decision-making patterns illuminates the levels of self-awareness experienced by each member, his ability to engage in problem solving, and how he used or did not use relationships with others to work out problems relevant to his role. These dimensions can also be clarified as the members "process" whether and how to deal with such issues when they interact with each other. In such discussions, also, members will come to understand the kinds of role models they have or have not had and the types of models they still seek.

In addition to such people-oriented assessment, the members and the worker will engage in environment-oriented assessment to understand the nature of the anomie experienced by members, and environmental supports and changes required for clarifying one's norms and pursuing relevant goals. This is accomplished through looking at the kind of norms present in the member's personal situations and whether they are ambiguous, unacceptable to the member, or

[4]Ibid., p. 237.

conflicted. Examples include traditional norms in one's family or workplace that are not acceptable and normative conflicts in one's community, school, or peer group. The member may even report experiencing punishment in these systems for considering new role-related behaviors.

As the members begin to determine their values in anomie reduction groups, they will seek support from their environments. This requires the group to help the members determine which systems will be supportive, which can be changed to provide support, and whether the member can, with the help of other group members, even create new opportunity structures ranging from support groups to new conditions of employment.

During the group formation phase, in addition to assessment, the members will seek to clarify group purpose. This starts with a decision as to how the roles to be discussed in the group will be defined. Thus, in a men's consciousness-raising group, a discussion took place on whether all issues of concern to the members as men would be discussed or whether some were beyond the purview of the group. This determination of the scope of the group will also help the members to review the appropriateness of any previous decisions such as the number of times the group will meet. Individual goals should also be defined at this stage so that their attainment can be measured and ultimately the effectiveness of the group evaluated. In a women's group, for example, one member developed the goal of making a decision as to what she thought should be her obligations in her marriage. Another member set as her goal a determination as to what kind of lesbian life style will fit her personality and her needs.

In the formation phase the members will also consider the general types of procedures they plan on using to achieve their goals even though their ideas on this may change as events unfold in the group. They can be told by the worker that the following are the most common types of procedures:

> Exercises to help them become more aware of their own beliefs, wants, and preferred life styles
>
> Experiences to help them develop their self-concepts
>
> Problem-solving discussions, particularly around choices about which they are ambivalent
>
> Group discussion in which each member shares current and developing beliefs with others so that members will have a number of models available to expand their basis for choice
>
> Process-oriented discussions so that members may better see how they present themselves as well as how they use others for support or change
>
> Discussions of their life situations so they may compare their perceptions of reality with perceptions held by others.

GOAL PURSUIT TASKS

The workers, in choosing techniques to help the members, will make decisions on targets to be affected by these interventions. For the person experiencing anomie, the internal target is most frequently an attitude. Workers, therefore, will draw on their knowledge about how attitudes are formed and how attitude conflicts are resolved. For example, we often modify our attitudes by our understanding of the world and how our behaviors affect it. The workers, therefore, will direct their attention to the kinds of cognitions that help to form attitudes. For example, one group, in which prejudice against racial minorities was an issue, examined information on the accomplishments of members of that minority group as well as the damage to its members through lack of educational opportunity and exclusion from job markets.

Our attitudes are also linked to our emotions. Members in the group just mentioned feared members of the minority in question, but through discussion of their experiences, were able to see the irrationality of these fears. This led to a willingness to meet with some people who were members of the minority group to learn more about their concerns and consequently to a further reduction in their fears.

In an anomie reduction group, the members, after they have clarified their attitudes and the forces that have produced them, will usually seek to change aspects of their environments that are in conflict with their new values or that hinder achievement of objects based on such values. Members will decide to confront the actions of others who deny them opportunities to live according to their values; they will also seek to create opportunities for themselves or to challenge the ways they are prevented from gaining access to these opportunities. As an example, members of a gay group were more determined after a consciousness-raising group experience than before to challenge people who express stereotypes about gay persons and to demand their rights to hold jobs and secure promotions based on their skills rather than their sexual preferences.

Culbert presents a model for development of consciousness-raising groups that can be used to identify some of the major techniques used for anomie reduction. His first stage is incorporated in our discussion of group formation tasks in such groups, when members are helped to identify aspects of systems that are discrepant with their individual needs. Culbert's second stage is "understanding ourselves and the system."[5] In this phase, he recommends that members work to develop a better understanding of themselves, that is, "how we work and what we need" as well as of the systems with which they interact.

In the process of analysis of self and relevant systems, members sometimes tend to hold stereotyped perceptions or to make inferences from their existing picture of reality. The worker should seek to offset this limited way of thinking by asking members to examine their concrete experiences rather than their "pet theories." The members can discuss how such experiences relate to defects in their social situations as well as in incorrect or limited views of themselves. This process is enhanced when members ask themselves the following types of questions: If what I am feeling now (about my situation or my values or my needs) is an

[5]Ibid.

example of a more basic issue, what would that be? What is it about my qualities and the organizations, agencies, and other systems I have contact with that could have produced some of the conflicts I am experiencing?[6]

Members in the process of discussing such questions may discover both similarities and differences among themselves. When only a few people identify a particular conflict, this may indicate that the issue is related to their needs and abilities; when a larger number of group members discover similarities, this will usually indicate dysfunctions in their environments.

One of the exercises that can be used to help members to gain a clearer idea of how their social behaviors indicate their needs is "Role Nominations." In this exercise members are given a list of various "roles," such as initiator, encourager, and dominator. The members check off the roles that have been enacted by each of the group members during group meetings. The "nominations" for each member are then tallied and a group discussion of the results is held.[7]

Another exercise for this purpose is "Adjectives." In this activity, members are asked to think of the person with whom they have the most satisfactory relationship and to write three adjectives describing that person. Members then do the same for the person with whom they have the least satisfactory relationship. After this, the group worker explains that this can also tell a great deal about the values of the members. The members, usually in dyads, discuss what they have learned about themselves from this exercise.[8]

An understanding of relevant systems can be enhanced through answering questions such as the following:

1. What do you think your (boss, wife, teacher, and so on) expects of you and other people in the system?
2. How powerful is the person referred to in question 1 compared to others, including yourself?
3. How strongly does that person want to retain you as a member of the system?
4. Diagram the system in terms of its subsystems, for example, the people most closely allied to one another in the system; the people most antagonistic to one another.

In the third stage of a consciousness-raising group, Culbert states that the members should develop a better understanding of their relationship with the system. This should grow out of the previous stage when members increased their knowledge of both themselves and the system. He sees this understanding facilitated by responding to the following types of questions.[9]

---

[6]These questions are similar to some posed by Culbert, *Consciousness-Raising*, p. 238.

[7]For details on this exercise, see J. William Pfeiffer and John E. Jones, eds., *A Handbook of Structured Experiences for Human Relations Training*, Vol. II, rev. (La Jolla, Calif.: University Associates, 1974), pp. 72–75. The reader can consult this series of annual handbooks for many other useful group exercises.

[8]For details on this exercise, see J. William Pfeiffer and John E. Jones, eds., *Handbook of Structured Experiences for Human Relations Training*, Vol. V (LaJolla, Calif.: University Associates, 1975), pp. 114–15.

[9]Culbert, *Consciousness-Raising*, pp. 239–41.

1. What are the goals we hold for our interactions with the system and what means do we use to attain them?
2. How do you think the system views you?
3. How do we influence the system and how does it influence us?

A major function of group discussion of these questions is to point out the assumptions members make in their answers. Sometimes this will require the group members to confront the individual regarding any resistance to examining such assumptions.

Example. In a men's consciousness-raising group, a member stated that his wife expected him to make the major family decisions; she became quite upset when he refused to do so. The members pointed out that there were a series of assumptions here about what his wife "really" wanted and why she became upset. One member stated that he had had a similar pattern and later found out that his wife feared that he planned on leaving her when he refused to continue making decisions; she actually resented his power but feared being left alone even more.

The fourth stage, according to Culbert, is one of "formulating alternatives."[10] The ability to do this should flow from a better understanding of member-system transactions and related assumptions. Specifically, "We do this by noting how assumptions which have been characterized by our relationship with the system are inconsistent with what we have learned about our own needs, interests and ideals."[11] These alternatives, logically, can include changes in the system or changes in our behavior with reference to the system. In the example of the husband who thought he made too many decisions, the alternatives he listed included (1) developing a different pattern of decision making in the system, such as working toward consensus on issues; (2) engaging in mutual problem solving; and (3) changing his relationship to the system by refusing to make decisions and explaining the role he would like to have in the family. Group members are helpful in this process because of their ability to suggest alternatives. They can also help members to analyze the consequences for themselves as well as others of carrying out each alternative.

The final stage of such a group is "affecting the lives of others."[12] Culbert makes the excellent point that effective consciousness-raising requires that the member secure the support of others outside of the group in this endeavor. This requires that these outside people, to some degree, have their "consciousness raised." Women in a consciousness-raising group will require that men see how they also are oppressed by stereotyped male roles; gay persons will require "straight" people to see the limitations in some definitions of that role (for example, narrow definitions of male and female "behaviors"); adolescents will require that relevant adults question "adult" roles that are too rigid and

[10]Ibid., pp. 241–42.
[11]Ibid.
[12]Ibid., pp. 242–44.

authoritarian or even too flexible and seductive. The same can be said of the "alter" group in relationship to any role that serves as the focus of consciousness-raising.

In this last stage of the conciouness-raising group, the members will help each other to plan how to receive the aforementioned support and change. This can often be initiated by what Culbert calls "friendly dialogue," which can even lead to others seeking support for a reexamination of their positions through formation of their own groups. He also believes that, in this stage, members need support to work for long-term institutional changes in ways that guarantee the rights of others to do the same in their own interests.

EVALUATION

One of the major aspects of the evaluation of effectiveness of an anomie reduction group is the determination of whether members have clarified values related to the role dealt with in the group. To effect this, members can decide the values around which they experience the most conflict. At early meetings and at subsequent points in the life of the group, they can rate the certainty of their value stance.

Example. One group, devoted to helping adolescents with confusion on sexual issues, developed questions such as the following:

> Do you believe that people of your age, if they have "mature feelings," should have sexual intercourse if they wish?
>
> _____ yes   _____ no
>
> How certain are you of this belief?
>
> _____ Very certain
>
> _____ Somewhat certain
>
> _____ Slightly certain
>
> _____ Not certain at all

Members can also make ratings on additional scales to indicate how likely they are to declare their beliefs and act on them. Members can also indicate whether they have identified changes that they wish to make in themselves or their situations in order to actualize their values. Progress in accomplishing such changes can be charted using some of the types of measures described in Chapter 8.

On a group level, members can rate whether specific exercises, discussions, or meetings have helped with any of the preceding situations. The effectiveness of such events can also be assessed by using a value assessment instrument prior to and following the event.

AN EXAMPLE

A group of nine men came together through a series of mutual friends to examine aspects of the male role. They were dissatisfied with some of the ways they had been leading their lives and they attributed this to the changes taking place in sex roles in our society. They sought help from a local community mental health agency and were assigned a group worker from the staff of that agency to help facilitate their group. The following are excerpts from some meetings of the group.

First Meeting. The men began the meeting with a "round" in which each man spoke of his feelings about coming to the group. Some of these feelings included fears about confidentiality, eager anticipation about what the group could become, anxiety about being in a group composed only of men, and doubts about what such a group would accomplish. There was some "cross talk" but it was limited and guarded. The group worker spoke empathically about their feelings and acknowledged that these were realistic in a group such as this. He gave recognition to the members for taking the risk in coming and speaking openly about feelings.

Much of the first meeting was then spent on negotiation of group operating procedures such as meeting times, length of meetings, and rules about absences. The purposes of the group were also discussed, such as the idea that this was not a "therapy" group although the members expressed some ambiguity and confusion about the differences between this group and therapy. Some of the ideas around which there was a consensus were that the group was to help clarify what they wanted to be like as men; that they will have to discuss their relationships with women as well as other men; that this will entail self-disclosure; and that they wanted feedback from each other as well as an opportunity to compare experiences. It was also evident, by the end of the meeting, that a few of the men thought of themselves as "gay," several as "heterosexual," and at least two thought they might be "bisexual." Some others had lived their lives as heterosexuals but were not sure what their feelings were about other men as friends.

The men discussed how they would like to conduct their next meeting. The worker suggested that they spend some time telling about their lives so that they might get to know each other better. The worker asked at the end of the meeting how the members thought the meeting had gone and the members expressed positive reactions. He also asked if the members were committed to continuing the group and that also was strongly supported.

Second Meeting. At the second meeting, one of the men was not present and there was some speculation as to the meaning of his absence. The group again began with a "round." Several men spoke about how enthusiastic they were after the last meeting and how eager they were for this one. One member spoke of some anxiety about the variety of sexual orientations in the group. There was little response to this and the worker indicated that this might be a "scary" topic and that the group should discuss this further when they were "ready."

The group spent the bulk of the meeting with two members telling their "stories." The first to speak, Bob, was 30 years old and a professional psychologist. He talked about his family composition as he was growing up and the sadness he still feels about the fact that his father died when he was an adolescent. He indicated that he was married and had recently become a father of a son and this had caused him to think a lot about himself and *his* father. He offered a number of recollections of his father—some were very positive, although he also spoke of situations when his father had been uncaring or even hostile to him. With some anxiety, he spoke about a homosexual "affair" he had before he was married while he was a college student. He had, however, discussed this with his wife and had reached an agreement with her that he would seek no sexual experiences with either sex outside of marriage. This was said somewhat blandly and this was commented on by one of the members. Almost all of the members asked Bob questions about his life or briefly indicated that they had had similar experiences or feelings.

Sixth Meeting. By the sixth meeting, all of the members had told their "stories" and one member had dropped out explaining that he did not have time for the group although several members thought he was intimidated by the frank tone of the meetings. One of the members said he still was not sure what the other members thought "masculinity" meant. When others echoed this concern, the worker suggested several exercises that could help. The worker had brought a large pad of newsprint and he asked members to suggest adjectives that are often applied to men. The list that was generated included "strong," "unemotional," "aggressive," and "athletic." The worker asked the men to suggest adjectives that they thought applied to themselves whether or not these were on the first list. The new list included "tender," "artistic," "unsure," and "funny." A lengthy discussion then took place about the similarities and differences between the lists and the reasons for these.

Eighth Meeting. At the eighth meeting, one member, Jim, said that he had a serious problem and he wanted to know what the rest of the members thought about it. He had been having an "affair" with a woman that his wife did not know about. With the help of the worker and the members, he talked about some of his reasons for the affair; these included his desire to "still be free"; his belief that people should act on their feelings; and also dissatisfactions he had regarding his relationship with his wife. The other members asked Jim questions to clarify the situation such as his sources of dissatisfaction with his wife and his expectations regarding the woman with whom he was having this relationship. Ultimately, the discussion moved to consideration of ways he could change his relationship with his wife as well as the implications of carrying out various alternatives.

The worker asked the members to consider whether there were some general issues in Jim's situation that affected all of them. This led to a discussion of the values and consequences of monogamous relationships as well as those that were not.

During the discussion of Jim's problem, one member, Harold, became quite critical of the self-centered way he thought Jim was handling his life. This led to a hostile exchange between Jim and Harold and it was obvious to the worker that the members were fearful such anger could "bust-up" the group. The worker, therefore, supported a discussion of the members' feelings and values regarding conflict and expressions of anger. While time constraints prevented this discussion from continuing too long, the members agreed this was an important topic for them.

Analysis. In this sample of some of the issues in a men's group, many of the principles previously discussed are illustrated; these include the effects of the similarity in role concerns and small size on what became a very cohesive group. The group also began in a fairly typical way to become acquainted with each other and to share role concerns. The worker was supportive during the formation period through his use of empathic responses and his identification of issues for discussion. When necessary, he supplied programmatic experiences to facilitate group development. He was aware of process issues such as the conflict that arose between Jim and Harold and the fears generated by early disclosure of intimate material. He also was aware when one person's input showed concerns that were universally felt such as the constraints placed on individuals through their relationships. The group still had not progressed to the point that members could begin to emphasize alternatives in their goals for themselves and their "systems" and to work toward these but that clearly was the group phase they were approaching.

SUMMARY

In this chapter, we reviewed the nature of anomie reduction groups and described their similarity to groups referred to as consciousness-raising. We discussed the worker's tasks in preplanning such groups, including decisions on composition and specific definitions of purpose. The phase of group formation was then considered and we described the assessment issues that are most prevalent in anomie reduction groups. In discussing the phases when goal attainment is at the forefront, we used a paradigm developed by Culbert to conceptualize the phases present in consciousness-raising and, perhaps, all anomie reduction groups. Some issues in evaluation of anomie reduction groups were described followed by a brief case example of one such group.

11

Working With Groups To Enhance Role Attainment

The role attainment purpose of groups is to help members to fulfill the requirements of roles that they aspire to or are already in. This might be a role of student, parent, spouse, employee, friend, or retired person. Examples of groups related to anticipated roles are those for people approaching retirement or graduation or parenthood. Examples of groups for people already in roles and experiencing difficulties in fulfilling role requirements, because of personal behaviors, barriers present in the situation, or both, are those for school children with classroom difficulties, for parents with problems in raising their children, and for teenagers who do not have friends. Role attainment groups, therefore, may be thought of as prevention-oriented compared to other types of groups.

The role attainment purpose is sometimes the major one fulfilled by the group. To some degree, however, it is present in all groups. Therefore, the approaches to group work described in this chapter may be appropriately used whenever this issue predominates.

Several strategies are used in groups with role attainment purposes and they shall often be referred to in this chapter. These strategies are: social skills training, task-centered group work, and behavior modification in groups.[1] All

---

[1] An introductory discussion of these shall be presented in this chapter. For more detailed discussions of task-centered group work, see Charles D. Garvin, "Practice with Task-Centered Groups," in *Task-Centered Practice with Groups and Families,* ed. Ann Fortune (New York:

these approaches have educational components, an emphasis on skill, and a concern with helping the member identify and contract for specific changes that will enhance personal functioning. Social skills training groups usually focus on specific components of social skills such as assertiveness, communication, and initiating and maintaining relationships. The techniques for training include presentation of models, discussion of principles, role playing, and homework assignments. Task-centered work involves helping members to select a task that, when carried out, will ameliorate a problem. Behavior modification in groups helps members to understand social-learning principles and to apply these in their lives. These social-learning principles include the modification of circumstances under which a behavior takes place or the likely consequences of behaving in specified ways—consequences that may be pleasant or aversive.

PREGROUP TASKS

One principle to follow in the composition of groups with a role attainment function is that members should have a similarity of relevant roles. This is because the strategy for work with such groups has a strong educational component and this can best be accomplished when members can be served by similar or common educational experiences, when they can accomplish tasks in the same sequence, or when the commonalities in members' roles facilitate the use of the group as a support system. There may also be common environmental barriers that can be overcome if the members of the group act together.

The worker, in assessing clients prior to the first meeting, will seek to learn the roles that are likely to be targeted by them as group members. This may require some prioritizing of their concerns prior to the beginning of the group. Thus an individual who sought help with parenting functions as well as assertiveness with her employer was asked to indicate which of these caused her the most concern. Since it was the parenting issue, she was invited to join a parents' skill-training group.

Prior to the first meeting, the worker should also assess the skills already possessed by the person in fulfilling the role, because while some homogeneity in this respect is not essential, it is desirable. Potential members also may vary in their skills and this can enrich the group. The group will have problems in establishing cohesiveness and developing a coherent program, however, if the differences are vast among members in the overall amount of skill. As an example, a member of one social skills group had always been very shy and had very few friends. Another member had many relationships but experienced considerable

---

Springer, 1985), pp. 45–77. For behavioral approaches in groups, see Sheldon Rose, *Group Therapy: A Behavioral Approach* (Englewood Cliffs, N.J.: Prentice-Hall, Inc., 1977). One detailed account of an aspect of social skills training is by Arthur J. Lange and Patricia Jakubowski, *Responsible Assertive Behavior* (Champaign, Ill.: Research Press, 1976).

difficulty in handling conflicts that arose in them. The former person required elementary training in initiating and sustaining conversations while the latter did not—it was in later phases of relationships that his problems occurred.

Role attainment groups are usually time-limited, short-term groups that meet from ten to twenty sessions. Because they usually prepare members for specific roles, their content is focused and their educational approach often allows for something analogous to a "curriculum." This short-term framework can be made more feasible if members are prepared for the group prior to the first meeting. In task-centered groups, for example, the worker will help the members to define the problem that concerned them as well as the role to which the problems are related. Then the initial activity of the group will be to clarify and reaffirm the relevant roles as well as the problems to be resolved—although the latter are sometimes modified as members experience the reality of the group. If work of this sort is not done in advance, the short-term plan for the group is sometimes unrealistic.

Example.   In the preparation of a group of young adults with problems in separating from their families, each prospective member was helped to clarify how he or she wished to work on functioning as an independent adult. One member defined the problem as handling parents imposing advice on him; another as establishing a separate residence against parental opposition; a third as helping the family to be less dependent on him for advice and direction. (This group provides the extended example used later in this chapter.)

In short-term groups, if the types of worker interventions are known in advance, these should also be explained to the members. In a task-centered group, members receive an explanation of the task concept. They are told that they will be helping each other to identify and work on tasks related to their problems. In assertiveness groups, members are often given "handouts" on the meaning of an assertive philosophy and are told about the sequence of activities (that is, learning about the meaning of assertion, assessing their own interactions, practicing, and then applying *new ways* of interacting).

When the type of intervention to be used is known, this will also have an impact on how members will be selected for the group. Some people will be able to make use of planned formats while others will not. This issue can be assessed by noting carefully the response of the prospective member during the worker's explanation. The option is always available to the worker to modify the format. Also, initial interviews will have disclosed that for some members one format will be more useful and appropriate than another.

If the role attainment group is one with a fairly structured program, the group can accommodate a larger number of members than other groups. Some groups, devoted to parent training, for example, will enroll as many as fifteen to twenty members. The worker can still, when appropriate, subdivide the group into "buzz groups" for further discussion of selected topics. The larger group can also be used by people who are fairly adequate in their role functioning, such as many parents, college students, employees, and trainees. On the other hand, if the members of such a group are young or vulnerable in other ways, or the technology calls for discussion and feedback, a size of about seven to ten members will be best. An example of this was a group that we categorized as a role attainment group: a group of retarded young adults seeking to learn how to meet their sexual and affectional needs in socially acceptable ways. Even though a "training" format was used, the amount of personal support and problem solving required in the group necessitated a small group.

In the formation of any type of role attainment group, the worker must be aware of stereotypes and biases that may develop. Gambrill and Richey have investigated a number of these as they relate to gender issues in social skills training.[2] Men and women entering a group may present a socially desirable image rather than one that truly meets their needs. Men may underestimate their social anxiety and women may overestimate their assertiveness since both of these responses are subject to gender stereotypes. Social workers involved with social skills groups may mistakenly expect men, more than women, to emphasize reduction of social anxiety since women might be defined as more emotional and excitable. Still another set of stereotypes cited by Gambrill and Richey relate to sexual orientation:

> For example, lesbian women may join a social skills group to increase contacts with other women, not with men, or their goals may be related to career advancement and not be relationship focused. The sexual orientation of group members may not be at all obvious. This discretionary visibility (whether sexual orientation is disclosed) may mislead a trainer into making faulty assumptions about desired goals. Reluctance to disclose a deviant sexual orientation may be increased by failure of the trainer to overtly recognize alternative life style.[3]

What this amounts to is that group workers must be sensitive to members' wishes regarding appropriate social behaviors rather than traditional views of how men, women, blacks, white, or members of any other group are *supposed to* behave.

GROUP FORMATION TASKS

In the first stage of group development, even though the purposes and procedures to be used in the group have been discussed individually, they should be discussed again in the group-as-a-whole. Members who did not "hear" everything will then have another opportunity to understand and react to the plans for the group. It is also likely that when members actually see who is present and hear something of their "story," they will want to modify the concerns they intended to bring to the group. The opposite can also happen: members who were reluctant to discuss some aspects of their lives, at least initially, when confronted with the actual group

---

[2]Eileen Gambrill and Cheryl Richey, "Gender Issues Related to Group Social Skills Training," *Social Work with Groups* VI (3/4) (Fall/Winter, 1983), 51–66.
[3]Ibid., p. 58.

composition may be more ready to do so because they feel that their similarity to other members reduces anxiety about reactions of other group members to their "deficiencies" or "weaknesses."

The amount of problem specification that takes place in a role attainment group will be related to the type of strategy the worker plans on using. If the group is similar to what Radin calls a "socioeducation" group[4] (for example, certain types of family life education), it may be sufficient for the worker to have an understanding of the major tasks called for by the role and to check this out with the group. Thus a worker in a parent education group will already have in mind the development of skills in discipline, self-care, preparation for schooling, and so on, and will ask the group members whether these are, in fact, on their "agenda." In contrast, in a task-oriented group, the worker will help the members to provide a fairly detailed description of their "problems" so that each member can be helped to develop tasks that are appropriate to their circumstances.

In behaviorally oriented, skill-training, and task-centered groups a further assessment of the members' role attainment concerns will take place so that interventions will be appropriate to these. In a behavioral group, this assessment will include a specification of: (1) the "antecedent conditions" in situations in which the member wishes to be able to act in a specified manner as well as (2) the types of consequences the member receives or will receive when he or she behaves appropriately or inappropriately. A considerable literature exists on ways members can help each other complete this type of behavioral analysis.[5] Because members share many similar experiences, they are often astute in suggesting antecedents and consequences to each other. The possibility of setting up role plays can also help members engage in this type of assessment in the group.

In task-centered groups, there is less emphasis on assessment; rather the members help each other devise tasks that will reduce problems. The process that most closely corresponds to assessment is that of designing a task that will be suitable for the person to accomplish, given his or her motivation, personal capacity, and the realities of the situation. After a task has been chosen, the members will—with the help of the worker—assist each other in assessing the kinds of barriers to accomplishing those tasks the members may encounter within themselves as well as in their environments.

Brim presents a framework that is useful in assessment relevant to role attainment. It can be used in a variety of social skill training situations. Specifically, he states: "There are three things a person requires before he is able to perfom satisfactorily in a role. He must know what is expected of him (both in behavior and in values), must be able to meet the role requirements, and must

[4]Norma Radin, "Socioeducation Groups," in *Individual Change Through Small Groups,* eds., Paul Glasser, Rosemary Sarri, and Robert Vinter (New York: Free Press, 1974), pp. 89–104.
[5]See Rose, *Group Therapy,* pp. 26–40; H. Lawrence and M. Sundel, "Behavior Modification in Adult Groups," *Social Work* XVII (1972), 34–43.

desire to practice the behavior and pursue the appropriate ends. It can be said that the purposes of socialization are to give a person knowledge, ability, and motivation.''[6] This is summarized by Brim in a six-cell table as follows:[7]

	Behavior	Values
Knowledge	A	B
Ability	C	D
Motivation	E	F

In discussing this table, Brim explains that "Cells A and B indicate respectively that the individual knows what behavior is expected of him and what ends he should pursue; E and F indicate that the individual is motivated to behave in the appropriate ways and to pursue the designated values; C and D indicate that the individual is able to carry out the behavior and hold appropriate values."[8] Some of the ways that the group and the worker can help assess the member relevant to Brim's formulation are now given.

Cell A. The member is asked to describe the behavior that he or she thinks is appropriate to the situation; alternatively, the members can be shown examples of appropriate and inappropriate behavior to see if they recognize what is called for in the situation.

Cell B. The member is asked what the goals or objectives of the behavior are.

Cell C. An examination is made of the member's ability to perform the behavior. This can be accomplished through the members either describing to the group how they acted in the relevant life situation or role playing a simulated version of the situation as the other members and worker identify their degree of skill.

Cell D. As Brim indicates,[9] some people are "unable" to hold certain values because of "conflict within the personality." This is illustrated through the example of a son who did not pursue the value of going to college because he perceived this as placing him in competition with his father's record.[10] Group workers

[6]Orville G. Brim, Jr. and Stanton Wheeler, *Socialization After Childhood: Two Essays* (New York: John Wiley, 1966), p. 25.
[7]Ibid.
[8]Ibid., pp. 25–26.
[9]Ibid., p. 26, footnote*.
[10]Ibid., p. 41.

deal with many group members who have difficulties with holding desired values because of psychological and social conflicts. Often these must be resolved by the members before they can invest themselves in role attainment activities.

The assessment of the inability to hold particular values is a subtle process. The sign of this often comes from the member's nonverbal cues. A member may proclaim commitment to a goal or a value while acting uncomfortable or showing inappropriate expression of emotion. Other members may see, in the member's behavior in the group or outside of it, that the individual's commitments are lacking or in conflict.

Cells E and F. Members should examine whether there are any reinforcers in the member's natural environment for engaging in the appropriate behaviors or for proclaiming the goals and values that will support these behaviors.

This type of assessment will help members and workers plan appropriate activities for role attainment. If, for example, values or motivation are lacking, the group's attention to increasing the members' abilities may be fruitless.

An analogous assessment of the environment must take place in role attainment groups. Members are unlikely to work very hard to adapt themselves to roles for which there will be no opportunity to pursue. School children who perceive that their teachers will not give them the help they need; trainees in job programs who know about racial or sex discrimination or a recession in the relevant industry; elderly people who are aware their families do not wish them to be active in the community—these people will be frustrated by programs geared only to these behaviors and skills. These systems can be assessed by examining the experiences members and others have had with such environments. On occasion, also, members will be asked by the group to test out the kinds of opportunities in relevant systems available for group members.

In examining opportunity structures, members should perceive whether role steps are defined and properly paced. Earlier we referred to a group of retarded young adults who were helped with affectional and sexual behaviors. In addition to their learning how to deal with such situations, appropriate opportunities had to be permitted them, such as social occasions with the opposite sex, dating, and ultimately, for some, engagement and marriage. These "steps" were not defined by their parents and caregivers or graded in any way. Thus, some members were given too much responsibility for social contacts and others too little. The worker, with the help of group members, undertook an assessment of this and as a result, meetings were held with people in the environment who could bring about the necessary changes related to clarifying and pacing such opportunities.

Based on these types of assessments, the worker and members will choose targets for the group's activities. As we discussed in reference to Brim's work, these targets may be any combination of members' behaviors, attitudes, and cognitions (knowledge) required for the roles the members seek to fulfill. Along with this, we have pointed out the futility of such role preparation when the environmental opportunities for role performance are limited. Thus associated aspects of the environment must also be targeted for change.

In a group of school children experiencing learning problems, the group worker and the members targeted the members' skill of paying attention to the teacher as well as the members' level of motivation for school success. In addition, the school was deficient in its opportunity structures in that remedial instruction to help these children "catch up" was lacking. The worker helped the members to compose a petition to their teacher and the principal in which this service was requested.

Also, during the formation period of the group, the members are helped to determine their role attainment goals. Almost always, in such groups, it is possible to attain a high level of precision in such formulations and this accomplishment, itself, goes a long way toward enhancing socialization processes in the group.

GOAL PURSUIT TASKS

One of the most frequently used procedures in social skills groups is behavioral rehearsal. In this activity the worker helps the members to role play or in other ways simulate the behaviors they seek to possess. The following are some of the steps in this process:

1. The member, through play or description, presents an example of the way the situation is customarily handled.
2. Members, with the help of the worker, suggest changes in the way the member acts. These changes are often guided by general principles that the group has learned. Examples of these from assertiveness training are "giving and receiving compliments," and "carrying on social conversations."[11]
3. The member has an opportunity to clarify suggestions from the group and to plan how he or she will act.
4. A member of the group is chosen to play the "alter" in the role play and is briefed by the member who is learning the behavior.
5. The role play is enacted.
6. After the role play, members *first* state the positive aspects of the performance. Members then make suggestions for improvements.
7. The member should plan occasions (homework assignments) outside the group to try out the behavior. At subsequent meetings, the member should report on this. Additional modifications and rehearsals may then be required.

Another major procedure in role attainment groups is modeling. A number of different people can model behaviors that the member desires to learn. Members who have successfully mastered the behavior can demonstrate it in role plays

[11]For exercises to teach these two skills, see Lange and Jakubowski, *Responsible Assertive Behavior,* pp. 74 and 77, respectively.

or can describe how they handled situations outside the group. The worker can also demonstrate behaviors. Members may select people outside of the group whose behavior they desire to emulate. Workers can also play tapes and films that present good examples of ways of handling situations relevant to the members' concerns.

In task-centered groups, any of the preceding procedures can be used to help in task accomplishment. The philosophy underlying task-centered work, however, calls for the maximum involvement of the group members in selecting their own tasks. The worker will illustrate the task concept by appropriate examples so that members will understand what is required. In our experience, the first members to select tasks do so slowly. The process, however, serves as a model for members who subsequently choose their tasks more quickly. In a homogeneous group, members may also select similar tasks and this is another reason for the acceleration in this process with time.

Rooney describes some innovative approaches for helping group members to define tasks as well as to accomplish them.[12] In working with a group of high school youths he proposed that members list their tasks as well as their progress on these tasks on long sheets of paper. These lists were then placed on the walls. He, as the worker, modeled this technique by creating his own list of tasks, such as activities he had promised to carry out to help the members achieve their goals. Members also formed a "buddy system" and worked in pairs to select means of overcoming barriers to task accomplishment.

During the task accomplishment phase, members are helped with their tasks as follows: they can rehearse them through group role plays or through verbally reviewing with other members how they plan to handle specific situations. They also will secure support from other members for carrying out their tasks. This support can be supplied as members empathize with each other regarding their feelings about their tasks, as they reinforce one another with praise or even through awarding "tokens," and as they encourage one another to "keep on."

Problem-solving activities will also be used as members encounter problems in carrying out their tasks. The customary problem-solving phases of collecting information, identifying alternatives, evaluating alternatives, and carrying out the most desired alternative will, consequently, be used in such task situations.

"Coaching" is another approach that can be used to help members carry out tasks. It can also be used in analogous situations in other kinds of role attainment groups.[13] Coaching involves helping the member to create a series of intermediate goals, secure information from other members on task activities, obtain support when it is needed, ask for advice, and even request that the worker or other members be present when the member works on the task in the actual life situation.

---

[12]Ronald Rooney, "Adolescent Groups in Public Schools," in *Task-Centered Practice,* eds. William J. Reid and Laura Epstein (New York: Columbia University Press, 1977), pp. 168–82.

[13]Anselem Strauss, "Coaching," in *Role Theory: Concepts and Research* (New York: John Wiley, 1966), pp. 350–53.

In behavioral groups used for role attainment purposes, a major emphasis is placed, throughout the life of the group, on helping members to define precisely their problems in role attainment and to monitor changes through such measures as behavioral counts. Members are assisted in helping each other develop behavioral change plans through acquiring an understanding of social-learning theory. In adult and other literate groups, this can be done by assisting the members to read and understand texts designed for the lay person.[14]

As in task-centered groups, members of behavioral groups are often given homework assignments. These involve either monitoring behaviors or trying out approaches to behavioral change. To enhance this, workers can issue assignment forms to members to keep in individual notebooks. Assignments are recorded as well as the effects of carrying out the assignment. These personal accounts also can have the effect of reinforcing the members' participation in the program.

The worker will also train the members in a variety of behavioral change procedures. These include choosing appropriate schedules of reinforcement and reinforcers, as well as procedures for altering dysfunctional thought processes and communication patterns.[15]

The sequence of activities in social skills training groups has been fairly standardized. First sessions are spent describing and planning subsequent ones. A sequence of skills are taught through exercises and "homework" assignments. Opportunity is provided for members to describe or enact experiences related to the skills and to engage in problem solving around problems. An assertiveness training group, for example, might offer exercises in the first meetings to teach members how to say "yes" and "no," how to initiate social conversations, how to identify personal rights, and how to assert these rights.[16]

Because of the problems some members have in learning and applying these types of skills, group workers have sought to understand how to overcome many obstacles, such as members' thought patterns that interfere with their ability to carry out desired behaviors. Members undergoing social skill training, therefore, should be taught how to recognize these patterns,[17] which include statements people make to themselves such as "one must have love all of the time from significant people," "one's life is bad when it does not go your way," "the solutions to life's problems should be found quickly," and "one cannot overcome the effects of past misfortunes."

When members find it difficult to apply some aspect of skill training to carry out a task, or to perform a behavioral assignment, the worker and members can ask about the person's thoughts under those circumstances. When these serve as barriers to success, the member can be taught to make other self statements that

[14]See, for example, Wesley C. Becker, *Parents Are Teachers: A Child Management Program* (Champaign, Il.: Research Press, 1971).

[15]See Rose, *Group Therapy,* pp. 86–102, for a discussion of these and other procedures.

[16]For descriptions of these exercises, see Lange and Jakubowski, *Responsible Assertive Behavior,* pp. 69–113.

[17]Many workers draw on the techniques of Albert Ellis for such cognitive changes; see A. Ellis and R.A. Harper, *A New Guide to Rational Living* (Englewood Cliffs, N.J.: Prentice-Hall, Inc., 1975).

will facilitate forward movement. For example, Lange and Jakubowski present a list of self statements that can help a person deal better with anger such as "This is going to upset me but I know how to deal with it," or "Getting upset won't help."[18] While this approach may appear simplistic to some readers, the effectiveness of such techniques has been well documented.[19]

Similarly, people involved in role attainment experiences will often be hindered by their emotional responses. Often these responses consist of anxiety in the face of trying out skills but they can also be excessive anger, jealousy, or sadness, the latter related to failures in carrying out tasks. Workers in such groups, therefore, must know how to respond empathically to such emotions and to help members to deal with them. Lange and Jakubowski, for example, describe several relaxation procedures that they recommend for use in assertiveness training groups.[20]

Because role attainment groups are so often oriented to educational procedures and task accomplishment, the worker should sometimes provide for a release of tension or a change of pace. Thus some of the "rounds" described in the previous chapter, in which members share their feelings at the moment, are appropriate. Members may also benefit from a "half-way-through " party or other social occasion. Rose, for example, described a social skill training group for fourth and fifth grade boys which met twice a week for half hour sessions for ten weeks.[21] At the first meeting members were given a cookie on entering and a token for sitting down. The children worked for tokens to be exchanged for such prizes as match box cars. When individual reinforcers were gradually withdrawn, group rewards included a field trip to the university to make a video tape and a picnic at the local park.

In the earlier days of group work, most workers were deployed in community centers and settlement houses. These agencies provided role attainment [that is, socialization] experiences through club activities and special interest groups (for example, arts and crafts, dramatics). These groups presumably attained their goals through the worker's facilitation of group development and group decision making and the selection of activities appropriate to the members' development tasks. While we are not offering in detail a discussion of group work in such situations, we believe that many of the procedures we have described throughout this book, and particularly in the Chapters on anomie reduction and role attainment, are useful to facilitate the members' role attainment in such groups.

---

[18]R.W. Novaco, *Anger Control: The Development and Evaluation of an Experimental Treatment* (Lexington, Mass.: Heath, 1975), as quoted in Lange and Jakubowski, *Responsible Assertive Behavior,* pp. 150–51.

[19]Ibid.

[20]Lange and Jakubowski, *Responsible Assertive Behavior,* pp. 169–72.

[21]Sheldon D. Rose and Alison Roessle, "A Social Skill Training Group for Fourth and Fifth Grade Boys," *Behavior Group Therapy* 1, no. 5 (September 1979), 2–12.

EVALUATION

In behaviorally oriented groups, workers will help members to evaluate their success in role attainment through devices previously described, such as behavioral counts, self reports of coping with targeted situations, and reports by significant others. The latter can include behavioral checklists completed by teachers, employers, and parents. Rose, for example, has developed a children's behavior code that was employed by observers in the child's academic classroom and gym class.[22] In one project Rose also used charts showing the number of behavioral assignments completed by each child.

Reid and his colleagues have developed a scale for evaluation of task-centered groups.[23] The problems on which members are working are listed and changes rated on a 10-point scale ranging from problem greatly aggravated to problem no longer present. The midpoint of the scale ("5") represents "no change"; smaller numbers represent degrees of problem aggravation and larger numbers represent degrees of problem alleviation. In the interest of reliability, workers secure these ratings from the client, a collateral person, and also make their own ratings.

Lange and Jakubowski discuss a number of measures for evaluating assertiveness training that can also be used for a broad range of social skills training groups. One category of measurement is so called "paper-and-pencil" measures. Examples of this are the College and Adult Self-Expressions Scales,[24] and the Gambrill-Richey Assertion Inventory.[25] Behavioral measures can also be used such as examining the behavior of members during role plays. The worker can create these although Lange and Jakubowski also cite some that have already been developed.[26] When such role plays are used, raters are trained to assign scores to the member along such dimensions as eye contact, length of conversation, loudness, and appropriateness of affect.

AN EXAMPLE

A group of three men and two women were organized into a group by a staff member of the counseling service of a university. All of these members had come to the agency asking for help with issues involving their emotional separation

[22]Ibid.

[23]See "Task-Centered Group Recording Guide III: Final Session," School of Social Service Administration, rev. (Chicago, Ill.: University of Chicago, 27 March 1977).

[24]J.P. Galassi, J.C. Delo, M.D. Galassi, and S. Bastein, "The College Self-Expression Scale: A Measure of Assertiveness," *Behavior Therapy* 5 (1974), 165–71.

[25]Eileen D. Gambrill and Cheryl A. Richey, "An Assertion Inventory for Use in Assessment and Research," *Behavior Therapy* 6 (1975), 350–62.

[26]R.M. McFall and A.R. Marston, "An Experimental Investigation of Behavior Rehearsal in Assertion Training," *Journal of Abnormal Psychology* 76 (1970), 295–303.

from their parents. The worker believed that a task-centered approach would help these members attain the role of an adult rather than a "child" in their "families of origin." Prior to the first meeting, the worker had ascertained that these clients wanted to work on this problem, and were willing to join a task-centered group after this approach was explained to them. The following are excerpts from several group meetings.

First Meeting. At the meeting, the members introduced themselves by name and told a little about their courses of study, their home communities, and their families. The worker explained again what a task-centered group was and some further questions about this approach were raised and answered. The worker suggested that members tell each other about their family concerns. The first member to speak, Jack, described his parents and particularly his father as only being able to converse with him if they were offering him advice. Another man, Bill, described the pressures he received from his family to get married. Sally was about to graduate and wanted help to resist pressures from her parents to live with them when she returned to her home community. Phil, stated his problem as dealing with his family's expectancy that now that he was the first member of the family to go to college, he could solve *all* the outstanding problems in his family. The worker encouraged the members to ask each other questions so that they could better understand each other's situations. This was done, although members primarily sought out similarities and differences in each other's family situations. The worker ended the meeting by suggesting that the topic of the second meeting should be to identify change goals for each member.

Fourth Meeting. The two intermediary meetings were devoted to helping each member list long- and short-term goals. Another purpose of this fourth meeting was to help each member select task(s) that will help them reach their goal.

Jack, whose problem was his "advice-offering parents," volunteered to "go first." His short-term goal was to discuss this problem with his parents in such a way that they would understand the kind of relationship he wanted with them, which was one in which each party would both give and receive advice. This type of goal obviously led to a definition of this task as conducting such discussions with his parents.

In the process of helping Jack to develop this goal and task statement, the main problem of the group members was the tendency to jump too quickly into making suggestions as to how Jack should solve his problem. The members also asked many questions of Jack that were not relevant to the purpose of defining goals and tasks. The worker used this situation to continue to educate group members about the model; in this case, he continued to define and illustrate what goal and task statements were. (In other task groups, the worker has role played this process with a co-worker.)

The remainder of the meeting was spent developing tasks for the other group members. The process did quicken as members learned more about the nature of such tasks.

Sixth Meeting. At the previous meeting, Jack had discussed with group members the kinds of statements he will make to his parents. At this meeting, the worker suggested that he role play these statements. Two members of the group agreed to role play the parents; by this time, they had heard enough from Jack that they thought they could do this realistically. The role play commenced and after about five minutes Jack seemed at a loss for words. The role play was stopped and the worker asked Jack to talk about his reactions. Jack indicated that he was feeling uncomfortable. After a little more reflection, he said that in some ways he was worried about how his "parents" were reacting. Sally wondered if he was concerned if his parents will still like him after this. Phil commented that perhaps he thought that his parents will begin to feel useless and old and that Jack would feel bad about being responsible for this. Jack said that both of these comments made sense. He wondered if the role players might have some feelings about what it was like to be his parents. A discussion then took place with the role players about their reactions. After this continued for a while, the worker asked if it was possible for Jack to ask for feedback from his actual parents on what they were feeling.

During this meeting, two other members asked for similar help with the planning of how to fulfill their tasks. Another two members briefly reported on their first steps in accomplishing their tasks and they were given support and encouragement from the other members.

Analysis. This example illustrates a number of processes typical of role attainment groups. The educational components are clear as members learn about tasks associated with attaining adult status in their families. Members also work at establishing clear goals related to their roles. Since all members experienced similar problems, they provided optimum levels of support and empathy to each other. The homogeneity of the group allowed members to work in unison at the various processes required by task-centered work. The group composition also provided many opportunities for members to experience vicariously the consequences of carrying out similar tasks.

SUMMARY

In this chapter we discussed the techniques and concepts that most pertain to role attainment groups. We noted that three approaches are frequently used in such groups: behavior modification, social skills training, and task-centered work. Pregroup tasks were discussed, such as group composition and member preparation. The ways that members are assessed in role attainment groups were portrayed, as well as specific assessment issues, when each of these major approaches is employed. The kinds of techniques workers use in the middle phase of the group were described, such as coaching, behavioral rehearsal, modeling, and reinforcement. The evaluation devices used by practitioners of these approaches were listed. The chapter concluded with a case example from a task-centered group.

12

Working With Groups In Social Control Situations

In the two previous chapters, we presented some of the ways to work with groups whose members are in transition from one role to another or from one stage of a role to a later stage. As we stated previously, members of such groups are being helped with socialization tasks and, as such, are usually viewed as healthy, nondeviant, or prosocial members of the society. Their group activities are considered by many, including the members themselves, to be educational and voluntary. The group experience may be thought of as prevention in that the members are learning to cope with situations that often cause the development of emotional illnesses and dysfunctional or illegal behavior in those who cannot cope.

In this chapter and the next, we shall describe how group workers facilitate groups for members who are viewed by society in opposite ways to the ones to which we have just referred, perhaps because of a failure in such socialization. Thus the latter members are characterized as criminals or delinquents on the one hand or as mentally or emotionally ill on the other. The group is considered as "treatment" or "rehabilitation" more often than as education. The overall function is one of *resocialization*.

At times the members who are recruited for such groups do not yet share some or all of the goals that the agency has identified in offering such group services. Part of the group, or even the entire group, in fact may never move to this commonality of purpose with the agency. We have termed this phenomenon "working with groups in social control situations." The social control aspect is justified by the agency by the fact that the society, through legislative processes, has established the social control function and has created judicial and executive procedures to determine the individuals to whom it should apply. Thus people who break the law are placed on probation or sent by the courts to training schools or prisons. In an analogous manner, people who behave in bizarre ways or whose behavior is considered to be a danger to themselves or others can also, by judicial decree, be placed in mental hospitals or other psychiatric facilities.

We do *not* believe that social work as a professional activity is controlled solely by the social mission of correctional or psychiatric institutions. This is similar to the work of teachers, doctors, or psychiatrists in such settings who supply professional services to "inmates" or "patients" in the interests of their individual growth and health needs. Such services do, however, complement the social control functions of the agency by making it more likely that the participants will be able to meet their own needs in socially acceptable ways.

Working with groups in these types of social control situations is closely related to the type of work with groups that we have termed "alternative role attainment," which shall be discussed in the next chapter. Thus when the purpose of the group, as we conceive it, has been achieved and the members have identified the commonality between their desires and the goals of the agency, presumably they will seek help in attaining these mutually held objectives and the function of the group then becomes one of resocialization—for roles that are "alternative" in contrast to the previous ones. It is also possible that a "common ground" between the members' and the agency's purposes will not be found and members will resist participation in the group, even after an extended period. In these cases, there may be no viable group work purpose that can be achieved. There are many measures, however, which we shall discuss later in this chapter, that workers can take to avoid such an impasse.

Many ethical issues confront the workers in these situations. One is whether they should ever seek to impose changes on a member that the member has not chosen. This is not a simple matter because there is a very thin line between *coercing* a member and *urging* a member to consider alternative values and behaviors that the worker thinks will be beneficial. The complicating factor here is the power the agency wields contrasted with the power of the member—especially when the agency controls the clients' access to discharge from the agency, thus the clients' freedom. The worker is, in reality, as well as in the perception of the member, associated with such power. The clients' willingness to participate in the group, for example, may be used for or against them in a discharge proceeding.

In addition, the worker can be caught between two values: one is that of self-determination in which members choose their own goals. The other is the respect the worker holds for the worth of the individual—what the individual is and may become—and this latter may justify strong measures to involve the member in activities that the worker believes have the potential of enhancing or even saving the life of the individual.

There are no easy answers to such questions and all workers, especially in social control settings, must struggle with them every day. We believe that the workers must discuss their dilemmas in this regard with members, especially if they expect the members to reciprocate and share *their* conflicts. Also, worker honesty in this regard is a first step in helping members to protect themselves from improper pressures.

Another struggle for workers is to avoid being inappropriately co-opted by the agency, especially when the program is more custodial than therapeutic. For example, we interviewed some inmates of a federal prison regarding their experiences with social workers, including those facilitating inmate groups. One social worker was criticized by the inmates because they felt he had accepted the guards' attitude toward prisoners during a session. An example they gave was that when a prisoner spoke to this worker of his desire for a pass to visit his seriously ill wife, the social worker was unreceptive and communicated his belief that prisoners were always trying to "con" the system and, therefore, the request was not merited.

Another type of ethical issue arises when the clients in a social control situation are diagnosed as psychotic or retarded or not of legal age. We believe that in these situations, the worker must consult with the families of such members regarding goals when the members are incapable of taking responsibility for themselves. Efforts, however, must always be made to secure informed consent whenever this is even remotely possible. The worker might even consider establishing an advisory group of clients with whom to consult on procedures for protecting client rights in group situations.

As in the other chapters in this part, we call the reader's attention to the fact that some groups are established primarily to fulfill social control functions. These are most frequently found in correctional settings. On the other hand, many agencies form groups in which social control represents one of several functions. An example of this is the use of groups in some school settings. A school, concerned about disruptive behavior (such as students ignoring teacher requests, committing vandalism, or aggressive acts against other students), may form groups for stopping this behavior in addition to supporting the education of the members. The presence of such "mixed" goals can pose difficulties for group members as they negotiate the purposes of the group with the worker. Sensitive negotiation skills as well as clear and honest statements from the worker are essential in such situations.

The strategies for group work in social control situations must address several common conditions. Group members are likely to be involuntary, at least at first. The fact that group attendance is seen as leading to some external benefit, such as a recommendation for parole or probation, does not mean that the member "really" wishes the group experience, but the group worker must respond to this issue as a first task. While any individual change effort will meet with some resistance, even in voluntary situations, groups in social change situations encounter this phenomenon to a great degree.

A second condition is that members' behavior is socially deviant. This means that their behavior has been fostered by the social forces that promote deviance: denial of access to social resources such as jobs and education; pressure from peers who are also deviant; suffering from the imposition of derogatory labeling, and so forth. Social control groups must confront these conditions that make it difficult, if not impossible, for the member to leave the deviant role. These conditions are often present to a great degree in poor communities and among those oppressed by virtue of their ethnicity. Social control groups must operate in ways that recognize these social conditions.

When groups are conducted in an institution for criminals or delinquents, the members are likely to be affected by the *inmate code.* This norm among inmates requires the individual to uphold his or her solidarity with other inmates by withholding information about them and by supporting them in any encounter with staff. As a result, members of groups in these settings resist discussing their reactions to each other in group meetings. Inasmuch as these reactions are the core of many group work approaches, workers must find ways of helping members to confront this code.

If the barriers caused by the inmate code are to be surmounted, there must be a commonality of group and agency purposes. Correctional institutions are often coercive and punitive and this can undermine the development of self-disclosure and confrontation in the group. The worker, consequently, must seek to "humanize" the correctional setting.

The group can play a role in this humanization. For example, the author consulted in a state prison with a worker who sought to train inmates as group workers for other inmates. The process included a strategy of lobbying with the prison administration to secure legitimacy for this approach, then a pilot program was conducted. Because of the success of the program, several guards were also trained as group workers and some groups were co-led by an inmate and a guard, both supervised by the worker. This gradually led to a different and more positive attitude of guards to prisoners and each group began to see the other as individuals rather than as clones.

Even in benign settings that have social control functions, members will often resist a reconsideration of their values and behaviors. The strategies employed by group workers in such situations involve the creation of a strong and supportive group in which members are aware of their caring for each other. In this climate the members will employ techniques with one another that are confrontive and direct. A great deal of controversy exists, however, among group workers regarding interventions that involve strong confrontations.

PREGROUP TASKS

A major factor in selecting members for and composing groups in social control situations is the nature of potential group members' existing group interactions. The interactional and social-psychological conception of deviance utilized in our approach to group work holds that such antisocial behavior is maintained by their interactions with their families and their peer groups, particularly the latter.

This view requires the worker to examine the peer group interactions of potential group members. Frequently the worker will attempt to work with the peer group itself as a "natural" group. This is the approach taken in such services as street gang work with delinquent adolescents.[1] In residential institutions with delinquents, the group, for group work purposes, is often the living group such as the "cottage" because this is the place that delinquent norms may be maintained.

In any case, in a pregroup assessment the worker will seek to determine the members' subcultural identifications. Members will be asked about the groups they belong to and the activities of such groups. The kinds of behavior the members condone should be investigated. Particularly important to note are the possible conflicts among the members of such groups regarding their beliefs. This may indicate whether some motivation for change can come from such peer groups.

Motivation to either examine one's values and behaviors or change them is also assessed during pregroup interviews. Few potential members are likely to have strong motivation for change or, if they have, to admit it to people perceived to be in authority positions. Nevertheless, such motivation will make it more likely that the group will achieve the agency's objectives and the presence of it in some members will facilitate consideration of alternative lifestyles in the group. The worker can assess this by asking the potential members about times they may have considered alternative goals, how they might now respond to new opportunities, and whether family members or other people in their social network are likely to support their entry into new roles.

A problem in group composition has been that the population in an organization such as a prison may not allow for much heterogeneity among members in life experiences, behaviors, and values. Members will, therefore, reinforce each other in their commitments to deviance. This does not preclude the use of groups, however. The worker can confront members about their adherence to such beliefs when the group has developed sufficiently to support members in dealing with such confrontation constructively. This type of confrontation, however, usually requires the members to be involved in other programs in the agency so that staff and participants in all programs can work together to promote a consideration of new roles.

Even under optimal conditions, however, the group composition will sometimes work against the achievement of the agency's objectives. A technique that workers have used to offset this is to "seed" the group with people who have been in the program long enough to have begun the process of personal change. Such "members" provide important models of how to overcome the pull of past social forces.

---

[1]Irving Spergel, *Street Gang Work* (Reading, Mass.: Addison-Wesley, 1966).

Groups that seek to help members to consider alternatives in their lives as well as to attain related roles are usually not short-term groups but may involve members for many months. They may also be "open-ended" in that members "graduate" to new group experiences as they become ready to do so. It is also possible to have a planned sequence of groups—the first one, to orient the members to the program and promote a willingness to consider its values; the second, to help members make appropriate choices regarding their careers and begin to pursue them; and the last, either to facilitate termination from the program or to provide a supportive type of follow-up.

Members in many such programs are not prepared in any detail for the group. This is because of the importance of helping members to place most of their dependence on the group rather than on the worker. The group itself constitutes the strongest force for a reconsideration of norms. For this reason, also, such groups may not be as small as other social work groups and may have as many as ten to fifteen members. This allows for some members to be selected as models and for additional changes for heterogeneity and at the same time the group is not so large that a member becomes "lost."

GROUP FORMATION TASKS

In discussions of group development in this chapter we draw from the guided group interaction material, cited previously, as a model of how groups may develop in social control situations. Based on our reading and experience, we believe there are general elements of development in most groups of this sort. As the reader will find in reviewing the literature cited here, there is considerable empirical support for this approach.

When a group is started in a social control situation, it is often hard work to overcome the initial distrust and hostility displayed by the members toward the worker and the agency and sometimes toward each other. Empey and Erickson describe a number of techniques used in the initial stages of a guided group interaction experience that have relevance for other social control situations as well.[2] They assume that members will behave in a manner that is "erratic and defensive" and, therefore, "the concern of a group leader should be with fostering interaction among group members and instilling some confidence that it might eventually be effective and rewarding.[3]

The recommended techniques are those, therefore, that will "foster and reward interaction" and that will teach members "that whatever interaction took place in a group and whatever progress was made, would depend on them, not just staff."[4] This is accomplished by showing sincere interest in what members say and by avoiding stereotyped responses often made by workers in these settings such as "the stern disciplinarian, the loving father, the kindly friend, or the all-wise

[2]Empey and Erickson, *The Provo Experiment,* pp. 96–103.
[3]Ibid., p. 96.
[4]Ibid., pp. 103–35.

doctor." In a sense, this requires the worker to behave in a somewhat ambiguous manner which includes *not* declaring all of the rules and procedures to be followed in the group but casting these issues back to the members. This is in direct contrast to what workers do in role attainment groups.

In social control groups, the members often seek formulas for the group and for their tenure in the agency. They will ask what they should be doing in the group and how this relates to their "stay" in the agency, particularly if it is a residential one and they have been committed there. Workers in guided group interaction programs are taught to redirect these questions back to the members for *their* ideas.

Another technique to encourage interaction and to set the stage for a willingness to use the group for problem solving is to ask the members to tell their "stories" (their histories) and to talk about their interests and their feelings about the program. This has the additional benefit of aiding the members in their efforts to find out from the group worker whether he or she will be understanding, supportive, and nonjudgmental.

The worker who is inexperienced in service to such groups will fear that the kinds of processes just described will continue indefinitely and that nothing worthwhile will be accomplished. The experience of such programs as guided group interaction is that members become bored with this activity and see that it, in itself, will not lead to discharge from the program. The members are then ready to consider using the group for problem-solving activity. The worker promotes this next phase by helping the members to reflect on what they have been doing and why their inputs have been shallow. While a change in the group may not happen quickly, such discussion does prepare members to invest their energy in seeking the commonality between their needs and the agency goals.

Workers will receive a good deal of information during this formation period, however, that will help them formulate an assessment of the members. Such procedures as the members telling their "stories" will give information about the kinds of norms they are committed to and how these norms relate to their present and past social relationships. Whether members experience conflict about their deviance can be examined as well as their knowledge about the role alternatives and opportunities available to them.

Attention must also be paid to an assessment of the social barriers faced by the members. These include the effects of racism as well as of "deviant labels" that may have been placed upon them. Means will have to be sought to cope with these when they are operative.

Helping members to choose new personal goals in social control oriented settings must often be paralled by seeking changes at an agency level. Members who view the agency as unresponsive to their needs are unlikely to use the services of that agency to reexamine their own lives. The members have chosen their deviant careers in response to a lack of environmental opportunities and an unsympathetic environment, and an agency that recreates this will fail in accomplishing its purposes.

The assessment processes during this formation period must thus include an evaluation of agency conditions that are detrimental to group members. When this is done in good faith, it will encourage the members to look *also* within themselves for sources of their difficulties. The kinds of conditions that are frequently targeted in these circumstances are the resources the agency supplies the members (educational programs, recreation, physical facilities), the responsiveness of the staff to member concerns, the degree to which members can participate in agency decision making, the agency's procedures for disciplining members (use of punishment, arbitrary or excessive penalties, favoritism), and sexist and racist attitudes.

As implied by the preceding discussion, the development of the contract in social situations is more problematic than in any of the others we have outlined. This is because it requires members to agree voluntarily to reconsider and then to change basic values. *This process only occurs when the agency is responsive to member concerns.* The intervention target thus must include the transactions occurring between the individual, the group, and the agency. After each participant in the interaction has made some changes, a contract for further client change becomes a realistic option.

GOAL PURSUIT TASKS

As we have stated, Empey and Erickson present a model for the development of guided group interaction groups that can be drawn on for other social control oriented groups. There are some distinguishing features of their type of treatment, however, that are not present in other programs, including the fact that when guided group interaction is used as the treatment approach, the setting is frequently residential. The Provo, Utah, program was an exception in that the participants were assigned on the basis of a judicial process but lived in the community and only spent part of each day at the program center. Program features included group meetings and a paid work program, school attendance, or both.

The Provo program, like others of its kind, employed little overall formal structure to communicate to the boys that release from the program was simply a matter of conformity to the rules. The ambiguity created by this lack of structure, it was hypothesized, created anxiety that members turned to the group to relieve; it also elicited members' typical coping mechanisms and stimulated creativity in solving problems.

Because the boys were involved with each other outside of the group as well as in it, the group became the vehicle for dealing with many behaviors the boys observed and with which they confronted each other. The salience of the group was enhanced by granting it the power to help decide when each boy would be released. This was linked with whether the boy had worked on his problems in the group and had been open and honest with other members.

Earlier in this chapter we described the formation period in such groups. This period ends as the members become frustrated with unproductive uses of the group and consider the possibility of using the group for problem solving. Empey and Erickson refer to the next stage, then, as "stereotyped problem solving."[5] Members begin to raise concerns but are still well defended in the way that this is done. They ask the kinds of questions that they think they are expected to ask and they give answers of similar quality.

The group worker during this period must be very patient. Too early a confrontation will reinstitute the members' defensiveness and mistrust. On the other hand, the worker must be sensitive to genuine problem statements in contrast to the "role playing" of problem-solving processes members believe are of interest to the staff members.

The members' behavior during this period may appear, therefore, to be contradictory. Members are tentatively and ambivalently testing out the problem-solving potential of the group. Because this is a social control situation, steps in the direction of problem solving by some group members are seen by others as "giving in" to workers or currying favor with them and members will criticize each other for this. Thus, this phase is also marked by group conflict and the worker is in a more strategic position if he or she mediates it rather than bears the brunt of it.

Empey and Erickson note that this type of conflict is intensified in those institutional settings into which members bring events that have occurred outside of the group—members' antisocial acts, for example, which may have affected other group members. As they state:

> When a group encounters such problems, basic loyalties, basic beliefs, and commitments are subject to strain. Boys are torn between their own self-interests and those of others. In a prison, a rule that is enforced by staff as well as offenders is that everyone should do his own "time," and not mess with the "time" of others. Some of the same behavior can be expected in a community program. The pressures against those who would assume a reformer's role is [sic] considerable. That is why group members at this stage of development cannot be expected to run much risk in dealing with the problems that emerge.[6]

The worker's role in responding to this type of situation must involve a recognition of how difficult a period this is for members. What is at stake here, when members begin to discuss each other's behavior, is their choice between antisocial and prosocial norms. As members wrestle with the issues of their evaluation of each other's behavior, they begin, as Empey and Erickson point out, to take responsibility for making judgments rather than being solely the targets of judgments made by "authority." This conflict also results in members directing hostility displaced from each other to the worker.

Empey and Erickson remind the reader that discussion of behavior in this phase introduces members to the "reformation role"; this begins to make the

---

[5]Ibid., p. 103.
[6]Ibid., p. 104.

group a "medium for change" and is a modification of the traditional staff-client relationship. The overall dynamic, therefore, is still that of building an effective group rather than solving basic problems.[7]

The next phase in the group emerges as members begin to challenge some of each other's characteristic defenses. As Empey and Erickson wisely note, "Delinquents, like anyone else, do not enjoy a group in which daily interaction is characterized by perpetual tension, though they may not know what to do about it."[8] The alternative that the worker encourages is greater openness and honesty to "get beyond existing facades." The important ingredient here is a sense of timing. Too premature a pressure toward openness can coalesce the group around a strongly antisocial member as protection against the strong feelings that emerge.

If these issues are resolved to a sufficient degree, the phase that follows in the group is termed by Empey and Erickson "awareness of individual differences and alternatives." In this stage, members start to move away from stereotyped reactions to each other, and beliefs regarding "individual differences and needs" emerge. This is accompanied by more openness regarding oneself and one's reactions to others in the group. Even this, however, is frightening, and so this phase is marked by reactions such as reaffirmation of the value of deviant behavior. This conflict can also be reflected in the emergence of subgroups that represent each point of view.

Despite these continuing conflicts in the group, the presence of an increased number of members who are committed to openness allows for an investment in problem solving around current issues. The members who involve themselves this way will feel rewarded and the worker can help them to share their satisfactions with the others. This is correlated with the group beginning to perceive each member as unique rather than as a stereotype.

Because of the openness that has surfaced, the worker will bring problems to the group that affect the members. This will include such day-to-day issues as nonattendance of members as well as problems being experienced in other components of the agency's program, such as its school or vocational facilities.

Empey and Erickson call the next phase "group awareness"[9] as its objectives are to increase the members' understanding of "group structure and process and to maximize group problem solving." The explanation for this emphasis, is that since much of deviance is a *social* phenomena, an understanding of *social* processes is an important treatment goal.

The natural processes of the group support this phase in that members become concerned about the group as an entity. This interest is facilitated by the worker who actually, but in nontechnical terms, teaches about such group phenomena as unwritten norms, leadership, and sources of power in the group. This new "sophistication" will also contribute to the members' understanding the workers' actions and even criticizing them.

[7]Ibid., pp. 106–7.
[8]Ibid., p. 111.
[9]Ibid., pp. 119–25.

Thus in this phase, while members continue to solve individual and group problems, they will do so with a better understanding of the barriers to this process posed by group phenomena. This understanding also motivates the members to try to improve the operation of the group, such as by creating new group norms.

The final stage is termed "integration of group and program structure."[10] Empey and Erickson recognize that this phase might not be reached by many groups but when it does occur, members help to prepare new groups as well as take responsibility for the continuing development of the agency's services. In addition, members seek to extend the prosocial norms of the group into the other institutions of the community.

As an argument against the notion that the kind of group development described here is too idealistic a concept for "real" work with delinquents, Empey and Erickson cite research based on 1000 recorded group sessions representing 10 different groups. In this investigation it was found that "when groups remain closed, there was some rather clear-cut evidence that a developmental process does take place—a process in which therapist participation decreases, group-centered comments increase, greater member-risks occur in which candid and confrontive statements are made, and nontask-oriented comments decrease. The analysis revealed that this process is better described in terms of a developmental trend than in terms of sharply demarcated stages.[11] In this discussion, the authors state that movement may include regressive shifts as well as forward ones. The worker under such circumstances must identify themes and directions rather than look for group changes that are without ambiguity or that cover all members at the same time.

The group phases just outlined fit partly into our concept of a social control function and partly into an alternative role attainment function. As we stated earlier, it is unlikely that a social worker will think of the former without the latter. In view of the back and forth movement of the group described by Empey and Erickson, at any given moment some members may be settling on efforts to change themselves while others are still considering whether or not to formulate such a contract between themselves and the group. The continued pull from antisocial peers as well as others keeps the social control function of the agency ever present as a force in the members' lives.

The foregoing material represents a model of how groups with social control functions are likely to evolve. Practitioners with such groups, however, have used a variety of interventions drawn from different theoretical orientations. How these affect the group's development is not well understood and should be the target of further investigation. Workers with such groups can develop their own specific approaches by consulting a literature that includes experiences in

[10]Ibid., p. 134.
[11]Ibid.

social control settings with analytic,[12] behavior-modification,[13] problem-solving,[14] and therapeutic-community[15] technologies.

EVALUATION

In consonance with our concept of group work in social control situations as functioning to secure agreement among agency, group, and client on client goals, we have sought to identify ways of evaluating the attainment of such agreement. We reserve for the next chapter on "alternative role attainment" the issue of evaluating personal change in clients of psychiatric, correctional, and similar institutions with control functions *after* agreement about goals has been reached.

Because one of the steps in fulfilling the function of groups in social control settings is to secure the commitment of the member to the group, it is a vital component for evaluation. Workers should carefully monitor such variables as meeting attendance, promptness in attending meetings, and the proportion of members who actively participate in meetings, even if such participation is hostile. We believe that the issue of contract is crucial in these groups. Workers, therefore, should monitor when each member has arrived at a contract regarding goals with the worker, group, and agency. This also implies that "behavioral agreement" with the contract should be examined. Workers can create simple log sheets in which deviations from the contract on the part of member (perhaps of the agency, too) are recorded and then examined by the worker to help determine the future of the group.

Most groups related to this function must also be concerned about the honesty and openness of members because this is essential to a viable contract. Workers can develop "climate" questionnaires to evaluate the attainment of this condition. These consist of questions in which members rate the trust they place in other members and the worker, the likelihood that the group will be helpful to them, the amount of support they feel from the group and the freedom they have to say what is actually "on their minds." Such questionnaires are usually completed anonymously. Because of members' fears about confidentiality, they may even request that a person outside of the group, whom they trust, tabulate and report on the findings.

[12]R. Rappaport, "Group Therapy in Prison: A Strategic Approach," in *Group Counseling and Group Psychotherapy with Rehabilitation Clients,* ed. Milton Seligman (Springfield: Thomas, 1977).
[13]H. Novotny and J. Enomoto, "Social Competence Training as a Correctional Alternative," *Offender Rehabilitation* I (1976), 45–55.
[14]G. Kassebaum, D. Ward, and D. Wilner, *Prison Treatment and Parole Survival: An Empirical Assessment* (New York: Wiley, 1971).
[15]E. Studt, S. Messinger, and T. Wilson, *C-Unit: Search for Community in Prison* (New York: Sage, 1968).

AN EXAMPLE

An example of issues that workers encounter in social control groups is shown in this excerpt of a meeting in a prison.[16] As can be seen, the group had progressed past the phase of group formation and had entered the middle phase of development. The group was composed of twelve men (eight black and four white) whose offenses included murder, armed robbery, and rape. The group had been meeting for four months.

The group worker had an eclectic orientation toward his work. He used many of the approaches described in this book including techniques that were related to analytic as well as behavioral theories. An innovation that he had created for this group and others is the use of an inmate as a co-worker. Such inmates had been selected and trained by him on the basis of their participation in groups in which they demonstrated capabilities for helping others. The worker is Dr. S. and the inmate co-worker is F.

At the meeting, two new members were present for the first time: Bill and Ted. They had learned from informal discussions with group members outside the group that they would be expected to tell something about their "problems" and background at this meeting. This had been reinforced in a screening interview they held with the worker. Bill began talking when the group convened as if he had been cued to do this. He stated that his offense had been armed robbery but that his was not the usual case. He had come from a "good" family and had not been in trouble as a teenager. He had been married when he was seventeen to a woman he loved and with whom he had a close relationship. He had received training as a musician and earned his living playing with bands. The long times he had to be away from home stressed his marriage. His wife wanted him to come home more. Because of her loneliness, she began to see other men. Eventually they were divorced. He found a new woman who was well-off financially, who did many nice things for him but wanted to be able to depend on him in return. After a heated argument about this, he took her driving in her car and, with every intention of returning it, made her get out of the car at gunpoint. He was very surprised, consequently, when he was confronted by the police and arrested.

The other men in the group asked Bill many questions such as why he had possession of a gun and why the woman had called the police. Bill responded that he always carried a gun to defend himself and that this woman was simply very angry with him. The other members expressed disbelief and indicated that Bill was not taking any responsibility for what had happened. He continued to make defensive statements and another member, Frank, told him that in the group he would learn how to face what he did to bring trouble upon himself.

Ted then began to talk and told his story without any prompting. He had been involved in a series of burglaries since he was a young teenager. When he was seventeen (about three years before), he and a "rap-buddy" (partner in commit-

[16]This example was also reported by the author in Charles D. Garvin, "Resocialization: Group Work in Social Control and Correctional Settings," in *The Group Workers' Handbook: Varieties of Group Experience,* ed. Robert K. Conyne (Springfield: Thomas, 1985), pp. 128–31.

ting crimes) had been engaged in the burglary of a store. While it was in progress, the owner of the store apprehended them and drew a gun. Ted grabbed a hammer and hit this man on the head. The man was in a coma and was expected to die. His "rap-buddy" snitched on him and he was arrested. The buddy was not sentenced but Ted was given "seven to fourteen." The victim survived but due to the seriousness of the crime, Ted was tried as an adult and placed in an adult institution.

Ted indicated that he had a problem with violence and several members asked him to elaborate on this. He said he had been involved in at least a dozen fights, in the last facility he had been in. Nevertheless, he had been placed in solitary confinement a number of times. His first fight occurred when his "rap-buddy," in jail on another charge, had been transferred to the same institution in which Ted was a prisoner. Ted said that he was justified in attacking the buddy, but he was wrong in his earlier attack on the person he had robbed. He explained that several other fights had occurred as he sought to ward-off homosexual advances.

F. commented that Ted seemed to present himself as a "victim" who was forced by others to be violent. Within this institution, it was clearly understood that "victim" meant that one abdicated responsibility for one's own actions. Ted did not respond to this and the theme was picked up by several other men. One commented that he thought Ted was a danger to other people and was not ready for release to the community. Another asked Ted if he still would attack his "rap-buddy." Ted said he wouldn't because this matter was now settled.

At this point group discussion to define "snitching" took place for about five minutes. Several members indicated that they had come to the conclusion that it was not "snitching" if you told the truth about something, even if this implicated others in a crime. These men agreed that snitching meant telling lies that falsely implicated others when the liar was the culprit. This discussion was an outgrowth of Ted's criticism of his "rap-buddy" for snitching.

A black man in the group (Ted is white) asked Ted about his recent actions to relieve himself from his work assignment in the kitchen. Ted stated that he did not like kitchen work. The black member said that he knew Ted had been relieved of this assignment by writing a letter to the supervisor stating that he was being "pressed" by others on this work detail and he could not handle this pressure (probably a reference to his known violent reactions). He continued by stating that Ted had manipulated a situation for his own benefit in a way that could cause others to suffer. He pointed out that since Ted was white and the others on the detail were black, the charge of the white man would be believed, as it was often alleged, that the majority of black inmates harrassed the whites. Ted denied this charge and a lengthy discussion ensued in which black members (supported by one white member) sought to convince Ted of the results of his actions. One member also pointed out that this discussion was related to the earlier point that Ted saw himself as "victim" when he actually provoked others.

At this point, the session was about to run past its allocated time. Dr. S. indicated to Ted that his anger at others and the way he handled it may have been the result of some of his earlier experiences, perhaps family ones. He asked Ted to think about this and to present some of these thoughts at a future meeting.

This example illustrates several processes that are typical of groups in social control settings. We see the new members encouraged to tell their stories as a way of introducing themselves to other members, initiating interactions, and identifying problems to be worked on in the group.

Even though this was Ted's first meeting, the other members perceived that he was open to some confrontation. It is also likely that this confrontation took place because his actions were not only harmful to himself but to his fellow inmates. That this was not a beginning group is evidenced by the fact that the members were willing to confront one another and to deal with such problems as racism in the institution. The inmate code usually prevents such confrontation unless members have begun to abandon it during group sessions. Members, also, are not likely to deal with such issues as racism unless they have become convinced that the group is a place where issues can be dealt with effectively.

SUMMARY

In this chapter we discussed the character of group work in social control situations. The function of the group when the social control function is dominant is to help the members seek out the common ground between their goals and those of the group and the agency—perhaps even of the larger environment. This is a difficult and sometimes long-term process in which the agency must also indicate a willingness to change itself so as to relate more to member needs. The major worker skills in this situation are those of mediating among members, group, and agency.

At times, however, members need a good deal of support to enter into this process as well as to increase their motivation to do so. This motivation is sometimes increased by workers through their use of confrontation, their support of inter-member confrontation, their reminders of the short and long-term consequences of behavior, and their heightening anxiety through the deliberate use of ambiguity.

A general model for the development of such groups and the workers' changing roles in different phases of the group was drawn from experiences with delinquents in a guided group interaction program. That program identified phases moving from the group-building efforts to stereotyped and, then, more individualized forms of problem solving. Research was cited as to the validity of this concept of group development. This chapter concluded with an illustration of a prison group.

13

Working With Groups For Alternative Role Attainment

In Chapter 11 we discussed the use of groups to help members perform better in their roles. We indicated that such people are usually defined as "normal" and their group activities have educational foci. There is another category of people who also seek to attain new roles or fulfill the requirements of existing roles; they, however, are currently performing in ways that are regarded by others as "sick" or "deviant." They have a double burden then: to overcome the forces that make it difficult to relinquish their previous positions as well as to acquire new behaviors, insights, and ways of coping with desired roles.

An example is that of patients in a mental hospital who have been diagnosed as schizophrenics. As they develop skills to cope with life stresses, they must also overcome forces in the family, the community, and the workplace that define them as "sick." An effective group program must be focused on both of these dimensions: the adaptation to new roles as well as the overcoming of conflicts between the new and the old. As we indicated previously, this is the reason for using the term "alternative role attainment."

There are major differences as well as similarities in the situations of the various types of people who fall within the aspect of group work. In very general terms, for example, a psychotic child or adult in a hospital, a prisoner in a training school or reformatory, and a client of a family counseling agency are faced with acquiring new roles while coping with the effects of having performed in the old ones. Nevertheless, the psychological and social dynamics in each case are quite different and the ways workers deal with such members will reflect this. Thus, psychotic persons have few adaptive mechanisms and they must be helped to develop them. Prison inmates may "act out" when stressed and they must be helped to control their behavior and deal with stress differently. Each of these "dynamics" calls for different interventions with the individual as well as with the group and will be commented upon in the course of this chapter.

Because of the extensive discussion of work in correctional and other social control settings in the last chapter, we shall give more weight in this one to psychiatric settings. We believe that some concerns and processes in a correctional setting are similar to those in a psychiatric setting when the former is oriented to rehabilitation and once the social control issues have been, at least partially, resolved with members. This is also in recognition of the fact that it can be the operation of social factors that determines whether *some* people "end up" in prison or a mental hospital.

In discussing approaches to helping individuals in groups, we shall cite five types. The first, referred to by Rose as a "minimal skill training group," involves training people in social skills that they may almost totally lack and that are necessary for any kind of functioning outside of a psychiatric or other institution. These are similar to the social skills training approaches described in Chapter 11 and yet are contrived so as to take into consideration the needs and abilities of very emotionally impaired persons. A second is the activity-oriented group for people not able to function in "talk" groups. The third, typically considered to be "group psychotherapy," is for people who possess basic social skills and a considerable degree of reality testing and who are helped to overcome persistent patterns of responding to situations in self-defeating ways. The fourth is the transition group for people leaving such settings. The fifth, the so-called "patient government group," is designed to help people learn participatory democracy skills that exist (or should exist) in all communities. Such groups are formed in institutions to give patients a way of participating in making rules, planning programs, and solving organizational problems.

In all of these cases, however, work is required to alter environments that maintain people in "deviant" roles, although, in some, the individual and the group may be able to act more on their own behalf than others. In any case, individuals in these types of groups will experience conflict among the demands of differing systems and must be helped to cope with these conflicts so as to respond in functional ways.

PREGROUP TASKS

An assessment before the beginning of the group will include an identification of the roles with which the person seeks help. In a mental hospital or after-care program, those roles that are emphasized tend to be associated with peers, family, and employment. For people who are severely impaired, the roles may be even more fundamental such as "information seeker" (for example, asking directions), "consumer" (for example, how to make a purchase), or "initiator of relationships" (for example, making the acquaintance of someone else).

Since the purpose of the compositional principle often is to secure members who have similar levels of social functioning, this attribute must be assessed prior to starting the group. Some people in psychiatric settings have experienced a deterioration in their behavior and the worker may have to secure historical information from the prospective member as well as significant others. Such information includes the kinds of social interactions in which the client has engaged at different phases of his or her life and how well these were managed. For example, the worker will ask whether the individual has had friends during previous periods, whether they were of both sexes, and the kinds of activities engaged in with these friends. This helps the worker to compose groups of people with similar skill levels, even if these skills are not manifested currently. The skill level of the group will also determine the kinds of techniques the worker employs in the group.

Goldstein, Sprafkin, and Gershaw have developed and tested skill survey instruments that can be used.[1] One version is for the staff to complete and the other is for clients. On the survey, the rater indicates the level of skill on a five-point scale ranging from "never good at using the skill" to "always good at using the skill." Thirty-six skills are listed such as "starting a conversation," "listening," "expressing anger," "apologizing," "following instructions," and "decision making."

If the worker seeks to develop a minimal skill training group, a specific number of sessions are usually planned. The number varies, however, based on the level of social competence of the members. Even within this type of planning, the worker can establish either a continuous training experience or divide it into segments with in-between periods when members work on the skills they have already developed without attempting new material. More research is needed on the effectiveness of such varying arrangements. Group psychotherapy experiences in which members are helped to develop insight into their behavior while also having an opportunity to try out new behaviors in the group can, in contrast, be at least a year in duration. Transition groups may meet only three to five times. Patient government groups are ongoing.

In any case, members should be prepared for the group experience. In one type of minimal skill training, "structured learning therapy," potential members are informed of the types of skills that may be taught in the group. The skill checklist developed by therapists using that approach can communicate to potential members what some of the purposes of the group may be.

Goldstein and his colleagues consider the possibility that the client may not be able to comprehend the checklist in which case it can be administered by the worker as a questionnaire. In any event, the worker should discuss the types of

[1]Arnold P. Goldstein, Robert P. Sprafkin, and N. Jane Gershaw, *Skill Training for Community Living: Applying Structured Learning Therapy* (Elmsford, N.Y.: Pergamon Press, 1976), pp. 166–73.

skills that may be taught, describe the procedures that will be used at meetings (to be presented later in this chapter), and contract with the individual regarding skills he or she is interested in pursuing. People invited to join the group are given a "trainee's notebook," which includes details regarding times and places, rules such as attendance and participation, and a description of the therapeutic procedures. The notebook includes pages for notes on each session as well as records of homework assignments and progress made on these.

In Chapter 3 we presented Yalom's procedure for preparing members for group psychotherapy. Some of the issues he clarifies for members are appropriate to any group experience. Several things he tells members, however, are unique to the group psychotherapy experience. One is his preparation of members for analysis of "process" by telling them that they must be "honest and direct with the feelings in the group at that moment, especially their feelings toward the other group members and the therapists."[2] Frustration and confusion during the first dozen meetings are predicted. The difficulty many people have in expressing feelings in group psychotherapy sessions is described as well as "the tendencies of some to withdraw emotionally, to hide their feelings, to let others express feelings for them, to form concealing alliances with others."[3]

The long-term nature of group psychotherapy is also explained to members by Yalom as a product of changing behavior and attitudes that were created over many years. Rules are explained that may be required in group psychotherapy but not in other group experiences with other members outside the group. The members are told that such relationships may impede rather than enhance therapy because "friendships among certain group members may prevent them from speaking openly to one another in the group" because of loyalties that develop to those relationships.

Both minimal skill training and psychotherapy groups are usually small, consisting of five to seven members. The amount of individualization and support necessary for resocialization experiences requires this size. Activity-oriented and transition groups can sometimes be larger, depending on how their activities are structured. Patient government groups may be large, depending on the number of units that must be represented.

GROUP FORMATION TASKS

After the initial assessment that occurs prior to the first group meeting, additional and often more complex assessments take place, which may continue throughout the group's life. In selecting individualized goals during group formation, one of the first topics that must be attended to is the forces at play in each member's life that maintain dysfunctional patterns. This is because during the time the group meets, plans will have to be made to change these forces, to provide the member

---

[2]Irving D. Yalom, *The Theory and Practice of Group Psychotherapy,* 2nd ed. (New York: Basic Books, 1975), p. 291.
[3]Ibid., p. 292.

with better means of coping with them, or both. These forces include those from families and peer groups that reinforce antisocial patterns as well as those stemming from social institutions such as schools and places of employment that do the same.

These interactions are assessed by asking members to describe reactions of significant others to their problems and actions. Because of the similarities that often exist in the members' circumstances, they can help each other to identify these reactions. Also the worker may have information from other sources in the agency that can be contributed to this analysis regarding family, peer, and organizational responses.

As members, in the beginning meetings of the group, clarify their goals for participation in the group and as they review situations that hinder their goal attainment, the worker and other members should note how the members indicate they cope with identified conflicts. Some members are able to engage actively in problem-solving conflicts and decision-making efforts while others deny conflicts, minimize them, or are overwhelmed by them. In such cases, the worker and others will help the members to remove such barriers to their effort to attain alternative, more functional roles.

Once the member has begun to accomplish tasks to attain his or her goals in view of forces promoting old roles and behaviors, the type of relevant assessment is similar to that conducted in role attainment groups. As we stated in Chapter 11, when the worker's interventions are composed of behavioral modification techniques, an assessment will specify the "antecedent conditions" of the member's behavior as well as the consequences of acting in functional or dysfunctional ways. This assessment should include information on the types of behaviors and attitudes also described in Chapter 11, that is, member's knowledge, ability, and motivation with regard to both behavior and attitudes.

The availability of opportunity structures is also an essential element of moving from dysfunctional to functional role performance and must also be ascertained. For example, people released from mental hospitals or other psychiatric rehabilitation programs must be able to find jobs, secure needed services, and obtain training. The group should examine whether these are available and open to the members who need them. Members can be coached on how to approach these resources and the group can plan group actions to make them more accessible. An assessment of such opportunities is, therefore, an integral requirement for group work services. The patient government group should be primarily devoted to improving the agency's or institution's opportunity structures.

The targets of group work intervention in alternative role attainment situations are thus similar to those we described previously for role attainment situations, namely the member's knowledge, skill, and motivation for performing designated roles. The essential difference, however, is that *the conflicts encountered in moving out of deviant positions must be addressed.*

The resocialization aspects of such groups have other effects on group processes during group formation. Some members may continue to respond with either resistance or ambivalence to the social control aspects of the agency. This can be manifested in some members opposing others in the group who wish to adapt in new ways. The entire group may also occasionally move into a resistive mode that is more typical of social control situations. This may be a response to either pressures from the environment or overwhelming anxiety about the changes taking place. Whitaker and Lieberman in their model of group psychotherapy, discussed in Chapter 5, present an analytical framework that is also pertinent to understanding the formation period of alternative role attainment groups.[4] To briefly review their formulation, they indicate that members will experience wishes regarding their personal outcomes that are termed the "disturbing motive." While members may have different wishes, these become linked by the process of communication and association. In a similar fashion, some of the fears regarding these wishes also become linked and Whitaker and Lieberman term this the "reactive motive." These two motives form the "focal group conflict" for which, at any given time, the group seeks a solution. These solutions may either be facilitating or hindering.

During the formation period of alternative role attainment groups, members will wish that their relationships may become gratifying, their activities less likely to get them into trouble, or their strivings met with success. This feeling of hopefulness can be shared by all group members. On the other hand, fears will also be felt—that the group will represent another promise that is broken, that the members and the worker are not sincere in their offers to help, that the hindering forces of the environment will be more powerful than the group, or that the members, themselves, will lack sufficient motivation or wisdom to help themselves.

Hindering solutions in this kind of conflict will include persistent efforts to test the group without really investing in it, a denial of the reality of the conflict taking place, a false sense of optimism in the face of problems, or a projection of the conflict onto others. Facilitating solutions should include the willingness to pursue the desired goals while still seeking to overcome barriers, and a commitment to asking for help from others in this process as well as offering it. This can only be achieved, however, as the worker and the members engage in an examination of the focal conflicts in the formation period and the solutions that emerge.

GOAL PURSUIT TASKS

Workers will combine sets of procedures so as to correspond to the unique requirements of each group. However, it is most feasible in this chapter to describe separately those procedures that pertain to minimal skill training, group psychotherapy, transitional, activity-oriented, and patient government groups. When these are integrated it may be because members are able to use a set of techniques, after the group has been in existence for a while, that they were not ready for earlier or because the worker discovered gaps in skills that required departing from the planned approach.

[4]Dorothy S. Whitaker and Morton S. Lieberman, *Psychotherapy Through the Group Process* (New York: Lieber-Atherton, Inc., 1965), pp. 14–40.

Minimal Skill Training Groups

One model of a minimal skill approach is "structured learning therapy," developed by Goldstein and his colleagues.[5] This set of procedures was designed for people who function too poorly to be discharged from or remain out of mental hospitals. Under existing treatment programs such people sometimes spend years in psychiatric facilities during which they become even less able to function in the community.

Structured learning therapy, which has an impressive record of effectiveness,[6] combines elements of modeling, role playing, social reinforcement, and transfer of training techniques. The authors thoroughly examined the research related to each of these processes and developed a group training approach combining the most effective formats.

The modeling component includes securing the members' attention through physical and other arrangements that avoid distracting stimuli. Retention of the behaviors observed in the model is enhanced by helping the members to conceptualize the behaviors observed by learning a list of principles and relating these to a demonstration of related behaviors. The investigators assert that anxiety associated with the behaviors can also be reduced by having the models demonstrate a relaxed way of performing the skill.

The role-playing component is enhanced in the following ways: The members have a choice whether or not to take part in the role playing although they are asked to role-play skills they had committed themselves to acquire. They are also given an opportunity to improvise in the role plays. Finally, they are given verbal praise and other signs of approval for taking part.

The reinforcement principles that are part of structured learning therapy are: that reinforcement follows immediately after the desired behaviors, that reinforcement is contingent on the desired behaviors, and that reinforcement is on an intermittent schedule (that is, one that is randomly determined).

Transfer of training is enhanced by teaching principles of behavior to members as well as providing models of the behavior. In addition, members are given opportunities to practice the behavior under varying circumstances, including "homework" assignments related to performing the behaviors that are to be learned.

Structured learning therapy sessions are held as often as three times a week. The setting for meetings is similar to a classroom in that members sit at tables placed at either end of the worker's table and perpendicular to it. This leaves space at the opposite end of the worker's table for role plays to take place. This physical arrangement indicates to members that they are learners, encourages their receptivity to learning, and leads up to their involvement in later learning experiences.

After the initial meeting in which members become acquainted with each other and learn about the meeting format, the subsequent meetings utilize a common structure. They include a definition of the skill to be learned (for

[5]Goldstein, Sprafkin, and Gershaw, *Skill Training*.
[6]Ibid., pp. 126–45.

example, "starting a conversation") and the reasons for the skill. Members are given a "skill card" that outlines the "learning points" for that skill. The learning points, for example, for starting a conversation are:

1. Choose the right place and time.
2. Greet the other person.
3. Make small talk.
4. Judge if the other person is listening and wants to talk with you.
5. Open the main topic you want to talk about.[7]

After the learning points are reviewed, a demonstration tape of a role play is shown. While the role play unfolds the worker points on a chart to the learning points that are exemplified by the action at that moment. Following this, the members discuss their reactions to the role play and this gives the worker additional opportunity to resolve ambiguities and to provide encouragement for the next step in which the members themselves role play the skill. When these "rehearsals" are over, the role players are given feedback by other members and by the worker. A format for providing such feedback is also supplied in the text that includes such points as asking the "co-actor" in the role play how he or she was made to feel; the "audience" is asked how well the learning points were followed; the "main actor" is asked for self-evaluation; and the worker provides appropriate feedback for all desired responses.[8]

The final phase of the meeting is devoted to determining homework assignments. Each group member is asked to try out in the institution the skill that was learned in the group. Since the in-group role plays are based on people and incidents drawn from actual member situations, in most cases the member is asked to carry out the assignment in those same situations. The member's notebook contains pages in which the homework assignment is noted, along with the member's description of what happens, and his or her evaluation of it. At the subsequent meeting, time is set aside, usually at the beginning, for discussion of these reports. Goldstein and co-workers note, however, that people who function very poorly will not be asked to do this much writing; presumably reports are oral. The Goldstein, Sprafkin, and Gershaw text contains a good deal of information also on how to help members to develop complex skills such as job seeking, handling both positive and negative marital interactions, and dealing with crisis situations.

Group Psychotherapy

Group psychotherapy for alternative role attainment is hard to specify because the procedures are seldom well spelled out and there is a lack of consensus on what the process is. There is also a great deal of variance in outcomes and the variables that

---

[7] Ibid., p. 83.
[8] Ibid., pp. 50–51.

account for this are not clear.[9] The group psychotherapy literature presents it as a long-term process in which people become aware of their dysfunctional interactional patterns through feedback from group members and the worker. They are then able, in the group, to explore new ways of relating, which is facilitated by forces present in such groups that are strengthened by worker activities.

One such force is a norm of openness in discussing one's feelings about oneself and others. The worker reinforces the existence of this norm through modeling it as well as encouraging it in others. The worker also helps members to understand the value of the norm as well as confronting the group when members act in violation of it. Another norm that the worker supports is that members should continually monitor the functioning of their group and should seek to identify and resolve group conditions that are antitherapeutic through problem-solving activity. These group conditions include the presence of antagonistic subgroups, the abuse of power by members, and group climates that inhibit the members' progress (for example, depressed or hostile emotional tone during a session).

The worker in a group psychotherapy situation also tries to maintain a "here and now" focus. This means that concerns of the members regarding events in their "outside" lives or in their past histories are related to patterns in the group that represent contemporary manifestations of these issues. The following are some examples of this from psychotherapy groups:

Example. A member in one group psychotherapy session said, "My mother always dominated me." In response, the worker questioned, "Do you see anyone else in the group that you have some of the same feelings about?" In another group, one member said "I wish that I could tell my wife when I want her help, " to which the worker responded, "Is there anyone in the group that you would like to ask for help?"

The value of such "here and now" focus is to assist members in seeing how their current interactions are a continuation of patterns that have been dysfunctional in the past. Members can explore, as we have said, new ways of acting in the group as a safe environment for such testing. They should be helped by the members and the worker to try out this "interpersonal learning" in their other life roles. The worker's interventions for this purpose are not always as abrupt as the few examples just given. For some members, the worker will support a "there and then" focus so that the issue the member describes can be delineated clearly for both the member in question as well as for others.

In group psychotherapy, the worker will also use a number of procedures that are analogous to those used in individual psychotherapy. The difference for the skillful group worker is that it is not only the worker who utilizes the procedure. Members are also helped to use these processes appropriately with

---

[9]For a recent compilation of such research, see Richard L. Bednar and Theodore J. Kaul, "Experiential Group Research: Current Perspectives," in *Handbook of Psychotherapy and Behavior Change: An Empirical Analysis,* 2nd ed., eds. Sol L. Garfield and Allen Bergin (New York: John Wiley, 1978).

each other. One such procedure, for example, is interpretation. In discussing interpretation, some workers adopt a specific framework for making interpretations such as psychoanalytic theory in which an interpretation is defined as an action "through which the therapist makes material previously unconsciousness in the patient, conscious for him in a meaningful and affective way."[10] Some group therapists give a broader definition to interpretations as views of the causes of behavior that contrast (for whatever reason including unconscious processes) with the views of those events already held by the member. The member is exposed to "cognitive dissonance" between old and new ideas that is then resolved by changing one's thoughts and/or behaviors.[11]

The skillful worker will not present interpretations to members and will limit such presentations among members until a good deal of preparation takes place. This preparation includes a slow and careful effort to help the member to see that the two events whose connection is to be asserted through an interpretation do exist independently (for example, anger toward mother and toward wife) and that manifestations of one are regularly associated with the other. Unless this slow process occurs, the member is likely to deny any but the most simple and obvious patterns. Psychologically oriented group members are often prone to make "quick" interpretations, often as a means of competing with each other and the worker. Once this kind of behavior is "processed," however, members, through their knowledge of each other, will develop and share many insights regarding each other's behavior.

As we indicated in Chapter 3, workers engaged in group psychotherapy in in-patient settings frequently work with groups in which members attend for only a week or two after which they are discharged from the hospital and continue their treatment in the community. Yalom has developed a model for work with such groups.[12] In this model, the worker helps the members to select a highly specific and immediate goal that they can attain within a single meeting. This goal identification also helps the member to be clear about what he or she should continue to work to achieve in subsequent treatment after discharge from the hospital.

The group sessions begin with an explanation by the worker of the purpose of the group, namely to help members work on problems related to relationships with other people. Each member is then helped to identify a goal for the meeting and the worker is highly active in helping the member to set a goal that is attainable in that time frame. Examples of such problems are "to seek feedback on whether others find me hostile," "to initiate a relationship," " to learn how to refuse a request," or "to continue to relate when I feel anxious and eager to withdraw."

[10]Robert J. Lange, *The Technique of Psychoanalytic Psychotherapy* (New York: Jason Aronson, 1973), pp. 451–511.

[11]Leon Festinger, *A Theory of Cognitive Dissonance* (New York: Row, Peterson, 1957). For applications to a theory of interpretation, see Leon H. Levy, *Psychological Interpretation* (New York: Holt, Rinehart & Winston, 1963).

[12]Irving Yalom, *Inpatient Group Psychotherapy* (New York: Basic Books, 1983).

After each member has arrived at a goal, the worker supports interactions among members in which each can work on that goal. This can often happen simultaneously within the same conversation; some members can be trying out new ways of interacting while others are receiving feedback.

The meeting concludes with a review by the worker of what has been accomplished. This is often enhanced by observers whose presence is known to the members, who have been told that at the end of the meeting such observers will give feedback on their observations of interactions among members. The members are also given an opportunity to briefly give their reactions to the observer's comments. The observers utilized by Yalom are usually trainees in one of the mental health professions.

This model is employed with "higher functioning" patients who can sustain this amount of verbal interaction even though some may be delusional or may even manifest bizarre behavior. Yalom presents another model for lower functioning hospital patients in which the worker makes use of structured activities.

Activity Groups

The third type of alternate role attainment group is an activity-oriented group. These groups are formed in residential institutions, community-based institutions, and halfway houses for both children and adults to help group members whose functioning cannot be enhanced on primarily a "verbal" level (that is, through discussion and problem solving). Such people are usually excluded from "group psychotherapy" such as that just outlined. These groups make use of a variety of program media to attain their goals. See Chapter 5 for a full discussion of such media. The following are some examples of how such tools are used:

Arts and Crafts. Members are given opportunities to work with clay, paints, cloth and other materials. These media help them to express emotions, to communicate ideas to others, and to enhance their sense of creativity and individual accomplishment. Such projects may either be individual or may involve cooperation among group members depending on the effects that the worker desires to have on group and interpersonal processes.

Games and Sports. Members can be helped to assume roles related to their goals for being in the group by playing games (for example, assertive roles), to deal with interpersonal issues (for example, competition and cooperation), and to release tensions. These are obviously only a few of the benefits of this type of activity.

Cooking and Other Forms of Food Preparation. These activities often meet the needs of members to nurture and be nurtured. They can elicit concerns over these behaviors that are then "worked on" in the group.

Music and Dance. These activities are valuable in helping members to express emotions, to feel unity with others, and, in the case of dance, to improve body image and a sense of one's physical self.

Trips. Members can travel as a group to a variety of places that help them to learn skills and communicate concerns. Groups have gone to restaurants, stores, museums, amusement parks, and zoos.

Dramatics. This activity ranges from the use of role plays to improvised as well as formal dramatic activities. Drama can help members to learn more about roles of concern to them, to communicate repressed ideas and feelings, and to practice new behaviors. Learning the actual skills involved in acting and producing a drama can also lead to a heightened sense of self-esteem.

Transition Groups

The next type of alternative role attainment group is the transitional group. Institutions will form groups for people who are about to be discharged to the community. Such groups focus particularly on helping members to cope with community and family forces that can pressure them to return to their dysfunctional ways of adapting. Of particular importance in these groups is helping members to explain their institutionalization or treatment in appropriate ways. The group will also help members to make specific plans for work and living arrangements and, for social and supportive interactions.

The important consideration in planning such groups is to begin them sufficiently in advance of discharge so that they can fulfill their proper function. This will include the review of and in some cases the development of appropriate individual goals. The techniques used in such groups include rehearsal activities through role playing, homework assignments for members who have temporary "passes" into the community, educational programs, group trips, and opportunities for problem solving. Not the least of the critical tasks for such a group is to help members express and overcome ambivalence regarding leaving the institution. Members will, on the one hand, desire the autonomy, sense of accomplishment, freedom, and opportunity to develop themselves by a return to the community. On the other hand, they may be leaving a "safe" environment, one in which they can be relatively dependent and one in which less responsibility may have been expected of them because they were defined as "sick." It is rare for this ambivalence to be totally resolved, yet the balance must be tilted for any chance of a permanent return to the community.

Patient Government Groups

Group workers have facilitated patient government groups for many years. They are usually established in institutions to help patients participate in institutional decisions that affect them, the rules of the institution and its program. These groups are sometimes used to mediate disputes between patients and staff and among patient groups.

Patient government groups are usually modeled on a legislative body. Members are elected by constituent groups such as wards or cottages. Within the group, members take responsibility for all the leadership positions. Ideally, the staff member functions as a facilitator and consultant to the group.

The major task required of the group worker is to train the members in skills required for their respective roles. This includes member skills in agenda planning, problem solving, decision making, and encouraging maximum participation of all "representatives." Problems in such groups arise when the decisions the group is permitted to make are not "real" and members lose interest in the group. It is also possible that the members of the group have been ill prepared to carry out their roles, thus creating strong feelings of frustration among members and staff alike. When properly charged and constituted, such groups can contribute to feelings of worth and power on the part of the members. When the groups are artificial, they can add instead to the feelings of unreality and impotence that already plague the members.

EVALUATION

Several measures that are intrinsic to structured learning therapy help workers to evaluate it. These may also be used for similar minimal skill training experiences. First, group members are required to keep a trainee's notebook that calls for a series of self-evaluations. These consist of a narrative report of what happened when members carried out their homework assignment, a listing of the "learning points" followed, and an overall rating of how well the skill was performed (excellent, good, fair, poor). Workers can examine the learning points followed and the ratings for evidence of group effectiveness. The narrative report can be used to substantiate the members' ratings as well as their claim to having followed specified learning points.

The schedule that we described earlier that is used to assess members' entering skills can also be used as an "after" measure by both members and staff. It can help workers to compare groups that have been more and less effective in order to determine with whom the training has worked best and for whom additional ways of helping should be devised.

Yalom, in his discussion of the need for the practitioner to evaluate the outcomes of group psychotherapy, suggests that the beginning group psychotherapist develop an understanding of the complexity of outcome evaluation by interviewing people who have terminated. He states: "It is a very valuable exercise for the student to attempt to evaluate the degree of change, the nature of change, the mechanisms whereby the group experience effected the change, and the contributing role of other factors in the patient's environment. The exercise becomes richer yet if the student has available a tape of the initial interview to which he and the patient can listen."[13]

Yalom criticizes approaches for evaluating member progress that depend on instruments that are not specific to the members' treatment goals. He concludes, "I can think of no alternative except a laborious individualized (idiographic) approach to outcome."[14] This can be "an individualized outcome scale for each patient." He also cites one writer who asked experienced clinicians to state "what type of changes would occur if the patient were to improve in therapy."[15] At the conclusion of treatment, each prediction is examined and rated for attainment. Yalom has used procedures of this sort and has based ratings on an examination of videotaped interviews held before and after group therapy. Yalom asserts that the changes in patients after group therapy may be of a different order than after individual therapy and that measures should be directed at the appropriate type of outcomes. These include interpersonal skills, reaching out to others when stressed, the ability to sustain relationships, and empathy skills.

In an analogous manner, workers should evaluate the outcomes of activity groups in terms compatible with the reasons the activity was chosen. If a game was used to help members to become less stressed in competitive situations, means should be devised to secure self-reports as well as observations of the members' responses to competition. If an art project is chosen to help members to become more comfortable with disclosure, the number of self-disclosure statements before and after the experience should be counted. If a musical session is held to increase group cohesiveness and member comfort, these variables should also be measured before and after the activity.

It is also important to plan a follow-up after members have completed a transition group. This can be accomplished by interviewing members after the group in reference to the purposes of the group. If the group was established to help members take steps to find employment, their employment plans should be examined both before and after the group. If members are to be helped to explain the facts of their treatment appropriately, they can be asked how they would handle this both before and after the group. Through such devices, the techniques used in such groups will be improved and our knowledge of the value of such experience enhanced. Patient government groups can be evaluated by assessing the quality of group decisions as well as member satisfaction with them. Leadership skills of members should also be assessed.

Since we stated that a unique aspect of all these groups is to help members reduce the conflict between old and new roles, this dimension should be examined. When the group ends, one way of doing this is to ask members about some of their perceptions and attitudes regarding previous roles. Some examples of such questions are as follows:

[13]Yalom, *Group Psychotherapy.* p. 519.
[14]Ibid., p. 520.
[15]Ibid.

1. Are there people who approved of the ways you acted before you entered the group, ways in which you no longer act? How do you feel about them now?
2. If you meet a person who tries to get you to perform [a "deviant" act] or makes you feel you want to do this, what would you do? How would you feel?

AN EXAMPLE

This example is from a transition group formed to help adolescents about to leave a residential treatment center.

First Meeting. As the meeting began, Tim said that John should tell the group what had happened to him on his last visit home. The worker asked John if he wanted to do so and John said that he did. He had gone to his former school to apply for readmission. While he was there, a boy asked him where he had been for the past term. When he said he had been in a hospital, the boy responded that he hoped it was not one of those places for crazy kids. John was so upset after this conversation that he went home without registering for school. The worker said that he could see how difficult this was for John. He asked if any of the other members had had something like that happen to them. Rick said that when he was last home, several of his old friends seemed unwilling to talk to him when he approached them on the street. Tim added that when he was home and relatives were visiting his parents, they also seemed to avoid talking to him. The worker said that a number of the members had similar concerns about family and friends. He asked if any of the others had thought of ways of handling this.

Jack said he did not like to talk to anyone about "this place." Al said that he told people he was just away at school. He planned on telling the local school, when he returned home, that the school he had been going to had lost his records. Tim thought Al would be in for a lot of trouble if the school ever found out he was lying. Al responded by saying that it would be a lot better than people finding out where you had been. Rick thought, on the other hand, that it might be possible to explain things to people in a way they would understand. The worker summarized the ideas that had been presented and said that he recognized that John still did not have an answer as to what he could have done when he went to the school.

The worker said that he had some tape recordings of how members of groups like this one had talked to peers as well as relatives or people in school about where they had been. He asked if the boys would like to hear these so they could discuss some of the alternatives they could use. He added this might help John decide what he wanted to do. The members all agreed this was a good idea and the worker played the first tape in which a boy was talking to his friend "back home." He told his friend that he had been upset about a lot of things that had happened to him. He had gone to a special school where they help young people learn how to handle their problems without becoming so upset. The school employed doctors and social workers as well as teachers but this did not mean that you were "crazy."

John thought there were some ideas on this tape that he could use. He was not sure, however, about telling others about "seeing doctors." The worker asked the boys what they thought about this and there was a lot of discussion about doctors seeing you when you are sick and whether they were thought of as "sick."

The worker said that he could see that there was a lot more about this they wanted to discuss and perhaps they could go on with it at the next meeting as the time was up. He also had some more tapes they could hear and discuss.

Analysis. In the incident just described, we can see the conflicts the boys face in interactions between their "sick roles" and the roles they seek to assume when they leave the institution. The worker had not yet helped the boys to recognize this conflict, as such. He had, however, responded to their feelings so that they will be more able to deal with them. He also sought to increase their skill in overcoming obstacles to performing their new roles as well as their understanding of what had happened to them while in placement. The group was developing as a supportive and safe place to deal with these issues. Not the least of the facets of this experience was the fact that the worker saw the members as competent to cope with the difficult problems they faced. He used models in the form of tapes at this meeting but planned to move to such action-oriented approaches as role plays in which the members practiced ways of handling situations such as those described here.

SUMMARY

In this chapter, we presented the issues members confront in groups devoted to helping them move from "sick" or "deviant" roles into more functional ones. Of particular importance was the recognition of the kinds of conflicts encountered in this situation and the role of the group in helping members cope with such conflicts. In addition to discussing assessment issues and the ways in which groups are formed in the light of these, we discussed a range of types of groups fulfilling the purposes of alternative role attainment. These groups were categorized as those supplying minimal skill training, those devoted to group psychotherapy, those utilizing activity bases, those conducted at the point of transition to the community, and those involving patients in governance. The means of evaluating such groups were described and an example of a transitional group was presented.

14

Working
With Oppressed People
In Groups

Throughout its history, group work has made a contribution to people experiencing social oppression. At some times this contribution was less than other times, as during reactionary periods in the larger society or in the profession of social work. We believe, however, that social work has a special commitment to those who are oppressed and in this chapter we intend to focus on practice issues related to this commitment. We have sought to raise issues of this type throughout the book but wish to highlight them here.[1]

We define oppression as the destructive effects of social institutions on people when such institutions damage their identities, denigrate their life styles, and deny them access to opportunities. This oppression becomes social oppression when it is based on attributes people share. The most apparent examples of this are the sexism directed at women and the racism directed at members of ethnic groups such as blacks, Hispanics, Native-Americans, and Asian-Americans. Others who experience such oppression are members of sexual minorities such as gay men and lesbians, age groups such as the elderly, handicapped people, those who are stigmatized by a label such as "mental

[1]This chapter draws upon Charles D. Garvin, "Work with Disadvantaged and Oppressed Groups," in *Individual Change Through Small Groups,* 2nd ed., eds. Martin Sundel, Paul Glasser, Rosemary Sarri, and Robert Vinter (New York: The Free Press, 1985), pp. 461–72.

patient" and "offender," individuals from nontraditional families, and the working and non-working poor. Even then, this is a partial list and it can be extended by reflecting on the frequent creation of self-help groups for those who experience rejection from human service institutions.

Goldenberg presents an excellent description of oppression when he writes:

> Oppression is, above everything else, a condition of being, a particular stance one is forced to assume with respect to oneself, the world, and the exigencies of change. It is a pattern of hopelessness and helplessness, in which one sees oneself as static, limited, and expendable. People only become oppressed when they have been forced (either subtly or with obvious malice) to finally succumb to the insidious process that continually undermines hope and subverts the desire to "become."[2]

The kinds of oppression that are experienced by the individuals we have listed include the poor schools often found in black neighborhoods, the poverty found on many Indian reservations, the antagonism displayed by many teachers when a Hispanic or Asian-American child speaks in a language other than English, the probing questions directed at a female applicant regarding her responsibilities for her children, the gay man or lesbian who is passed over for promotion, and the fully qualified older adult who is encouraged to retire.

Still other examples are the physically handicapped person whose school library is not accessible to wheelchairs, the ex-offender or mental patient who has been abandoned by friends and family, and the single parent who finds that schools, workplaces, and other "opportunity structures" are unnecessarily stressful because of rigid schedules and policies. Poor people are also stigmatized by educational and social institutions in ways that perpetuate their poverty cycle.

There are good reasons for the use of group work by socially oppressed people. They often wish to offer support to and secure support from others in a similar status. Under this circumstance, the oppressed person may wish to join a group that is homogeneous in respect to the oppressed status or seek membership in a group that is heterogeneous in order to overcome the isolation that is produced by the oppression. In either case, the oppressed person is likely to want help in learning to cope with or to change social institutions. Often, the member may want the group to take some action because she or he recognizes that many people acting together possess more power to change social conditions than an individual alone.

The motivation and skills to change oppressive situations is related to what is frequently termed *empowerment*. In a book that has made a major contribution to our understanding of this, Solomon defines empowerment as:

> . . . a process whereby persons who belong to a stigmatized social category throughout their lives can be assisted to develop and increase skills in the exercise of interpersonal influence and the performance of valued social roles. Power is an interpersonal

---

[2]Ira Goldenberg, *Oppression and Social Intervention* (Chicago: Nelson-Hall, 1978), p. 2.

phenomena: if it is not interpersonal it should probably be defined as "strength." However, the two concepts—power and strength—are so tightly interrelated that they often are used interchangeably. In any event, the transformation of the abstraction of power into an observable reality will be the dominant theme of the chapters that follow.[3]

Groups can facilitate empowerment in ways that are not available to other social-work modalities. With reference to Solomon's emphasis on skills, members can help each other to learn how to assert themselves, how to select and implement appropriate change strategies, and how to defend themselves against retaliation. They can learn these things as they seek to mold the group as well as institutions in the environment to their needs. The relationship that exists between being empowered in the group and in the larger society is one that should be reinforced by the worker. Members, for example, may play a passive role with respect to change processes, particularly those that involve conflict, as these occur in the group. They can be helped to "work out" this withdrawal in the group as a means of avoiding such withdrawal outside of the group.

Workers can enhance empowerment through groups by applying the following principles: members must understand that the group is *their* group and they are responsible for its direction. This does not mean that they may not have to deal with policies and procedures of the agency, but they must he helped to see how they can affect these procedures and what the consequences are of violating them. Then the members can decide to take on these consequences and the worker can help members to assume this responsibility.

Members are also empowered when they understand that their lives are affected by environmental forces, but that they have the responsibility and the capacity to seek a change in that environment. Sue analyzes this by distinguishing between *locus of control* and *locus of responsibility.*[4] The former dimension refers to the individuals' attributions as to the causes of events that affect them: an "external locus of control" is one in which the individual believes that his or her life is primarily affected by random external events while an "internal locus of control" is one in which the individual believes his or her life is primarily affected by events under his or her control. The empowered individual does not take responsibility for the oppressive circumstances he or she faces but is able to see how these have been created by historical as well as current structural circumstances.

The locus of responsibility dimension differs from locus of control in that it refers to the one who has responsibility to work for change in an oppressive environment. The person with an external locus of responsibility expects others to do this while the person with an internal locus of responsibility understands that he or she must take part in such change efforts. In brief, then, the empowered individual has an external locus of control orientation with an internal locus of responsibility. The ways for workers to facilitate this are drawn from the consciousness-raising orientation we described in Chapter 10.

[3]Barbara Solomon, *Black Empowerment* (New York: Columbia University Press, 1976), p. 6.

[4]Derald W. Sue, *Counseling the Culturally Different: Theory and Practice* (New York: John Wiley, 1981), pp. 74–80.

Group workers seeking to help members understand the forces affecting their lives, as well as their capacity for changing them, can learn a great deal from the writings of the Brazilian educator Paulo Freire.[5] Freire presents many of his ideas in the context of programs he developed to reduce adult illiteracy in Brazil. He concluded that adults will be enhanced in becoming literate if they connect literacy to the idea that culture is created by human beings and can be altered in the same way. This connection is developed through the emergence of a *critical consciousness* in which people come to understand the forces that maintain their oppressive social circumstances, whether these forces occur in their schools, workplaces, or communities. The highest form of critical consciousness is referred to by Freire as *critical transitive consciousness*. He defines this as:

> The critically transitive consciousness is characterized by: depth in the interpretation of problems, by the substitution of causal principles for magical explanations; by the testing of one's "findings" and by openness to revision; by the attempt to avoid distortion when perceiving problems and to avoid preconceived notions when analyzing them; by refusing to transfer responsibility; by rejecting passive positions; by soundness of argumentation; by the practice of dialogue rather than polemics; by receptivity to the new for reasons beyond mere novelty and by the good sense not to reject the old just because it is old—by accepting what is valid in both old and new.[6]

Group workers seeking to enhance empowerment will provide opportunities to further member's critical consciousness. Examples of this are:

> A group worker in a support group for women who had been abused helped them to examine the many ways society makes it possible for men to abuse women. These included the nonresponsiveness they initially experienced when they asked for help and the "message" many received from their families that they were responsible for how they were treated by men.

> A group worker in a mothers' group composed of black women who were raising children in the absence of a male partner discussed with them the penalties their families faced from the welfare system when they sought to create two-parent families.

> A newly assigned group worker in a group of elderly members found that the group had officers who had been appointed by her predecessor. She was told by that worker that the members would be upset if they faced a competitive election. She returned to the group and initiated a discussion of this. She helped the members to examine the many times that others assumed they wished to be told what to do when this was untrue. The members also came to realize that others often stated this as the reason when actually they wished to keep things "simple" for themselves.

As we described in Chapter 2, the agency context for group work service has a major influence upon that service and this is particularly true for work with oppressed people. Many of our agencies, themselves, commit institutional forms of racism as well as institutional biases against members of the group oppressed

---

[5]Paul Freire, *Education for Critical Consciousness* (New York: Seabury Press, 1973).
[6]Ibid., p. 18.

for reasons other than race. Chesler describes these biases in regard to blacks,[7] although they undoubtedly occur for all the other oppressed groups we have listed. These are (1) blaming the victim; (2) focusing on the pathology rather than the strength of the victim; (3) blaming cultural values of the victims for their detrimental situations; (4) using racism to maintain the status quo; (5) assuming that members of the group will remain dependent permanently.

Consequently, the agency that seeks to serve oppressed people and understand the social basis of their oppression will certainly not confine its services to one-to-one or even group forms but will expect its workers to act as brokers and advocates on behalf of clients. This means that the agency will allow workers time for such activities, will hire workers who are oriented in this way, and will train workers to be more effective agents for social change. As Pinderhughes has pointed out, there is a correlation between workers seeking to empower themselves and those who seek to facilitate clients in this process.[8] Furthermore, workers with and on behalf of group members who try to change oppressive conditions will encounter conflict and the agency will have to support workers when this happens or workers are likely to reduce these types of activities that are essential for change to occur.

The agency that provides a good environment for change to occur does not "colonize" the oppressed group but encourages its members to participate at all levels of agency decision making:[9] these include the governing boards of private agencies and the advisory boards of public ones. Members of the oppressed group will also be recruited through affirmative action procedures for all levels of staff. The most direct consequences for these "noncolonial" policies is that information will be readily available regarding the group, stereotypes will be challenged, and role models will be present for members.

It can be anticipated that most agencies that seek to effectively serve oppressed people will find that they have some shortcomings related to the kinds of conditions we have just described. The agency should, consequently, seek feedback from members regarding these dimensions and help in changing them. Agency good faith is demonstrated when it does this.

PREGROUP TASKS

Any planning of group services for oppressed people must be done jointly with those who are similarly oppressed—with individuals who actually will become members of the group or with those in a similar status. This principle is consistent

---

[7]Mark A. Chesler, "Contemporary Sociological Theories of Racism" in *Toward the Elimination of Racism,* ed. P. Katz (New York: Pergamon, 1976), pp. 21–72.

[8]Elaine Pinderhughes, "Empowerment for our Clients and for Ourselves," *Social Casework* 64 (June, 1983), pp. 331–38.

[9]For an excellent discussion of "colonization" as this process has implications for social agencies, see Robert Blauner, "Internal Colonialism and Ghetto Revolt," *Social Problems* 16 (Spring, 1969), 393–408.

with the goal of empowerment since, from the beginning, actions affecting oppressed people are taken *with* rather than *for* them. At times, also, the agency (often together with group representatives) will undertake a needs assessment of a sampling of relevant people within the agency's catchment in order to determine the needs to be met through group services. This needs assessment can be conducted through such devices as a door-to-door survey or "hearings" held in the agency or a "neutral" spot in the community.

This type of beginning led one agency to provide family-type programs for Hispanics within the neighborhood, rather than separating family members from one another. Another agency in a Chinese-American neighborhood developed a series of educational activities for youth who wished to learn more about their history and culture. Still another institution in a largely black area organized a series of youth-oriented programs to help members deal with school and occupation related problems.

Agencies concerned about oppression not based on ethnicity have established still other types of services. One agency created a group for former prison inmates who wished to help each other in dealing with employment issues. The group members also wished to change the image that existed in the community of ex-offenders. A university counseling service conducted a needs assessment together with several gay men and lesbians and consequently established several "coming out" groups whose purpose was to help members clarify identity issues for themselves and consequently to decide how and when to express this identity to others such as family members and friends. In addition, the counseling service sponsored a conference for parents of homosexuals, a "defense" committee to respond to charges of harassment of homosexuals in the university, and a planning committee for gay and lesbian social centers.

As we indicated earlier in this chapter, preparation of agency staff should precede the first meeting of the groups. Unless the agency is largely composed of members of the targeted population, a process of staff consciousness-raising should take place. This might include learning about the needs of the group as well as its history and current situation.

Elsewhere, we categorized the information that workers should have in order to offer effective service to oppressed groups.[10] Briefly our categories are the following:

1. Communications. This refers to the language utilized by the group members and the rules as to who speaks to whom and about what. The language may be Spanish, Chinese, or native-American; a nonstandard form of English such as black-English; or the argot used by some homosexuals or members of a criminal sub-culture. The group worker should be familiar with the language or be prepared to compensate for this through, for example, the use of an indigenous

---

[10]Charles Garvin and Brett Seabury, *Interpersonal Practice in Social Work: Processes and Procedures* (Englewood Cliffs, N.J.: Prentice-Hall, 1984), pp. 321–29.

person as a co-facilitator. The rules regarding communications processes and structures are important to know since they will affect how the worker thinks about group composition or how the group will react to topics introduced by the worker.

2. Habitat. This refers to how members are likely to view as well as utilize their physical space, where the worker and the members decide to hold their meetings, and how the space for the meeting is arranged. There could be problems, for example, if the agency held a meeting of an almost exclusively Catholic group of Hispanics in a local Protestant church; yet, it could be an asset to conduct this meeting in the local Catholic church attended by the members. Some ethnic group workers might prefer the typical circle arrangement for group meetings while members of another group might be most comfortable when the worker locates himself or herself in a way that denotes a different status.

3. Social Structure. This refers to the social stratification of the larger oppressed community with which the members identify. When speaking of an ethnic group, this includes the structure of the family, economic, and social institutions of the ethnic group. Other oppressed groups also have internal structures, as described by Kassebaum, Ward, and Wilner in their discussion of a prison.[11] Within this setting, prisoners were categorized as "square johns," "right guys," "con-politicians," and "outlaws." Another example is that of the gay male subculture in which distinctions are usually made between those who wear female clothes and those who do not, those who dress in leather and those who do not, and so forth. The worker must understand these categories as they will also have implications for group composition, group goals, and the interactions that arise among members once the group has begun.

4. Socialization. This refers to how the individuals associated with the oppressed group are helped to enter into social roles that exist within their culture and to learn the behaviors required for these roles. Examples of this are the roles associated with stages of the life cycle unique to each ethnic group, such as the preparation for puberty ceremonies found in many native-American tribes. With regard to women, there are many ways that they are taught the appropriate feminine roles for the expectations of the larger culture. Within a prison, there is an inmate culture with its own values that are taught to the newcomer. The purposes developed for groups by oppressed people often are to further this type of socialization.[12] Workers should also be sensitive to occasions when members may

---

[11]G. Kassebaum, G. Ward, and D. Wilner, *Prison Treatment and Parole Survival: An Empirical Assessment* (New York: Wiley, 1971).

[12]For an example of this, see E.D. Edwards, M.E. Edwards, G.M. Daines, and F. Eddy, "Enhancing Self-Concept and Identification with 'Indianness' of American Indian Girls," *Social Work with Groups,* 1, no. 3 (1978), 309–18.

wish to use the group to alter a socialization pattern. This is often found in women's groups in which the members seek to change the roles traditionally assigned to women in the family, community, and workplace.

5. Economy. This refers to how the group is affected by the economic institutions and practices of the larger society, as well as the internal economy within the oppressed group. Ethnic groups such as blacks, Hispanics, and native-Americans have been systematically exploited by the economic institutions of the society, as attested to by their income and occupational distributions. The same has been true of women. Homosexuals, the elderly, and ex-offenders find it difficult to be successful in many occupations because of prejudice against them. It is hard, therefore, to imagine a group composed of members of these populations that does not, in some way, deal with issues related to economic factors.

6. Beliefs and Sentiments. This refers to the belief systems that emerge as people with similar concerns or destinies interact with one another. These beliefs are embedded in the religion, folklore, literature, "sayings," music, and poetry that group members identify as their own. These beliefs have a great deal of impact on selection of partners for intimate relationships, discipline of children, behavior toward others who are and are not in the in-group, and treatment of illness (both mental and physical). This does not imply that all people who consider themselves part of the group will think alike but, rather, that some beliefs will be more characteristic of one group than another. For example, members of many native-American groups will hold the value that it is inappropriate to insist on a change in another's behavior and that it is essential to respect another's privacy and independence.[13] Group workers, in this case, should emphasize group approaches in which members have an opportunity to observe others as models rather than being offered advice and direction when this has not been requested.

In keeping with the empowerment focus of all work with oppressed people, the potential members of the group or others in a similar status should participate in pregroup tasks such as deciding on group composition, size, format, and purpose. There is no one preferred condition: decisions on these matters will depend on the purposes that have been chosen as a basis for initial planning. As we have suggested, many purposes will require that the group be homogeneous in that all members experience oppression in similar ways: as blacks, women, poor people, and so forth. On some occasions, these members may wish to interact with others from a different status in order to receive feedback, learn how to assert themselves, or create a coalition for social change. The latter may be an important strategy when several groups discover that they have an adversary in common.

The above planning steps may require that an agency change its image in the community. The agency should seek publicity for its program in the media and should utilize existing networks. An example of this was a new agency to serve

---

[13]E. Daniel Edwards and Margie E. Edwards, "Group Work Practice with American Indians," *Social Work with Groups* 7 (Fall, 1984), 12.

homosexuals. The agency arranged interviews on television programs for its staff who were then also invited to speak to local homosexual groups. Posters on agency services were placed in gay bars and businesses. Physicians and other health services utilized by homosexuals were contacted as well as a local church that had been established by and for homosexuals.

GROUP FORMATION TASKS

Some of the aspects of formation that may be prolonged for other types of groups occur rapidly in groups of people who perceive each other as having experienced the same types of oppression. Members assume (although this may not always be a fact) that they have had similar experiences, perceive things in a similar way, speak the same language, and may even know many of the same people. In fact they may already be acquainted with one another. Members are likely, therefore, to be ready to "get down to business."

That business will initially consist of determining individual and group goals. As in any other group, this involves an assessment of the relevant circumstances. As a result of this, members may discover that their previous experiences have not been as similar as they had thought and some of their values and goals may differ. These issues should either be reconciled or members should seek a way to proceed with multiple agendas.

One value to which we subscribe with reference to such groups is that individual and group goals should be chosen with consideration for their effects on others who are similarly oppressed. This is because of the negative social and political implications of some individuals making gains at the expense of others. When some blacks, or handicapped people, or women become symbols of how open the opportunities are for social mobility, this can be used to deny opportunities to others. This phenomenon of "tokenism" has many insidious consequences. An example of this was when several gay group members sought employment in a firm that was boycotted by the gay community. Their energies were then drained into a struggle within the gay community rather than into creating job opportunities.

As the worker and members consider the goals toward which they will work and the means to be used to attain them, they must assess member competencies, particularly as these relate to seeking to create environmental changes. This places the emphasis on member strengths and member learning. This perspective is highly compatible with that of Maluccio,[14] who views the member as a learner and assessment as a process of determining competence rather than deficits. We believe that this perspective, especially with regard to oppressed people, removes many barriers between members and worker and reduces resistance.

Because of the focus on coping with an oppressive environment, members will seek to assess their relevant environments as part of the goal setting process. This assessment will include such factors as the investment of the people in the environment status quo, how decisions for change are made and who can make

[14]Anthony Maluccio, *Promoting Competence in Clients* (New York: The Free Press, 1981).

them, who in the environment has the power to influence the decision makers and how they may be reached (the existence of allies), and what is likely to make others in the environment aware of the need for change.

An important issue for members to assess is what the likelihood is for some form of retribution for the change effort and what the form of this retribution might be. There is seldom a situation in which people can work for change without risks and members should learn this "fact of life." Nevertheless, they can choose when and how to take risks—an important principle to learn.

GOAL PURSUIT TASKS

During the phase when the group members are working to attain their goals, they will engage in two types of activities: those to increase their competence and those to bring about change in their environment. In this chapter we shall describe how to increase their competence. The approaches to bring about changes used by oppressed people in groups were described in Chapter 7.

As we stated in the introductory section of this chapter, an important aspect of becoming empowered is to increase one's critical consciousness. This can be done through several procedures, one of which is for members to review their life stories. The focus of this review should be upon how past experiences have caused members to devalue themselves in ways that were inappropriate and destructive. In one group, for example, Hispanic members spoke of how the response of others to their use of Spanish led to feelings of inferiority rather than pride in their culture. In another group, women members discovered how the response of others to their assertiveness led to inhibiting the expressions of their own needs and interests.

Another approach to consciousness raising is for members to examine their current interactions with people who do not share their oppressed status (blacks with whites, women with men, gays with straights, and so forth) and to identify how they respond to these in powerless ways. It often helps to examine these interactions in light of the concept of "false consciousness," which refers to an acceptance of the values of one's oppressor when this is dysfunctional to meeting one's own needs. Examples of this are black people who believe that blacks are unmotivated, poor people who believe that those without material resources are entirely responsible for their lack of opportunity, women who believe that others of their gender are happy and content to be dependent on men, and handicapped people who believe they do not have the right to seek intimate relationships.

All of these myths must be challenged as part of the empowerment process. Values-clarification exercises are a way of accomplishing this. These exercises help members examine their values and evaluate them critically. A useful type of exercise is to choose some statement and ask members to rate how they agree or disagree with it (5–strongly agree; 4–agree; 3–neutral; 2–disagree; 1–strongly disagree). Members then join other members who have made the same rating and discuss in that subgroup why they think as they do. Subgroups report to each other their reasons and the entire group discusses the kinds of issues that have surfaced through this process. Workers can draw upon a substantial literature of values clarification to discover appropriate exercises.[15]

In addition to consciousness raising, members must be helped to acquire skills directly associated with competence in securing a more humane environment. One important category of such skills is *assertiveness*. This type of behavior is derived from the idea that all human beings have the right to express their needs, wishes, and feelings in ways that do not infringe on the rights of others,[16] even though people associated with all oppressed groups are likely to have been discouraged or even punished for being assertive. A number of authors have focused on helping women to regain their assertiveness. This type of specialized investigation of how to help oppressed people, in view of their unique circumstances, should be extended.[17]

Other skills that members may seek to acquire relevant to their empowerment are how to engage in constructive confrontation, how to appropriately express anger, how to negotiate, and how to present information to support one's position. Workers can also help members to learn how to defend their rights aggressively when this is made necessary by the intransigence of an adversary. This involves identifying vulnerable positions of others, eliciting help from people who have authority over an adversary, and threats to employ legal action.

Negotiation skills are particularly important. As described by Ury and Fisher,[18] the successful negotiator must bargain in ways that recognize each person's *interests* rather than *positions*. An interest is what each party seeks to receive from the interchange while a position is a specific "solution" that an individual seeks to defend. For example, if a member of a group has a child who has special educational needs, having these needs met is an interest while having them met through an assignment to a specific program is a position. The desire of the school to secure needed services for each child while minimally disrupting existing arrangements is an interest; meeting the needs of the aforementioned child through a tutoring arrangement is a position.

Fisher and Ury also describe how successful negotiators seek to separate relationship issues from substance ones, help participants perceive each other's situations accurately, respond to feelings, and try to create innovative solutions. All of these skills can be taught to group members through simulation of actual or illustrative situations during group sessions.

[15]See, for example, Sidney B. Simon, Leland N. Howe, and Howard Kirschenbaum, *Values Clarification: A Handbook of Practical Strategies for Teachers and Students* (New York: Hart, 1972).
[16]See Chapter 7 for information on assertiveness training.
[17]See, for example, B.S. Brockway, "Assertive Training for Professional Women," *Social Work* 21 (1976), 498–505; M.M. Linehan and K.J. Egan, "Assertion Training for Women," in *Research and Practice in Social Skills Training* eds. A.S. Bellack and M. Hersen (New York: Plenum, 1979); and M.L. MacDonald, "Assertion Training for Women," in *Social Skills Training: A Practical Handbook for Assessment and Treatment* eds. J.P. Curran and P.M. Monti (New York: The Guilford Press, 1982).
[18]Roger Fisher and William Ury, *Getting to Yes: Negotiating Agreement Without Giving In* (New York: Penguin Books, 1981).

While treatment groups often adopt a "blame the victim" posture, this does not contradict the idea that all of the techniques described in this book may be required by oppressed people if by treatment we mean help in modifying one's behaviors, cognitions, or affects that hinder the member from attaining his or her goals. Thus, someone who is oppressed may need help to improve the quality of his or her relationships, reduce a feeling of depression or anxiety, or raise a sense of self-esteem. While becoming an active social change agent (and, we hope, achieving some success) may ameliorate these problems, this is not inevitable. The agency, however, that offers treatment to oppressed people will be unlikely to emphasize pathology or view the coping behaviors of oppressed people as signs of "illness." It will not degrade people by the loose application of labels.

Workers will be on the alert for suitable social-action projects: those that will enhance members' competence to cope with the environment, raise their self-esteem, and teach skills in working with others. These projects must not be too insignificant or too ambitious. Early group workers were noted for the energy they brought to improving garbage collection or securing stop signs at busy intersections. During the 1960s, workers went to the other extreme and encouraged members to join rent strikes, welfare department sit-ins, and picket lines without warning these members about the likelihood of retaliation and the ability of the targeted institutions to procrastinate. Many group members in the 1980s, on the other hand, did participate in voter registration drives, which helped members to see immediate results (a newly registered voter) while increasing their investment in political processes. We hope that while members may not have found that they affected election results in the short run, this did not erase the beneficial effects of their activity.

Another type of activity for these members to engage in is to create a network with others who share similar concerns. The role of the worker is to facilitate the ways oppressed individuals can communicate with and support one another. The worker helps members locate others who may wish to join their group or form additional groups and helps members become knowledgeable about other existing groups and organizations and how they might interact with them.

Many years ago, as a group worker in a settlement house, I was approached by a group of black teenage young women to sponsor their "club," which they had named, "Better Human Relations Builders." They wanted to do something to combat racism but were not sure how to proceed. I helped them to contact the National Association for the Advancement of Colored People, as well as other organizations, for program ideas and support. A highlight of the year we spent together was our attendance at a civil rights rally where the members first experienced the large movement of which they were becoming a part.

Nothing we have stated is meant to imply that oppressed people should always be isolated in groups with others in a similar status. Homogeneous groups are often valuable because of the support they provide, their concern for a reaffirmation of identity, and the energy they can bring to social-change activities. An oppressed person may join a group with others who are not oppressed in the same way. This can be valuable for all as members discover how oppression diminishes the oppressor as well as the oppressed and as all explore the true meaning of justice.

EVALUATION

One of the most important ways to measure the outcome of a group experience involving oppressed people should be whether they have been empowered. As we indicated earlier, empowerment involves an increase in the use of skills to influence others and an increase in the performance of valued social roles.

Skills to influence others are demonstrated in specific situations. One way, therefore, to measure them is to ask members about situations in which they sought to use influence and the kinds of influence they employed. Some simple set of categories such as the following could be utilized: reward, coercion, expertise, reference to one's position, or the respect can be rated by comparing it to a standard provided by the group, the worker, or the member. For some evaluation purposes, it may be sufficient to know that the member has sought to influence situations in which he or she previously would have behaved in a passive manner.

Another way of measuring social influence is by the use of an assertiveness scale. One that has been frequently used was devised by Gambrill and Richey.[19]

Members can also role play situations in the group and can be evaluated by other group members. The ratings will focus upon behaviors that have been targeted in the group, such as persistence in presenting one's argument; resistance to discounting, discourteous, or rejecting behavior of the "other"; appropriate and ethical increases in aggressiveness; or the selection of a strategy that is appropriate to the situation.

If members have been focusing on self-esteem or identity issues, an evaluation measure appropriate to these should be employed. Workers can use or adapt measures of self-esteem developed by such investigators as Gergen and Morse,[20] Fitts,[21] or Kelly.[22] Measures of identity can also be devised in which members are asked about their feelings of status as a member of an ethnic grop, as a woman, as a gay person, and so forth. They can also be asked about the frequency with which they interact with others in a similar status, partake of relevant cultural and educational offerings, or attend relevant events.

Since empowerment "begins" in the group experience itself, the worker should gather data on whether or not this has been manifested. This includes:

[19]Eileen Gambrill and Cheryl Richey, "An Assertion Inventory for Use in Assessment and Research," *Behavior Therapy* 6 (1975), 350–62.

[20]K.J. Gergen and S.J. Morse, "Self-consistency: Measurement and Validation," *Proceedings of the 75th Annual Convention of the American Psychological Association* 2 (1967), 207–8.

[21]W.F. Fitts, *Tennessee Self-Concept Scale Manual* (Nashville: Counselor Recordings and Tests, 1965).

[22] See his Role Construct Repertory Test in G.A. Kelly, *The Psychology of Personal Constructs* (New York: Norton, 1955).

1. Have group members developed some form of structure through which they can take responsibility for their group? Is this structure working as planned?
2. Have group members initiated goals and activities or do they depend on the worker for this?
3. Do members express their beliefs and intentions regarding the group or do they signal otherwise by not paying attention to events in the group, speaking about irrelevant matters, attending infrequently, and so on.
4. Do members challenge agency actions that interfere with group autonomy?

It is also important to evaluate whether members are developing their critical consciousness. One way to do this is to note, when examples of oppression are presented in the group, whether members seek to analyze the social forces at play, who profits from the oppression, and the psychological consequences of the oppression. It is essential to note whether members even identify instances of oppression or whether they personalize these as proof of their own inadequacy, immorality, or fate.

AN EXAMPLE

This example is from a group of seven black teenage young women who were meeting in a school setting. Their group worker was also a black woman who was a graduate student in a school of social work. The members of the group had not been doing well in school; several had been involved in fights with other youths. Two members of the group were mothers of infants who were being cared for by their own mothers. The following events took place in the seventh meeting of the group.

Meeting. Mary had been elected president of the group at the previous meeting. She entered the meeting this week about ten minutes after the others had arrived and immediately began talking to Lisa about a teacher who had thrown her out of class that day. Several members began to criticize her for coming late, especially since she was their president. It appeared likely that a real confrontation was in the offing. I (the worker) interrupted and said that I thought what was happening resulted from their not having been given much opportunity to learn to govern themselves in group. Perhaps, also, Mary had some feelings about her new responsibility and that this had something to do with how she was acting.

Alicia said that I was right. Even when she had been a member of the school's student council, the sponsoring teacher had conducted the meetings. Cecelia gave another example of a club in a neighborhood community center in which the staff member assigned to the group had always "been in charge." Mary said that this had always been how it happened to her. She admitted that she was nervous and had come close staying away from this meeting altogether. Frankie said that it didn't matter to her and wasn't it the job of the staff to run things. Mary responded that this wasn't right. They would never learn how to do things for themselves if this always happened and this was the reason she was in the group.

I thought this was a good time to move things on, therefore I suggested we talk some more about the job of the president so that Mary, as well as future presidents, could do it well and not be so nervous. I added that they might always be a "little nervous" but they could still do the job. For example, whenever I came to a meeting, I was always a little tense about how things were going to go and whether I would be able to be as helpful as possible.

I then wondered if they wanted to talk about this topic of the president's tasks. All of the members said that they did. Mary said that T.J. who had been elected secretary could write down their suggestions. I said I thought this was a good idea and that these suggestions could be put on the blackboard (we were meeting in a classroom) so we could think about them. An animated discussion then took place in which such items were listed: saying when it was time for the meeting to begin, calling on each person to speak, insisting that members raise their hands when they want to talk, reminding members not to speak when they were not called on, and asking the members at the beginning of the meeting to make a list of what they were going to talk about that afternoon.

After this discussion, Mary said she could start to practice these things by asking us to make a list of what we wanted to talk about for the rest of the meeting. Mary wanted to talk to everyone regarding what to do about having been being thrown out of class. No one else had any suggestions for topics so we decided to discuss the issue and then have our refreshments. T.J. said that probably Mary had brought this on herself as she usually did by cussing or fighting. Alicia immediately answered that she knew the teacher was one who always looked for a chance to pick on a black student. I commented that we were making a mistake by either blaming ourselves or someone else without getting all the facts first. Lisa said that was right and she asked Mary to tell exactly what happened.

In the subsequent discussion we learned that Mary had been using curse words in class but that she had done this because she felt provoked when the teacher said. "You all never do your work," and Mary interpreted this as an attack on all black students. This led to a spirited discussion that we had to end before any conclusions were reached because the time allocated for our meeting had come to an end. I suggested that Mary put this topic on her list for the next meeting. I also asked if she wanted to meet with me after the meeting to discuss what she was going to do about the class in the meantime. She said that she did.

Analysis. As we have indicated throughout this chapter, a major issue for work with oppressed people is empowerment. We see this manifested at the very beginning of the meeting as the worker supported the members in setting up a structure for governing their own group. This structure, however, had not yet begun to work as Mary was uncomfortable and unskilled with reference to her position. The worker addressed both of these issues while taking the opportunity to increase all of the members' competence in fulfilling a leadership role.

In addition, the worker sought to increase the critical consciousness of the group by discussing Mary's classroom problem and helping them to learn how to assess both their own responsibility for events as well as the forces present in the actual situation. This process was begun and is likely to continue for some time with reference to Mary's situation, as well as situations encountered by other members. A challenge to the worker will be how to help the members to conceptualize this kind of analysis so that they can use it beyond the specific situation under consideration. While this assessment process might take place in any type of group, it is important to note that the issue of racism was raised here and this offers the group an opportunity to learn more about how to understand and deal with that reality.

SUMMARY

In this chapter, we discussed the special aspects of group work with members who have been and are being socially oppressed. Such oppression was defined as "the destructive effects by social institutions on people when such institutions damage their identities, denigrate their life styles, and deny them access to opportunities" based on "attributes they share with others." We identified a number of populations to which this applies, such as many ethnic groups, women, and sexual minorities.

We discussed empowerment, attributions regarding themselves and their environments, lack of critical consciousness, and the conditions present in agencies serving them, which are common issues facing members. Following this, we described typical issues facing such groups in their various phases. This included joint planning between agency and group representatives in the pregroup phase as well as preparation of agency staff in this phase; the assessment of member competency and environmental conditions in the formation phase; and alternative strategies for the goal pursuit phase such as skills training, consciousness raising, social action, and creation of support from a network.

Evaluation issues were discussed with reference to all of these types of interventions including measurement of critical consciousness, social competence, and empowerment. We concluded the chapter with an example of a group of young black women who were coping with issues of empowerment and critical consciousness.

15

Working
With Committees
And
Other Task Groups

There are many types of groups in which social workers participate either as facilitators or members. Throughout this book, we have primarily emphasized groups composed of clients who have joined the group as a means of attaining personal goals. Group workers may be involved with other groups as part of their professional work and can use their knowledge of group processes to help those groups to achieve their purposes. Because there are differences as well as similarities in the ways workers can help these two types of groups, we have included this chapter on committees and other task groups.

While there may be a wide range of groups in which social workers are involved, the two major categories are (1) staff groups created in the agency to enhance the agency's functioning and (2) community groups created outside of the agency that benefit "classes" of clients (such as the "elderly," "handicapped," "poor," "homeless," and so forth). The staff groups include staff administrative meetings, teams, committees with specific charges such as to recommend a new policy or program, and in-service training. Community groups include councils consisting of representatives of several organizations, social action groups acting to change social conditions, and committees created as components of a neighborhood organization devoted to social planning and neighborhood development. Each type of agency or community group has unique requirements that go well beyond the scope of this chapter; consequently, we shall broadly describe some of the ways of facilitating these two somewhat general sets of groups.[1]

As a general term for the types of groups we shall be discussing, we use *task group*. Toseland and Rivas define this as "any group in which the major purpose is neither intrinsically nor immediately linked to the needs of the members of the group. In task groups, the overriding purpose is to accomplish a mandate and complete the work for which the group was convened."[2]

It is important for the reader to recognize that it is not always possible to draw a clear line between treatment groups and task groups. Sometimes a worker will create a task group composed of agency clients because of the therapeutic benefits for those clients. An example of this is the patient government group we discussed as part of alternative role attainment in Chapter 13. On the other hand, community organizers engaged in "grass roots" work with people in a community may encounter group members who seek to discuss personal problems during committee meetings and the other group members may decide to deal with these to a limited degree.

Nevertheless, it is useful to maintain a distinction between treatment and task groups and to be aware of the difficulties that arise when the line becomes blurred. These difficulties consist of a failure of the group to accomplish its mission because of individual needs, intragroup conflict, loss of members frustrated by group ineffectiveness, and a lack of help to members who are seeking it because there is, in fact, no mandate for treatment to occur.

While we shall become more specific in this chapter as to the procedures that are employed in task groups, we shall also point out some general similarities and differences between task and treatment groups. As the reader will see, the differences may at times be relative rather than absolute and, even then, this depends on the specific type of task or treatment group under consideration.

First is the structure of the meeting. Many types of treatment groups have an agenda, but it is often "loose" and consists of a series of topics. An exception is a skills training group that has a highly structured meeting plan. Virtually all task groups have a specific agenda for the meeting and we shall describe important considerations for the creation of this agenda later in this chapter.

Second, many agenda items in a task group call for specific decisions as to actions to be taken. The less formal "topics" in a treatment group may or may not lead to specific actions and when the discussion is of an individual's behavior, that individual may or may not enact the recommendations made by others in the group.

Third, task groups usually have a formal process of decision making such as majority rule and voting procedures. These procedures are seldom used in treatment groups where decisions, if they are made, are often in the form of a group "consensus."

---

[1]Readers interested in more extensive discussions of work with different types of task groups can consult John E. Tropman, *Effective Meetings: Improving Group Decision-Making* (Beverly Hills: Sage, 1980) and Steve Burghardt, *Organizing for Community Action* (Beverly Hills: Sage, 1982).

[2]Ronald Toseland and Robert Rivas, *An Introduction to Group Work Practice* (New York: Macmillan, 1984), p. 15.

Fourth, especially as a task group increases in size, there may be formal rules as to how members are "recognized" to speak, how "motions" for action may be made, and so forth.[3] Treatment groups are much more likely to be conducted on an informal basis.

Fifth, members are usually selected for a treatment group based on their individual needs as well as how their participation will help meet others' needs. Members are selected for a task group almost exclusively in terms of the composition that is most likely to help the group achieve its mission.

Sixth, treatment groups always insist on confidentiality. Task groups, on the other hand, usually create minutes of meetings and these minutes may be required to be made public.

Last (and certainly not least), the role of the group worker is likely to be different. In a treatment group, the worker has a central position as a group facilitator. In a task group, the group worker may simply be another member, may be the formal chairperson, or may "staff" a group which has a chair as well as other appointed "officers." The role of "staff" to a group has unique requirements that we shall also describe later.

Task groups go through the same phases as any other group; therefore, we shall continue our discussion utilizing the same phase structure as we employed in the preceding chapters on practice variations.

PREGROUP TASKS

As with any other type of group, the purpose for which the group is formed will help to determine many other conditions such as group composition and size. The purpose is usually determined by the agency or community organization that creates the group and is often communicated to the potential group members in written form. This is often referred to as the group's *mandate*. When the group begins to meet, the members usually review this mandate and if it is unclear, ask for clarification.

As we stated earlier, the composition of the group should be determined by the human resources the group will require in order to accomplish its purposes. These resources include both the attributes of members as well as their location in the organizational structure. Thus, if a task group is to plan a fund-raising event, it should include people who are capable of planning the event and carrying out the tasks related to it such as publicity, budget, and recruitment of workers. If another task group is to assess the health needs of a community, it should include representatives of various age groups, ethnic groups, social classes, and both genders.

Various compositional problems are likely to occur in task groups. One that arises in an agency is whether different levels of the agency hierarchy should be represented, such as line staff, supervisors, and administrators as well as people

---

[3]Task groups often use what has been referred to as parliamentary procedure such as that embodied in H. Robert, *Robert's Rules of Order* (Glenview, Ill.: Scott, Foresman and Co., 1970).

from various departments. Again, the purpose of the group will help the convenors make this decision and the effect of the presence or absence of any contigent should be considered. Another is the presence of individuals in the group who are in conflict as individuals or in conflict by virtue of membership in groups that are at conflict. The likelihood of conflict does not, in itself, militate against including any individual. The convenors, however, will have to consider how to help the group cope with this issue—a topic we shall consider later.

A phenomenon that convenors must consider is that of the "hidden agenda." This refers to the fact that members of task groups may have personal goals that they wish to pursue in the group, but they do not express this openly because these goals are not directly related to the purpose of the group and may even be contrary to it. A hidden agenda may also relate to the member's identification with another group that he or she may officially or unofficially represent. The convenor—as well as any subsequent officer, staff person, or facilitator—can make some informed guesses about hidden agendas and, on the basis of this, come to some conclusions about group composition or, at least, how this will be dealt with once the group has begun.

The convenor of a group in an agency will also be cognizant of how the group's composition relates to the "informal" system of the organization. The informal system represents relationships among staff that arise among them by virtue of their interactions with each other rather than by virtue of formal job requirements. Thus, staff form relationships with each other at lunch, around the coffee machine, or after duty hours. Staff may use the informal system to create cooperative arrangements that are not mandated by the agency or, in contrast, to complain about the agency and to hinder its efforts. The convenor should try to understand how the group's composition intersects with the informal system and, consequently, how members are likely to want to use the group.

Often the convenors will seek volunteers for the group rather than appointing specific individuals because of their role in the agency. This most often occurs in community organizations who seek to recruit people in the neighborhood for active roles in meeting community needs. There are several ways to do this. We think the least effective way is through a newspaper announcement, posters in businesses, or a circular sent out to people on a mailing list. Individuals are unlikely to respond to these anonymous approaches unless the issue is a "hot" one as, for example, after some crisis has occurred in the community or in response to an issue that people think will seriously affect their well-being (a fire has demonstrated the lack of safety of dwellings; a factory is to be built that makes the community a less desirable place to live).

Instead, a personal form of appeal is better. This can be in the form of home visits in the community, telephone calls, speeches before local groups, or a table in a shopping center with staff or volunteers present. Ideally, also, a professional staff person should be teamed up with indigenous community members with whom recruits can identify. As a further guarantee of meeting attendance, the staff member or a volunteer should call the community resident to remind her or him of the meeting. If transportation, baby sitting, or fears of coming alone are manifest, some plan should exist to address these needs. These measures will ensure that the bane of the organizer's life—a meeting that is called to which no one comes—will not occur.

The size of the group will also be related to its purpose. We have found when the purpose of the group is to create a plan to be considered subsequently by a large, representative body, the smallest size group that can bring the required knowledge and experience to the task is best. On the other hand, if the group must accomplish a task that requires the support and approval of a wide range of people, the most representative group is best, even if it is fairly large (more than fifteen people). A large group may have to subdivide itself into smaller task forces in order to accomplish its mission.

Some task groups with a range of purposes or steadily evolving purposes may be created for either a long or indefinite period. Otherwise, if there are only a few purposes, the group should be created for a limited period of time. This will aid in the recruitment of members who may be willing to commit their energies to a short-term group but hesitate to take on long-term commitments.

The role of staff members should also be clarified in advance so that prospective members can adapt to this. There are several roles that are performed by trained group workers:

1. *Member* The worker may simply be a member of the group. Examples of this are staff committees and representative community groups.
2. *Officer* The worker may hold office in the group such as its chair or secretary.
3. *Staff* This is a position frequently held by the group worker. In this situation, the group has officers and members and these roles are separate from that of the worker who is not a member. According to Tropman[4] the roles of the staff person are:

resource person

consultant

technician

catalyst

enabler

tactician

assistant to the chair

Since the role of *staff* may be an unfamiliar one, we shall discuss it now in detail. The staff person usually functions as an aid to the chair although he or she may, at times, be assigned to help other group members accomplish their tasks. In relationship to the chair, the staff person will secure information, analyze options, make recommendations, and suggest strategies. The staff person will usually consult with the chair about the agendas for coming meetings and notify members of these. The staffer is also likely to prepare the minutes of previous meetings and to distribute these with the agenda of the coming one. The staffer will maintain the group's files and make them available to members as they are needed.

An important factor in holding productive meetings is the way the agenda has been constructed. The agenda lists the topics to be considered at the meeting in

[4]Tropman, *Effective Meetings*, p. 52.

order and sometimes indicates how much time is to be allocated to each. Tropman recommends the following order:[5]

1. Enter brief, agenda-relevant minutes.
2. Make informative announcements.
3. Decide on less controversial items.
4. Consider most difficult item.
5. Break.
6. Talk over "for discussion only" items.
7. Consider the least difficult item(s) and call for adjournment.

Tropman recommends that less controversial items be handled first as they help participants to develop confidence and to "open up." By then (about one-third of the way through the meeting), latecomers will have arrived and those who have to leave early will still be present. The energy level of members will be high.

After a difficult item has been dealt with, members may need a "break" that may be either a time to stretch or a longer peiod when members might refill their coffee cups. A more relaxed discussion of items that do not yet require action might take place. Tropman believes that some quick, noncontroversial items may be resolved just before the close of the meeting so that it ends on a high note of success, especially if earlier items involved controversy and tension.

GROUP FORMATION TASKS

During the first meetings of the group, the major issues that the group will deal with will be purpose, membership, structure, operating procedures, and work plan. We shall discuss each of these in turn.

The purpose of the group, often referred to as its mandate, should be the first topic considered. The agency or community organization that convenes the task group will specify, usually in writing, the mission of the group. This may also be derived from the minutes of the meeting at which the group was proposed. If the group worker is appointed as a staff person for the task group, he or she will be expected to clarify the group's mandate. Otherwise, a staff person or officer of the "parent" organization could be invited to attend the group's initial meeting for this purpose. Along with this clarification, the group should be informed of other expectations of the "parent" such as the resources it will supply as well as those the task group should secure on its own; the time within which outcomes should be produced; the reports that the task group should submit to the parent (or other groups) and at what intervals; and any other constraints that are placed on the task group.

It is possible that the individuals invited to join the task group will have some objection to the mandate created by the "parent." This should be recognized and discussed. Many task groups have foundered because of conflicts between them and the organization because of a failure to consider reactions to initial mandates.

At times, the parent organization will have determined the membership of the task group as well as its officers and will have done so in consultation with the person designated as the task group chair. The members of the task group should have the right to ask for and receive information as to the basis for this selection. Sometimes, the task group will have the responsibility of adding additional members as needed, and selecting some or all of its officers. In this latter circumstance, an assessment of how many members and what kinds of officers the group will need in order to accomplish its purposes should be made by the existing members. They will then have to plan ways to recruit the additional members they will need.

Groups should also discuss the attributes and experiences they require in their officers and this will often help members to be more objective in their selection of such persons. They should also determine the length of time officers will serve. We have not found it desirable to have officers rotate after one or a few meetings unless a staff person will provide continuity for the group.

Structural decisions must then be made and these include when and where the group will meet, how meetings will be called, how members will be notified of meetings, what the responsibilities of members are, and how many members must be present for business to be conducted (that is, the size of a quorum). How decisions will be made (by majority vote, consensus, two-thirds) should also be clarified as well as whether the group will use formal procedures such as those embodied in *Robert's Rules of Order.*[6]

Many groups find it useful to have a discussion at an early meeting as to group norms. These might include the following:

1. The responsibility members have to notify the group if they cannot fulfill a responsibility they have assumed or if they wish to withdraw from the group
2. The way members may help one another to remain task oriented
3. Whether the group is willing to engage in "process" discussions in which members seek to assess how well the group is functioning as a group and how its deliberations may be improved
4. Whether members should feel free to disagree publicly with majority decisions of the group if they were not in the majority. This can also be an issue for a group officer—even the chair—who does not agree with the majority of members in the group

During the formation period, if the group has several purposes or one complex purpose, it should develop a work plan. This includes whether the group will divide itself into subcommittees where each will work on a different purpose or aspect and whether a time period should be established during which the group will work on each purpose. If the group must accomplish a series of complex steps

[6]See footnote 3.

in order to have completed its work by a specific date, the members may wish to employ a procedure like the Program Evaluation and Review Technique (PERT).[7] This technique helps members to create a chart by starting at the "end" with the final product and due date and working backward listing each prior task and when it must be accomplished in order for the group to meet its deadline.

GOAL PURSUIT TASKS

A major part of the activity of most task groups is problem solving. Anyone who seeks to facilitate task groups should understand the ways groups can best engage in problem solving, as we described in Chapter 5. In addition to the procedures we described there, several additional ones are often used in task groups.

Brainstorming as well as other procedures we shall describe are means of overcoming two major blocks to effective problem solving. One is that people tend to think in ways that are similar to those they have used in the past, even when these are not productive. The other is that some members of groups have higher status than others and their ideas tend to be accepted while those of lower status members tend to be rejected. Some means must be used, therefore, to encourage groups to look at ideas generated by all group members, not just a select few.

Brainstorming involves asking members to provide possible alternative solutions to the group problem without any evaluation as to the positives or negatives until all the solutions have been listed. These are often written on a blackboard or newsprint so that members can review all possibilities without immediately linking them to the specific member who made them. A brief discussion usually precedes the introduction of brainstorming in groups unfamiliar with it. Members are informed that people often withhold creative solutions for fear that others will regard them as too "way out." Group members must get past this informal censorship in order to tap their most creative capacities. The brainstorming session is then introduced by stating several "rules" that apply.

Another means of generating new ideas is to encourage members to draw upon analogies as a way of bringing thoughts about a very different situation to the problem at hand. Gordon[8] and Prince[9] have done a great deal of work in showing how this method works.

The worker, in utilizing analogies, will first explain to the members that he or she is introducing a different means for considering an issue. When approval has been secured for this, the worker will ask the question, "How is this situation like. . . ?" This sentence may be completed with a noun that refers to an external real situation, a fantasy, or the persons themselves.

An example of this occurred in a staff committee that was trying to understand a particularly difficult family situation. The chairperson of the meeting

---

[7]D. Cook, *Program Evaluation and Review Technique: Application in Education,* Cooperation Research Monograph 17 (Washington, D.C.: United States Office of Education, 1966).

[8]W. Gordon, *Synectics: The Development of Creative Capacity* (New York: Harper & Row, 1961).

[9]G. Prince, *The Practice of Creativity* (New York: Harper & Row, 1970).

asked "How is the M. situation like a horserace?" Some of the answers that were provided by the staff present were the following:

> Everyone is trying to outdistance the other, even if the other is hurt in the process and even if he or she has to resort to "dirty tricks."
>
> In this effort, each person remains in the same track.
>
> Each person is looking for cheers from the "audience."
>
> There are a few clear "front runners" and the others have little hope of obtaining what they want.
>
> In the process of "running," many family members have "forgotten" why they are in the race.

After this list was completed, the group discussed each comparison further as well as the implications it held for helping the family. The group members stated that they had come up with many new ideas not thought of previously. The skill of the chairperson lay in providing an analogy that had the potential to help the members generate such thoughts.

Several procedures have been developed to help members focus on objective factors rather than personal ones. (This is referred to in the social psychological literature as a "process loss.") One is the *Delphi Method*. As described by Zander,[10] the first step in a "Delphi" is for the members to complete a questionnaire about their opinions, usually devised by the group worker. The results are reported to participants as part of a second questionnaire, in which members are also asked to react to the results of the first questionnaire. During this process new ideas may be generated and these are added to the subsequent questionnaires.

The Delphi procedure is particularly useful when group members come from different backgrounds or professions. Because of the anonymity that it guarantees, members react to the ideas rather than to their judgments about whether people from a particular group are likely to have good ideas. It was called Delphi (after the site of the oracle in ancient Greece which foretold the future) because it is often used to pool the individuals' predictions about the future when these individuals possess different yet valid types of information.

The author utilized this method, for example, as part of a project to predict the likely future goals for mental health services so that staff development could be future oriented rather than primarily "catching up with yesterday."[11] Readers can consult the work of Dalkey for details on how to set up a Delphi.[12]

Still another method for facilitating problem solving in groups is the *Nominal Group Technique*. Toseland and Rivas,[13] who have experimented with the technique recommend that it be used with six to nine people (so that larger groups should be divided). Before the meeting, the worker writes a clear statement

---

[10]Alvin Zander, *Groups at Work* (San Francisco: Jossey-Bass, 1977), pp. 78–79.

[11]Charles Garvin, "Training and the Future of Mental Health Services: Steps Towards a Service Society," in *The Michigan Study of Mental Health Continuing Education,* by A. Lauffer (Ann Arbor: School of Social Work, The University of Michigan, 1977), pp. 31–50.

[12]N.C. Dalkey, "The Delphi Method: An Experimental Study of Group Opinion," *Management Science* (June, 1969).

[13]Toseland and Rivas, *An Introduction to Group Work Practice,* pp. 285–89.

of the problem on a work sheet and duplicates this sheet for every participant. Members are asked to work individually at first by writing their ideas about or responses to the problem on the sheet.

After sufficient time has elapsed for each member to have written something, the worker proceeds to the next step. Each member, in turn, is asked to provide one idea, which the worker writes on a large pad of newsprint or on a blackboard. Members are explicitly prevented from giving all of their ideas at once. They are encouraged, however, to think of new ideas by building on those presented by others. The worker continues calling on each person, in turn, in additional rotations until all the ideas have been listed. Members, however, do not criticize each other's ideas at this point.

The next stage involves clarifying the ideas that have been listed after which the group is helped to rank order the ideas. Members are asked to list the best five (or four or six, or whatever the worker thinks will produce a suitable range of alternatives) on cards. These "votes" are then listed on the chart. The items that have received some predetermined number of votes can then be further ranked by members in order to create a "short list." Further discussion should take place if there are major discrepancies in the rank ordering of different members in order to clarify the basis for such disagreements. Research on and description of Nominal Group Technique is available in the work of Delbecq and his colleagues.[14]

In addition to introducing such devices as brainstorming, Delphi, and nominal group technique, workers who seek to facilitate task groups will be on the lookout for several problems that hinder the work of such groups: lack of interest, uneven verbal input, and restraints on discussion. Zander in a summary of the techniques used by facilitators to deal with these problems suggests the following:[15] Lack of interest can be countered by posing an interesting issue that members will want to discuss; by raising issues in ways that require interaction among members; by providing an experience for the group that will raise interest in the topic (such as a field visit or an interesting speaker); and by making sure that topics are placed on the agenda that have been suggested by members.

Verbal input can be made more even by creating small subgroups to develop points of view about different aspects of the topic, by highlighting differences of opinion, and by appointing a member or members to observe and report on the group's process. Members can also be asked to prepare a statement about their point of view in advance. Participation is enhanced when members are given a brief period of silence to consider their point of view and even to make a few notes.

When the discussion appears to lag, the facilitator can summarize the points that have been made thus far, or can ask if a member or the chair would be willing

---

[14]A. Delbecq, A. Van de Ven, and D. Gustafson, *Group Techniques for Program Planning: A Guide to Nominal Group and Delphi Processes* (Glenview, Ill.: Scott, Foresman, and Co., 1975); A Van de Ven and A. Delbecq, "Nominal versus Interacting Group Processes for Committee Decision-Making Effectiveness," *Academy of Management Journal* 9 (1971), 203–12.

[15]Alvin Zander, *Making Groups Effective* (San Francisco: Jossey-Bass, 1982), pp. 42–43.

to do this. The facilitator can indicate unresolved issues or those about which there are differences. This also may be the point at which the worker introduces one of the techniques discussed in another part of this section.

Earlier in this chapter we made reference to *Robert's Rules of Order.* In small task groups, it is unlikely that the members will wish to draw upon all the formal rules embodied in such parliamentary procedure. Burghardt recommends a modified version, however, that he believes is useful in groups that must frequently make formal decisions.[16] In this version, group members operate by making and seconding motions; calling or moving the "question" which serves to end debate on the issue; making amendments to motions; and making procedural motions.

When the group is considering an issue, the chairperson can ask for or the facilitator can suggest that someone "make a motion." This requires stating in clear terms the action that member wishes the group to take. If there is support for the motion, it is "seconded." If not, another person usually arises to state a different motion on the issue.

After the motion has been made and seconded (and usually recorded by the secretary for the minutes), the chair calls for discussion on the motion. When anyone thinks that sufficient discussion has taken place for all points of view to have been expressed, that person can either "call for" or "move" the question. In the former case, the chair will ask if there are any objections to "calling the question" and, if not, the motion will be voted on. If the member has "moved" the question, a vote is taken as to whether the group is *ready to vote on the issue itself.* If a majority votes in favor of *this* motion, the main motion is then voted on.

Sometimes, it appears likely that a motion will be passed if it is modified in some manner. An individual can then "move" to amend the motion in some way. The original maker and seconder of the motion will often agree with the amendment and it is then incorporated in the original motion as a "friendly amendment." If it is not agreed to in this way, the amendment must be voted on by the members (before they vote on the original motion) and it is only incorporated if the majority of the group agree to it.

Procedural requests (usually referred to by the member who makes them as *points of order)* include requests for information about the topic, the time remaining in the meeting, or other pertinent issues. Procedural motions include motions to "table the motion" and to adjourn the meeting. The move to "table" is often made when the member thinks that the group should have more time to think about the issue or to get more information. When the motion has been presented by a subcommittee, those members are usually expected to secure more information, rethink the issue, and so forth. Points of order may be handled by the chair if he or she thinks them appropriate. Procedural motions are voted upon and passed by the majority of the group present.

As we have stated earlier, the group members should decide in their first meetings how and to what degree they wish to use such decisional procedures. The important thing to remember is that they are tools for groups to use in the ways

---

[16]Steve Burghardt, *Organizing for Community Action* (Beverly Hills: Sage Publications, 1982), pp. 54–57.

they think will best expedite their deliberations. In large groups, however, *Robert's Rules of Order* are usually adhered to more firmly than in small groups, and members may have to be instructed in their use.

EVALUATION

In general, many of the procedures described in Chapter 8 that relate to changes in group or environmental conditions can be used in task groups. In addition, a number of procedures can be used to assess the unique aspects of such groups. Tropman, in a series of exercises at the end of his succinct discussion of effective meetings, provides items that could be used by workers, observers, or members to evaluate aspects of their groups.[17] Some of those we have found most useful from his work as well as our own are the following:

1. Membership
   1.1. Does the group represent all of the interests that it should?
   1.2. Does the group consist of members that cover the range of skills the group requires to accomplish its mission?
2. Mission
   2.1. Is the purpose of the group clear?
   2.2. How well do members agree with the purpose?
3. Task Group Functioning
   3.1. How well do the members know their membership roles?
   3.2. Do you think the group makes good decisions?
   3.3. How well are all members involved in decision making?
   3.4. Does the group operate on the basis of an agenda?
   3.5. Do members have an opportunity to contribute to the agenda and are they notified of its content before meetings?
   3.6. Does the agenda take into consideration the proper placement of important and/or controversial items so that members have become involved in the meeting yet are not too exhausted to give proper consideration to them (usually in the middle third of the meeting)?
   3.7. Have members accepted and do they effectively employ procedural rules that help them make decisions?
   3.8. Does the group employ procedures to help members be more creative and objective in decision making?
4. The Staffer Role
   4.1. Does this person provide information to the chair and the members that they need?
   4.2. Does this person give technical assistance-training?
   4.3. Does this person help in the creation of an agenda and its distribution in a timely fashion?
   4.4. Does this person help members analyze choices?
   4.5. Does this person help to set the stage for the meeting (set-up of room, availability of materials that are needed)?

---

[17]Tropman, *Effective Meetings,* pp. 93–109.

5. The Chairperson
    5.1. Does this person prepare for meetings in advance?
    5.2. Does this person act impartially?
    5.3. Does this person conduct meetings in an orderly fashion?
    5.4. Does this person work with staff person[s] when they are assigned?
    5.5. Does this person model good committee behavior for members (such as promptness, good listening, objectivity, preparation such as reading reports in advance of meeting)?

The above points are meant to be suggestive and can be added to in numerous ways or modified by creating rating scales (for example, ranging from "5"—accomplished at a high level to "1"—totally missing). Members can use selected items by completing questionnaires during a meeting, by holding an open discussion on appropriate points, or by appointing different individuals or subgroups to assess different aspects of group functioning.

AN EXAMPLE

The following is an example of part of a meeting of a "block club" that was organized in the neighborhood of a community center. The center hoped eventually to create such clubs in all of the blocks in its area. The purpose of the block clubs is to help the residents identify and work toward ways of making their block a better place to live. This might require members of several or all of the block clubs to work together for community-wide change. For that purpose, the center had created a block-club federation, and each individual group selected two representatives to attend the federation. This meeting was to be the fifth for this group.

Meeting between staffer and chair. Immediately after the fourth meeting, Ms. J., the block-club worker who was trained in group work and who had her Master's degree, met with Ms. F. who had just been elected the chairwoman of the club. They talked about how things were going in the group and about the agenda for the next meeting. Ms. F. said that she was worried because none of the Hispanic residents had attended any of the meetings (Ms. F. was a black woman). The worker, who was also black, had visited the homes of several Hispanic residents prior to the first meeting and had called them before each meeting, but to no avail. Ms. J. and Ms. F. decided that this should be one of the items on the agenda of the next meeting.

They also discussed the survey that Ms. J. had made of block concerns when she visited the residents. Those that had been mentioned most frequently were the number of robberies in the neighborhood, the fights between black and Hispanic teenagers, the lack of any medical services in the immediate neighborhood, the many days the school had been closed for teacher meetings thereby causing working parents to have child-care problems, and the threat that a number of apartment buildings in the block would be torn down so that the city could build a new fire station. Ms. J. and Ms. F. thought that the next meeting should devote some time also to selecting the group's first project.

Ms. F. said that she didn't know how to handle Mr. Y. who had attended every meeting. Every chance he had he complained about the poor reception on his TV. The other members resented his interruptions because they thought these had little to do with the purposes of the meeting. Ms. J. suggested that Ms. F. explain to the members that when they were discussing a particular point on the agenda, she would have to interrupt anybody not speaking on that topic. She also suggested that since Mr. Y. was a custodian at the local school, he could be told that the group would value his opinions about how the children in the neighborhood behaved when this topic was discussed.

Based on this discussion, Ms. J. wrote down the following agenda and agreed to have it distributed from door to door. Several members of the club said that their children would do this chore.

Agenda for fifth meeting

1. Introduction of new members
2. Minutes of the fourth meeting
3. Information about a fund-raising event sponsored by the federation
4. Decision regarding a group project
5. Discussion regarding how representative the block club is
6. Decision regarding how frequently the group will meet
7. Selection of temporary representatives to the Federation

Meeting. Eleven people attended the fifth meeting of the group, including two Hispanic residents. Since the previous meetings had never had more than nine in attendance, this was an improvement. Ms F. called the meeting to order and asked the worker, who had taken the minutes of the previous meeting, to read them. After this, she asked if there were any additions to the minutes and none were made. Ms. F. then introduced Mr. H., Mr. O., and Ms. T. who were attending for the first time. She had approached them before the beginning of the meeting and had obtained their names, addresses, and phone numbers.

Following this, Ms. F. called on the worker to explain about the fund-raising event. The worker explained that it was a bake sale and that the federation hoped that as many residents as possible from each group would bake and donate cakes. Mr. Y. said that he didn't see how anyone in his family could bake a cake with all of the rumbling caused by street repairs. He then continued to ramble on about this. Ms. F. said that the group could decide to take this up as an issue, but this wasn't the time to discuss it at any length.

Ms. F. then stated that the group should begin to decide on its projects. She called on the worker to tell about the neighborhood survey. While she was doing this, Mr. P. asked whether the survey was any good inasmuch as he had never been asked his opinion. The worker explained that she did visit homes at various times of the day and evening so that different family members could be interviewed, and she had talked to about 40 percent of the families on the block. She was sorry she had missed Mr. P., however, he would have a good chance to give his opinions now.

The worker listed the topics that had been suggested by the residents as well as the response to questions about what they would like to see improved in the neighborhood. She suggested a way of selecting the ones to work on first by allowing each person to pick three topics and then seeing which topic received the most "votes." First, she suggested, they could discuss each one in order to clarify what the issue was. Afterwards, they could create committees around the topics that had received the largest vote so that people could work on the topic about which they had the greatest concern.

The above presentation and discussion took about a half hour while the clarification and selection took another hour. This left a half hour of the two-hour meeting for the last three items on the agenda. Space here does not permit our giving further details on this meeting.

Analysis. This excerpt demonstrates several aspects of work with a task group. In this example, the group worker is functioning as staff person for the committee. In this role, she provides support for the chair and fulfills tasks between meetings that will help the group to function. We see that a major part of her work involves helping the chair to prepare the agenda and securing information for the committee—in this case, the results of a survey.

We see that the worker helps the chair and the group to keep a *task focus* rather than a focus on meeting individual needs. On the other hand, she does help the group to draw upon the strengths of members so that individuals will find the group rewarding. She also is concerned that the group maintains the interest of the members by focusing upon concerns of theirs related to the overall purpose of the group. She provides techniques that will help the group make decisions such as the approach she used to prioritize neighborhood concerns. Individual motivation is also maintained by each member selecting the issue to work on that each is most interested in.

SUMMARY

In this chapter we discussed the ways in which workers facilitate task groups in the agency and in the community. These ways draw upon the same small-group knowledge base as that utilized with treatment groups. Because, however, the focus is upon accomplishing a task rather than changing the situations of individual members, the ways of facilitating such groups involve the use of some techniques that are not customarily employed in treatment groups.

We followed the same outline as that drawn upon in the previous chapter and described pregroup, formation, goal pursuit, and evaluation processes. The pregroup activities include a decision by the agency or community organization that creates the group as to its purpose or mandate and includes staff training, decision making, or carrying out an activity such as fund raising or publicizing events. Another pregroup activity is choosing members for the group or determining that the chairperson and possibly a few others will do this. Major compositional issues are to ensure that the group represents the right factions and that it includes members who possess the range of expertise necessary to accomplish the group's purpose. If the group is to recruit its own members, an effective means of attracting people must be used. Another important issue is to determine whether the group worker will be a member, officer, or staff person of the group.

During the group's first meetings, members will clarify the group's purpose and will negotiate any disagreements they have about this with the agency or community organization. They will also deal with membership issues, if they are expected to expand the group's size. They will resolve structural issues such as choosing officers and they will clarify how decisions will be made such as whether or not they will employ formal parliamentary procedure. A work plan and time schedule will also be devised.

As the group moves on to accomplish its purposes, it will have to devise means for reaching decisions as objectively and creatively as possible. For these reasons, workers have employed the methods of brainstorming, Delphi questionnaires, Nominal Group Technique, and the use of analogies. These procedures were described in this chapter, as well as others, for overcoming apathy and uneven participation during meetings.

Following this discussion of goal-pursuit methods in task groups, we presented a list of items that can be used to evaluate the functioning of task groups. The chapter ended with an example of a task group that was created by a community organization program.

Bibliography

Acosta, F.X., and J. Yamamoto, "The Utility of Group Work Practice for Hispanic Americans," *Social Work with Groups* VII (1984), 63–73.

Back, K.W., *Beyond Words: The Story of Sensitivity Training and Encounter Movement.* New York: Russell Sage, 1972.

Bales, Robert F., *Interaction Process Analysis: A Method for the Study of Small Groups.* Reading, Mass.: Addison-Wesley, 1950.

———. "Task Roles and Social-Emotional Roles in Problem Solving Groups," in *Readings in Social Psychology,* (3rd ed.), eds. E.E. Maccoby, T.M. Newcomb, and E.T. Hartley, pp. 437–47. New York: Holt, Rinehart & Winston, 1958.

Bednar, Richard L., and Theodore J. Kaul, "Experiential Group Research: Current Perspectives," in *Handbook of Psychotherapy and Behavior Change: An Empirical Analysis* (2nd ed.), eds. Sol L. Garfield and Allen Bergin, pp. 769–816. New York: John Wiley, 1978.

Berne, Eric, *Transactional Analysis in Psychotherapy.* New York: Grove Press, 1961.

Bernstein, Douglas A., and Thomas D. Borkovec, *Progressive Relaxation Training: A Manual For the Helping Professions.* Champaign, Ill.: Research Press, 1973.

Bernstein, Saul, ed., *Explorations in Group Work.* Boston: Boston University School of Social Work, 1965.

Bertcher, Harvey J., and Frank Maple, "Elements and Issues in Group Composition," in *Individual Change Through Small Groups,* eds. Martin Sundel, Paul Glasser, Rosemary Sarri, and Robert Vinter, pp. 180–202. New York: Free Press, 1985.

Bettelheim, Bruno, *A Home for the Heart.* New York: Knopf, 1974.

Bion, W.R., *Experiences in Groups.* New York: Basic Books, 1959.

Blauner, Robert, "Internal Colonialism and Ghetto Revolt," *Social Problems* 16 (Spring, 1969), 393–408.

Brim, Orville G., Sr., and **Stanton Wheeler,** *Socialization After Childhood: Two Essays.* New York: John Wiley, 1966.

Brockway, B.S., "Assertive Training for Professional Women," *Social Work* 21 (1976), 498–505.

Burghardt, Steve, *Organizing for Community Action.* Beverly Hills: Sage, 1982.

Burrow, T. "The Basis of Group Analysis," *British Journal of Medical Psychology* 8, Pt 3 (November, 1928), 198–206.

Cartwright, Dorwin, and **Alvin Zander,** eds., *Group Dynamics: Research and Theory* (3rd ed.). New York: Harper & Row, Pub., 1968.

Chesler, Mark, "Contemporary Sociological Theories of Racism," in *Toward the Elimination of Racism.* ed. P. Katz. pp. 21–72. New York: Pergamon, 1976.

Chu, J., and **S. Sue,** "Asian/Pacific Americans and Group Practice," *Social Work with Groups* VII (1984), 23–36.

Churchill, Sallie R., "Social Group Work: A Diagnostic Tool in Child Guidance," *American Journal of Orthopsychiatry* 35 (April 1965), 581–88.

Clark, Frank W. and others, eds., *The Pursuit of Competence in Social Work.* San Francisco: Jossey-Bass, 1979.

Cloward, Richard A., and **Lloyd E. Ohlin,** *Delinquency and Opportunity.* Glencoe, Ill.: Free Press, 1969.

Compton, Beulah R., and **Burt Galoway,** eds., *Social Work Processes* (rev. ed.). Homewood, Ill.: Dorsey Press, 1979.

Cook, D., *Program Evaluation and Review Technique: Application in Education.* Cooperation Research Monograph 17. Washington, D.C.: United States Office of Education, 1966.

Coyle, Grace L., *Studies in Group Behavior.* New York: Harper & Row, Pub., 1937.

———. *Group Experience and Democratic Values.* New York: Women's Press, 1947.

———. *Group Work with American Youth.* New York: Harper & Row, Pub. 1948.

Croxton, Tom A., "The Therapeutic Contract in Social Treatment," in *Individual Change Through Small Groups,* eds., Martin Sundel, Paul Glasser, Rosemary Sarri, and Robert Vinter, pp. 159–79. New York: Free Press, 1985.

Culbert, Samuel A., "Consciousness Raising: A Five Stage Model for Social and Organizational Change," in *The Planning of Change* (3rd ed.), eds. Warren G. Bennis and others, pp. 231–45. New York: Holt, Rinehart & Winston, 1976.

Dalkey, N.C. "The Delphi Method: An Experimental Study of Group Opinion," *Management Science* (June, 1969).

Davis, Allen, "Settlements: History," in *Encyclopedia of Social Work* (vol. 2), pp. 1175–80. New York: National Association of Social Workers, 1971.

Davis, Larry, "Essential Components of Group Work with Black Americans," *Social Work with Groups* VII (1984), 97–109.

Delbecq, A., A. Van de Ven, and **D. Gustafson,** *Group Techniques for Program Planning: A Guide to Nominal Group and Delphi Processes.* Glenview, Ill.: Scott, Foresman and Co., 1975.

Dewey, John, *How We Think.* Lexington, Mass.: Heath, 1933.

Edwards, E.D., M.E. Edwards, G.M. Daines, and **F. Eddy,** "Enhancing Self-Concept and Identification with 'Indianness' of American Indian Girls," *Social Work with Groups* I (1978), 309–18.

Edwards, E. Daniel, and **Margie E. Edwards,** "Group Work Practice with American Indians," *Social Work with Groups* 7 (Fall, 1984), 7–22.

Ellis, A., and **R.A. Harper,** *A New Guide to Rational Living.* Englewood Cliffs, N.J.: Prentice-Hall, Inc., 1975.

Empey, LaMar, and **Maynard L. Erickson,** *The Provo Experiment: Evaluating Community Control of Delinquency.* Lexington, Mass.: Heath, 1972.

Ezriel, H., "Psychoanalytic Group Therapy," in *Group Therapy,* eds. L.R. Wolberg and E.K. Schwartz, pp. 191–202. New York: Intercontinental Medical Book Corporation, 1973.

Fairweather, George W., ed., *Social Psychology in Treating Mental Illness: An Experimental Approach.* New York: John Wiley, 1964.

Fairweather, George and others, *Community Life for the Mentally Ill: An Alternative to Institutional Care.* Chicago: Aldine, 1969.

Festinger, Leon. "Informal Social Communication," *Psychological Review* LVII (1950), 271–82.

Fischer, Joel, *Effective Casework Practice.* New York: McGraw-Hill, 1978.

Fischer, Joel, and **Harvey Gochros,** *Planned Behavior Change: Behavior Modification in Social Work.* New York: The Free Press, 1975.

Fisher, Roger, and **William Ury,** *Getting to Yes: Negotiating Agreement Without Giving In.* New York: Penguin Books, 1981.

Fitts, W.F., *Tennessee Self-Concept Scale Manual.* Nashville: Counselor Recordings and Tests, 1965.

Follett, Mary Parker, *The New State,* New York: Longmans, 1926.

Framo, James. "Symptoms from a Family Transactional Viewpoint," in *Progress in Group and Family Therapy,* eds. Clifford Sager and Helen Kaplan, pp. 271–308. New York: Brunner/Mazel, 1972.

Freire, Paulo, *Education for Critical Consciousness.* New York: Seabury Press, 1973.

Galinsky, Maeda, and **Janice Schopler,** "Warning: Groups May be Dangerous," *Social Work* 22 (1977), 89–94.

Gambrill, Eileen, and **Cheryl A. Richey,** "An Assertion Inventory for Use in Assessment and Research," *Behavior Therapy* 6 (1975), 350–62.

_____. "Gender Issues Related to Group Social Skills Training," *Social Work With Groups* VI (Fall/Winter, 1983), 51–66.

Garfield, Sol. L., and **Allen Bergin,** eds., *Handbook of Psychotherapy and Behavior Change: An Empirical Analysis* (2nd ed.). New York: John Wiley, 1978.

Garvin, Charles, "Education for Generalist Practice: A Comparative Analysis of Current Modalities," in *Teaching for Competence in the Delivery of Direct Services.* New York: Council on Social Work Education, 1976.

_____. "Training and the Future of Mental Health Services: Steps Toward a Service Society," in *The Michigan Study of Mental Health Continuing Education,* ed. Armand Lauffer, pp. 31–50. Ann Arbor: University of Michigan School of Social Work, 1977.

_____. "Group Process: Usage and Uses in Social Work Practice," in *Individual Change Through Small Groups,* eds., Martin Sundel, Paul Glasser, Rosemary Sarri, and Robert Vinter, pp. 203–25. New York: Free Press, 1985.

_____. "Resocialization: Group Work in Social Control and Correctional Settings," in *The Group Worker's Handbook: Varieties of Group Experience,* ed. Robert Conyne. pp. 113–34. Springfield: Thomas, 1985.

_____. "Practice with Task-Centered Groups," in *Task Centered Practice with Groups and Families,* ed. Anne Fortune, pp. 45–77. New York: Springer, 1985.

_____. "Work with Disadvantaged and Oppressed Groups," in *Individual Change through Small Groups,* eds. Martin Sundel, Paul Glasser, Rosemary Sarri, and Robert Vinter, pp. 461–72. New York: The Free Press, 1985.

Garvin, Charles D., and **Paul H. Glasser,** "Social Group Work: The Preventative and Rehabilitative Approach," in *Individual Change Through Small Groups,* eds. Martin Sundel, Paul Glasser, Rosemary Sarri, and Robert Vinter, pp. 35–49. New York: Free Press, 1985.

Garvin, Charles, and **Brett Seabury.** *Interpersonal Practice in Social Work: Processes and Procedures.* Englewood Cliffs, N.J.: Prentice-Hall, 1984.

Garvin, Charles D., William Reid, and **Laura Epstein,** "A Task-Centered Approach," in *Theories of Social Work with Groups,* eds. Robert W. Roberts and Helen Northen, pp. 238–67. New York: Columbia University Press, 1976.

Garvin, Charles and others, "Group Work Intervention in the Social Environment," in *Individual Change Through Small Groups,* eds. Martin Sundel, Paul Glasser, Rosemary Sarri, and Robert Vinter, pp. 273–93. New York: Free Press, 1985.

Geller, Janet A., "Reaching the Battering Husband," *Social Work With Groups* 1 (Spring, 1978), 27–38.

Gergen, K.J., and S.J. Morse, "Self-consistency: Measurement and Validation," *Proceedings of the 75th Annual Convention of the American Psychological Association* 2 (1967), 207–8.

Glasser, Paul H., and Charles D. Garvin, "An Organizational Model," in *Theories of Social Work with Groups,* eds. Robert W. Roberts and Helen Northen, pp. 75–115. New York: Columbia University Press, 1976.

———. "Social Group Work: The Organizational and Environmental Approach," in *Encyclopedia of Social Work* Vol. II, pp. 1338–50. New York: National Association of Social Workers, 1977.

Glasser, Paul, Rosemary Sarri, and Robert Vinter, eds., *Individual Change Through Small Groups.* New York: Free Press, 1974.

Glassman, Urania, and Len Kates, "The Technical Development of the Democratic Humanistic Norms of the Social Work Group," New York: Adelphi University School of Social Work, no date (Mimeographed).

Goldenberg, Ira, *Oppression and Social Intervention.* Chicago: Nelson-Hall, 1978.

Goldstein, Arnold P., and Frederick H. Kanfer, eds., *Maximizing Treatment Gains: Transfer Enhancement in Psychotherapy.* New York: Academic Press, 1979.

Goldstein, Arnold, Kenneth Heller, and Lee Sechrest, *Psychotherapy and the Psychology of Behavior Change.* New York: John Wiley, 1966.

Goldstein, Arnold P., Robert P. Sprafkin, and N. Jane Gershaw, *Skill Training for Community Living: Applying Structured Learning Therapy.* Elmsford, N.Y.: Pergamon Press, 1976.

Gordon, W., *Synectics: The Development of Creative Capacity.* New York: Harper & Row, 1961.

Gottman, D.M., and S.R. Leiblum, *How to Do Psychotherapy and How to Evaluate It.* New York: Holt, Rinehart & Winston, 1974.

Hartford, Margaret E., *Working Papers Toward a Frame of Reference for Social Group Work.* New York: National Association of Social Workers, 1962.

———. *Groups in Social Work.* New York: Columbia University Press, 1972.

———. "Group Methods and Generic Practice," in *Theories of Social Work with Groups,* eds. Robert W. Roberts and Helen Northen, pp. 45–74. New York: Columbia University Press, 1976.

Hartman, Ann, "Anomie and Social Casework," *Social Casework* 50 (1969), 131–37.

Hasenfeld, Yeheskel, "Organizational Factors in Service to Groups," in *Individual Change Through Small Groups,* eds. Martin Sundel, Paul Glasser, Rosemary Sarri, and Robert Vinter, pp. 294–309. New York: Free Press, 1985.

Hersen, M., and D.H. Barlow, *Single Case Experimental Designs.* Elmsford, N.Y.: Pergamon Press, 1976.

Ho, M.K., "Social Group Work with Asian/Pacific-Americans," *Social Work with Groups* VII (1984), 49–61.

Hoehn-Saric, R. and others, "Systematic Preparation of Patients for Psychotherapy: Effects on Therapy Behavior and Outcome," *Journal of Psychiatry Research,* II (1964), 267–81.

Howe, Irving, *World of our Fathers.* New York: Simon & Schuster, 1976.

Hynes, K., and J. Werbin, "Group Psychotherapy for Spanish Speaking Women," *Psychiatric Annals* VII (1977), 622–27.

Kaiser, Clara A., *The Group Records of Four Clubs.* Cleveland: Western Reserve University, 1930.

Kassebaum, G., D. Ward, and D. Wilner, *Prison Treatment and Parole Survival: An Empirical Assessment.* New York: Wiley, 1971.

Kelly, G.A., *The Psychology of Personal Constructs.* New York: Norton, 1955.

Kelley, Harold H., and **John W. Thibaut,** "Group Problem Solving," in *The Handbook of Social Psychology* (2nd ed.), eds. Gardner Lindzey and Elliot Aronson, pp. 1–101. Reading, Mass.: Addison-Wesley, 1969.

Kiresuk, Thomas J., and **Geoffrey Garwick,** "Basic Goal Attainment Procedures," in *Social Work Processes* (2nd ed.), eds. Beulah R. Compton and Burt Galaway. Homewood, Ill.: Dorsey Press, 1979.

Klein, Alan F., *Society, Democracy, and the Group.* New York: Morrow, 1953.

———. *Effective Group Work.* New York: Association Press, 1972.

Konopka, Gisela. *Therapeutic Group Work with Children.* Minneapolis, Minn.: University of Minnesota Press, 1949.

———. *Social Group Work: A Helping Process* (2nd ed.). Englewood Cliffs, N.J.: Prentice-Hall, Inc., 1972.

Kübler-Ross, Elisabeth, *On Death and Dying,* New York: Macmillan, 1964.

Lang, Norma C., "A Broad Range Model of Practice with the Social Work Group," *Social Service Review* 46 (1972), 76–89.

———. "A Comparative Examination of Therapeutic Uses of Groups in Social Work and in Adjacent Human Service Professions: Part II—The Literature from 1969-1978," *Social Work with Groups* 2, no. 2 (Fall 1979), 197–220.

Lange, Arthur J., and **Patricia Jakubowski,** *Responsible Assertive Behavior.* Champaign,Ill.: Research Press, 1976.

Laqueur, H., **H. Laburt,** and **G. Morong,** "Multiple Family Therapy: Further Developments," *International Journal of Social Psychiatry* (1964) Congress Issue, 70–80.

Lawrence, Harry, "The Origins of Social Group Work," (unpublished manuscript, p. 13) quoted in Scott Briar, "Social Casework and Social Group Work: Historical Foundations," in *Encyclopedia of Social Work* II, p. 1241. New York: National Association of Social Workers, 1971.

Lawrence, Harry, and **Martin Sundel,** "Behavior Modification in Adult Groups," *Social Work* 17 (1972), 34–43.

Lieberman, Morton A., "Group Methods," in *Helping People Change,* eds. Frederick A. Kanfer and Arnold P. Goldstein, pp. 433–86. New York: Pergamon Press, 1975.

Lieberman, M.A., **I. Yalom,** and **M. Miles,** *Encounter Groups: First Facts.* New York: Basic Books, 1973.

Lindeman, Eduard C., *The Community.* New York: Association Press, 1921.

Linehan, M.M., and **K.J. Egan,** "Assertion Training for Women," in *Research and Practice in Social Skills Training,* eds. A.S. Bellack and M. Hersen, pp. 237–72. New York: Plenum, 1979.

London, Perry, *Behavior Control.* New York: Harper & Row, Pub., 1971.

McCorkle, Lloyd W., **Albert Elias,** and **F. Lovell Bixby,** *The Highfields Story.* New York: Holt, Rinehart and Winston, 1958.

MacDonald, M.L., "Assertion Training for Women," in *Social Skills Training: A Practical Handbook for Assessment and Treatment,* eds. J.P. Curran and P.M. Monti. New York: The Guilford Press, 1982.

McGrath, Joseph E., *Groups: Interaction and Performance.* Englewood Cliffs, N.J.: Prentice-Hall, 1984.

Maluccio, Anthony, ed. *Promoting Competence in Clients.* New York: The Free Press, 1981.

Martin, P.Y., and **K.A. Shanahan,** "Transcending the Effects of Sex Composition in Small Groups," *Social Work with Groups* VI (1983), 19–32.

Meadow, Diane, "Connecting Theory and Practice: The Effect of Pregroup Preparation on Individual and Group Behavior," No Date (Mimeographed).

Middleman, Ruth. *The Non-Verbal Method in Working with Groups.* New York: Association Press, 1968.

Middleman, Ruth R., and **Gale Goldberg,** *Social Service Delivery: A Structural Approach to Social Work Practice.* New York: Columbia University Press, 1974.

Middleman, Ruth, and **Gale Goldberg,** "Social Group Work," in *Encyclopedia of Social Work.* New York: National Association of Social Workers, in press.

Mills, Theodore M., *The Sociology of Small Groups.* Englewood Cliffs, N.J.: Prentice-Hall, Inc., 1967.

Moos, Rudolf, *Evaluating Treatment Environments: A Social Ecological Approach.* New York: John Wiley, 1974.

Moreno, J.L., *Psychodrama* (rev. ed.). Beacon, N.Y.: Beacon House, Inc., 1964.

Murphy, Marjorie, *The Social Group Work Method in Social Work Education.* New York: Council on Social Work Education, 1959.

Newsletter, W.I., "What Is Social Group Work?" in *Proceedings of the National Conference on Social Work,* pp. 291–99. Chicago: University of Chicago Press, 1935.

Northen, Helen, *Social Work With Groups.* New York: Columbia University Press, 1969.

_____. "Psychosocial Practice in Small Groups," in *Theories of Social Work With Groups,* eds. Robert W. Roberts and Helen Northen, pp. 116–52. New York: Columbia University Press, 1976.

Novotny, H., and **J. Enomoto,** "Social Competence Training as a Correctional Alternative," *Offender Rehabilitation* I (1976), 45–55.

Papell, Catherine P., and **Beulah Rothman,** "Social Group Work Models: Possession and Heritage," *Journal of Education for Social Work,* 2, no. 2 (Fall 1966), 66–77.

Parloff, Morris B., Irene E. Waskow, and **Barry E. Wolfe,** "Research on Therapist Variables in Relationship to Process and Outcome," *Handbook of Psychotherapy and Behavior Change: An Empirical Analysis* (2nd ed.), eds. Sol L. Garfield and Allen Bergin, pp. 233–82. New York: John Wiley, 1978.

Perls, Fritz, R.F. Hefferline, and **Paul Goodman,** *Gestalt Therapy.* New York: Julian Press, 1951.

Pfeiffer, J. William, and **John E. Jones,** eds. *A Handbook of Structured Experiences for Human Relations Training.* LaJolla, Calif.: University Associates, 1974 (issued annually).

Pincus, Allen, and **Anne Minahan,** *Social Work Practice: Model and Method.* Itasca, Ill.: F.E. Peacock, 1973.

Pinderhughes, Elaine, "Empowerment for our Clients and for Ourselves," *Social Casework* 64 (June, 1983), 331–38.

Prince, G., *The Practice of Creativity.* New York: Harper & Row, 1970.

Rappaport, R., "Group Therapy in Prison: A Strategic Approach," in *Group Counseling and Group Psychotherapy with Rehabilitation Clients,* ed. Milton Seligman, pp. 115–31. Springfield, Mass.: Thomas, 1977.

Rathus, S.A., "A 30-Item Schedule for Assessing Assertive Behavior," *Behavior Research and Therapy* Vol. 11 (1973), 398–406.

Redl, Fritz, and **David Wineman,** *Controls from Within.* New York: Free Press, 1956.

Reid, William, *The Task Centered System.* New York: Columbia University Press, 1978.

Reid, William, and **Laura Epstein,** *Task-Centered Casework.* New York: Columbia University Press, 1972.

_____. *Task Centered Practice.* New York: Columbia University Press, 1977.

Richmond, Mary, "Some Next Steps in Social Treatment," *Proceedings of the National Conference of Social Work, 1920,* pp. 254–58. New York: Columbia University Press, 1939.

Robert, H., *Robert's Rules of Order.* Glenview, Ill.: Scott, Foresman, and Co., 1970.

Roberts, Robert W. and **Helen Northen,** eds., *Theories of Social Work with Groups.* New York: Columbia University Press, 1976.

Rooney, Ronald, "Adolescent Groups in Public Schools," in *Task-Centered Practice,* eds. William J. Reid and Laura Epstein, pp. 168–82. New York: Columbia Press, 1977.

Rose, Sheldon, *Treating Children in Groups.* San Francisco: Jossey-Bass, 1972.

_____. *Group Therapy: A Behavioral Approach.* Englewood Cliffs, N.J.: Prentice-Hall, Inc., 1977.

———. *A Casebook in Group Therapy.* Englewood Cliffs, N.J.: Prentice-Hall, 1980.

———. "Use of Data in Identifying and Resolving Group Problems in Goal Oriented Treatment Groups," *Social Work with Groups* VII (Summer, 1984), 23–36.

Rose, S.D., J.J. Gayner, and J.L. Edelson, "Measuring Interpersonal Competence," *Social Work,* 22 (1977), 125–29.

Sarri, Rosemary, and Maeda Galinsky, "A Conceptual Framework for Group Development," in *Individual Change Through Small Groups,* eds. Martin Sundel, Paul Glasser, Rosemary Sarri, and Robert Vinter, pp. 70–86. New York: Free Press, 1985.

Schopler, Janice, and Maeda Galinsky, "Meeting Practice Needs: Conceptualizing the Open-Ended Group," *Social Work with Groups* VII (1984), 3–21.

Schopler, Janice H., Maeda Galinsky, and Mark Alicke, "Goals in Social Group Work Practice: Formulation, Implementation, and Evaluation," in *Individual Change Through Small Groups,* eds. Martin Sundel, Paul Glasser, Rosemary Sarri, and Robert Vinter, pp. 140–58. New York: Free Press, 1985.

Schulman, Evaline D., *Intervention in Human Services* (2nd ed.). St. Louis, Mo.: C.V. Mosby, 1978.

Schutz, William, C., *Firo: A Three Dimensional Theory of Interpersonal Orientations.* New York: Holt, Rinehart & Winston, 1958.

———. *Here Comes Everybody.* New York: Harper & Row, 1971.

Schwartz, William, "The Social Worker in the Group," in *New Perspectives on Service to Groups,* pp. 7–29. New York: Columbia University Press, 1961.

———. "Social Group Work: The Interactionist Approach," *Encyclopedia of Social Work* (vol. 2), pp. 1252–63. New York: National Association of Social Workers, 1971.

———. "Neighborhood Centers and Group Work," in *Research in the Social Services: A Five Year Review,* ed. Henry S. Maas, pp. 130–91. New York: National Association of Social Workers, 1971.

———. "Between Client and System: The Mediating Function," in *Theories of Social Work with Groups,* eds. Robert W. Roberts and Helen Northen, pp. 171–97. New York: Columbia University Press, 1976.

Shaffer, John B.P., and David Galinsky, *Models of Group Therapy and Sensitivity Training.* Englewood Cliffs, N.J.: Prentice-Hall, Inc., 1974.

Shalinsky, William I., "The Effects of Group Composition on Aspects of Group Functioning" (unpublished DSW dissertation, Western Reserve University, 1967).

Shaw, Marvin E., *Group Dynamics: The Psychology of Small Group Behavior.* New York: McGraw-Hill, 1976.

Sherman, T.M., and W.H. Cormier, "The Use of Subjective Scales for Measuring Interpersonal Reactions," *Journal of Behavior Therapy and Experimental Psychology,* 3 (1972), 279–80.

Shulman, Lawrence, "Scapegoats, Group Workers, and Pre-emptive Intervention," *Social Work* 12, no. 2 (1967), 37–43.

Simon, Sidney B., Leland W. Howe, and Howard Kirschenbaum, *Values Clarification: A Handbook of Practical Strategies for Teachers and Students.* New York: Hart Pulishing Co., Inc., 1972.

Siporin, Max, *Introduction to Social Work Practice.* New York: Macmillan, 1975.

Slavson, S.R., *Creative Group Education.* New York: Association Press, 1937.

Smalley, Ruth E., *Theory for Social Work Practice.* New York: Columbia University Press, 1967.

Solomon, Barbara, *Black Empowerment.* New York: Columbia University Press, 1976.

Somers, Mary Louise, "Problem Solving in Small Groups," in *Theories of Social Work with Groups,* eds. Robert W. Roberts and Helen Northen, pp. 331–67. New York: Columbia University Press, 1976.

Spergel, Irving, *Street Gang Work: Theory and Practice.* Reading, Mass.: Addison-Wesley, 1966.

Studt, E., S. Messinger, and **T. Wilson,** *C-Unit: Search for Community in Prison.* New York: Sage, 1968.

Sue, Derald, *Counseling the Culturally Different.* New York: John Wiley, 1981.

Sundel, Martin, Paul Glasser, Rosemary Sarri, and **Robert Vinter,** eds., *Individual Change Through Small Groups,* (2nd ed.). New York: Free Press, 1985.

Thibaut, John W., and **Harold H. Kelley,** *The Social Psychology of Groups.* New York: John Wiley, 1959.

Toseland, Ronald, and **Robert Rivas,** *An Introduction to Group Work Practice.* New York: Macmillan, 1984.

Traux, C.B., R.R. Carkhuff, and **I. Rodman, Jr.,** "Relationships Between Therapist Offered Conditions and Patient Change in Group Psychotherapy," *Journal of Clinical Psychology* 21 (1965), 327–29.

Traux, C.B., J. Wittmer, and **D.G. Wargo,** "Effects of the Therapeutic Conditions of Accurate Empathy, Non-possessive Warmth, and Genuineness on Hospitalized Mental Patients During Group Therapy," *Journal of Clinical Psychology* 27 (1971), 137–42.

Trecker, Harleigh B., ed., *Group Work: Foundations and Frontiers.* New York: Whiteside, Inc., 1955.

──────. ed., *Group Work in the Psychiatric Setting.* New York: Whiteside, Inc., 1956.

Tropman, John E. *Effective Meetings: Improving Group Decision Making.* Beverly Hills: Sage, 1980.

Tropp, Emanuel, "Social Group Work: The Developmental Approach," *Encyclopedia of Social Work* (vol. 2), pp. 1246–52. New York: National Association of Social Workers, 1971.

──────. "Developmental Theory," in *Theories of Social Work with Groups,* eds. Robert W. Roberts and Helen Northen, pp. 198–237. New York: Columbia University Press, 1976.

Van de Ven, A., and **A. Delbecq,** "Nominal versus Interacting Group Processes for Committee Decision-Making Effectiveness," *Academy of Management Journal* 9 (1971), 42–43.

Vinter, Robert D., "Group Work: Perspectives and Prospects," in *Social Work With Small Groups,* pp. 128–49. New York: National Association of Social Workers, 1959.

──────. "Analysis of Treatment Organizations," *Social Work* 8 (1963), 3–15.

──────. "Social Group Work," in *Encyclopedia of Social Work,* pp. 715–24. New York: NASW, 1965.

──────. "Program Activities: An Analysis of Their Effects on Participant Behavior," in *Individual Change Through Small Groups,* eds. Martin Sundel, Paul Glasser, Rosemary Sarri, and Robert Vinter, pp. 226–36. New York: Free Press, 1985.

──────. "The Essential Components of Group Work Practice," in *Individual Change Through Small Groups,* eds. Martin Sundel, Paul Glasser, Rosemary Sarri, and Robert Vinter, pp. 11–34. New York: Free Press, 1985.

Vorrath, Harry, and **Larry Brendtro,** *Positive Peer Culture.* Chicago: Aldine, 1974.

Weiner, M.F., *Therapist Disclosure: The Use of Self in Psychotherapy.* Boston: Butterworths, 1978.

Whitaker, Dorothy Stock, and **Morton A. Lieberman,** *Psychotherapy Through the Group Process.* New York: Atherton Press, 1965.

Williamson, Margaretta, *The Social Worker in Group Work.* New York: Harper & Row, Pub., 1929.

Wilson, Gertrude, "From Practice to Theory: A Personalized History," in *Theories of Social Work with Groups,* eds. Robert W. Roberts and Helen Northen, pp. 1–44. New York: Columbia University Press, 1976.

Wilson, Gertrude, and **Gladys Ryland,** *Social Group Work Practice,* Boston, Mass.: Houghton-Mifflin, 1949.

Wolpe, Joseph, *The Practice of Behavior Therapy* (2nd ed.). Elmsford, N.Y.: Pergamon Press, 1973.

Yalom, Irvin D., *The Theory and Practice of Group Psychotherapy* (2nd ed.). New York: Basic Books, 1975.

_____. *Inpatient Group Psychotherapy.* New York: Basic Books, 1983.

Zander, Alvin. *Groups at Work.* San Francisco: Jossey-Bass, 1977.

_____. *Making Groups Effective.* San Francisco: Jossey-Bass, 1982.

Index